Sustainability

A BEDFORD SPOTLIGHT READER

Sustainability

A BEDFORD SPOTLIGHT READER

Christian R. Weisser
Penn State Berks

Bedford/St. Martin's
Boston | New York

For Bedford/St. Martin's

Publisher for Composition and Business and Technical Writing: Leasa Burton
Executive Editor: John E. Sullivan III
Publishing Services Manager: Andrea Cava
Production Supervisor: Victoria Anzalone
Marketing Manager: Jane Helms
Project Management: Books By Design, Inc.
Senior Art Director: Anna Palchik
Text Design: Castle Design
Cover Design: William Boardman
Cover Photo: Bumblebee in Flight, © Paul Earle Photography/Getty Images
Composition: Achorn International, Inc.
Printing and Binding: RR Donnelley and Sons

Manufactured in the United States of America.

9   8   7   6   5   4
f   e   d   c   b   a

For information, write: Bedford/St. Martin's, 75 Arlington Street, Boston,
   MA 02116   (617-399-4000)

ISBN 978-1-4576-3431-4

Acknowledgments

The Bedford Spotlight Reader Series is a new line of single-theme readers, each featuring Bedford's trademark care and quality. The readers in the series collect thoughtfully chosen readings sufficient for an entire writing course — about forty selections — to allow instructors to provide carefully developed, high-quality instruction at an affordable price. Bedford Spotlight Readers are designed to help students make inquiries from multiple perspectives, opening up topics such as money, food, sustainability, and gender to critical analysis. An Editorial Board, made up of a dozen compositionists at schools focusing on specific themes, has assisted in the development of the series.

Spotlight Readers offer plenty of material for a composition course while keeping the price low. Combine a Spotlight Reader with a handbook or rhetoric and save 20 percent off the combined price. Or package your Spotlight Reader with *Critical Reading and Writing: A Bedford Spotlight Rhetoric*, a brief rhetoric covering the essentials of critical reading, the writing process, and research, for free (a $10 value).

Each volume in the series offers multiple perspectives on the topic and its effects on individuals and society. Chapters are built around central questions such as "What Are the Foundations of Sustainability?" and "What Rituals Shape Our Gender?" and so offer numerous entry points for inquiry and discussion. High-interest readings, chosen for their suitability in the classroom, provide a mix of genres and disciplines, as well as accessible and challenging selections to allow instructors to tailor their approach to each classroom. Each chapter thus brings to light related — even surprising — questions and ideas.

A rich editorial apparatus provides a sound pedagogical foundation. A general introduction, chapter introductions, and headnotes provide context. Following each selection, writing prompts provide avenues of inquiry tuned to different levels of engagement, from reading comprehension ("Understanding the Text"), to critical analysis ("Reflection and Response"), to the kind of integrative analysis appropriate to the research paper ("Making Connections"). A Web site for the series offers support for teaching: **bedfordstmartins.com/spotlight**.

Preface for Instructors

In many ways, sustainability is the perfect subject for a college writing course. Its importance is obvious, since sustainability focuses on life itself and humanity's future on planet Earth. Its relevance is clear, because debates and conversations about sustainability surround us every day in media, politics, and other public and private venues. Sustainability is personal, and students are quick to recognize that their lifestyles, consumer habits, food preferences, modes of transportation, careers, and countless other aspects of their lives are shaped by sustainable (or unsustainable) choices. Its complexity is both a challenge and an attribute; grappling with the diverse and sophisticated issues surrounding sustainability can help students develop critical thinking skills in ways that an easy or simple subject (with clear answers) might not allow. And sustainability is comprehensive and inherently inter-disciplinary — nearly every social, academic, and professional arena contributes to the sustainability conversation.

Most important, though, sustainability is discursive and rhetorical. College writing courses are fundamentally about analyzing and creating texts, and sustainability is a concept that is shaped and molded through texts of many types. Each text in this book can be seen as a different rhetorical act that seeks to change the ways we consider or define sustainability. These texts all contribute, in some way, to our understandings of sustainability, and they all hope to influence our thoughts and actions. Students will develop their own rhetorical abilities as a result of the reading, writing, and thinking they will do in a course using this book, and those persuasive skills will carry over to other aspects of their personal, professional, and civic lives. In that way, *Sustainability* is more about helping students to think and communicate than it is about any particular subject.

This book is informed by my ongoing interest in environments, ecologies, networks, and the ways in which writing shapes and is shaped through discursive systems. One of the things I've learned about systems over the years is that they are healthiest when they are most diverse. A thriving, sustainable system hinges upon variety, openness, interaction, and diversity; systems fail when they are closed, isolated, or dominated by any one thing, activity, or approach. When I first started thinking about a textbook about sustainability nearly ten years ago, the principle of diversity was a guiding concept. My goal was to create a book that would contain a diverse and comprehensive range of subjects, genres, opinions, perspectives, and voices on sustainability. Rather than trying to advance any particular position or subject, I wanted to present as much of the conversation about sustainability as possible. I wanted my students (and other readers of this book) to encounter and engage with the diversity that makes sustainability such a promising yet challenging topic.

Of course, the book I originally envisioned would not fit on any bookshelf. It was necessary to choose representative texts about sustainability rather than including everything that's been said and written on the subject. However, I think this book does a pretty good job of capturing the essence of the conversation — I hope you will agree. The collection begins with several landmark historical texts about nature and the environment that have influenced our conceptions of sustainability. Understanding how our contemporary discussions of sustainability are informed by preceding texts is important, and I believe students benefit from the contextual readings in environmental writing that appear early in this book. Most of the readings that follow are current, and they cover a wide range of questions and perspectives. The selections in Chapter 2, in particular, are intended to demonstrate the diversity of opinion on sustainability. It is likely that you will disagree with some of the perspectives in this collection — I certainly do — but it is vital to expose students to the wide-ranging viewpoints surrounding sustainability, allowing them to situate their own beliefs in the process. Similarly, the readings in Chapters 4 and 5 reveal the ways in which sustainability is at once an inherently local issue, requiring local solutions, while at the same time a transnational issue, in that solutions to the big problems of resource use, equity, and humanity's future must be conceived and addressed on a global scale. Collectively, the readings in this book cover a wide range of subjects and viewpoints regarding sustainability.

Sustainability includes literary texts, government reports, journalistic accounts, scholarly and scientific articles, personal narratives, blog entries, Web-based texts, and arguments of various sorts; these texts reveal the diversity of genres, styles, and voices in the sustainability conversation. The book also includes images of some iconic people, places, and events influencing our notions of sustainability — I encourage you to discuss the impact of these images with your students. Each chapter is grouped to highlight the interaction and negotiation between voices and perspectives on sustainability, and the introductions, headnotes, and inquiry-based questions are intended to spark productive discussion and critical engagement. In short, this book is designed to provide real opportunities for students to think and write about the complex issues surrounding sustainability.

It is worth noting that this printed book is a static text about a dynamic, constantly evolving subject; the conversation develops every day, while a printed text is rooted in time. Likewise, a print publication like this one is (currently) unable to include the many multimedia texts that increasingly influence the sustainability conversation. For that reason, I encourage you to visit **bedfordstmartins.com/spotlight** for materials that will enhance your class and your students' currency and engagement with sustainability, including a variety of links to multimedia, such as videos and Web sites, you may find useful. In addition, you'll find syllabi and assignments that you may find helpful as you prepare your own classes on sustainability and writing. I encourage you to send me your recommendations for related material, since the site will be updated with new and important texts about the subject.

As a final note: sustainability is more than just the subject of this book — it is also a guiding principle in the production and distribution of the text itself. I commend Bedford/St. Martin's and Macmillan for their efforts to produce this book in sustainable ways. Please see page xi for more information on sustainability at Macmillan.

Acknowledgments

Many people helped in the creation and development of this book. First, I'd like to acknowledge the students who helped me to understand why sustainability and writing are important to them. Numerous students at Penn State Berks offered insights and ideas about the readings, questions, and other materials through courses on sustainability, writing, and rhetoric. I am grateful for the assistance of Penn State students who helped with various stages of research for this book, including Kara Kennedy, Lydia Conrad, Ashley Offenback, and Jacob Kraus. I also would like to thank the amazing students in my Sustainability and Rhetoric course at Middlebury College, who served as the "test pilots" of this book when I taught a winter seminar there in 2014.

I deeply appreciate the many generous scholars and colleagues who have contributed to my thinking about sustainability, writing, and rhetoric. My biggest debt is to my friend and ongoing collaborator Sid Dobrin. Our work together through *Natural Discourse: Toward Ecocomposition*,

Ecocomposition: Theoretical and Pedagogical Approaches, and other scholarly projects has had a fundamental influence on my thinking and on this textbook. Equally important, Sid has been a model for how to take the work very seriously without taking yourself too seriously in the process. Also important to me were the conversations about sustainability, writing, rhetoric, discourse, ecocomposition, and ecology I have had with colleagues and friends including Jimmie Killingsworth, Marilyn Cooper, Steve Brown, Derek Owens, Jon Isham, Bill McKibben, Julie Drew, Joe Hardin, Chris Keller, Michelle Ballif, Anis Bawarshi, Bradley Dilger, Mary Jo Reiff, Raul Sanchez, Gary Olson, Peter Goggin, John Ackerman, Byron Hawk, Peter Vandenberg, Paul Heilker, and too many others to mention. In their own ways, each of these people has helped to shape the direction and focus of this book.

I would like to acknowledge the staff, faculty, and administrators at Penn State Berks for their support of my research and writing endeavors. I am particularly appreciative of the Research Development Grant I received from Penn State in 2014, which gave me time and resources to complete this book.

I am grateful to all the reviewers who provided thoughtful and detailed feedback during the book's development process: Marilyn M. Cooper, Michigan Tech; Sid Dobrin, University of Florida; Darrel Elmore, Florida International University; Peter N. Goggin, Arizona State University; Brad Monsma, California State University, Channel Islands; Amy Patrick Mossman, Western Illinois University; and Heidi Stevenson, Northern Michigan University.

I owe a massive thank you to the wonderful people I have worked with at Bedford/St. Martin's. First and foremost is executive editor John Sullivan, who has patiently guided me through every stage of this book. John's keen editorial eye, his helpful advice about content and structure, and most of all his enthusiasm for the subject of sustainability have steered this book in all the right directions. I also thank Leasa Burton and Sophia Snyder for encouraging me to take on this project and for their open-mindedness in considering what it could become. I recognize the many other people at Bedford/St. Martin's who contributed to the development, editing, and marketing of this book, including Emily Rowan, Jane Helms, Karen Henry, Sue Brown, Andrea Cava, Nancy Benjamin, Amy Gershman, Kalina Ingham, Martha Friedman, Jenn Kennett, Sarah D'Stair, and Rachel Childs.

I couldn't write a book like *Sustainability* without the support of my family. They have willingly accompanied me on countless hikes; snowboarding trips; adventures in rivers, lakes, and oceans; and other outdoor expeditions while I subconsciously considered, planned, and wrote (in my mind) this book. They have also patiently and sometimes quietly tolerated the many hours I spent in front of a computer screen making this book a reality. I do it all for them and couldn't do it without them.

I dedicate this book to my father-in-law Don Kasun. He gave me some excellent advice in the early stages of this book: include as many perspectives as possible, and allow people to make up their own minds. That advice became a guiding principle for the book, and it has resulted in a more comprehensive and inclusive collection. I continue to benefit from Don's advice on this and on so many things in my life, and I am grateful for his influence.

Contribution

A portion of my proceeds from this book will go to Surfrider Foundation USA, a grassroots nonprofit environmental organization that works to protect the world's oceans, beaches, and waterways. Surfrider was my first contact with sustainability issues more than three decades ago, and the foundation's efforts still inspire and motivate me to stay involved. Check them out: www.surfrider.org.

Christian R. Weisser

A Note on Sustainability from Macmillan

At Macmillan, Sustainability Is More Than an Aspiration — It's Part of Our Mission

At Macmillan, we take great pride in the work we do. We view our role not only as a corporate contributor, but also as a global citizen. We strongly believe that finding a sustainable future is necessary not only in our business, but also for our world. Because of this, we have committed to addressing sustainability in the most serious way.

Corporate Sustainability as Mission at Macmillan

In 2009, corporate sustainability became part of the very mission of Macmillan. Not just as a press release, not just around the edges, but woven into the very fabric of our company. As part of this effort, we decided to focus on CO_2 emissions as our most pressing issue, with a goal of a 65 percent reduction in our carbon footprint (over our 2009 baseline) by the end of the current decade in 2020. If you do not share our conviction in the likelihood of greenhouse gas (GHG) emissions leading to a climate crisis — because it is not an absolutely proven fact — perhaps you might agree that the consequences of its being ultimately proven true are so dire that it is more prudent to take preventative action now rather than past the point where a catastrophic situation is beyond remedial action.

As Publishers, We Know We Have Certain Responsibilities to Society

First, we took a year to conduct a comprehensive investigation of our practices and to determine our carbon footprint. Next, we established employee-led committees to look at all aspects of our business and to make ongoing recommendations on how we can reduce CO_2 emissions.

The biggest area of environmental impact for a book publisher remains paper consumption. Paper combined with transportation, printing, and distribution of books accounts for over 80 percent of Macmillan's carbon footprint. Because of this, our initial effort has been dedicated to looking at every possible way we can reduce the carbon emissions resulting from our paper usage.

Making Great Strides

We have made great strides in becoming more efficient in our paper consumption and rigorously well informed regarding our purchasing decisions. This dedication has been rewarded with a significant decline in our scope emissions from our paper usage by 25 percent over each of the past two years. Said another way, we have reduced the CO_2 intensity per ton of purchased paper required to print our books by 44 percent over our 2009 baseline.

Looking Ahead

Even with this early success, we are still at the very beginning of following through on our commitment. Macmillan's sustainability effort now covers every aspect of our working day, processes, and all the steps required to publish, print, and sell books — everything our companies can control or influence in their relationship with employees, vendors, authors, stores, and readers.

Sustainability has become part of our everyday discussion and a key factor in our business decisions. It is as important as our company growth, as important as our profitability. It may be even more important. All companies will need to address sustainability issues sooner rather than later if they hope to stay in business. It's more than "doing well by doing good"; it's the basic allegiance that any global citizen should pledge.

Please visit **sustainability.macmillan.com** for more information.

Bedford/St. Martin's offers resources and format choices that help you and your students get even more out of your book and course. To learn more about or to order any of the following products, e-mail sales support (sales_support@bfwpub.com), visit the Web site at **macmillanhighered.com/spotlight**, or contact your Bedford/St. Martin's sales representative.

Select Value Packages

Add value to your book by packaging any Bedford/St. Martin's text with *Sustainability*. To learn more about package options for any of the following products, contact your Bedford/St. Martin's sales representative or visit **macmillanhighered.com/sustainability/catalog**.

LearningCurve for Readers and Writers, Bedford/St. Martin's adaptive quizzing program, quickly learns what students already know and helps them practice what they don't yet understand. Gamelike quizzing motivates students to engage with their course, and reporting tools help teachers discern their students' needs. *LearningCurve for Readers and Writers* can be packaged with *Sustainability* at a significant discount. An activation code is required. To order *LearningCurve* packaged with the print book, use ISBN 978-1-4576-7936-0. For details, visit **macmillanhighered.com/englishlearningcurve**.

i·series, the popular series from Bedford/St Martin's, presents multimedia tutorials in a flexible format — because there are things you can't do in a book.

- *ix visualizing composition 2.0* helps students put into practice key rhetorical and visual concepts. To order *ix visualizing composition 2.0* packaged with *Sustainability*, use ISBN 978-1-4576-7937-7.
- *i·claim: visualizing argument* offers a new way to see argument — with six multimedia tutorials, an illustrated glossary, and a wide array of multimedia arguments. To order *i·claim: visualizing argument* packaged with *Sustainability*, use ISBN 978-1-4576-7931-5.

***Portfolio Keeping*, Third Edition, by Nedra Reynolds and Elizabeth Davis** provides all the information students need to use the portfolio method successfully in a writing course. *Portfolio Teaching*, a companion guide for instructors, provides the practical information instructors and writing program administrators need to use the portfolio method successfully in a writing course. To order *Portfolio Keeping* packaged with *Sustainability*, use ISBN 978-1-4576-7934-6.

A *Reader's Guide to College Writing*, by John J. Ruszkiewicz gives students an insider's view of the way critical reading really works and how a writer's rhetorical choices lead to powerful writing. In dynamic, pocket-sized lessons, readers are drawn into the conversation with a wise, helpful, and fun professor who knows just the right example to illustrate a concept. To order *A Reader's Guide to College Writing* packaged with *Sustainability*, use ISBN 978-1-319-01078-2.

***EasyWriter*, Fifth Edition, by Andrea Lunsford** distills Andrea Lunsford's teaching and research into the essentials that today's writers need to make good choices in any rhetorical situation. To order *EasyWriter* packaged with *Sustainability* use ISBN 978-1-4576-9536-0.

Make Learning Fun with *Re:Writing 3*

New open online resources with videos and interactive elements engage students in new ways of writing. You'll find tutorials about using common digital writing tools, an interactive peer review game, Extreme Paragraph Makeover, and more — all for free and for fun. Visit **bedfordstmartins.com/rewriting**.

Instructor Resources

You have a lot to do in your course. Bedford/St. Martin's wants to make it easy for you to find the support you need — and to get it quickly.

TeachingCentral offers the entire list of Bedford/St. Martin's print and online professional resources in one place. You'll find landmark reference works, sourcebooks on pedagogical issues, award-winning collections, and practical advice for the classroom — all free for instructors.

Bits collects creative ideas for teaching a range of composition topics in an easily searchable blog format. A community of teachers — leading scholars, authors, and editors — discuss revision, research, grammar and style, technology, peer review, and much more. Take, use, adapt, and pass the ideas around. Then, come back to the site to comment or share your own suggestions.

The Bedford Coursepack for Composition is available for the most common course management systems — Blackboard, Angel, Desire2Learn, Canvas, Moodle, and Sakai — and allows you to easily download digital materials from Bedford/St. Martin's for your course. To see what's available in the Bedford Coursepack for Composition, visit **macmillanhighered.com/coursepacks**.

Contents

Introduction for Students   1

Chapter 1   What Are the Foundations of Sustainability?   19

Henry David Thoreau, *Where I Lived, and What I Lived For*   22
A famed American author and philosopher describes his two-year experiment living in a cabin in the woods, contemplating the individual's place in the world and in nature.

John Muir, *The American Forests*   37
A writer and naturalist—often called "the father of the environmental movement"—describes the decline of American forests in the nineteenth century and the need for conservation.

Rachel Carson, *The Obligation to Endure*   49
A scientist and writer suggests that pesticides may do more harm than good and that long-term public health and safety must be considered.

Aldo Leopold, *Thinking Like a Mountain*   57
A conservationist describes watching a wolf die and the realization this brought him about the interconnections between man, animals, and nature.

David Suzuki, *The Sacred Balance: Rediscovering Our Place in Nature*   61
A scientist and environmental activist explores human society's impact on the natural world, both for the planet and for the people living on it.

Donella Meadows, Jorgen Randers, and Dennis L. Meadows, *Limits to Growth: Tools for the Transition to Sustainability*   70
A team of scientists analyzes the impact of worldwide population growth, global consumption patterns, and the dwindling supply of resources.

Chapter 3   How Do Crises and Disasters Create Challenges for Sustainability?   151

Chapter 5   How Is Sustainability a Transnational Issue?   255

Introduction for Students

Sustainability: A Bedford Spotlight Reader is a textbook for college writers. As you can see by surveying the table of contents, all of the articles and essays included in the book are focused on one particular theme: sustainability and humanity's impact on planet Earth. You may be wondering why a college writing textbook would be "about" something so specific; there is a good explanation for this, having to do with what college writing — and thinking — is. This introduction will explain what it means to be a college writer, provide a brief overview of sustainability and why it is an appropriate subject for a college writing course, and describe the organization and apparatus of this book.

What Is College Writing?

College writing represents a conjunction of skills that includes not just writing but also critical reading and critical thinking. *Critical reading* means being able to comprehend complex texts by reading closely, working to understand terms and theories, applying your own knowledge to them, cross-referencing other sources, asking questions of the text, and using strategies like note-taking and journal-keeping that result in enhanced understanding of a piece of writing. *Critical thinking* means being able to evaluate the merit of what you are studying by reflecting on and judging the information and arguments you are engaged with by thinking about them from multiple perspectives, probing their claims, recognizing biases, and questioning assumptions made by the authors. This conjunction of critical reading, critical thinking, and writing are part of the intellectual framework you will need to be successful in your academic and professional life — no matter what you choose to do.

Some students might say to themselves, "I am going to college to become a dentist, so when am I ever going to need to write a paper about sustainability?" Or, "I am majoring in criminal justice, so why do I need to learn about environmental issues?" These are understandable questions, but there are answers to them most educated people would agree with. First, the intellectual processes involved in comprehending complex ideas, applying those ideas to your own observations and experiences, formulating rational questions (and provisional answers to the dilemmas posed by your questions), and producing negotiated responses all constitute a basic structure inherent in every academic field and professional environment. The abilities you develop as a college writer in this course, and through this subject, will help you in all of your other classes as well as in your personal and professional life because nearly every facet of life requires effective reasoning and communicating. Second, it is vital to your college studies to cultivate curiosity about subjects that may seem initially uninteresting to you or unrelated to your future career. Developing skills as a critical thinker, reader, and writer will allow you to engage with new ideas and subjects in potentially exciting and challenging ways. This is one of the fundamental lessons of college studies: not all themes will immediately engage you or seem directly relevant, but all of your studies will contribute to your development as a critical thinker, an effective writer and communicator, and a valuable member of society.

As you advance in college, and eventually graduate — and perhaps move on to graduate or professional school or your first "real" job — you will transform in many ways. One of the major aspects of this transformation involves moving from student to professional, a turn from being a receiver of knowledge to being a producer of knowledge. To be a producer of knowledge means simply that you will be shaping the world by contributing your ideas and practices to it, and overwhelmingly you will do this through language: listening, reading, speaking, thinking, and writing. To be able to contribute to professional organizations and social institutions capably, responsibly, intelligently, and sensitively is a long-term goal that college writing can help you achieve.

What Is Sustainability?

You've probably heard the term "sustainability" in some context. It is likely that you've used some product or service that was labeled as sustainable, or perhaps you are aware of a campus or civic organization that focuses on sustainability. You may even recognize that sustainability has to do with preserving or maintaining resources; we often associate sustainability with things like recycling, using renewable energy sources like solar and wind power, and preserving natural spaces like rain forests and coral reefs. However, unless you have an inherent interest in sustainability, you probably haven't thought much about what the term actually means. In fact, many people do not have a clear sense of what sustainability is or why it is so important. The following description will provide a starting point for your investigations of sustainability, but your own ideas and perspectives will emerge as you get further into the subject through this book and through your class discussions and activities.

Simply put, sustainability is the capacity to endure or continue. If a thing or an activity is sustainable, it can be reused, recycled, or repeated in some way because it has not exhausted all of the resources or energy required to create it. Sustainability can be broadly defined as the ability of something to maintain itself, and biological systems such as wetlands or forests are good examples of sustainability because they remain diverse and productive over long periods of time. Seen in this way, sustainability has to do with preserving resources and energy over the long term rather than exhausting them quickly to meet short-term needs or goals.

Many current discussions about sustainability focus on the ways in which human activity — and human life itself — can be maintained in the future without exhausting all of our current resources. Historically, there has been a close correlation between the growth of human society and environmental degradation — as communities grow, the environment often declines. Sustainability seeks new ways of addressing that relationship, which would allow human societies and economies to grow without destroying or over-exploiting the environment or ecosystems in which those societies exist. The most widely quoted definition of sustainability comes from the Brundtland Report by the World Commission on Environment and Development in 1987, which defined sustainability as meeting "the needs of the present without compromising the ability of future generations to meet their own needs."

In other words, sustainability is based on the idea that human society should use industrial and biological processes that can be sustained indefinitely or at least for a very long time and that those processes should be cyclical rather than linear. The idea of "waste" is important here; a truly sustainable civilization would have little or no waste, and each turn of the industrial cycle would become the material for the next cycle. A basic premise of sustainability, then, is that many of our current practices are unsustainable and that human society will need to change to ensure that people in the future live in a world that is virtually no worse than the one we inherited.

As a quick example of sustainability, think about aluminum soda cans. In the past, many soda cans were used and thrown away without a whole lot of thought. Their creation, use, and disposal was a linear process, and lots of soda cans wound up in landfills and trash dumps. The practice of throwing them away was unsustainable because ready sources of aluminum are limited and landfills and trash dumps were filling with wasted cans. Consequently, governments and private corporations began to recycle aluminum soda cans, and today more than 100,000 soda cans are recycled each minute in the United States. In fact, today's typical used soda can returns as a new can in

iStockPhoto

just sixty days. A billion-dollar recycling industry has emerged, creating jobs and profits for the workers and businesses employed in that enterprise, while at the same time using limited resources more thoughtfully and reducing the impact on the environment. The process has become cyclical, resulting in the continued use of materials, rather than linear, in which a soda can is used once and then becomes waste. Many questions remain about the actual benefits of recycling — some of which you can read about in this book — but most people agree that recycling is a more-sustainable solution than pitching our used soda cans into the trash.

But sustainability is about more than just the economic benefits of recycling materials and resources. Although the economic factors are important, sustainability also accounts for the social and environmental consequences of human activity. This concept, referred to as the "three pillars of sustainability," asserts that true sustainability depends on three interlocking factors: social equity, environmental preservation, and economic viability. Some describe this three-part model as People, Planet, Profit. First, people and communities must be treated fairly and equally — particularly with regard to eradicating global poverty and ending the environmental exploitation of poor countries and communities. Second, sustainable human activities must protect the earth's environment. And, third, sustainability must be economically feasible — human development depends on the long-term production, use, and management of resources as part of a global economy. Only when all three of these pillars are incorporated can an activity or enterprise be described as sustainable. The following diagram illustrates the ways in which these three components intersect:

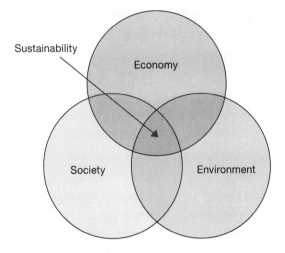

As this model should make clear, sustainability must consider the environment, society, and the economy to be successful. In fact, the earliest definitions of sustainability account for this relationship. The term *sustainability* first appeared in forestry studies in Germany in the 1800s, when forest overseers began to manage timber harvesting for continued use as a resource. In 1804, German forestry researcher Georg Hartig described sustainability as "utilizing forests to the greatest possible extent, but still in a way that future generations will have as much benefit as the living generation" (Schmutzenhofer 1992).[1] Although our current definitions are quite different and much expanded from Hartig's, sustainability still accounts for the need to preserve natural spaces, to use resources wisely, and to maintain them in an equitable manner for all human beings, both now and in the future.

Our current definitions of sustainability — particularly in the United States — are deeply influenced by our historical and cultural relationship with nature. Many American thinkers, writers, and philosophers have focused on the value of natural spaces, and they have contributed to our collective understanding about the relationship between humans and the environment.

---

[1]Quoted in K. F. Wiersum, "200 Years of Sustainability in Forestry: Lessons from History," *Environmental Management* 19 (3): 321–29.

Some of their writing is featured early in this book, and their ideas contributed to the environmentalist movement that emerged in the second half of the twentieth century. Environmentalism advocates for the protection and restoration of nature, and grassroots environmental organizations lobby for changes in public policy and individual behavior to preserve the natural world. The Sierra Club, for example, is one of the oldest, largest, and most influential environmental organizations in the United States; you can read an essay by its founder, John Muir, in Chapter 1.

Environmentalism and sustainability have a lot in common. In fact, some people think that our current conversations about sustainability are the next development or evolution of environmentalism. However, earlier environmental debates often pitted the environment against the economy — nature vs. jobs — and this dichotomy created a rift between those supporting one side of the debate against the other. The battle between the "tree huggers" and the "greedy industrialists" left a lot of people out of the conversation. Many current discussions involving sustainability hope to bridge that gap by looking for possibilities that balance a full range of perspectives and interests — a win-win solution rather than a win-lose scenario. Sustainability encourages and provides incentives for change rather than mandating change, and the three pillars of sustainability emphasize this incorporation. Many sustainability advocates imagine new technologies as mechanisms to protect the planet while also creating economic opportunities and growth; other sustainable approaches simply endorse new ways of thinking and acting. In essence, sustainability looks for coordinated innovation to create a future that merges environmental, economic, and social interests rather than setting them in opposition.

As you read the essays and articles in this book, all of which focus in one way or another on sustainability, you should think about how each of the authors operates from a different perspective, how the readings might influence your own definition of sustainability and, perhaps most important, what you should do to create a more sustainable world. It is likely that your views and perspectives on sustainability will change as you make your way through this textbook, and your critical reading and thinking skills will certainly develop as you become a more analytical writer.

Why Should I Study Sustainability in a College Writing Course?

In short, "sustainability" is a topic that will allow you to practice and hone your critical reading, thinking, and writing skills. You might ask, then, "Why sustainability? Why not something else?" This is a fair question. Sustainability is among the best single themes for a college writing course for the reasons outlined in this section.

Sustainability Is Important

In some ways, sustainability is the most important conversation taking place in our society today. The earth is our home, and it provides all of the things we need for our survival and nourishment. However, that home has limited resources, and our collective future will depend on the successful management and use of those resources. We are living in a critical time, in which global supply of natural resources and ecosystem services is declining dramatically, while demand for these resources is escalating. From pollution, to resource depletion, to loss of biodiversity, to climate change, a growing human footprint is evident. This is not sustainable. We need to act differently if the world and its human and nonhuman inhabitants are to thrive in the future. Sustainability is about how we can preserve the earth and ensure the continued survival and nourishment of future generations. You and everyone you know will be affected in some way by the choices our society makes in the future regarding the earth and its resources. In fact, your very life may well depend on those choices.

Sustainability Is Relevant

Sustainability impacts nearly all human endeavors, and it is tied to nearly every social, academic, and professional arena. When you consider sustainability in relation to science, business, economics, political science, art, music, literature, history — or indeed any field of study — you will no doubt see that ideas and assumptions about sustainability are important both to the shape of those fields and to the work done within them. Further, the readings in this collection are particularly relevant to American readers and writers because debates and conversations about sustainability can be found all around us — in the news, on television, in film, and perhaps even among people in your own family or social circles. Therefore, understanding sustainability will help you understand an important facet of your future life and work. This relevancy will allow you to respond to these readings in a way that wouldn't be possible with a less-accessible or less-timely theme. Because sustainability spans many fields of study, it offers a convenient research topic that accommodates diverse interests and many different kinds of writing (including personal, analytical, and argumentative).

Sustainability Is Complex

Sustainability is a complex subject that involves many different topics, conversations, and perspectives. Much of what we think and do concerning sustainability emerges from "expert" opinions on scientific, economic, and political issues, and it may seem daunting to try to form your own opinions based on your limited knowledge. Even the experts often disagree, and it can be confusing and difficult to sort through the complexity of the issues involved in the sustainability conversation. In fact, you may feel as if the subject is better left to those experts to address. However, you should recognize that it is that very complexity that makes the subject of sustainability worth addressing. Sustainability is a broad and diverse subject with no clear answer or set of answers. Consequently, it will allow you to form your own opinions; use research, reasoning, and evidence to support your claims; and contribute to the conversation in your own way. As you engage with the issues surrounding sustainability, you will develop your critical thinking skills in ways that an easy or simple subject (with clear answers) might not allow. Addressing the complex subject of sustainability will help prepare you to address other complex issues and subjects in your professional, personal, and social life.

Sustainability Is Interdisciplinary

Along with its complexity, sustainability is also an interdisciplinary subject. This means that it can be addressed or analyzed from many different academic perspectives and that various "disciplines" can be combined in its understanding. Interdisciplinary thinking is about crossing the boundaries of specific, traditional fields of study to look at a problem or subject in more holistic, comprehensive ways. In this respect, sustainability combines a variety of disciplines, including science, economics, politics, humanities, and others. In fact, it is hard to think of an academic discipline that could not contribute to the sustainability conversation. Your academic program or major — whatever it may be — can be a useful perspective on sustainability, and you can learn a great deal about the subject by exploring it through a range of disciplines and perspectives.

Sustainability Is a "Discourse"

All intellectual endeavors involve participation in an ongoing conversation called a "discourse." This is not the same type of conversation you might have with a roommate or with a group of friends; it is the type of conversation that takes place among many people over many years in various methods of expression: books, essays, articles, speeches, and other kinds of articulations. All university students are expected to develop skills to absorb, assimilate, and synthesize information gathered from various sources within various discourses and to find their own voice within them. This is a basic pattern in the creation of knowledge. Sustainability is an emerging conversation or "discourse" in our society — its definition is still developing, and the reading, writing, thinking, and talking that you do can contribute to that definition. This book offers a range of interrelated readings focusing on the discourse of sustainability; learning how to evaluate and analyze that discourse and how to shape your own voice and perspective within that discourse is an important skill.

Sustainability Is Political

Because sustainability is concerned with how we use limited resources on the earth, it is essentially a political issue. Each of the debates surrounding sustainability are political, since they seek to change the ways people think and act, often with the goal of influencing public policy and law. The essays and articles in this book emerge from a wide variety of political perspectives, ranging from liberal to conservative, and one goal of this book is to expose student readers to these varying perspectives so that they can develop their own opinions and beliefs. The book is intentionally designed to offer varying perspectives, even when these perspectives seem to be in opposition. As you read this book, think about the political perspective of each of the authors and the ways in which their politics inform their message.

Sustainability Is Rhetorical

Simply defined, rhetoric is about the ways in which speakers or writers attempt to persuade or motivate an audience. An effective writer will make careful choices in the language, delivery, timing, and other factors involved in a piece of writing because he or she wants those words to be understood, accepted, and acted on. Each selection in this book can be seen as a different rhetorical act that seeks to change the ways we consider or define sustainability. They all contribute, in some way, to our understanding of sustainability, and they all hope to influence our thoughts and actions. Because sustainability is such an important, complex, and political issue, it is vital to analyze the words and images that are used to define it. You will develop your abilities to understand rhetoric as you read further into this collection, and you will certainly develop your own rhetorical abilities as a result of the reading, writing, and thinking you will do. These persuasive abilities will carry over to other aspects of your personal, professional, and civic life.

Sustainability Is Personal

Sustainability affects each of us on a personal level. The communities we live in, the foods we eat, our modes of transportation, the jobs we pursue — each of these aspects of our lives and countless others are shaped by sustainable (or unsustainable) choices. By learning more about sustainability, you will learn more about the world you live in and the influence it has on your own personal well-being. Furthermore, each of us has the ability to choose sustainable behaviors to improve our own lives and the lives of those around us. Your own perspective on sustainability will likely evolve as you consider the essays and articles in this book, and that will shape your values and decision-making, enabling you to create a healthier, happier, and more sustainable lifestyle for yourself.

The Units in This Book

Sustainability is a vast subject, and many experts devote themselves to just one small aspect of it. Scientists, politicians, businesspeople, writers, journalists, and others are involved in the sustainability conversation, and, as noted earlier in this introduction, they often speak different "discourses" focused on their own specialization and expertise regarding sustainability. In fact, even the experts in sustainability can be uninformed about certain aspects of this complex and expansive topic. For instance, a climate change researcher may understand the science behind global weather patterns, but she may not fully understand how political leaders might respond to environmental changes. Likewise, an economist may be able to predict the financial impact of an increasing population on a third-world country, but he may not be able to account for the ways in which new technologies might alleviate some of that impact. Writers and journalists, in particular, struggle with the vast amount of information they encounter when researching sustainability issues, and they often seek input and advice from trusted experts as they report on sustainability issues to the public at large.

It is impossible to know everything about sustainability, and this book certainly does not aim to make you an expert on every facet of sustainability. However, the collection does provide a broad overview of many key questions relating to sustainability in the world today. Most of the pieces you will read are current, and many are selected from popular media sources like newspapers, Web sites, and blogs. As a result, they should be easy to digest and understand — and I hope you find them interesting and informative. A few pieces are selected from expert sources, but even those are relatively short and accessible for general readers. The goal is to expose you to the general conversations taking place regarding sustainability and prepare you to contribute to the ongoing discourse about how we will manage our planet's resources in the future. You will certainly play a role in this discussion one way or another, and this book may help you to contribute in a more effective and active way as a student, citizen, or employee — or perhaps even as an expert on some sustainability-related topic in your own right.

This book is designed around the following six key questions relating to sustainability, each with a corresponding chapter.

Chapter 1: What Are the Foundations of Sustainability?

This chapter's goal is to establish a "sustainability literacy" by exposing you to many classic or landmark texts in sustainability and environmentalism. The chapter reflects on and establishes definitions of key terms, such as "sustainability," "environmentalism," "ecology," "conservation," and so on. The reading selections lay the groundwork for the other chapters and conversations in this book by providing necessary background for sustainability readings and discussions.

Chapter 2: How Is Sustainability a Political Issue?

This chapter highlights important texts involving sustainability and environment as political and social topics. It focuses on human relationships with and in environments and the ways in which persuasive discourse shapes our public perceptions of those places. The central purpose of this chapter is to provide a range of perspectives from liberal to conservative, comparing and contrasting the ways they use language to shape public understanding about sustainability. It highlights major media outlets on different ends of the political spectrum as key participants in debates concerning sustainability and environmentalism.

Chapter 3: How Do Crises and Disasters Create Challenges for Sustainability?

This chapter addresses several recent environmental disasters, with a focus on those in the United States. Drawing on media, governmental, and scientific publications, the chapter describes the ways in which disasters create challenges and opportunities for sustainability. The reading selections cover three of the more-recent environmental disasters (Hurricane Katrina, Hurricane Sandy, and the BP oil spill in the Gulf of Mexico), as well as the important issue of species extinction.

Chapter 4: How Is Sustainability Connected to Local and Urban Environments?

This chapter looks at sustainability efforts in cities, suburbs, and other urban areas. The chapter's goal is to erase the dichotomy of environmentalism as a focus on preserving "natural" places, while highlighting the ways in which sustainability has been discussed as a personal and social activity. The reading selections address food and consumption, the pros and cons of recycling, the growth of "green jobs," campus sustainability efforts, the environmental impact of cell phones and personal electronics, and other related topics.

Chapter 5: How Is Sustainability a Transnational Issue?

This chapter highlights sustainability and environmental preservation as global, transnational issues. The chapter examines worldwide issues of population, resource use, global climate change, and the limits of global food production. To correspond with Chapter 3 (recent environmental disasters), this chapter also includes reading selections focusing on global environmental challenges, including the sustainable recovery efforts after the earthquake in Haiti and the environmental effects of the tsunami in Japan.

Chapter 6: How Are Tourism and Recreation Connected to Sustainability?

This chapter examines the role of tourism, leisure activities, and recreation in creating a more sustainably minded public. It begins by focusing on the ways ecotourism can both harm and help to protect environments through sustainable planning and development. Other reading selections address high-interest activities (including surfing, skiing, and hunting) and the ways in which these activities shape sustainability. The chapter also addresses the role of zoos and public aquariums in educating people about sustainability.

· · ·

By concentrating on these key questions relating to sustainability, you will develop a broad understanding of the conversation today. In fact, I believe that by the end of your course, you will know much more about sustainability than most people in our society. You will be a sustainability expert as a result of the reading, research, writing, discussing, and exploring that you will do. Each chapter is designed to add a new dimension to understanding sustainability — how it developed, how it is political, how disasters have shaped sustainability, how it affects local and global communities, and how it relates to tourism and recreation. Each reading in the chapters is intended to be put into conversation with the others, so as you read, note where intersections and discrepancies appear. Part of critical thinking and reading involves integrating sources, allowing them to "speak to" one another by noting where they agree and disagree, where they help clarify and expand one another, and where one sheds new light on another.

Across all the chapters, you will see many opportunities to share your experiences and personal perspectives about sustainability; to add your observations about the current state of the earth and what the future might look like; to place the readings in relation to one another; to engage with scientific, political, ethical, and economic issues related to sustainability; and in general to work within the discourse of sustainability to challenge the readings as much as they will challenge you. Most of all, I hope you will see that the intellectual processes you will engage in by reading, thinking, and writing within this discourse will translate to the kind of applications of critical reading, thinking, and writing you will perform throughout college and into your personal and professional life.

A Note on the Questions

At the end of each essay or article, you will find three sets of questions to help you think about the readings. The first set, "Understanding the Text," is designed to help you comprehend the reading on its own terms. These questions ask for clarification of the main point or theme in the articles, interpretations of the meaning of unique claims, and extrapolations of the examples and illustrations the author uses to support his or her overall positions. These are "reading comprehension" questions that can help you read the pieces closely and understand the author. Consider them as author-centered questions because they focus on understanding the author's main point or perspective.

The second set of questions, "Reflection and Response," asks for your contributions of examples, gathered through your experiences and observations, and your opinions or ideas about the articles as a whole or about their specific claims. These questions are intended to bring you into the conversation. Consider them as reader-centered questions because they focus on your own perspective and responses to the readings.

The third set of questions, "Making Connections," is designed to help you think of the readings as parts of larger conversations rather than as individual perspectives. These are often more complex writing prompts that ask you to consider reading in clusters, to look for correlations between different writers, and to examine sources outside this book. These questions also ask you to think further, to include your own claims and examples, or to offer counterclaims and counterexamples. Because each question calls for understanding various texts, positioning yourself within the conversation, and combining and cross-referencing other texts, you can think of these as discourse-centered questions.

I cannot predict how your instructor will use this text — and I would not want to suggest one way of using it that would be better than another. Each instructor will use it in his or her own way, based on the objectives of the class. Some teachers may select a few of the chapters in this book and investigate them exhaustively. Others may use all of the chapters in the book but perhaps in a different order than they appear. Your instructor's goals will also determine the types of assignments and questions you will draw from the book. One instructor may prefer to focus on the "Reflection and Response" questions, for instance, in a writing class that favors expressive essay writing or writing from experience. Another may value research-based writing and stay in the "Making Connections" section more often than not. Still another may prefer to modify these questions, combine them, or even ignore them and invent his or her own writing assignments. No matter how these readings are used, however, two things are certain: (1) this subject matter opens multiple ways to learn college writing; and (2) the readings elicit an important thread running through all good writing: *relevancy*. The relevancy of sustainability provides an undeniable immediacy and importance to whatever kind of work you produce about it. After all, these readings address the fundamental role of human beings and our future on earth. What could be more relevant and important than that?

On a personal note, I want you to know that this is one of the first writing textbooks devoted to this emerging and progressive topic. Sustainability is a cutting-edge subject for a writing class, and I think you are lucky to be taking a course that addresses it. I am deeply interested in your questions, ideas, and perspectives on sustainability and on this book. Please feel free to e-mail me at crw17@psu.edu.

Good luck with your writing!

Christian R. Weisser
Penn State Berks
Courtesy Christian R. Weisser

© Paul Earle Photography/Getty Images

What Are the Foundations of Sustainability?

Sustainability is an important subject in our world today, but few people have a clear sense of what sustainability means or where the term came from. You probably recognize that sustainability is somehow tied to preserving resources and protecting the environment, but it is likely that your definitions do not extend much further. That's okay — you will know far more about the foundations of sustainability after you've read, discussed, and written about the selections in Chapter 1.

The goal of this chapter is to help you establish a *sustainability literacy* — a basic understanding of what sustainability is all about and how the term and its related concepts have evolved. To develop this understanding, you will read and consider some of the primary texts that are central to the sustainability conversation. These readings will serve as a background to other selections in this book — in fact, many of the authors in Chapter 1 are referenced throughout the rest of the collection. In a way, you can consider some of the authors in this chapter as the forerunners of contemporary sustainability because what they said and did has had a big impact on our current views. This background will be tremendously useful as you begin to understand and participate in your own conversations about sustainability.

You may notice that the early selections in this chapter — written by Thoreau, Muir, Carson, and Leopold — do not reference or use the word *sustainability* directly. For those writers, the term was not yet a part of their vocabulary. What these authors offer, however, are some fundamental perspectives on human relationships to the world. This chapter is loosely chronological, and the early authors included here are pioneers. Many of them explored the natural world while also writing about it, giving us valuable insights on places, ecologies, and environments. Thoreau and Muir are among the first American writers to extol the value of natural places, so you should read their essays carefully to see how they begin the conversations. Leopold builds on this premise of the value of nature to consider the relationships and interconnections among all living things. Carson explores the impact of chemicals on natural systems and on our own bodies, and her book *Silent Spring*, which is excerpted here, is often credited as the impetus for the

American environmental movement. In many ways, the thoughts and writings of these four authors serve as a precursor to our contemporary understanding of sustainability.

The selections in the middle of the chapter — Suzuki and Meadows et al. — are more current, and they reflect on human culture and its relationship with the environment. This is a vital aspect of the sustainability conversation, and these pieces will provide further groundwork for understanding the connections between society and our planet's systems and resources. Suzuki and Meadows et al. introduce the notion of time (past, present, and future) as a significant aspect of sustainability. Together, these articles encourage you to think more broadly and deeply about humanity's place in the world.

The final piece in the chapter addresses sustainability directly and is intended to give you a fuller understanding of the term. Goffman introduces the economic and scientific aspects of sustainability, which will be examined in more depth throughout the book.

Collectively, the seven essays in Chapter 1 provide a background to the sustainability conversation, preparing you for more-specific and more-detailed discussions that will follow. One of your goals as you read this chapter — perhaps this is a goal of your course — should be to look for the connections between the concepts of nature, environment, ecology, and sustainability. Although these concepts and terms are not identical, they are inextricably linked. Understanding these key words will help you develop your sustainability literacy and will enable you to form your own perspectives on sustainability.

Where I Lived, and What I Lived For

Henry David Thoreau

Henry David Thoreau was one of the most important American authors of the nineteenth century. *Walden*, from which this essay is excerpted, is his most famous work. Published in 1854, *Walden* describes Thoreau's two-year experience living in a cabin he built himself in woodland close to Walden Pond, a few miles outside the town of Concord, Massachusetts. Thoreau writes: "I went to the woods because I wished to live deliberately, to front only the essential facts of life, and see if I could not learn what it had to teach." *Walden* remains a best-selling book today, and many readers are drawn to Thoreau's belief in finding truth and meaning in natural settings.

Thoreau's experiment in living simply and deliberately was inspired by the Transcendentalist philosophy, which identifies a spiritual connection between humans and nature. In many ways, the Transcendentalist movement was a precursor to more contemporary environmental and sustainable movements, as it highlights the individual's place in the world and in nature.

As you read this selection, think about what Thoreau is saying about a "deliberate" life in harmony with nature. Why did he choose to live away from other people? What does he say about simplicity and the necessities of life? What does he suggest about modern society?

At a certain season of our life we are accustomed to consider every spot as the possible site of a house. I have thus surveyed the country on every side within a dozen miles of where I live. In imagination I have bought all the farms in succession, for all were to be bought, and I knew their price. I walked over each farmer's premises, tasted his wild apples, discoursed on husbandry with him, took his farm at his price, at any price, mortgaging it to him in my mind; even put a higher price on it — took everything but a deed of it — took his word for his deed, for I dearly love to talk — cultivated it, and him too to some extent, I trust, and withdrew when I had enjoyed it long enough, leaving him to carry it on. This experience entitled me to be regarded as a sort of real-estate broker by my friends. Wherever I sat, there I might live, and the landscape radiated from me accordingly. What is a house but a *sedes*, a seat? — better if a country seat. I discovered many a site for a house not likely to be soon improved, which some might have thought too far from the village, but to my eyes the village was too far from it. Well, there I might live, I said; and there I did live, for an hour, a summer and a winter life; saw how I could let the years run off, buffet the winter through, and see the spring come

Walden Pond, near Concord, Massachusetts.

in. The future inhabitants of this region, wherever they may place their houses, may be sure that they have been anticipated. An afternoon sufficed to lay out the land into orchard, wood-lot, and pasture, and to decide what fine oaks or pines should be left to stand before the door, and whence each blasted tree could be seen to the best advantage; and then I let it lie, fallow, perchance, for a man is rich in proportion to the number of things which he can afford to let alone.

My imagination carried me so far that I even had the refusal of several farms — the refusal was all I wanted — but I never got my fingers burned by actual possession. The nearest that I came to actual possession was when I bought the Hollowell place, and had begun to sort my seeds, and collected materials with which to make a wheelbarrow to carry it on or off with; but before the owner gave me a deed of it, his wife — every man has such a wife — changed her mind and wished to keep it, and he offered me ten dollars to release him. Now, to speak the truth, I had but ten cents in the world, and it surpassed my arithmetic to tell, if I was that man who had ten cents, or who had a farm, or ten dollars, or all together. However, I let him keep the ten dollars and the farm too, for I had carried it far enough; or rather, to be generous, I sold him the farm for just what I gave for it, and, as he was not a rich man, made him a present of ten dollars, and still had my ten cents, and seeds, and materials for a wheelbarrow left. I found thus that I had been a rich man without any damage to my poverty. But I retained the landscape, and I have since annually carried off what it yielded without a wheelbarrow. With respect to landscapes,

> "I am monarch of all I *survey,*
> My right there is none to dispute."

I have frequently seen a poet withdraw, having enjoyed the most valuable part of a farm, while the crusty farmer supposed that he had got a few wild apples only. Why, the owner does not know it for many years when a poet has put his farm in rhyme, the most admirable kind of invisible fence, has fairly impounded it, milked it, skimmed it, and got all the cream, and left the farmer only the skimmed milk.

"A man is rich in proportion to the number of things which he can afford to let alone."

The real attractions of the Hollowell farm, to me, were: its complete retirement, being, about two miles from the village, half a mile from the nearest neighbor, and separated from the highway by a broad field; its bounding on the river, which the owner said protected it by its fogs from frosts in the spring, though that was nothing to me; the gray color and ruinous state of the house and barn, and the dilapidated fences, which put such an interval between me and the last occupant; the hollow and lichen-covered apple trees, nawed [*sic*] by rabbits, showing what kind of neighbors I should have; but above all, the recollection I had of it from my earliest voyages up the river, when the house was concealed behind a dense grove of red maples, through which I heard the house-dog bark. I was in haste to buy it, before the proprietor finished getting out some rocks, cutting down the hollow apple trees, and grubbing up some young birches which had sprung up in the pasture, or, in short, had made any more of his improvements. To enjoy these advantages I was ready to carry it on; like Atlas,° to take the world on my shoulders — I never heard what compensation he received for that — and do all those things which had no other motive or excuse but that I might pay for it and be unmolested in my possession of it; for I knew all the while that it would yield the most abundant crop of the kind I wanted, if I could only afford to let it alone. But it turned out as I have said.

Atlas: a Greek mythological figure who holds the earth on his shoulders.

All that I could say, then, with respect to farming on a large scale — 5
I have always cultivated a garden — was, that I had had my seeds
ready. Many think that seeds improve with age. I have no doubt that
time discriminates between the good and the bad; and when at last I
shall plant, I shall be less likely to be disappointed. But I would say to
my fellows, once for all, As long as possible live free and uncommit-
ted. It makes but little difference whether you are committed to a
farm or the county jail.

Old Cato, whose "De Re Rustica" is my "Cultivator," says — and the
only translation I have seen makes sheer nonsense of the passage —
"When you think of getting a farm turn it thus in your mind, not to
buy greedily; nor spare your pains to look at it, and do not think it
enough to go round it once. The oftener you go there the more it will
please you, if it is good." I think I shall not buy greedily, but go round
and round it as long as I live, and be buried in it first, that it may
please me the more at last.

The present was my next experiment of this kind, which I propose
to describe more at length, for convenience putting the experience of
two years into one. As I have said, I do not propose to write an ode to
dejection, but to brag as lustily as chanticleer in the morning, standing on his roost, if only to wake my neighbors up.

When first I took up my abode in the woods, that is, began to
spend my nights as well as days there, which, by accident, was on
Independence Day, or the Fourth of July, 1845, my house was not finished for winter, but was merely a defense against the rain, without
plastering or chimney, the walls being of rough, weather-stained
boards, with wide chinks, which made it cool at night. The upright
white hewn studs and freshly planed door and window casings gave
it a clean and airy look, especially in the morning, when its timbers
were saturated with dew, so that I fancied that by noon some sweet
gum would exude from them. To my imagination it retained throughout the day more or less of this auroral character, reminding me of a
certain house on a mountain which I had visited a year before. This
was an airy and unplastered cabin, fit to entertain a travelling god,
and where a goddess might trail her garments. The winds which
passed over my dwelling were such as sweep over the ridges of mountains, bearing the broken strains, or celestial parts only, of terrestrial
music. The morning wind forever blows, the poem of creation is un-
interrupted; but few are the ears that hear it. Olympus° is but the
outside of the earth everywhere.

Olympus: mountain where Greek gods were thought to live.

The only house I had been the owner of before, if I except a boat, was a tent, which I used occasionally when making excursions in the summer, and this is still rolled up in my garret; but the boat, after passing from hand to hand, has gone down the stream of time. With this more substantial shelter about me, I had made some progress toward settling in the world. This frame, so slightly clad, was a sort of crystallization around me, and reacted on the builder. It was suggestive somewhat as a picture in outlines. I did not need to go outdoors to take the air, for the atmosphere within had lost none of its freshness. It was not so much within doors as behind a door where I sat, even in the rainiest weather. The Harivansa° says, "An abode without birds is like a meat without seasoning." Such was not my abode, for I found myself suddenly neighbor to the birds; not by having imprisoned one, but having caged myself near them. I was not only nearer to some of those which commonly frequent the garden and the orchard, but to those smaller and more thrilling songsters of the forest which never, or rarely, serenade a villager — the wood thrush, the veery, the scarlet tanager, the field sparrow, the whip-poor-will, and many others.

I was seated by the shore of a small pond, about a mile and a half 10 south of the village of Concord and somewhat higher than it, in the midst of an extensive wood between that town and Lincoln, and about two miles south of that our only field known to fame, Concord Battle Ground; but I was so low in the woods that the opposite shore, half a mile off, like the rest, covered with wood, was my most distant horizon. For the first week, whenever I looked out on the pond it impressed me like a tarn high up on the side of a mountain, its bottom far above the surface of other lakes, and, as the sun arose, I saw it throwing off its nightly clothing of mist, and here and there, by degrees, its soft ripples or its smooth reflecting surface was revealed, while the mists, like ghosts, were stealthily withdrawing in every direction into the woods, as at the breaking up of some nocturnal conventicle. The very dew seemed to hang upon the trees later into the day than usual, as on the sides of mountains.

This small lake was of most value as a neighbor in the intervals of a gentle rain-storm in August, when, both air and water being perfectly still, but the sky overcast, mid-afternoon had all the serenity of evening, and the wood thrush sang around, and was heard from shore to shore. A lake like this is never smoother than at such a time; and

---

Harivansa (Harivamsa): ancient religious Hindu text.

the clear portion of the air above it being, shallow and darkened by clouds, the water, full of light and reflections, becomes a lower heaven itself so much the more important. From a hill-top near by, where the wood had been recently cut off, there was a pleasing vista southward across the pond, through a wide indentation in the hills which form the shore there, where their opposite sides sloping toward each other suggested a stream flowing out in that direction through a wooded valley, but stream there was none. That way I looked between and over the near green hills to some distant and higher ones in the horizon, tinged with blue. Indeed, by standing on tiptoe I could catch a glimpse of some of the peaks of the still bluer and more distant mountain ranges in the northwest, those true-blue coins from heaven's own mint, and also of some portion of the village. But in other directions, even from this point, I could not see over or beyond the woods which surrounded me. It is well to have some water in your neighborhood, to give buoyancy to and float the earth. One value even of the smallest well is, that when you look into it you see that earth is not continent but insular. This is as important as that it keeps butter cool. When I looked across the pond from this peak toward the Sudbury meadows, which in time of flood I distinguished elevated perhaps by a mirage in their seething valley, like a coin in a basin, all the earth beyond the pond appeared like a thin crust insulated and floated even by this small sheet of interverting water, and I was reminded that this on which I dwelt was but *dry land.*

Though the view from my door was still more contracted, I did not feel crowded or confined in the least. There was pasture enough for my imagination. The low shrub oak plateau to which the opposite shore arose stretched away toward the prairies of the West and the steppes of Tartary, affording ample room for all the roving families of men. "There are none happy in the world but beings who enjoy freely a vast horizon" — said Damodara, when his herds required new and larger pastures.

Both place and time were changed, and I dwelt nearer to those parts of the universe and to those eras in history which had most attracted me. Where I lived was as far off as many a region viewed nightly by astronomers. We are wont to imagine rare and delectable places in some remote and more celestial corner of the system, behind the constellation of Cassiopeia's Chair, far from noise and disturbance. I discovered that my house actually had its site in such a withdrawn, but forever new and unprofaned, part of the universe. If it were worth the while to settle in those parts near to the Pleiades or the Hyades, to Aldebaran or Altair, then I was really there, or at an equal remoteness from the life which I had left behind, dwindled and twinkling with as fine a ray to my nearest neighbor; and to be seen only in moonless nights by him. Such was part of creation where I had squatted, —

"There was a shepherd that did live,
  And held his thoughts as high
As were the mounts whereon his flocks
  Did hourly feed him by."

What should we think of the shepherd's life if his flocks always wandered to higher pastures than his thoughts?

Every morning was a cheerful invitation to make my life of equal simplicity, and I may say innocence, with Nature herself. I have been as sincere a worshipper of Aurora° as the Greeks. I got up early and bathed in the pond; that was a religious exercise, and one of the best things which I did. They say that characters were engraven on the bathing tub of King Tching Thang to this effect: "Renew thyself completely each day; do it again, and again, and forever again." I can understand that. Morning brings back the heroic ages. I was as much affected by the faint hum of a mosquito making its invisible and unimaginable tour through my apartment at earliest dawn, when I was sitting with door and windows open, as I could be by any trumpet that ever sang of fame. It was Homer's requiem; itself an Iliad and Odyssey in the air, singing its own wrath and wanderings. There was something cosmical about it; a standing advertisement, till forbidden, of the everlasting vigor and fertility of the world. The morning, which is the most memorable season of the day, is the awakening hour. Then there is least somnolence in us; and for an hour, at least, some part of us awakes which slumbers all the rest of the day and night. Little is to be expected of that day, if it can be called a day, to which we are not awakened by our Genius, but by the mechanical nudgings of some servitor, are not awakened by our own newly acquired force and aspirations from within, accompanied by the undulations of celestial music, instead of factory bells, and a fragrance filling the air — to a higher life than we fell asleep from; and thus the darkness bear its fruit, and prove itself to be good, no less than the light. That man who does not believe that each day contains an earlier, more sacred, and auroral hour than he has yet profaned, has despaired of life, and

Aurora: the Roman goddess of dawn.

is pursuing a descending and darkening way. After a partial cessation of his sensuous life, the soul of man, or its organs rather, are reinvigorated each day, and his Genius tries again what noble life it can make. All memorable events, I should say, transpire in morning time and in a morning atmosphere. The Vedas° say, "All intelligences awake with the morning." Poetry and art, and the fairest and most memorable of the actions of men, date from such an hour. All poets and heroes, like Memnon, are the children of Aurora, and emit their music at sunrise. To him whose elastic and vigorous thought keeps pace with the sun, the day is a perpetual morning. It matters not what the clocks say or the attitudes and labors of men. Morning is when I am awake and there is a dawn in me. Moral reform is the effort to throw off sleep. Why is it that men give so poor an account of their day if they have not been slumbering? They are not such poor calculators. If they had not been overcome with drowsiness, they would have performed something. The millions are awake enough for physical labor, but only one in a million is awake enough for effective intellectual exertion, only one in a hundred millions to a poetic or divine life. To be awake is to be alive. I have never yet met a man who was quite awake. How could I have looked him in the face?

We must learn to reawaken and keep ourselves awake, not by mechanical aids, but by an infinite expectation of the dawn, which does not forsake us in our soundest sleep. I know of no more encouraging fact than the unquestionable ability of man to elevate his life by a conscious endeavor. It is something to be able to paint a particular picture, or to carve a statue, and so to make a few objects beautiful; but it is far more glorious to carve and paint the very atmosphere and medium through which we look, which morally we can do. To affect the quality of the day, that is the highest of arts. Every man is tasked to make his life, even in its details, worthy of the contemplation of his most elevated and critical hour. If we refused, or rather used up, such paltry information as we get, the oracles would distinctly inform us how this might be done. 15

I went to the woods because I wished to live deliberately, to front only the essential facts of life, and see if I could not learn what it had to teach, and not, when I came to die, discover that I had not lived. I did not wish to live what was not life, living is so dear, nor did I wish to practice resignation, unless it was quite necessary. I wanted to live deep and suck out all the marrow of life, to live so sturdily and

Vedas: Hindu book of knowledge.

Spartan-like as to put to rout all that was not life, to cut a broad swath and shave close, to drive life into a corner, and reduce it to its lowest terms, and, if it proved to be mean, why then to get the whole and genuine meanness of it, and publish its meanness to the world; or if it were sublime, to know it by experience, and be able to give a true account of it in my next excursion. For most men, it appears to me, are in a strange uncertainty about it, whether it is of the devil or of God, and have *somewhat hastily* concluded that it is the chief end of man here to "glorify God and enjoy him forever."

Still we live meanly, like ants; though the fable tells us that we were long ago changed into men; like pygmies we fight with cranes; it is error upon error, and clout upon clout, and our best virtue has for its occasion a superfluous and evitable wretchedness. Our life is frittered away by detail. An honest man has hardly need to count more than his ten fingers, or in extreme cases he may add his ten toes, and lump the rest. Simplicity, simplicity, simplicity! I say, let your affairs be as two or three, and not a hundred or a thousand; instead of a million count half a dozen, and keep your accounts on your thumb-nail. In the midst of this chopping sea of civilized life, such are the clouds and storms and quicksands and thousand-and-one items to be allowed for, that a man has to live, if he would not founder and go to the bottom and not make his port at all, by dead reckoning, and he must be a great calculator indeed who succeeds. Simplify, simplify. Instead of three meals a day, if it be necessary eat but one; instead of a hundred dishes, five; and reduce other things in proportion. Our life is like a German Confederacy, made up of petty states, with its boundary forever fluctuating, so that even a German cannot tell you how it is bounded at any moment. The nation itself, with all its so-called internal improvements, which, by the way are all external and superficial, is just such an unwieldy and overgrown establishment, cluttered with furniture and tripped up by its own traps, ruined by luxury and heedless expense, by want of calculation and a worthy aim, as the million households in the land; and the only cure for it, as for them, is in a rigid economy, a stern and more than Spartan simplicity of life and elevation of purpose. It lives too fast. Men think that it is essential that the *Nation* have commerce, and export ice, and talk through a telegraph, and ride thirty miles an hour, without a doubt, whether *they* do or not; but whether we should live like baboons or like men, is a little uncertain. If we do not get out sleepers, and forge rails, and devote days and nights to the work, but go to tinkering upon our *lives* to improve *them*, who will build railroads? And if railroads are not built, how shall we get to heaven in season? But if we stay at home and mind our business, who will want railroads? We do not ride on the railroad; it rides upon us. Did you ever think what those sleepers are that underlie the railroad? Each one is a man, an Irishman, or a Yankee man. The rails are laid on them, and they are covered with sand, and the cars run smoothly over them. They are sound sleepers, I assure you. And every few years a new lot is laid down and run over; so that, if some have the pleasure of riding on a rail, others have the misfortune to be ridden upon. And when they run over a man that is walking in his sleep, a supernumerary sleeper in the wrong position, and wake him up, they suddenly stop the cars, and make a hue and cry about it, as if this were an exception. I am glad to know that it takes a gang of men for every five miles to keep the sleepers down and level in their beds as it is, for this is a sign that they may sometime get up again.

Why should we live with such hurry and waste of life? We are determined to be starved before we are hungry. Men say that a stitch in time saves nine, and so they take a thousand stitches today to save nine tomorrow. As for *work,* we haven't any of any consequence. We have the Saint Vitus' dance,° and cannot possibly keep our heads still. If I should only give a few pulls at the parish bell-rope, as for a fire, that is, without setting the bell, there is hardly a man on his farm in the outskirts of Concord, notwithstanding that press of engagements which was his excuse so many times this morning, nor a boy, nor a woman, I might almost say, but would forsake all and follow that sound, not mainly to save property from the flames, but, if we will confess the truth, much more to see it burn, since burn it must, and we, be it known, did not set it on fire — or to see it put out, and have a hand in it, if that is done as handsomely; yes, even if it were the parish church itself. Hardly a man takes a half-hour's nap after dinner, but when he wakes he holds up his head and asks, "What's the news?" as if the rest of mankind had stood his sentinels. Some give directions to be waked every half-hour, doubtless for no other purpose; and then, to pay for it, they tell what they have dreamed. After a night's sleep the news is as indispensable as the breakfast. "Pray tell me anything new that has happened to a man anywhere on this globe" — and he reads it over his coffee and rolls, that a man has had his eyes gouged out this morning on the Wachito River, never dreaming the while that he lives in the dark unfathomed mammoth cave of this world, and has but the rudiment of an eye himself.

St. Vitus' dance: disease characterized by involuntary jerking movements.

For my part, I could easily do without the post-office. I think that there are very few important communications made through it. To speak critically, I never received more than one or two letters in my life — I wrote this some years ago — that were worth the postage. The penny-post is, commonly, an institution through which you seriously offer a man that penny for his thoughts which is so often safely offered in jest. And I am sure that I never read any memorable news in a newspaper. If we read of one man robbed, or murdered, or killed by accident, or one house burned, or one vessel wrecked, or one steamboat blown up, or one cow run over on the Western Railroad, or one mad dog killed, or one lot of grasshoppers in the winter — we never need read of another. One is enough. If you are acquainted with the principle, what do you care for a myriad instances and applications? To a philosopher all *news,* as it is called, is gossip, and they who edit and read it are old women over their tea. Yet not a few are greedy after this gossip. There was such a rush, as I hear, the other day at one of the offices to learn the foreign news by the last arrival, that several large squares of plate glass belonging to the establishment were broken by the pressure — news which I seriously think a ready wit might write a twelve-month, or twelve years, beforehand with sufficient accuracy. As for Spain, for instance, if you know how to throw in Don Carlos and the Infanta, and Don Pedro and Seville and Granada, from time to time in the right proportions — they may have changed the names a little since I saw the papers — and serve up a bull-fight when other entertainments fail, it will be true to the letter, and give us as good an idea of the exact state or ruin of things in Spain as the most succinct and lucid reports under this head in the newspapers: and as for England, almost the last significant scrap of news from that quarter was the revolution of 1649; and if you have learned the history of her crops for an average year, you never need attend to that thing again, unless your speculations are of a merely pecuniary character. If one may judge who rarely looks into the newspapers, nothing new does ever happen in foreign parts, a French revolution not excepted.

What news! how much more important to know what that is which was never old! "Kieou-pe-yu (great dignitary of the state of Wei) sent a man to Khoung-tseu to know his news. Khoung-tseu caused the messenger to be seated near him, and questioned him in these terms: What is your master doing? The messenger answered with respect: My master desires to diminish the number of his faults, but he cannot accomplish it. The messenger being gone, the philosopher remarked: What a worthy messenger! What a worthy messenger!" The preacher, instead of vexing the ears of drowsy farmers on their day of rest at

20

the end of the week — for Sunday is the fit conclusion of an ill-spent week, and not the fresh and brave beginning of a new one — with this one other draggle-tail of a sermon, should shout with thundering voice, "Pause! Avast! Why so seeming fast, but deadly slow?"

Shams and delusions are esteemed for soundest truths, while reality is fabulous. If men would steadily observe realities only, and not allow themselves to be deluded, life, to compare it with such things as we know, would be like a fairy tale and the Arabian Nights' Entertainments. If we respected only what is inevitable and has a right to be, music and poetry would resound along the streets. When we are unhurried and wise, we perceive that only great and worthy things have any permanent and absolute existence, that petty fears and petty pleasures are but the shadow of the reality. This is always exhilarating and sublime. By closing the eyes and slumbering, and consenting to be deceived by shows, men establish and confirm their daily life of routine and habit everywhere, which still is built on purely illusory foundations. Children, who play life, discern its true law and relations more clearly than men, who fail to live it worthily, but who think that they are wiser by experience, that is, by failure. I have read in a Hindoo book, that "there was a king's son, who, being expelled in infancy from his native city, was brought up by a forester, and, growing up to maturity in that state, imagined himself to belong to the barbarous race with which he lived. One of his father's ministers having discovered him, revealed to him what he was, and the misconception of his character was removed, and he knew himself to be a prince. So soul," continues the Hindoo philosopher, "from the circumstances in which it is placed, mistakes its own character, until the truth is revealed to it by some holy teacher, and then it knows itself to be *Brahme*." I perceive that we inhabitants of New England live this mean life that we do because our vision does not penetrate the surface of things. We think that that *is* which *appears* to be. If a man should walk through this town and see only the reality, where, think you, would the "Milldam" go to? If he should give us an account of the realities he beheld there, we should not recognize the place in his description. Look at a meeting-house, or a court-house, or a jail, or a shop, or a dwelling-house, and say what that thing really is before a true gaze, and they would all go to pieces in your account of them. Men esteem truth remote, in the outskirts of the system, behind the farthest star, before Adam and after the last man. In eternity there is indeed something true and sublime. But all these times and places and occasions are now and here. God himself culminates in the present moment, and will never be more divine in the lapse of all the ages. And we are enabled to apprehend at all what is sublime and noble only by the perpetual instilling and drenching of the reality that surrounds us. The universe constantly and obediently answers to our conceptions; whether we travel fast or slow, the track is laid for us. Let us spend our lives in conceiving then. The poet or the artist never yet had so fair and noble a design but some of his posterity at least could accomplish it.

Let us spend one day as deliberately as Nature, and not be thrown off the track by every nutshell and mosquito's wing that falls on the rails. Let us rise early and fast, or break fast, gently and without perturbation; let company come and let company go, let the bells ring and the children cry — determined to make a day of it. Why should we knock under and go with the stream? Let us not be upset and overwhelmed in that terrible rapid and whirlpool called a dinner, situated in the meridian shallows. Weather this danger and you are safe, for the rest of the way is down hill. With unrelaxed nerves, with morning vigor, sail by it, looking another way, tied to the mast like Ulysses.° If the engine whistles, let it whistle till it is hoarse for its pains. If the bell rings, why should we run? We will consider what kind of music they are like. Let us settle ourselves, and work and wedge our feet downward through the mud and slush of opinion, and prejudice, and tradition, and delusion, and appearance, that alluvion which covers the globe, through Paris and London, through New York and Boston and Concord, through Church and State, through poetry and philosophy and religion, till we come to a hard bottom and rocks in place, which we can call *reality*, and say, This is, and no mistake; and then begin, having a *point d'appui*, below freshet and frost and fire, a place where you might found a wall or a state, or set a lamp-post safely, or perhaps a gauge, not a Nilometer, but a Realometer, that future ages might know how deep a freshet of shams and appearances had gathered from time to time. If you stand right fronting and face to face to a fact, you will see the sun glimmer on both its surfaces, as if it were a cimeter, and feel its sweet edge dividing you through the heart and marrow, and so you will happily conclude your mortal career. Be it life or death, we crave only reality. If we are really dying, let us hear the rattle in our throats and feel cold in the extremities; if we are alive, let us go about our business.

Time is but the stream I go a-fishing in. I drink at it; but while I drink I see the sandy bottom and detect how shallow it is. Its thin

Ulysses: a character in Homer's *Iliad* and *Odyssey*.

current slides away, but eternity remains. I would drink deeper; fish in the sky, whose bottom is pebbly with stars. I cannot count one. I know not the first letter of the alphabet. I have always been regretting that I was not as wise as the day I was born. The intellect is a cleaver; it discerns and rifts its way into the secret of things. I do not wish to be any more busy with my hands than is necessary. My head is hands and feet. I feel all my best faculties concentrated in it. My instinct tells me that my head is an organ for burrowing, as some creatures use their snout and fore paws, and with it I would mine and burrow my way through these hills. I think that the richest vein is somewhere hereabouts; so by the divining-rod and thin rising vapors I judge; and here I will begin to mine.

Understanding the Text

1. What does Thoreau mean when he says, "A man is rich in proportion to the number of things which he can afford to let alone" (par. 1)? How does this concept relate to what you know about environmentalism and sustainability?

2. How does Thoreau describe his location in paragraphs 10–13? Why is this important?

3. In paragraphs 14–15, Thoreau talks about waking up each morning. What does "waking up" mean to him literally, symbolically, and spiritually?

4. Near the end of this passage, Thoreau writes that "Time is but a stream I go a-fishing in" (par. 23). What is Thoreau saying about his place in the world?

Reflection and Response

5. Thoreau talks a lot about ownership. What are the benefits and liabilities of ownership? Do you agree or disagree with Thoreau's perspective?

6. What do you make of the many references to classical mythology in this excerpt? Why do you think Thoreau included them? What do they add to the text?

7. The word "simplicity" is used repeatedly in this text. Why does Thoreau repeat the term so often? What is his point?

8. How does Thoreau's location affect his way of thinking? Would he have had a different perspective if he had lived in a more urban environment? How does your landscape and location affect the way you think about things?

Making Connections

9. Thoreau is associated with the Transcendentalist philosophy. Do some research on Transcendentalism. What are its central beliefs? How does Transcendentalism relate to environmentalism and sustainability?

10. What is Walden Pond like today? How is it different from the place Thoreau lived? What would Thoreau think if he visited Walden Pond right now?

11. In paragraph 19, Thoreau discusses the communication technologies of his day. What is he saying about the ways in which we communicate? How does this relate to the communication technologies you use in your everyday life? How does technology connect or disconnect us from other people?

The American Forests

John Muir

John Muir is often described as the "father of the environmental movement" because he was one of the earliest and most persuasive advocates of environmental preservation in the United States. Born in Scotland in 1838, Muir moved to the United States as a boy and spent much of his early life exploring the American wilderness. After traveling to California, he spent many years exploring and writing about the Sierra Nevada mountain area. His writing and advocacy for the region helped to establish the Yosemite and Sequoia National Parks.

Muir published a dozen books and hundreds of articles about his experiences in the wilderness, and his work has been read by millions. It is no understatement to say that Muir fundamentally shaped the way Americans envision their relationship with the natural world. Hiking trails, monuments, beaches, glaciers, bridges, and even a college have been named in his honor. Later in his life, Muir founded the Sierra Club, one of the oldest and most influential environmental organizations in the United States.

The essay excerpted here, "The American Forests," originally appeared in *The Atlantic* magazine in 1897. Muir wrote the essay to raise awareness about the decline of American forests, and the essay is often credited as one of the inspirations for the establishment of the U.S. Forest Service. Pay attention to Muir's central idea and the way he conveys it. What point is he making about natural resources? What does he hope to accomplish? How does he use language to persuade readers?

The forests of America, however slighted by man, must have been a great delight to God; for they were the best he ever planted. The whole continent was a garden, and from the beginning it seemed to be favored above all the other wild parks and gardens of the globe. To prepare the ground, it was rolled and sifted in seas with infinite loving deliberation and forethought, lifted into the light, submerged and warmed over and over again, pressed and crumpled into folds and ridges, mountains and hills, subsoiled with heaving volcanic fires, ploughed and ground and sculptured into scenery and soil with glaciers and rivers, — every feature growing and changing from beauty to beauty, higher and higher. And in the fullness of time it was planted in groves, and belts, and broad, exuberant, mantling forests, with the largest, most varied, most fruitful, and most beautiful trees in the world. Bright seas made its border with wave embroidery and icebergs; gray deserts were outspread in the middle of it, mossy tundras on the north, savannas on the south, and blooming prairies and plains; while lakes and rivers shone through all the vast forests and openings, and happy birds and beasts gave delightful animation. Everywhere, everywhere over all the blessed continent, there were beauty, and melody, and kindly, wholesome, foodful abundance.

These forests were composed of about five hundred species of trees, all of them in some way useful to man, ranging in size from twenty-five feet in height and less than one foot in diameter at the ground to four hundred feet in height and more than twenty feet in diameter, — lordly monarchs proclaiming the gospel of beauty like apostles. For many a century after the ice-ploughs were melted, nature fed them and dressed them every day; working like a man, a loving, devoted, painstaking gardener; fingering every leaf and flower and mossy furrowed bole; bending, trimming, modeling, balancing, painting them with the loveliest colors; bringing over them now clouds with cooling shadows and showers, now sunshine; fanning them with gentle winds and rustling their leaves; exercising them in every fibre with storms, and pruning them; loading them with flowers and fruit, loading them with snow, and ever making them more beautiful as the years rolled by. Wide-branching oak and elm in endless variety, walnut and maple, chestnut and beech, ilex and locust, touching limb to limb, spread a leafy translucent canopy along the coast of the Atlantic over the wrinkled folds and ridges of the Alleghanies,° — a green billowy sea in summer, golden and purple in autumn, pearly gray like a steadfast frozen mist of interlacing branches and sprays in leafless, restful winter.

To the southward stretched dark, level-topped cypresses in knobby, tangled swamps, grassy savannas in the midst of them like lakes of light, groves of gay sparkling spice-trees, magnolias and palms, glossy-leaved and blooming and shining continually. To the northward, over Maine and the Ottawa, rose hosts of spiry, rosiny evergreens, — white pine and spruce, hemlock and cedar, shoulder to shoulder, laden with purple cones, their myriad needles sparkling and shimmering, covering hills and swamps, rocky headlands and domes, ever bravely aspiring and seeking the sky; the ground in their shade now snow-clad and frozen, now mossy and flowery; beaver meadows here and there, full of lilies and grass; lakes gleaming like eyes, and a silvery embroidery of rivers and creeks watering and brightening all the vast glad wilderness.

Alleghanies: the Allegheny Mountains, which run through Pennsylvania, Maryland, West Virginia, and Virginia.

Thence westward were oak and elm, hickory and tupelo, gum and liriodendron, sassafras and ash, linden and laurel, spreading on ever wider in glorious exuberance over the great fertile basin of the Mississippi, over damp level bottoms, low dimpling hollows, and round dotting hills, embosoming sunny prairies and cheery park openings, half sunshine, half shade; while a dark wilderness of pines covered the region around the Great Lakes. Thence still westward swept the forests to right and left around grassy plains and deserts a thousand miles wide: irrepressible hosts of spruce and pine, aspen and willow, nut-pine and juniper, cactus and yucca, caring nothing for drought, extending undaunted from mountain to mountain, over mesa and desert, to join the darkening multitudes of pines that covered the high Rocky ranges and the glorious forests along the coast of the moist and balmy Pacific, where new species of pine, giant cedars and spruces, silver firs and sequoias, kings of their race, growing close together like grass in a meadow, poised their brave domes and spires in the sky three hundred feet above the ferns and the lilies that enameled the ground; towering serene through the long centuries, preaching God's forestry fresh from heaven.

Here the forests reached their highest development. Hence they 5 went wavering northward over icy Alaska, brave spruce and fir, poplar and birch, by the coasts and the rivers, to within sight of the Arctic Ocean. American forests! the glory of the world! Surveyed thus from the east to the west, from the north to the south, they are rich beyond thought, immortal, immeasurable, enough and to spare for every feeding, sheltering beast and bird, insect and son of Adam; and nobody need have cared had there been no pines in Norway, no cedars and deodars on Lebanon and the Himalayas, no vine-clad selvas in the basin of the Amazon. With such variety, harmony, and triumphant exuberance, even nature, it would seem, might have rested content with the forests of North America, and planted no more.

So they appeared a few centuries ago when they were rejoicing in wildness. The Indians with stone axes could do them no more harm than could gnawing beavers and browsing moose. Even the fires of the Indians and the fierce shattering lightning seemed to work together only for good in clearing spots here and there for smooth garden prairies, and openings for sunflowers seeking the light. But when the steel axe of the white man rang out in the startled air their doom was sealed. Every tree heard the bodeful sound, and pillars of smoke gave the sign in the sky.

I suppose we need not go mourning the buffaloes. In the nature of things they had to give place to better cattle, though the change might

John Muir in 1902.

have been made without barbarous wickedness. Likewise many of nature's five hundred kinds of wild trees had to make way for orchards and cornfields. In the settlement and civilization of the country, bread more than timber or beauty was wanted; and in the blindness of hunger, the early settlers, claiming Heaven as their guide, regarded God's trees as only a larger kind of pernicious weeds, extremely hard to get rid of. Accordingly, with no eye to the future, these pious destroyers waged interminable forest wars; chips flew thick and fast; trees in their beauty fell crashing by millions, smashed to confusion, and the smoke of their burning has been rising to heaven more than two hundred years. After the Atlantic coast from Maine to Georgia had been mostly cleared and scorched into melancholy ruins, the overflowing multitude of bread and money seekers poured over the Alleghanies into the fertile middle West, spreading ruthless devastation ever wider and farther over the rich valley of the Mississippi and the vast shadowy pine region about the Great Lakes. Thence still westward the invading horde of destroyers called settlers made its fiery way over the broad Rocky Mountains, felling and burning more fiercely than ever, until at last it has reached the wild side of the continent, and entered the last of the great aboriginal forests on the shores of the Pacific.

Surely, then, it should not be wondered at that lovers of their country, bewailing its baldness, are now crying aloud, "Save what is left of the forests!" Clearing has surely now gone far enough; soon timber will be scarce, and not a grove will be left to rest in or pray in. The remnant protected will yield plenty of timber, a perennial harvest for every right use, without further diminution of its area, and will continue to cover the springs of the rivers that rise in the mountains and give irrigating waters to the dry valleys at their feet, prevent wasting floods and be a blessing to everybody forever.

Every other civilized nation in the world has been compelled to care for its forests, and so must we if waste and destruction are not to go on to the bitter end, leaving America as barren as Palestine or Spain. In its calmer moments in the midst of bewildering hunger and war and restless over-industry, Prussia has learned that the forest plays an important part in human progress, and that the advance in civilization only makes it more indispensable. It has, therefore, as shown by Mr. Pinchot, refused to deliver its forests to more or less speedy destruction by permitting them to pass into private owner-ship. But the state woodlands are not allowed to lie idle. On the con-trary, they are made to produce as much timber as is possible without spoiling them. In the administration of its forests, the state right-eously considers itself bound to treat them as a trust for the nation as a whole, and to keep in view the common good of the people for all time.

In France no government forests have been sold since 1870. On the other hand, about one half of the fifty million francs spent on for-estry has been given to engineering works, to make the replanting of denuded° areas possible. The disappearance of the forests in the first place, it is claimed, may be traced in most cases directly to mountain pasturage. The provisions of the code concerning private woodlands are substantially these: No private owner may clear his woodlands without giving notice to the government at least four months in ad-vance, and the forest service may forbid the clearing on the following grounds: to maintain the soil on mountains, to defend the soil against erosion and flooding by rivers or torrents, to insure the existence of springs and watercourses, to protect the dunes and seashore, etc. A proprietor who has cleared his forest without permission is subject to heavy fine, and in addition may be made to replant the cleared area.

In Switzerland, after many laws like our own had been found wanting, the Swiss forest school was established in 1865, and soon after the Federal Forest Law was enacted, which is binding over nearly two thirds of the country. Under its provisions, the cantons

10

denuded: to make naked or bare; strip.

must appoint and pay the number of suitably educated foresters required for the fulfillment of the forest law; and in the organization of a normally stocked forest, the object of first importance must be the cutting each year of an amount of timber equal to the total annual increase, and no more.

The Russian government passed a law in 1888, declaring that clearing is forbidden in protection forests, and is allowed in others "only when its effects will not be to disturb the suitable relations which should exist between forest and agricultural lands."

Even Japan is ahead of us in the management of her forests. They cover an area of about 29,000,000 acres. The feudal lords valued the woodlands, and enacted vigorous protective laws; and when, in the latest civil war, the Mikado government destroyed the feudal system, it declared the forests that had belonged to the feudal lords to be the property of the state, promulgated a forest law binding on the whole kingdom, and founded a school of forestry in Tokio. The forest service does not rest satisfied with the present proportion of woodland, but looks to planting the best forest trees it can find in any country, if likely to be useful and to thrive in Japan.

In India systematic forest management was begun about forty years ago, under difficulties — presented by the character of the country, the prevalence of running fires, opposition from lumbermen, settlers, etc. — not unlike those which confront us now. Of the total area of government forests, perhaps 70,000,000 acres, 55,000,000 acres have been brought under the control of the forestry department, — a larger area than that of all our national parks and reservations. The chief aims of the administration are effective protection of the forests from fire, an efficient system of regeneration, and cheap transportation of the forest products; the results so far have been most beneficial and encouraging.

"Now it is plain that the forests are not inexhaustible, and that quick measures must be taken if ruin is to be avoided."

It seems, therefore, that almost every civilized nation can give us 15 a lesson on the management and care of forests. So far our government has done nothing effective with its forests, though the best in the world, but is like a rich and foolish spendthrift who has inherited a magnificent estate in perfect order, and then has left his rich fields and meadows, forests and parks, to be sold and plundered and wasted at will, depending on their inexhaustible abundance. Now it is plain that the forests are not inexhaustible, and that quick measures must be taken if ruin is to be avoided. Year by year the remnant is growing smaller before the axe and fire, while the laws in existence provide neither for the protection of the timber from destruction nor for its use where it is most needed. . . .

It is not generally known that, notwithstanding the immense quantities of timber cut every year for foreign and home markets and mines, from five to ten times as much is destroyed as is used, chiefly by running forest fires that only the federal government can stop. Travelers through the West in summer are not likely to forget the firework displayed along the various railway tracks. Thoreau,° when contemplating the destruction of the forests on the east side of the continent, said that soon the country would be so bald that every man would have to grow whiskers to hide its nakedness, but he thanked God that at least the sky was safe. Had he gone West he would have found out that the sky was not safe; for all through the summer months, over most of the mountain regions, the smoke of mill and forest fires is so thick and black that no sunbeam can pierce it. The whole sky, with clouds, sun, moon, and stars, is simply blotted out. There is no real sky and no scenery. Not a mountain is left in the landscape. At least none is in sight from the lowlands, and they all might as well be on the moon, as far as scenery is concerned.

The half dozen transcontinental railroad companies advertise the beauties of their lines in gorgeous many-colored folders, each claiming its as the "scenic route." "The route of superior desolation" — the smoke, dust, and ashes route — would be a more truthful description. Every train rolls on through dismal smoke and barbarous melancholy ruins; and the companies might well cry in their advertisements: "Come! travel our way. Ours is the blackest. It is the only genuine Erebus° route. The sky is black and the ground is black, and on either side there is a continuous border of black stumps and logs and blasted trees appealing to heaven for help as if still half alive, and their mute eloquence is most interestingly touching. The blackness is perfect. On account of the superior skill of our workmen, advantages of climate, and the kind of trees, the charring is generally deeper along our line, and the ashes are deeper, and the confusion and desolation displayed can never be rivaled. No other route on this continent so fully illustrates the abomination of desolation." Such a claim would be reasonable, as each seems the worst, whatever route you chance to take.

Thoreau: Henry David Thoreau (1817–1862), U.S. naturalist and author.
Erebus: in classical mythology, it is the darkness under the earth, imagined either as the abode of sinners after death or of all the dead.

Of course a way had to be cleared through the woods. But the felled timber is not worked up into firewood for the engines and into lumber for the company's use; it is left lying in vulgar confusion, and is fired from time to time by sparks from locomotives or by the workmen camping along the line. The fires, whether accidental or set, are allowed to run into the woods as far as they may, thus assuring comprehensive destruction. The directors of a line that guarded against fires, and cleared a clean gap edged with living trees, and fringed and mantled with the grass and flowers and beautiful seedlings that are ever ready and willing to spring up, might justly boast of the beauty of their road; for nature is always ready to heal every scar. But there is no such road on the western side of the continent. Last summer, in the Rocky Mountains, I saw six fires started by sparks from a locomotive within a distance of three miles, and nobody was in sight to prevent them from spreading. They might run into the adjacent forests and burn the timber from hundreds of square miles; not a man in the State would care to spend an hour in fighting them, as long as his own fences and buildings were not threatened.

Notwithstanding all the waste and use which have been going on unchecked like a storm for more than two centuries, it is not yet too late, though it is high time, for the government to begin a rational administration of its forests. About seventy million acres it still owns, — enough for all the country, if wisely used. These residual forests are generally on mountain slopes, just where they are doing the most good, and where their removal would be followed by the greatest number of evils; the lands they cover are too rocky and high for agriculture, and can never be made as valuable for any other crop as for the present crop of trees. It has been shown over and over again that if these mountains were to be stripped of their trees and underbrush, and kept bare and sodless by hordes of sheep and the innumerable fires the shepherds set, besides those of the millmen, prospectors, shake-makers, and all sorts of adventurers, both lowlands and mountains would speedily become little better than deserts, compared with their present beneficent fertility. During heavy rainfalls and while the winter accumulations of snow were melting, the larger streams would swell into destructive torrents; cutting deep, rugged-edged gullies, carrying away the fertile humus and soil as well as sand and rocks, filling up and overflowing their lower channels, and covering the lowland fields with raw detritus.° Drought and barrenness would follow.

---

detritus: any disintegrated material; debris or dirt.

In their natural condition, or under wise management, keeping 20
out destructive sheep, preventing fires, selecting the trees that should
be cut for lumber, and preserving the young ones and the shrubs and
sod of herbaceous vegetation, these forests would be a never failing
fountain of wealth and beauty. The cool shades of the forest give rise
to moist beds and currents of air, and the sod of grasses and the various flowering plants and shrubs thus fostered, together with the network and sponge of tree roots, absorb and hold back the rain and the
waters from melting snow, compelling them to ooze and percolate
and flow gently through the soil in streams that never dry. All the
pine needles and rootlets and blades of grass, and the fallen decaying
trunks of trees, are dams, storing the bounty of the clouds and dis-
pensing it in perennial life-giving streams, instead of allowing it to
gather suddenly and rush headlong in short-lived devastating floods.
Everybody on the dry side of the continent is beginning to find this
out, and, in view of the waste going on, is growing more and more
anxious for government protection. The outcries we hear against forest reservations come mostly from thieves who are wealthy and steal
timber by wholesale. They have so long been allowed to steal and destroy in peace that any impediment to forest robbery is denounced as
a cruel and irreligious interference with "vested rights," likely to en-
danger the repose of all ungodly welfare.

Gold, gold, gold! How strong a voice that metal has!

"O wae for the siller, it is saepreva 'lin'."

Even in Congress, a sizable chunk of gold, carefully concealed, will
outtalk and outfight all the nation on a subject like forestry, well
smothered in ignorance, and in which the money interests of only a
few are conspicuously involved. Under these circumstances, the bawl-
ing, blethering oratorical stuff drowns the voice of God himself. Yet
the dawn of a new day in forestry is breaking. Honest citizens see that
only the rights of the government are being trampled, not those of the
settlers. Merely what belongs to all alike is reserved, and every acre
that is left should be held together under the federal government as a
basis for a general policy of administration for the public good. The
people will not always be deceived by selfish opposition, whether
from lumber and mining corporations or from sheepmen and prospectors, however cunningly brought forward underneath fables and gold.

Emerson° says that things refuse to be mismanaged long. An exception would seem to be found in the case of our forests, which have

---

Emerson: Ralph Waldo Emerson (1803–1882), U.S. essayist and poet.

been mismanaged rather long, and now come desperately near being like smashed eggs and spilt milk. Still, in the long run the world does not move backward. The wonderful advance made in the last few years, in creating four national parks in the West, and thirty forest reservations, embracing nearly forty million acres; and in the planting of the borders of streets and highways and spacious parks in all the great cities, to satisfy the natural taste and hunger for landscape beauty and righteousness that God has put, in some measure, into every human being and animal, shows the trend of awakening public opinion. The making of the far-famed New York Central Park was opposed by even good men, with misguided pluck, perseverance, and ingenuity; but straight right won its way, and now that park is appreciated. So we confidently believe it will be with our great national parks and forest reservations. There will be a period of indifference on the part of the rich, sleepy with wealth, and of the toiling millions, sleepy with poverty, most of whom never saw a forest; a period of screaming protest and objection from the plunderers, who are as unconscionable and enterprising as Satan. But light is surely coming, and the friends of destruction will preach and bewail in vain.

The United States government has always been proud of the welcome it has extended to good men of every nation, seeking freedom and homes and bread. Let them be welcomed still as nature welcomes them, to the woods as well as to the prairies and plains. No place is too good for good men, and still there is room. They are invited to heaven, and may well be allowed in America. Every place is made better by them. Let them be as free to pick gold and gems from the hills, to cut and hew, dig and plant, for homes and bread, as the birds are to pick berries from the wild bushes, and moss and leaves for nests. The ground will be glad to feed them, and the pines will come down from the mountains for their homes as willingly as the cedars came from Lebanon for Solomon's temple. Nor will the woods be the worse for this use, or their benign influences be diminished any more than the sun is diminished by shining. Mere destroyers, however, tree-killers, spreading death and confusion in the fairest groves and gardens ever planted, let the government hasten to cast them out and make an end of them. For it must be told again and again, and be burningly borne in mind, that just now, while protective measures are being deliberated languidly, destruction and use are speeding on faster and farther every day. The axe and saw are insanely busy, chips are flying thick as snowflakes, and every summer thousands of acres of priceless forests, with their underbrush, soil, springs, climate, scenery, and religion, are vanishing away in clouds of smoke, while, except in the national parks, not one forest guard is employed.

All sorts of local laws and regulations have been tried and found wanting, and the costly lessons of our own experience, as well as that of every civilized nation, show conclusively that the fate of the remnant of our forests is in the hands of the federal government, and that if the remnant is to be saved at all, it must be saved quickly.

Any fool can destroy trees. They cannot run away; and if they 25 could, they would still be destroyed, — chased and hunted down as long as fun or a dollar could be got out of their bark hides, branching horns, or magnificent bole backbones. Few that fell trees plant them; nor would planting avail much towards getting back anything like the noble primeval forests. During a man's life only saplings can be grown, in the place of the old trees — tens of centuries old — that have been destroyed. It took more than three thousand years to make some of the trees in these Western woods, — trees that are still standing in perfect strength and beauty, waving and singing in the mighty forests of the Sierra. Through all the wonderful, eventful centuries since Christ's time — and long before that — God has cared for these trees, saved them from drought, disease, avalanches, and a thousand straining, leveling tempests and floods; but he cannot save them from fools, — only Uncle Sam can do that.

Understanding the Text

1. How does Muir describe the variation in American forests from region to region?

2. How does Muir use the passage of time — past, present, and future — to make a point about the American forests?

3. How do the policies regarding deforestation in other countries differ from those Muir describes? Why does he make this comparison?

Reflection and Response

4. Why does Muir use so much description of the forests and landscape? What is the purpose of this thick description?

5. At times, Muir uses biblical or spiritual terminology. Why do you think he would link the earth and forests to God? How did this appeal to his audience?

6. What impact does the last paragraph of this piece have on you? What was Muir's intended purpose?

Making Connections

7. Muir mentions Thoreau's fear for the forests and their future (par. 16). What are the other similarities between Thoreau's essay (earlier in this chapter) and Muir's?

8. Do some research on Yosemite or Sequoia National Parks. What role did Muir play in their creation? Do you think he would be pleased with their current state?

9. Muir was one of the founders of the Sierra Club, a prominent environmental organization. Visit the Sierra Club's Web site and look for similarities between the essay you've just read and the content you find on the Web site. In what ways are Muir's ideas present in the organization today? How is it different from what he might have envisioned?

10. In what ways does this essay foreshadow current environmental and sustainability issues? In what ways are the issues it describes different from our current issues?

The Obligation to Endure

Rachel Carson

Writer, scientist, and conservationist Rachel Carson was born on a small family farm in Springdale, Pennsylvania, in 1907. Carson graduated from Pennsylvania College for Women (now Chatham College) in 1929; studied at the Marine Biological Laboratory in Woods Hole, Massachusetts; and received her master's degree in zoology from Johns Hopkins University in 1932. She began her career as an aquatic biologist for the U.S. Bureau of Fisheries and became a full-time writer in the 1950s.

Carson is known for two best-selling books: *The Sea Around Us* (1951) and *Silent Spring* (1962). Her early writing, including *The Sea Around Us*, focuses on the beauty of nature and combines scientific study and poetic description. Her later work focuses on the dangers of pesticides and other chemicals and their widespread use after World War II. Carson wrote *Silent Spring* to warn the public about the long-term effects of these chemicals, challenging the practices of agricultural scientists and the U.S. government. The basic premise of "The Obligation to Endure," the second chapter in *Silent Spring*, is that pesticides may do more harm than good and that public health and safety must be considered.

After the publication of *Silent Spring*, Carson was attacked as an alarmist by some in the chemical industry and in government, but she continued to speak out about the dangers of pesticides to humans, animals, and ecosystems. Testifying before Congress in 1963, Carson called for new policies to protect human health and the environment. Her work led to a nationwide ban on DDT and other pesticides, and it contributed to the creation of the U.S. Environmental Protection Agency (EPA). Carson was posthumously awarded the Presidential Medal of Freedom by President Jimmy Carter.

The history of life on earth has been a history of interaction between living things and their surroundings. To a large extent, the physical form and the habits of the earth's vegetation and its animal life have been molded by the environment. Considering the whole span of earthly time, the opposite effect, in which life actually modifies its surroundings, has been relatively slight. Only within the moment of time represented by the present century has one species — man — acquired significant power to alter the nature of his world.

During the past quarter century this power has not only increased to one of disturbing magnitude but it has changed in character. The most alarming of all man's assaults upon the environment is the contamination of air, earth, rivers, and sea with dangerous and even lethal materials. This pollution is for the most part irrecoverable; the chain of evil it initiates not only in the world that must support life but in living tissues is for the most part irreversible. In this now universal contamination of the environment, chemicals are the sinister and little recognized partners of radiation in changing the very nature of the world — the very nature of its life. Strontium 90, released through nuclear explosions into the air, comes to earth in rain or drifts down as fallout, lodges in soil, enters into the grass or corn or wheat grown there, and in time takes up its abode in the bones of a human being, there to remain until his death. Similarly, chemicals sprayed on croplands or forests or gardens lie long in soil, entering into living organisms, passing from one to another in a chain of poisoning and death. Or they pass mysteriously by underground streams until they emerge and, through the alchemy of air and sunlight, combine into new forms, that kill vegetation, sicken cattle, and work unknown harm on those who drink from once pure wells. As Albert Schweitzer has said, "Man can hardly even recognize the devils of his own creation."

> "The history of life on earth has been a history of interaction between living things and their surroundings."

It took hundreds of millions of years to produce the life that now inhabits the earth, eons of time in which that developing and evolving and diversifying life reached a state of adjustment and balance with its surroundings. The environment, rigorously shaping and directing the life it supports, contained elements that were hostile as well as supporting. Certain rocks gave out dangerous radiation; even within the light of the sun, from which all life draws its energy, there were short-wave radiations with power to injure. Given time — time not in years but in millennia — life adjusts, and a balance has been reached. For time is the essential ingredient; but in the modern world there is no time.

The rapidity of change and the speed with which new situations are created follow the impetuous and heedless pace of man rather than the deliberate pace of nature. Radiation is no longer merely the background radiation of rocks, the bombardment of cosmic rays, the ultraviolet of the sun that have existed before there was any life on earth; radiation is now the unnatural creation of man's tampering with the atom. The chemicals to which life is asked to make its adjustment are no longer merely the calcium and silica and copper and all the rest of the minerals washed out of the rocks and carried in rivers to the sea; they are the synthetic creations of man's inventive mind, brewed in his laboratories, and having no counterparts in nature.

To adjust to these chemicals would require time on the scale that 5 is nature's; it would require not merely the years of a man's life but the life of generations. And even this, were it by some miracle possible, would be futile, for the new chemicals come from our laboratories in an endless stream; almost five hundred annually find their way into actual use in the United States alone. The figure is staggering and its implications are not easily grasped — 500 new chemicals to which the bodies of men and animals are required somehow to adapt each year, chemicals totally outside the limits of biologic experience.

Among them are many that are used in man's war against nature. Since the mid-1940s over 200 basic chemicals have been created for use in killing insects, weeds, rodents, and other organisms described in the modern vernacular as "pests"; and they are sold under several thousand different brand names.

These sprays, dusts, and aerosols are now applied almost universally to farms, gardens, forests, and homes — nonselective chemicals that have the power to kill every insect, the "good" and the "bad," to still the song of birds and the leaping of fish in the streams, to coat the leaves with a deadly film, and to linger on in soil — all this though the intended target may be only a few weeds or insects. Can anyone believe it is possible to lay down such a barrage of poisons on the surface of the earth without making it unfit for all life? They should not be called "insecticides," but "biocides."

The whole process of spraying seems caught up in an endless spiral. Since DDT° was released for civilian use, a process of escalation has been going on in which ever more toxic materials must be found. This has happened because insects, in a triumphant vindication of Darwin's principle of the survival of the fittest, have evolved super races immune to the particular insecticide used, hence a deadlier one has always to be developed and then a deadlier one than that. It has happened also because, for reasons to be described later, destructive insects often undergo a "flareback," or resurgence, after spraying, in numbers greater than before. Thus the chemical war is never won, and all life is caught in its violent crossfire.

Along with the possibility of the extinction of mankind by nuclear war, the central problem of our age has therefore become the

---

DDT: $C_{14}H_9Cl_5$; potent chemical used as an insecticide, prohibited for agricultural use in the United States since 1973.

contamination of man's total environment with such substances of incredible potential for harm — substances that accumulate in the tissues of plants and animals and even penetrate the germ cells to shatter or alter the very material of heredity upon which the shape of the future depends.

Some would-be architects of our future look toward a time when it   10
will be possible to alter the human germ plasm by design. But we may easily be doing so now by inadvertence, for many chemicals, like radiation, bring about gene mutations. It is ironic to think that man might determine his own future by something so seemingly trivial as the choice of an insect spray.

All this has been risked — for what? Future historians may well be amazed by our distorted sense of proportion. How could intelligent beings seek to control a few unwanted species by a method that contaminated the entire environment and brought the threat of disease and death even to their own kind? Yet this is precisely what we have done. We have done it, moreover, for reasons that collapse the moment we examine them. We are told that the enormous and expanding use of pesticides is necessary to maintain farm production. Yet is our real problem not one of overproduction? Our farms, despite measures to remove acreages from production and to pay farmers not to produce, have yielded such a staggering excess of crops that the American taxpayer in 1962 is paying out more than one billion dollars a year as the total carrying cost of the surplus-food storage program. And is the situation helped when one branch of the Agriculture Department tries to reduce production while another states, as it did in 1958, "It is believed generally that reduction of crop acreages under provisions of the Soil Bank will stimulate interest in use of chemicals to obtain maximum production on the land retained in crops."

All this is not to say there is no insect problem and no need of control. I am saying, rather, that control must be geared to realities, not to mythical situations, and that the methods employed must be such that they do not destroy us along with the insects.

The problem whose attempted solution has brought such a train of disaster in its wake is an accompaniment of our modern way of life. Long before the age of man, insects inhabited the earth — a group of extraordinarily varied and adaptable beings. Over the course of time since man's advent, a small percentage of the more than half a million species of insects have come into conflict with human welfare in two principal ways: as competitors for the food supply and as carriers of human disease.

Disease-carrying insects become important where human beings are crowded together, especially under conditions where sanitation is poor, as in time of natural disaster or war or in situations of extreme poverty and deprivation. Then control of some sort becomes necessary. It is a sobering fact, however, as we shall presently see, that the method of massive chemical control has had only limited success, and also threatens to worsen the very conditions it is intended to curb.

Under primitive agricultural conditions the farmer had few insect 15 problems. These arose with the intensification of agriculture — the devotion of immense acreages to a single crop. Such a system set the stage for explosive increases in specific insect populations. Single-crop farming does not take advantage of the principles by which nature works; it is agriculture as an engineer might conceive it to be. Nature has introduced great variety into the landscape, but man has displayed a passion for simplifying it. Thus he undoes the built-in checks and balances by which nature holds the species within bounds. One important natural check is a limit on the amount of suitable habitat for each species. Obviously then, an insect that lives on wheat can build up its population to much higher levels on a farm devoted to wheat than on one in which wheat is intermingled with other crops to which the insect is not adapted.

The same thing happens in other situations. A generation or more ago, the towns of large areas of the United States lined their streets with the noble elm tree. Now the beauty they hopefully created is threatened with complete destruction as disease sweeps through the elms, carried by a beetle that would have only limited chance to build up large populations and to spread from tree to tree if the elms were only occasional trees in a richly diversified planting.

Another factor in the modern insect problem is one that must be viewed against a background of geologic and human history: the spreading of thousands of different kinds of organisms from their native homes to invade new territories. This worldwide migration has been studied and graphically described by the British ecologist Charles Elton in his recent book *The Ecology of Invasions.* During the Cretaceous Period,° some hundred million years ago, flooding seas cut many land bridges between continents and living things found themselves confined in what Elton calls "colossal separate nature reserves." There, isolated from others of their kind, they developed many new species. When some of the land masses were joined again, about 15 million years ago, these species began to move out into new territories — a movement that is not only still in progress but is now receiving considerable assistance from man.

The importation of plants is the primary agent in the modern spread of species, for animals have almost invariably gone along with the plants, quarantine being a comparatively recent and not completely effective innovation. The United States Office of Plant Introduction alone has introduced almost 200,000 species and varieties of plants from all over the world. Nearly half of the 180 or so major insect enemies of plants in the United States are accidental imports from abroad, and most of them have come as hitchhikers on plants.

In new territory, out of reach of the restraining hand of the natural enemies that kept down its numbers in its native land, an invading plant or animal is able to become enormously abundant. Thus it is no accident that our most troublesome insects are introduced species.

These invasions, both the naturally occurring and those dependent on human assistance, are likely to continue indefinitely. Quarantine and massive chemical campaigns are only extremely expensive ways of buying time. We are faced, according to Dr. Elton, "with a life-and-death need not just to find new technological means of suppressing this plant or that animal"; instead we need the basic knowledge of animal populations and their relations to their surroundings that will "promote an even balance and damp down the explosive power of outbreaks and new invasions." Much of the necessary knowledge is now available but we do not use it. We train ecolo-

20

Cretaceous Period: from 135 million to 63 million years ago; end of the age of reptiles; appearance of modern insects and flowering plants.

gists in our universities and even employ them in our governmental agencies, but we seldom take their advice. We allow the chemical death rain to fall as though there were no alternative, whereas in fact there are many, and our ingenuity could soon discover many more if given opportunity.

Have we fallen into a mesmerized state that makes us accept as inevitable that which is inferior or detrimental, as though having lost the will or the vision to demand that which is good? Such thinking, in the words of the ecologist Paul Shepard, "idealizes life with only its head out of water, inches above the limits of toleration of the corruption of its own environment. . . . Why should we tolerate a diet of weak poisons, a home in insipid surroundings, a circle of acquaintances who are not quite our enemies, the noise of motors with just enough relief to prevent insanity? Who would want to live in a world which is just not quite fatal?"

Yet such a world is pressed upon us. The crusade to create a chemically sterile, insect-free world seems to have engendered a fanatic zeal on the part of many specialists and most of the so-called control agencies. On every hand there is evidence that those engaged in spraying operations exercise a ruthless power. "The regulatory entomologists . . . function as prosecutor, judge and jury, tax assessor and collector and sheriff to enforce their own orders," said Connecticut entomologist Neely Turner. The most flagrant abuses go unchecked in both state and federal agencies.

It is not my contention that chemical insecticides must never be used. I do contend that we have put poisonous and biologically potent chemicals indiscriminately into the hands of persons largely or wholly ignorant of their potentials for harm. We have subjected enormous numbers of people to contact with these poisons, without their consent and often without their knowledge. If the Bill of Rights contains no guarantee that a citizen shall be secure against lethal poisons distributed either by private individuals or by public officials, it is surely only because our forefathers, despite their considerable wisdom and foresight, could conceive of no such problem.

I contend, furthermore, that we have allowed these chemicals to be used with little or no advance investigation of their effect on soil, water, wildlife, and man himself. Future generations are unlikely to condone our lack of prudent concern for the integrity of the natural world that supports all life.

There is still very limited awareness of the nature of the threat. 25 This is an era of specialists, each of whom sees his own problem and is unaware of or intolerant of the larger frame into which it fits. It is also an era dominated by industry, in which the right to make a dollar at whatever cost is seldom challenged. When the public protests, confronted with some obvious evidence of damaging results of pesticide applications, it is fed little tranquilizing pills of half truth. We urgently need an end to these false assurances, to the sugar coating of unpalatable facts. It is the public that is being asked to assume the risks that the insect controllers calculate. The public must decide whether it wishes to continue on the present road, and it can do so only when in full possession of the facts. In the words of Jean Rostand,° "The obligation to endure gives us the right to know."

Jean Rostand: (1894–1977), French biologist and philosopher.

Understanding the Text

1. What does Carson say about the power of humans to alter the natural world? In what ways is this power new, unique, or dangerous?

2. Why does Carson suggest that these chemicals should be called "biocides" rather than "insecticides"? What is the difference between these terms? Which term is more accurate?

3. In what two principle ways do insects conflict with humans? Does Carson believe that pesticides and other chemicals are the best methods for addressing these conflicts?

Reflection and Response

4. How does Carson appeal directly to the public? Is the public her primary audience in this piece? What other audiences do you think she imagined?

5. How does this excerpt discuss the notion of time? What are the differences in time that Carson discusses? How might these differences affect humans and natural environments?

6. The image on page 52 is taken from Carson's original text of *Silent Spring*. What does this image convey? How does it seek to persuade readers without using words? Do you think the image adds meaning to Carson's work?

Making Connections

7. Carson's work is credited for the ban of some pesticides, including DDT. Do some research to learn about DDT. How is it different from or similar to other pesticides that are still on the market?

8. Research some natural ways to control the pests that may destroy crops or gardens. Are these methods as effective as traditional pesticides? Which methods seem most appropriate to you?

9. Do some research on the EPA. What are the agency's goals? How are these goals similar to or different from Carson's ideas in this reading selection?

Thinking Like a Mountain

Aldo Leopold

Aldo Leopold (1887–1948) was an American writer, scientist, and conservationist. Leopold studied forestry at Yale University, worked for the U.S. Forest Service, and later became a professor of game management at the University of Wisconsin. Leopold is best known for his book *A Sand County Almanac* (1949), which has sold more than two million copies. The book is admired for its depiction of the land as a living organism, and "Thinking Like a Mountain" is one of the most famous passages in it.

Leopold was influential in the development of modern environmental ethics and in the movement for wilderness conservation. His ethics of nature and wildlife preservation had a profound impact on the environmental movement, and, like other environmentalists of his time, he warned of the dangers of short-term or limited thinking about natural resources. This essay describes Leopold's experience watching a wolf die and the realization this brought him about the interconnections among humans, animals, and nature. As you read the essay, think about what Leopold is saying about our connection to and dependence on the natural world.

A deep chesty bawl echoes from rimrock to rimrock, rolls down the mountain, and fades into the far blackness of the night. It is an outburst of wild defiant sorrow, and of contempt for all the adversities of the world.

Every living thing (and perhaps many a dead one as well) pays heed to that call. To the deer it is a reminder of the way of all flesh, to the pine a forecast of midnight scuffles and of blood upon the snow, to the coyote a promise of gleanings to come, to the cowman a threat of red ink at the bank, to the hunter a challenge of fang against bullet. Yet behind these obvious and immediate hopes and fears there lies a deeper meaning, known only to the mountain itself. Only the mountain has lived long enough to listen objectively to the howl of a wolf.

Those unable to decipher the hidden meaning know nevertheless that it is there, for it is felt in all wolf country, and distinguishes that country from all other land. It tingles in the spine of all who hear wolves by night, or who scan their tracks by day. Even without sight or sound of wolf, it is implicit in a hundred small events: the midnight whinny of a pack horse, the rattle of rolling rocks, the bound of a fleeing deer, the way shadows lie under the spruces. Only the ineducable tyro can fail to sense the presence or absence of wolves, or the fact that mountains have a secret opinion about them.

My own conviction on this score dates from the day I saw a wolf die. We were eating lunch on a high rimrock, at the foot of which a turbulent river elbowed its way. We saw what we thought was a doe fording the torrent, her breast awash in white water. When she climbed the bank toward us and shook out her tail, we realized our error: it was a wolf. A half-dozen others, evidently grown pups, sprang from the willows and all joined in a welcoming mêlée of wagging tails and playful maulings. What was literally a pile of wolves writhed and tumbled in the center of an open flat at the foot of our rimrock.

In those days we had never heard of passing up a chance to kill a   5 wolf. In a second we were pumping lead into the pack, but with more excitement than accuracy: how to aim a steep downhill shot is always confusing. When our rifles were empty, the old wolf was down, and a pup was dragging a leg into impassable slide-rocks.

We reached the old wolf in time to watch a fierce green fire dying in her eyes. I realized then, and have known ever since, that there was something new to me in those eyes — something known only to her and to the mountain. I was young then, and full of trigger-itch; I thought that because fewer wolves meant more deer, that no wolves would mean hunters' paradise. But after seeing the green fire die, I sensed that neither the wolf nor the mountain agreed with such a view.

• • •

Since then I have lived to see state after state extirpate° its wolves. I have watched the face of many a newly wolfless mountain, and seen the south-facing slopes wrinkle with a maze of new deer trails. I have seen every edible bush and seedling browsed, first to anaemic desuetude, and then to death. I have seen every edible tree defoliated to the height of a saddlehorn. Such a mountain looks as if someone had given God a new pruning shears, and forbidden Him all other exercise. In the end the starved bones of the hoped-for deer herd, dead of its own too-much, bleach with the bones of the dead sage, or molder under the high-lined junipers.

> "In wildness is the salvation of the world."

I now suspect that just as a deer herd lives in mortal fear of its wolves, so does a mountain live in mortal fear of its deer. And perhaps with better cause, for while a buck pulled down by wolves can

extirpate: to remove or destroy totally; exterminate.

be replaced in two or three years, a range pulled down by too many deer may fail of replacement in as many decades.

So also with cows. The cowman who cleans his range of wolves does not realize that he is taking over the wolf's job of trimming the herd to fit the range. He has not learned to think like a mountain. Hence we have dustbowls, and rivers washing the future into the sea.

· · ·

We all strive for safety, prosperity, comfort, long life, and dullness. 10 The deer strives with his supple legs, the cowman with trap and poison, the statesman with pen, the most of us with machines, votes, and dollars, but it all comes to the same thing: peace in our time. A measure of success in this is all well enough, and perhaps is a requisite to objective thinking, but too much safety seems to yield only danger in the long run. Perhaps this is behind Thoreau's dictum: In wildness is the salvation of the world. Perhaps this is the hidden meaning in the howl of the wolf, long known among mountains, but seldom perceived among men.

Understanding the Text

1. Why did Leopold kill the wolf? What did he learn from his experience?
2. Why does a mountain live "in mortal fear of its deer" (par. 8)?
3. What is the connection among wolves, deer, and the mountains in this essay? By extension, what is Leopold saying about the role of humans in this relationship?

Reflection and Response

4. What does it mean to "think like a mountain" (par. 9)?
5. In what ways does the wolf's howl have "meaning"? Do wolves, deer, people, and mountains communicate in different ways?
6. How does this excerpt address the notion of time? What does Leopold suggest about the perception of time?
7. Why does Leopold divide this essay into sections? Does each section have a different focus? How do these sections affect the way you read this essay?

Making Connections

8. Near the end of this passage, Leopold references Thoreau's dictum: "In wildness is the salvation of the world" (par. 10). What does this mean? Reread

Thoreau's writing earlier in this chapter and look for similarities between the two writers' ideas as well as Thoreau's influences on Leopold's thinking.

9. How is "thinking like a mountain" related to what you know about sustainability? Do you think this short phrase captures the essence of sustainability? Why or why not?

10. Find an example of a natural place that has been damaged or destroyed by human activity. How does this relate to Leopold's essay?

The Sacred Balance: Rediscovering Our Place in Nature

David Suzuki

David Suzuki (b. 1936) is a Canadian academic and an environmental activist. Suzuki earned a Ph.D. in zoology from the University of Chicago in 1961, and he was a professor in the genetics department at the University of British Columbia from 1963 until 2001. Suzuki was the host of several popular television and radio series about nature and the environment, including the long-running CBC Television science magazine, *The Nature of Things*, which was aired in more than forty countries.

The Sacred Balance was published in 2007 and was later adapted into a series of documentary films. The book highlights humankind's interconnection with the earth and with other living creatures. As you read the prologue to the book, think about the qualities that have made humans successful as a species and how some of those same qualities may threaten our future health and well-being.

Suppose that 200,000 years ago, biologists from another galaxy searching for life forms in other parts of the universe had discovered Earth and parked their space vehicle above the Rift Valley in Africa. At the moment of our species' birth, mammoths, sabre-toothed cats, huge moa birds and giant sloths still roamed the planet. Those intergalactic visitors would have gazed upon vast grasslands filled with marvellous plants and animals, including a newly evolved species, *Homo sapiens*.°

It is highly unlikely that those alien scientists would have concentrated their attention on this infant upright ape species in anticipation of its meteoric rise to preeminence a mere two hundred millennia later. After all, those early humans lived in small family groups that didn't rival the immense herds of wildebeest and antelope. In comparison with many other species, they weren't especially large, fast or strong, or endowed with special sensory acuity. Those early humans possessed a survival trait that was invisible because it was locked within their skulls and only revealed through their behavior. Their immense and complex brains conferred tremendous intelligence, along with a vast capacity for memory, an insatiable curiosity

Homo sapiens: the species to which human beings belong.

61

and an astonishing creativity — abilities that more than compensated for their physical and sensory deficiencies.

That newly evolved human brain invented a novel concept called the "future." In reality, all that exists is the present and our memories of what is past, but by creating the notion of a future, we were unique in recognizing that we could influence events to come by what we do in the present. By looking ahead, we could anticipate potential danger and opportunities. Foresight was the great advantage that catapulted *Homo sapiens* into a position of dominance on the planet.

The eminent Nobel laureate François Jacob suggests that the human brain is "hardwired" to require order. Chaos is terrifying to us, because without some appreciation of cause and effect, we have no possibility of understanding and controlling the cosmic forces impinging on our lives. Early humans recognized that there are patterns in nature that are predictable — diurnal rhythm, or the movement of the sun; movement of the moon and stars; tides; seasons; animal migration; and plant succession. They were able to exploit these regularities for their own benefit and to avoid potential hazards.

Over time, every human society evolved a culture that inculcated   5
an understanding of its place on Earth and in the cosmos. The collective knowledge, beliefs, languages and songs of each society make up what anthropologists call a worldview. In every worldview, there is an understanding that everything is connected to everything else, that nothing exists in isolation. People have always known that we are deeply embedded in and dependent upon the natural world.

In such a world of interconnectedness, every action has consequences, and since we were part of that world, we had a responsibility to act properly to keep the world in order. Many of our rituals, songs, prayers and ceremonies were reaffirmations of our dependence on nature and our commitment to behave properly. That is how it has been for most of human existence all over the world.

From Naked Ape to Superspecies

But suddenly in the last century, *Homo sapiens* has undergone a radical transformation into a new kind of force that I call a "superspecies." For the first time in the 3.8 billion years that life has existed on Earth, one species — humanity — is altering the biological, physical and chemical features of the planet on a geological scale. That shift to superspecies has occurred with explosive speed through a number of factors. One is population. It took all of human existence to reach a billion people in the early nineteenth century. A hundred years later, when I was born, in 1936, there were two billion people on Earth. In my lifetime, global population has tripled. Thus, by virtue of our numbers alone, our species' "ecological footprint" on the planet has grown explosively — we all have to eat, breathe and drink, and clothe and shelter ourselves.

We are now the most numerous mammalian species on the planet, but unlike all the others, our ecological impact has been greatly amplified by technology. Virtually all of modern technology has been developed within the past century, thereby escalating both the scale and scope of our ability to exploit our surroundings. Resource exploitation is fueled by an exploding consumer demand for products, and the fulfilment of that demand has become a critical component of economic growth. Hyperconsumption in the developed world serves as the model for people in developing countries now that globalization has rendered the entire world population a potential market. Taken together, human numbers, technology, consumption and a globalized economy have made us a new kind of force on the planet.

Throughout our evolutionary past, we were a local, tribal animal. We may have encountered a hundred humans over a range of a few hundred kilometers in a lifetime. We didn't have to worry about tribes on the other side of a mountain or across an ocean; nor did we have to consider the collective impact of our entire species, because our ecological footprint was so much lighter and nature seemed vast and endlessly self-renewing. Our new status of superspecies has been achieved so rapidly that we are only now becoming aware of a new level of collective responsibility, which reflects a dawning realization that taken all together, human activity is the main cause of the current decline in the biosphere's rich diversity and productivity that support all life on earth.

A Shattered World

As we have shifted our status to superspecies, our ancient understanding of the exquisite interconnectivity of all life has been shattered. We find it increasingly difficult to recognize the linkages that once gave us a sense of place and belonging. After all, we are flooded with food and goods that come from all parts of the world, so we scarcely notice that it's the middle of winter when we are buying fresh strawberries and cherries. The constraints of locality and seasons are pushed aside by the global economy. Exacerbating the fragmentation of the world has been the stunning shift from predominant habitation in rural village communities to concentration in large cities. In big cities, it becomes easy to assume that we differ from all other species in that we create our own habitat and thereby escape the constraints of nature. It is nature that cleanses water, creates air, decomposes sewage, absorbs garbage, generates electricity and produces food, but in cities, these "ecosystem services" are assumed to be performed by the workings of the economy.

To make matters worse, as we look toward more and more esoteric sources for our information, the context, history and background needed to set new "facts" or events in place are lost, and our world is broken up into disconnected bits and pieces. While we look to science to reveal the secrets of the cosmos, its primary methodology of reductionism focuses on parts of nature. And as the world around us is examined in pieces, the rhythms, patterns and cycles within which those pieces are integrated are lost, and any insights we gain become illusions of understanding and mastery. Finally, as transnational corporations, politics and telecommunications move onto the global stage, the sense of the local is decimated.

This, then, is where we are at the beginning of the third millennium. With explosive speed, we have been transmogrified from a species like most others that live in balance with their surroundings into an unprecedented force. Like a species introduced into a new environment free of constraints, we have expanded beyond the capacity of our surroundings to support us. It is clear from the history of the past two centuries that the path we embarked on after the Industrial Revolution is leading us increasingly into conflict with life support systems of the natural world. Despite forty years of experience in the environmental movement we have not yet turned onto a different path.

The Growth of Environmentalism

Like millions of people around the world, I was galvanized° in 1962 by Rachel Carson's° eloquent call to action in her book *Silent Spring*. We were swept up in what was to become the "environmental movement." In British Columbia, that meant protesting such threats as the American testing of nuclear weapons at Amchitka in the Aleutian

---

galvanized: startled into sudden activity; stimulated.
Rachel Carson: (1907–1964), U.S. marine biologist and author.

Islands (a protest that gave birth to Greenpeace° in Vancouver), clear-cut logging throughout the province, proposed offshore drilling for oil, the planned dam at Site C on the Peace River, and air and water pollution from pulp mills. In my mind, the problem was that we were taking too much from the environment and putting too much waste back into it. From that perspective, the solution was to set limits on how much and what could be removed from the biosphere for human use and how much and what could be put back into our surroundings, then make sure to enforce the regulations. So in addition to protesting, marching and blockading, many of us were lobbying politicians to set aside more parks, to enact Clean Water and Clean Air legislation, to pass Endangered Species Acts and to establish the agencies to enforce the regulations. When *Silent Spring* was published in 1962, no government on Earth had a Minister or Department of the Environment.

But Carson's book itself offered evidence of the need for a deeper analysis. As I read the book, I was shocked to realize that the experimental systems scientists study in flasks and growth chambers are artifacts, simplifications meant to mimic reality but lacking the context within which those simplified systems exist and devoid of the rhythms, patterns and cycles that impinge on the Earth. This realization came to me as a profound shock and impelled me to look beyond the lab into the real world.

The more involved I became in environmental issues, the clearer 15 it became to me that my rather simple-minded approach wouldn't work, because we were too ignorant to anticipate the consequences of our activity and to set appropriate limits. Carson's book dealt with DDT.° In the 1930s when Paul Mueller, working for the chemical company Geigy in Switzerland, discovered that DDT killed insects, the economic benefits of a chemical pesticide were immediately obvious. Trumpeting the imminent scientific conquest of insect pests and their associated diseases and damage to crops, Geigy patented the discovery and went on to make millions, and Mueller was awarded the Nobel Prize in 1948. But years later, when bird watchers noted the decline of eagles and hawks, biologists investigated and discovered the hitherto unknown phenomenon of "biomagnification," whereby compounds become concentrated as they are ingested up the food chain. How could limits have been set on DDT in the early 1940s

Greenpeace: an organization founded in 1971 that stresses the need to maintain a balance between human progress and environmental conservation.
DDT: $C_{14}H_9Cl_5$; potent chemical used as an insecticide, prohibited for agricultural use in the United States since 1973.

when we didn't even know about biomagnification as a biological process until birds began to disappear?

Similarly, CFCs° were hailed as a wonderful creation of chemistry. These complex molecules were chemically inert, so they didn't react with other compounds and thus made excellent fillers in aerosol cans to go along with substances such as deodorants. No one anticipated that because of their stability, CFCs would persist in the environment and drift into the upper atmosphere, where ultraviolet radiation would break off ozone-scavenging chlorine free radicals. Most people had never heard of the ozone layer, and certainly no one could have anticipated the long-term effects of CFCs, so how could the compounds have been regulated? I have absolutely no doubt that genetically modified organisms (GMOs) will also prove to have unexpected negative consequences despite the benefits claimed by biotech companies. But if we don't know enough to anticipate the long-term consequences of human technological innovation, how can its impact be managed? For me as a scientist, this posed a terrible conundrum.

A Way Out

I gained an important insight to free me from this quandary in the late 1970s. As host of the long-running television series *The Nature of Things,* I learned of the battle over clearcut logging in the Queen Charlotte Islands, off the coast of British Columbia. For thousands of years, the islands have been home to the Haida, who refer to their lands as Haida Gwaii. The forestry giant MacMillan Bloedel had been clearcutting huge areas of the islands for years, an activity that had generated increasingly vocal opposition. It was a good story, and I proposed to report it. In the early 1980s, I flew to Haida Gwaii to interview loggers, forestry officials, government bureaucrats, environmentalists and natives. One of the people I interviewed was a young Haida artist named Guujaaw who had led the opposition to logging for years.

Unemployment was very high in the Haida communities, and logging generated desperately needed jobs for the Haida. So I asked Guujaaw why he opposed the logging. He answered, "Our people have determined that Windy Bay and other areas must be left in their natural condition so that we can keep our identity and pass it on to

---

CFCs: chlorofluorocarbons, chemical compound used in various industrial, commercial, and household items that are hastening the depletion of the ozone layer.

following generations. The forests, those oceans, are what keep us as Haida people today." When I asked him what would happen if the logging continued and the trees were cleared, he answered simply, "If they're logged off, we'll probably end up the same as everyone else, I guess."

It was a simple statement whose implications escaped me at the time. But on reflection, I realized that he had given me a glimpse into a profoundly different way of seeing the world. Guujaaw's statement suggested that for his people, the trees, the birds, the fish, the water, and wind are all parts of Haida identity. Haida history and culture and the very meaning of why Haida are on earth reside in the land.

Ever since that interview, I have been a student learning from encounters with indigenous people in many parts of the world. From Japan to Australia, Papua New Guinea, Borneo, the Kalahari, the Amazon and the Arctic, aboriginal people have expressed to me that vital need to be connected to the land. They refer to Earth as their Mother, who they say gives birth to us. Moreover, skin enfolds our bodies but does not define our limits because water, gases and heat dissipating from our bodies radiate outward, joining us to the world around us. What I have learned is a perspective that we are an inseparable part of a community of organisms that are our kin.

In 2001, U.S. president Bill Clinton joined with scientists to announce the completion of the Human Genome Project,° which elucidated the complete sequence of three billion letters in a single human nucleus. While politicians and scientists speculated about the potential benefits of understanding diseases, new drugs and cures for many ailments, the most amazing revelation was all but ignored. Not only is the human genome nearly identical to our closest relatives, the Great Apes, as well as our pet dogs and cats, we carry thousands of genes identical to those in fish, birds, insects and plants, a revelation that we share genes with all other life forms to whom we are related by our shared evolutionary history.

Changing Our Perspective

In 1990, my wife, Tara Cullis, and I established an organization that would examine the root causes of ecological destruction so that we could seek alternatives to our current practices. We decided to draft a document that would express the foundation's worldview and

Human Genome Project: a federally funded U.S. scientific project to identify both the genes and the entire sequence of DNA base pairs that make up the human genome.

perspective and could be offered to the Earth Summit in Rio de Janeiro in 1992. We called it a Declaration of Interdependence. Tara and I formulated a rough draft and asked for input from Guujaaw, ethnobiologist Wade Davis and the children's singer Raffi. When I was working on the first draft, I tried writing "We are made up of molecules from the air, water and soil," but this sounded like a scientific treatise and failed to convey the simple truth of our relationship with Earth in a powerful, emotional way. After spending days pondering the lines, I suddenly thought, "We *are* the air, we *are* the water, we *are* the earth, we *are* the Sun."

> "We are intimately fused to our surroundings and the notion of separateness or isolation is an illusion."

With this realization, I also saw that environmentalists like me had been framing the issue improperly. There is no environment "out there" that is separate from us. We can't manage our impact on the environment if we *are* our surroundings. Indigenous people are absolutely correct: we are born of the earth and constructed from the four sacred elements of earth, air, fire and water. (Hindus list these four and add a fifth element, space.)

Once I had finally understood the truth of these ancient wisdoms, I also realized that we are intimately fused to our surroundings and the notion of separateness or isolation is an illusion. Through reading I came to understand that science reaffirms the profundity of these ancient truths over and over again. Looked at as biological beings, despite our veneer of civilization, we are no more removed from nature than any other creature, even in the midst of a large city. Our animal nature dictates our essential needs: clean air, clean water, clean soil, clean energy. This led me to another insight, that these four "sacred elements" are created, cleansed and renewed by the web of life itself. If there is to be a fifth sacred element, it is biodiversity itself. And whatever we do to these elements, we do directly to ourselves.

As I read further, I discovered the famed psychologist Abraham Maslow, who pointed out that we have a nested series of fundamental needs. At the most basic level, we require the five sacred elements in order to live rich, full lives. But when those basic necessities are met, a new set of needs arises. We are social animals, and the most profound force shaping our humanity is love. And when that vital social requirement is fulfilled, then a new level of spiritual needs arises as an urgent priority. This is how I made the fundamental reexamination of our relationship with Earth that led to *The Sacred Balance.*

In the years since, I have yet to meet anyone who would dispute the reality and primacy of these fundamental needs. And everything in my reading and experiences since then has merely reaffirmed and amplified my understanding of these basic needs. The challenge of this millennium is to recognize what we need to live rich, rewarding lives without undermining the very elements that ensure them.

Understanding the Text

1. What characteristics enabled humans to survive and become the dominant species on the planet?

2. How does Suzuki define a "superspecies," and what factors have contributed to the impact of humans on the global environment?

3. According to Suzuki, what are the solutions to our global environmental problems? What are the major features and movements within environmentalism that have influenced Suzuki's thinking?

Reflection and Response

4. The introduction to this piece asks you to imagine that you're a biologist from another planet, visiting earth 200,000 years ago. Why does Suzuki create this fictional situation? What does he hope readers will gain from it?

5. What is the "sacred balance" that Suzuki refers to in the title of the essay?

6. Suzuki writes that "we have expanded beyond the capacity of our surroundings to support us" (par. 12). Do you agree with this statement? Why or why not?

7. What does Suzuki mean when he writes, "We *are* the air, we *are* the water, we *are* the earth, we *are* the Sun" (par. 22)? Does he mean this literally or metaphorically?

Making Connections

8. Suzuki mentions the impact that *Silent Spring* had on the world. What other books, speeches, or movies may have had similar impacts on our collective thinking about environmentalism and sustainability?

9. In the section titled "A Shattered World," Suzuki talks about the "reductionist" methodology that predominates science. How is this similar to what Fritjof Capra suggests in his essay in Chapter 4? What alternatives do the two authors offer?

10. Suzuki suggests that humans are unique because of our ability to envision a future but that we have neglected this ability with regard to global sustainability. Think of something that you do on a daily or weekly basis that might work for you now but may be unsustainable (or unhealthy) in the long run.

Limits to Growth: Tools for the Transition to Sustainability

Donella Meadows, Jorgen Randers, and Dennis L. Meadows

In 1972, a team of scientists from the Massachusetts Institute of Technology created a computer model to analyze the impact of worldwide population growth and the dwindling supply of resources. The results were published in the best-selling book *Limits to Growth*, which speculated that unchecked consumption and population growth was leading the earth toward "overshoot" of its carrying capacity, followed by disaster.

The following excerpt is part of the team's "30-year update" of the book, and it offers an analysis of present and future trends in resource use and the possible outcomes of our current growth and consumption patterns. As you read this passage, consider the ways that the authors envision the future and consider your own role in the process.

"We must be careful not to succumb to despair, for there is still the odd glimmer of hope."

—EDOUARD SAOUMA, 1993

We have been writing about, talking about, and working toward sustainability for over three decades now. We have had the privilege of knowing thousands of colleagues in every part of the world who work in their own ways, with their own talents, in their own societies toward a sustainable society. When we act at the official, institutional level and when we listen to political leaders, we often feel frustrated. When we work with individuals, we usually feel encouraged.

Everywhere we find folks who care about the earth, about other people, and about the welfare of their children and grandchildren. They recognize the human misery and the environmental degradation around them, and they question whether policies that promote more growth along the same old lines can make things better. Many of them have a feeling, often hard for them to articulate, that the world is headed in the wrong direction and that preventing disaster will require some big changes. They are willing to work for those changes, if only they could believe their efforts would make a positive difference. They ask: What can I do? What can governments do? What can corporations do? What can schools, religions, media do? What can citizens, producers, consumers, parents do?

Experiments guided by those questions are more important than any specific answers, though answers abound. There are "50 simple things you can do to save the planet." Buy an energy-efficient car, for one. Recycle your bottles and cans, vote knowledgeably in elections — if you are among those people in the world blessed with cars, bottles, cans, or elections. There are also not-so-simple things to do: Work out your own frugally elegant lifestyle, have at most two children, argue for higher prices on fossil energy (to encourage energy efficiency and stimulate development of renewable energy), work with love and partnership to help one family lift itself out of poverty, find your own "right livelihood," care well for one piece of land, do whatever you can to oppose systems that oppress people or abuse the earth, run for election yourself.

All these actions will help. And, of course, they are not enough. Sustainability and sufficiency and equity require structural change; they require a revolution, not in the political sense, like the French Revolution, but in the much more profound sense of the ag-

> "Sustainability and sufficiency and equity require structural change; they require a revolution."

ricultural or industrial revolutions. Recycling is important, but by itself it will not bring about a revolution.

What will? In search of an answer, we have found it helpful to try   5 to understand the first two great revolutions in human culture, insofar as historians can reconstruct them.

The First Two Revolutions: Agriculture and Industry

About 10,000 years ago the human population, after millennia of evolution, had reached the huge (for the time) number of about 10 million. These people lived as nomadic hunter-gatherers, but in some regions their numbers had begun to overwhelm the once abundant plants and game. To adapt to the problem of disappearing wild resources they did two things. Some of them intensified their migratory lifestyle. They moved out of their ancestral homes in Africa and the Middle East and populated other areas of the game-rich world.

Others started domesticating animals, cultivating plants, and staying in one place. That was a totally new idea. Simply by staying put, the proto-farmers altered the face of the planet, the thoughts of humankind, and the shape of society in ways they could never have foreseen.

For the first time it made sense to own land. People who didn't have to carry all their possessions on their backs could accumulate things, and some could accumulate more than others. The ideas of wealth, status, inheritance, trade, money, and power were born. Some people could live on excess food produced by others. They could become full-time toolmakers, musicians, scribes, priests, soldiers, athletes, or kings. Thus arose, for better or worse, guilds, orchestras, libraries, temples, armies, competitive games, dynasties, and cities.

As its inheritors, we think of the agricultural revolution as a great step forward. At the time it was probably a mixed blessing. Many anthropologists think that agriculture was not a better way of life, but a necessary one to accommodate increasing populations. Settled farmers got more food from a hectare than hunter-gatherers did, but the food was of lower nutritional quality and less variety, and it required much more work to produce. Farmers became vulnerable in ways nomads never were to weather, disease, pests, invasion by outsiders, and oppression from their emerging ruling classes. People who did not move away from their own wastes experienced humankind's first chronic pollution.

Nevertheless, agriculture was a successful response to wildlife 10 scarcity. It permitted yet more population growth, which added up over centuries to an enormous increase, from 10 million to 800 million people by 1750. The larger population created new scarcities, especially in land and energy. Another revolution was necessary.

The industrial revolution began in England with the substitution of abundant coal for vanishing trees. The use of coal raised practical problems of earthmoving, mine construction, water pumping, transport, and controlled combustion. These problems were solved relatively quickly, resulting in concentrations of labor around mines and mills. The process elevated technology and commerce to a prominent position in human society — above religion and ethics.

Again everything changed in ways that no one could have imagined. Machines, not land, became the central means of production. Feudalism gave way to capitalism and to capitalism's dissenting offshoot, communism. Roads, railroads, factories, and smokestacks appeared on the landscape. Cities swelled. Again the change was a mixed blessing. Factory labor was even harder and more demeaning than farm labor. The air and waters near the new factories turned unspeakably filthy. The standard of living for most of the industrial workforce was far below that of a farmer. But farmland was not available; work in a factory was.

It is hard for people alive today to appreciate how profoundly the industrial revolution changed human thought, because that thought still shapes our perceptions. In 1988 historian Donald Worster described the philosophical impact of industrialism perhaps as well as any of its inheritors and practitioners can:

The capitalists . . . promised that, through the technological domination of the earth, they could deliver a more fair, rational, efficient and productive life for everyone. . . . Their method was simply to free individual enterprise from the bonds of traditional hierarchy and community, whether the bondage derived from other humans or the earth. . . . That meant teaching everyone to treat the earth, as well as each other, with a frank, energetic, self-assertiveness. . . . People must . . . think constantly in terms of making money. They must regard everything around them — the land, its natural resources, their own labor — as potential commodities that might fetch a profit in the market. They must demand the right to produce, buy, and sell those commodities without outside regulation or interference. . . . As wants multiplied, as markets grew more and more far-flung, the bond between humans and the rest of nature was reduced to the barest instrumentalism.

That bare instrumentalism led to incredible productivity and a world that now supports, at varying levels of sufficiency, 6,000 million people — more than 600 times the population existing before the agricultural revolution. Far-flung markets and swelling demands drive environmental exploitation from the poles to the tropics, from the mountaintops to the ocean depths.

The success of the industrial revolution, like the previous suc- 15 cesses of hunting-gathering and of agriculture, eventually created its own scarcity, not only of game, not only of land, not only of fuels and metals, but of the total carrying capacity of the global environment. Humankind's ecological footprint had once more exceeded what was sustainable. Success created the necessity for another revolution.

The Next Revolution: Sustainability

It is as impossible now for anyone to describe the world that could evolve from a sustainability revolution as it would have been for the farmers of 6000 BCE to foresee the corn and soybean fields of modern Iowa, or for an English coal miner of CE 1800 to imagine an automated Toyota assembly line. Like the other great revolutions, the coming sustainability revolution will also change the face of the land and the foundations of human identities, institutions, and cultures. Like the previous revolutions, it will take centuries to unfold fully — though it is already under way.

Of course no one knows how to bring about such a revolution. There is not a checklist: "To accomplish a global paradigm shift, follow these 20 steps." Like the great revolutions that came before, this one can't be planned or dictated. It won't follow a list of fiats from government or a proclamation from computer modelers. The sustainability revolution will be organic. It will arise from the visions, insights, experiments, and actions of billions of people. The burden of making it happen is not on the shoulders of any one person or group. No one will get the credit, but everyone can contribute.

Our systems training and our own work in the world have affirmed for us two properties of complex systems germane to the sort of profound revolution we are discussing here.

First, information is the key to transformation. That does not necessarily mean more information, better statistics, bigger databases, or the World Wide Web, though all of these may play a part. It means relevant, compelling, select, powerful, timely, accurate information flowing in new ways to new recipients, carrying new content, suggesting new rules and goals (rules and goals that are themselves information). When its information flows are changed, any system will behave differently. The policy of glasnost, for example — the simple opening of information channels that had long been closed in the Soviet Union — guaranteed the rapid transformation of Eastern Europe beyond anyone's expectations. The old system had been held in place by tight control of information. Letting go of that control triggered total system restructuring (turbulent and unpredictable, but inevitable).

Second, systems strongly resist changes in their information 20 flows, especially in their rules and goals. It is not surprising that those who benefit from the current system actively oppose such revision. Entrenched political, economic, and religious cliques can constrain almost entirely the attempts of an individual or small group to operate by different rules or to attain goals different from those sanctioned by the system. Innovators can be ignored, marginalized, ridiculed, denied promotions or resources or public voices. They can be literally or figuratively snuffed out.

Only innovators, however — by perceiving the need for new information, rules, and goals, communicating about them, and trying them out — can make the changes that transform systems. This important point is expressed clearly in a quote that is widely attributed to Margaret Mead,° "Never deny the power of a small group of committed individuals to change the world. Indeed that is the only thing that ever has."

We have learned the hard way that it is difficult to live a life of material moderation within a system that expects, exhorts, and rewards consumption. But one can move a long way in the direction of moderation. It is not easy to use energy efficiently in an economy that produces energy-inefficient products. But one can search out, or if necessary invent, more efficient ways of doing things, and in the process make those ways more accessible to others.

Above all, it is difficult to put forth new information in a system that is structured to hear only old information. Just try, sometime, to question in public the value of more growth, or even to make a distinction between growth and development, and you will see what we mean. It takes courage and clarity to challenge an established system. But it can be done.

In our own search for ways to encourage the peaceful restructuring of a system that naturally resists its own transformation, we have tried many tools. The obvious ones are . . . rational analysis, data gathering, systems thinking, computer modeling, and the clearest words we can find. Those are tools that anyone trained in science and economics would automatically grasp. Like recycling, they are useful, necessary, and they are not enough.

We don't know what will be enough. But we would like to conclude   25
by mentioning five other tools we have found helpful. We introduced and discussed this list for the first time in our 1992 book [*Limits to Growth*]. Our experience since then has affirmed that these five tools are not optional; they are essential characteristics for any society that hopes to survive over the long term. We present them here again . . . "not as the ways to work toward sustainability, but as some ways."

"We are a bit hesitant to discuss them," we said in 1992, "because we are not experts in their use and because they require the use of words that do not come easily from the mouths or word processors of scientists. They are considered too 'unscientific' to be taken seriously in the cynical public arena."

What are the tools we approached so cautiously? They are visioning, networking, truth-telling, learning, and loving. It seems like a feeble list, given the enormity of the changes required.

Margaret Mead: (1901–1978), American cultural anthropologist.

But each of these exists within a web of positive loops. Thus their persistent and consistent application initially by a relatively small group of people would have the potential to produce enormous change — even to challenge the present system, perhaps helping to produce a revolution.

"The transition to a sustainable society might be helped," we said in 1992, "by the simple use of words like these more often, with sincerity and without apology, in the information streams of the world." But we used them with apology ourselves, knowing how most people would receive them.

Many of us feel uneasy about relying on such "soft" tools when the   30
future of our civilization is at stake, particularly since we do not know how to summon them up, in ourselves or in others. So we dismiss them and turn the conversation to recycling or emission trading or wildlife preserves or some other necessary but insufficient part of the sustainability revolution — but at least a part we know how to handle.

Understanding the Text

1. What are the first two major "revolutions" the authors describe in this essay? How did those revolutions change human life? What were the positive and negative aspects of the two revolutions?

2. What is the next revolution that the authors call for? What would such a revolution entail?

3. The authors suggest that *information* and *innovators* will be essential in transforming society. How do they define these two terms?

4. How do the authors define a sustainable society?

Reflection and Response

5. Near the beginning of this essay, the authors describe a number of practical, personal strategies for sustainability. Do these strategies make a difference? Discuss the role of the individual and of society in enacting sustainability.

6. How do we typically define a revolution? What are the similarities and differences of a political revolution and a structural societal revolution? Is "revolution" the best term to use in our discussions of the future?

7. The authors suggest that it is impossible to predict how the world might evolve through a sustainability revolution. How would you envision it?

Making Connections

8. The authors offer five tools or characteristics for creating a sustainable society: visioning, networking, truth-telling, learning, and loving. How could these characteristics be useful? Do they seem unconventional, coming from a group of scientists? Read more of *Limits to Growth* to gather information.

9. This essay and the previous one (Suzuki's "The Sacred Balance") look far back in history to suggest something about our current culture and our future. Compare the two essays. What do they have in common? How do they differ?

Defining Sustainability, Defining the Future

Ethan Goffman

Ethan Goffman is an environmental writer who lives in the Washington, D.C., region. He is an associate editor of the online magazine *Sustainability: Science, Practice, & Policy*, and he is on the executive committee of the Montgomery County, Maryland, Sierra Club.

Goffman's "Defining Sustainability, Defining the Future" (2005) examines the economic and historical roots of sustainability, offering examples and definitions of the ways in which sustainable thinking is tied to a culture's success or failure. As you read the essay, think about the ways in which economic and environmental issues are related.

A new concept in environmental and human affairs was introduced with the Brundtland° Declaration of 1987: "Sustainable development is development that meets the needs of the present without compromising the ability of future generations to meet their own needs." Implicit in this often-quoted definition is the idea that the natural environment faces stress and overexploitation and will not be able to indefinitely meet escalating human demands.

By itself, the Brundtland definition is insufficient. How does one define "needs," as opposed to wants or even excessive luxury? Is a lowering of living standards acceptable? Is barely enough to eat and minimal shelter good enough? What about education and medical care? Does sustainability imply some equity in distribution of goods, or might an increasing gap between rich and poor meet the sustainability test (if environmental and population stability are achieved)? Is ecosystem health important for itself, or only as it sustains humans?

The Brundtland Declaration suggests some answers. Linking global inequity to environmental degradation, it calls for a decrease in consumption in the wealthy global north, together with development for the impoverished global south.[1] In this, it foreshadows today's environmental justice movement. The implicit problem here is that the wealthy are often protected from the environmental costs of their lifestyles, while the poor often lack the means to care for their immediate environment.

Brundtland: the Brundtland Commission, a UN organization of world leaders formed in 1983 whose mission was to unite countries to pursue sustainable development together. See the selection "Our Common Future" on page 92.

If sustainability implies a linking of problems of consumption and poverty with pollution, resource degradation, and conflict, the solutions also require novel linkages. Regarding sustainability, science cannot exist in a vacuum, but must interact with politics, with policy, with governance issues that reach into people's daily lives. Economic factors structure how, where, and how much the environment will be exploited. Communication between different sectors — which too often exist as compartmentalized units — is crucial. Environmental scientists can no longer be content merely with doing "good" science; discussion and persuasion become part of the scientist's role.

How we proceed toward sustainable development depends upon perception. If people perceive resource depletion, they will recycle; if they perceive an unlimited amount of extractable resources, or forthcoming technological answers to all problems, they will not. Similarly, if people believe that automobile emissions are causing dangerous global warming they will buy more fuel-efficient cars, and seek other alternatives. However citizens must also feel empowered, must believe that their efforts and decisions have some meaning, in order to work toward sustainable lifestyles.

Individual perceptions extend to the collective social will, and hence to political and policy operations, which can institutionalize what may begin as lifestyle choices. Regarding automobiles, monetary incentives often prompt people to "do the right thing." Prohibitions are a more heavy-handed policy instrument, as in absolute limits on gas mileage. Incentives and prohibitions are generated, and need to be supported, by policy and government. In moving toward sustainability, the beliefs of key policy-makers, the system of governance, and the role of local, national, and international organizations all play a part.

The overlapping roles of governance, social values, and economic needs generate the interdisciplinary nature of sustainability science. To break down barriers between disciplines that too often remain discrete, and to encourage exploration of practical policy options, CSA° and the USGS's° National Biological Information Infrastructure have launched the e-journal *Sustainability: Science, Practice, and Policy.* "This is an important endeavor as it aims at answering fundamental questions on what prevents the wide replication of best known practices in sustainable development," writes Klaus Töpfer, executive director of the United Nations Environment Programme. "I

CSA: Community Services Administration.
USGS: United States Geological Survey.

hope that the journal will catalyze debate between different disciplines that include practitioners and policymakers."

Given its interdisciplinary nature, a question remains as to whether "sustainability science" is more of a traditional science, a social science, or something different and more improvisational, more an art than a science. In the narrowest sense of experimentation and replication it cannot be called a traditional science (although many contributing fields are certainly traditional sciences). In the ultimate sense, that empirically events are occurring in our ecosystems, and that these will have definite effects, it is a science, albeit one that affects every human being's daily life. The eventual impact of today's decisions, then, provides a final test of sustainability.

Economic and Historical Roots

The link between economics and the environment is crucial, particularly in a globalizing world. Historically economics, dating back to Adam Smith's° *The Wealth of Nations,* has largely disregarded environmental issues.

True, Smith included "land" among his original economic factors, [10] but mainly as a resource to be exploited.[2] Later economists downgraded the importance of land and other environmental factors, assuming a virtually unlimited amount of natural goods to be harvested and used by humans.

The problematic exception is Thomas Malthus, who in 1798 published *An Essay on the Principle of Population,* warning that while population increased exponentially food production increased only incrementally.[3] Population was thus bound to vastly overshoot subsistence, leading to mass poverty and starvation. This set the terms for an environmental limit to ever-expanding human needs.

In terms of today's wealthier societies, Malthus was quite wrong, as technological advances have allowed food production, along with numerous other goods and services, to advance at an even faster rate than population. Yet elsewhere, local environment has proved unable to meet daily needs. One question for future sustainability is whether resource use will be able to continually shift as needed, or whether all resources will eventually be exhausted. A related question is how heavy a price increasing pollution, including hazardous wastes and such threshold effects as global climate change, will ex-

Adam Smith: (1723–1790), a Scottish economist.

act. Economists refer to these costs, which are not paid by those who harvest or produce goods, as *externalities*.

Meanwhile, Malthus has proved right in numerous local circumstances, as various groups of people have exceeded the *carrying capacity* of their environments and paid the price. A favorite example of environmentalists and sustainability scientists is Easter Island, discovered in 1722 by Europeans who were amazed by the enormous stone statues that confronted them on an otherwise barren landscape. Speculation on the mystery of who put them there would last for centuries.

Today we believe we know the answer. Leaders of the Polynesian civilization that settled the island erected these statues as enormous symbols of their prestige. The drive for status overrode ecological considerations, leading them to denude the island, cutting down ever-more trees upon which to drag ever-larger boulders, in the quest to make ever-larger statues. That the island was isolated, with a fragile ecosystem, made it particularly prone to environmental collapse.

Although environmentalists use Easter Island as a symbol of what   15
may happen to our own society, global ecosystems are, of course, far more complex and resilient, while our technology and our ability to communicate and change give us much greater ability to adapt. Yet, as Jared Diamond° documents in his book *Collapse: How Societies Choose to Fail or Succeed*, other societies have overexploited their available ecosystems, precipitating disasters similar to that predicted by Malthus.[4]

The Maya present one of the most dramatic cases; their civilization largely collapsed, probably during the ninth century AD, leaving vast ruins replete with abandoned temples and monuments. Diamond explains the collapse as "population growth outstripping available resources," along with deforestation, conflict, drought, and inaction by Mayan kings.[5] The explanation goes beyond ecological determinism; despite difficult circumstances, Diamond believes that better decision-making by the Maya would have forestalled collapse.

Societies facing overpopulation and ecological stress have not always failed. Sometimes, Diamond explains, they have realized their situation and adapted environmental management strategies that allow long-term success. Japan is a prime example. In the 17th century the island nation faced a population explosion that threatened to overrun the resources available in its limited space. Deforestation

Jared Diamond: (b. 1937), an American evolutionary biologist, physiologist, biogeographer, lecturer, and nonfiction author.

was a particular threat. According to Diamond, a combination of forward-looking forestry practices and rather draconian population measures enabled Japan to avoid the Malthusian fate of the Maya, to move toward its dynamic role in recent world history.[6]

Where Are We Now?

Sustainability science, then, implicitly holds that what happened to Easter Island and the Maya may happen to us on a global scale, that we are in a condition of *overshoot* in which environmental systems will not sustain our collective lifestyle. Foresight, wisdom, and better decision-making are thus necessary for our global civilization to ultimately succeed.

That we may be facing environmental limits was a key point brought into consciousness by the Club of Rome's 1972 report *The Limits to Growth,* a crucial predecessor of the sustainability movement, that predicted an eventual crisis as the world ran out of critical goods. Using computer modeling, and extrapolating from statistics over the previous 70 years, the report concluded that, "if the present growth trends in world population, industrialization, pollution, food production, and resource depletion remain unchanged, the limits to growth on this planet will be reached sometime within the next one hundred years." The report was not fatalistic, however, but argued that, "it is possible to alter these growth trends and to establish a condition of ecological and economic stability that is sustainable far into the future."[7] From its inception onward, the report has been harshly criticized, for instance for assuming exponential growth in population and resource use but only incremental change in technology.

A similar, but more cataclysmic, theory had been advanced in 1968 by Paul Ehrlich, whose *The Population Bomb* updated Malthus, predicting that, "in the 1970's the world will undergo famines — hundreds of millions of people will starve to death."[8] By contrast Ehrlich's intellectual opponent, Julian Simon, believed that human creativity and technological development would allow substitution of resources to the point that an infinitely growing population would be able to continue to improve standards of living virtually forever: "We have in our hands now — actually in our libraries — the technology to feed, clothe, and supply energy to an ever-growing population for the next 7 billion years."[9]

That both Simon and Ehrlich made preposterous statements — Simon's made preposterous by a basic mathematical knowledge of exponential growth, Ehrlich's by time — provides a warning of the dangers of letting ideology transcend facts. Yet in their argument of a race between human invention and environmental capacity lies a basic understanding of the challenge of sustainability. It comes down to the idea that resource renewal and substitution, together with the creative use of endless new technology, will allow endless economic growth, versus the idea that population growth, per capita resource use growth, and *threshold effects* spell eventual doom.

Although specific societies have lost the race between growth and destruction, the overall global trend has been toward improved living standards, as measured by such key indicators as life expectancy, health, resource use, and technology. Yet past performance is no guarantee of the future. Given that the earth is finite, and given rising resource use by a rising population, without careful planning we will, at some point, lose on a global scale. Employing a much broader range of data than that employed by Ehrlich in 1968, sustainability scientists believe that we are somewhere near the tipping point and that we must begin to decrease our per capita resource use and must monitor and manage the environment far more wisely.

The recent devastation of New Orleans provides a dramatic example of how, even in a technologically advanced society that has shown long-term improvement of human welfare, environmental stresses plus a natural disaster may lead to a local collapse, one that better prior planning would have alleviated. Sitting well below sea level, with the Mississippi River folding around it, and near numerous lakes and the Gulf of Mexico, New Orleans has long been vulnerable to flooding. To protect itself, the city built an extensive levee system. When Hurricane Katrina hit, however, the levees acted as a giant bowl, keeping water in, in turn drowning the pumps normally used to prevent flooding. Toxic and human wastes stirred up in

> "Sustainability seeks healthy human societies as its ultimate goal, but sees environmental health as crucial to achieving this goal."

this cesspool have added to the trouble. The prior destruction of wetlands, which had acted as a natural buffer absorbing water from hurricanes, was another factor increasing Katrina's impact. Ironically, the levees built to protect the city from flooding due to the river helped dry up these wetlands.[10]

At least prior to Katrina, in the United States, many of the worst environmental predictions had failed to occur. Forests have revived, local air is often cleaner, and notable species such as the Bald Eagle have been taken off the endangered species list. These facts, however, are not an argument that we can do nothing and human creativity will solve all problems. They show, rather, that an awareness of environmental problems can lead to good environmental management, and that such management can then make an impact. The Bald Eagle really was threatened, and earlier species such as the Passenger Pigeon did go extinct. California really was plagued by smog alerts, and Cleveland's Cuyahoga River actually was so polluted that it caught fire several times.[11]

Environmental management has certainly had its successes at a national level, but voracious resource use has created a wider threat. And poor countries often neglect basic environmental standards. Environmental scientists warn that solutions to escalating global threats require foresight and planning. . . .   25

Shifting Definitions

Despite a clear environmental danger, and with the terms "sustainability" and "sustainable development" in ever-broader use, definitions remain contested. Critics contend that "sustainability" has become such an overused word as to lose much of its meaning. Julianne Lutz Newton and Eric T. Freyfogle, for instance, believe that "sustainability" has no clear goal, confusing sustaining natural systems with other human goals and values. They question sustainability's usefulness in synthesizing "three strands — the human health/social justice strand, the biodiversity/ecological process strand, and the agrarian strand."[12]

On the most basic level, Paul Reitan points out that, "surely no one would want simply to sustain the maximum number of humans organized into societies, knowing that that would mean existence at the barest, meanest survival level."[13] Attempting to untangle and sharpen definitions, Julian Marshall and Michael Toffel discuss the great range of uses of "sustainability," from simply "a new term for responsible environmental and labor management practices" to "a vast, diverse set of goals, such as poverty elimination and fair and transparent governance."[14] They then draw upon psychologist Abraham Maslow's Hierarchy of Needs, which ranges from basic physical survival, to social and individual needs, to artistic and spiritual values.

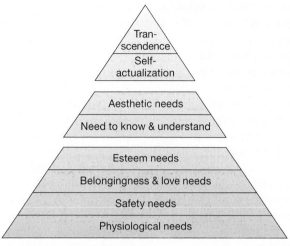

Maslow's Hierarchy of Needs

Transferring this to the realm of human and natural environment, Marshall and Toffel define four levels of sustainability, simplified as follows:

Marshall and Toffel suggest that a blurring of these meanings has led to a devaluation of the term "sustainability," and that the top level needs to be dropped outright. Sorting out which issues remain in the three highest levels, how to prioritize them, and what policies will best address them remains a formidable task.

Sustainability, then, seems best defined beyond the barest survival limits, to include basic health and human rights, yet limited in prescribing values systems. This still leaves it an arguable and vexed term — is democracy, for instance, a primary value from which sustainability flows, or might a more authoritarian system be better able to mandate sustainable practices (as with China's population control policies)? Yet it also seems as though, given its origins in international reports and conventions, sustainability seeks healthy human societies as its ultimate goal, but sees environmental health as crucial to achieving this goal.

Beyond a simple definition, the term "sustainability" exemplifies an awareness that environmental conservation alone is a problematic goal, since acting to enforce conservation always involves social and political issues. So Robert Paehlke defends the term: "as a social scientist, the concept is centered in economics, public policy, and ethics rather than in the biological sciences."[15] Depending on one's perspective, then, sustainability may be an anthropomorphic enterprise in which the sciences serve as instruments toward larger social goals, or the environmental and social sciences may be seen as relatively equal partners.

With human society given a central role, it may be unrealistic to ask for the clarity of purpose associated with the natural sciences. One group of scientists, however, proposes "connecting ecosystems models (a relatively well developed field within ecology) with models of human systems. . . . Few scholars in either area have communicated actively with scholars in the other; however, it is this combination of disciplines that is necessary to fully analyze today's environmental problems."[16] These model theories attempt connections, to simplify a fuzzy and astoundingly complex assemblage. It is a start. Sustainability issues, however, are likely to be played out in amorphous political realms in a process at least partly improvisational.

The challenge of sustainability, then, is one of doing good science, of collecting the best data and analyzing it in as many ways as possible, of never accepting any theory as final but continually testing, rethinking, and revising. It is also one of communication and connections, of acting within the social realm, of challenging people in their day-to-day lives and assumptions. It means that science cannot continue to operate in a pure realm removed from daily life, but must be intimately involved with politics and society.

Notes

1. World Commission on Environment and Development. 1987. The Brundtland Report: Our Common Future. Oxford University Press. See http://www.are .admin.ch/imperia/md/content/are/nachhaltigeentwicklung/brundtland bericht.pdf?PHPSESSID=a87facb795e0733fcc8db467b28f461d for an electronic version.

2. Smith, Adam. 1776. An Inquiry into the Nature and Causes of the Wealth of Nations. *The Wealth of Nations*. London: Methuen and Company. 1904, 5th edition.

3. Malthus, T. 1798. An Essay on the Principle of Population, as It Affects the Future Improvement of Society with Remarks on the Speculations of Mr. Godwin, M. Condorcet, and Other Writers. London: Printed for J. Johnson, in St. Paul's Church-Yard. See http://www.ac.wwu.edu/~stephan/malthus/malthus.0.html for an electronic version.

4. Diamond, J. 2005. *Collapse: How Societies Choose to Fail or Succeed*. New York: Viking.

5. Ibid., p. 176.

6. Ibid., p. 304 ff.

7. Club of Rome. 1972. *The Limits to Growth*. Washington, D.C.: Potomac Associates.

8. Ehrlich. 1968. *The Population Bomb*. New York: Ballantine Books, p. 11.

9. Simon, Julian. 1995. "The State of Humanity: Steadily Improving." Cato Policy Report 17 (5), September/October 1995: 131. See http://www.cato.org/pubs/policy_report/pr-so-is.html for an electronic version. See http://en.wikipedia.org/wiki/Julian_Simon for further discussion. See Ed Regis, 1997, The Doomslayer, *Wired* Magazine 5(2) for an influential article on Julian Simon (available at http://www.wired.com/wired/archive/5.02/ffsimon_pr.html).

10. The following sources present good discussions of New Orleans and its vulnerability to hurricanes: Hurricane risk for New Orleans. 2002. American Radio Works. Available at http://americanradioworks.publicradio.org/features/wetlands/hurricane1.html; Sullivan, B. 2005. Wetlands Erosion Raises Hurricane Risks. MSNBC. Available at http://www.msnbc.msn.com/id/9118570/; Available at http://www.publichealth.hurricane.lsu.edu/convert%20to%20tables/New%20Orleans%20Study%20Areatf.htm.

11. For more information, see Susan Griffith, 2004, Myths Surrounding Cuyahoga River Fire 35 Years Ago, Eurekalert, http://www.eurekalert.org/pub_releases/2004-06/cwru-msc061704.php.

12. Lutz Newton, J., & Freyfogle, E. 2005. Conservation Forum: Sustainability: A Dissent. *Conservation Biology* 19(1): 36–38, p. 29.

13. Reitan, P. 2005. Sustainability Science — and What's Needed Beyond Science. *Sustainability: Science, Practice, and Policy*. CSA & the National Biological Information Infrastructure. http://ejournal.nbii.org/archives/vol1iss1/communityessay.reitan.html.

14. Marshall, J., & Toffel, M. 2005. Framing the Elusive Concept of Sustainability: A Sustainability Hierarchy. *Environmental Science and Technology* 39(3): 673–82, p. 673.

15. Paehlke, R. 2005. Conservation Forum: Sustainability as a Bridging Concept. *Conservation Biology* 19(1): 36–38, p. 36.

16. Costanza, R., Low, B., Ostrom, E., & Wilson, J. 2001. Ecosystems and Human Systems: A Framework for Exploring the Linkages. In R. Costanza, B. Low, E. Ostrom, & J. Wilson (Eds.), *Institutions, Ecosystems, and Sustainability*. New York: Lewis Publishers, pp. 3–20.

Understanding the Text

1. How is sustainability dependent on people's perceptions of the world?
2. In what ways is sustainability tied to economic theory?
3. What examples does Goffman use to demonstrate cultures that were unsustainable? Why does he include these examples?
4. What is the "carrying capacity" of an environment? What can happen if the carrying capacity is exceeded?

Reflection and Response

5. Are incentives or prohibitions more effective in bringing about sustainability? What do you think our government should do to create a sustainable society? What should the government not do?
6. Do you think our culture could wind up like Easter Island and Mayan cultures? Why or why not?
7. This essay suggests that population is a major factor in environmental issues and sustainability. Do you believe that the population should be "controlled" in some way? If so, how should it be done?

Making Connections

8. A few essays in this chapter talk about "overshoot" as a critical factor in environmental issues. What exactly is overshoot? Why is it a problem?
9. Do further research on Abraham Maslow's "hierarchy of needs." How does this provide a framework for sustainable thinking? In what ways could the pyramid be revised or changed to account for nature or culture or both?
10. One purpose of this essay is to present a definition of sustainability. How does the author define it? How do you define it? Has your definition changed after reading this essay or other essays in this chapter?

How Is Sustainability a Political Issue?

Sustainability is a complex issue, and the conversations surrounding it involve a wide range of people, organizations, companies, institutions, governments, and nations. All of these participants in the conversation operate from their own perspective, and they all have different goals and motivations in engaging with sustainability. Each writer seeks to persuade others to think about the subject in certain ways and to act on those thoughts.

As you will discover through reading this chapter, these participants envision sustainability as a political issue — that is, they seek to sway public opinion and influence government policies to achieve their goals. Many of the authors in this chapter are politicians themselves or are active in politics, and for those individuals, shaping the opinions of the public is very important. In fact, most articles in this chapter are written for a general public audience. You are a part of that audience; as you read these selections, consider the ways in which each author attempts to change your thinking about sustainability.

The readings in this chapter are intentionally diverse. They cover a wide range of genres, from government reports to magazine articles to blog postings. All of these genres and many more are part of our collective public discourse about sustainability, and each genre and subject has a different goal. More important, the readings in Chapter 2 span the political spectrum from liberal to conservative. One primary goal of the chapter is to help you to compare and contrast the ways in which different groups and individuals use language to shape public understandings about sustainability. The chapter begins with articles from authors who are identified (or who self-identify) as politically liberal — most notably Gore, Orr, and Merchant. Political liberals are generally seen as the strongest advocates for environmental preservation and sustainability programs. The authors who appear later in this chapter are generally more skeptical of the goals, aims, and possibilities of sustainability and environmental efforts — including Lomborg, Miller, and Ross — and they represent more politically conservative views. The final reading selection, by Zorach, seeks to bridge the political gap between liberals and conservatives on the issue of sustainability. Your own perspective may fall somewhere along this political spectrum, and it may change as you read these articles — that's a good thing.

As you read, pay close attention to the ways in which key words like *environment* and *sustainability* are defined. Each author expresses a different outlook on these key terms, and consequently, suggests different methods of addressing the issues surrounding them. Although it may seem confusing to read contrasting or opposing definitions of a term like *sustainability*, keep in mind that these definitions can reveal the author's viewpoints, objectives, and goals concerning the subject.

Our Common Future: From One Earth to One World (Brundtland Report)

World Commission on Environment and Development

In 1983, the United Nations convened the World Commission on Environment and Development (WCED) to address the accelerating deterioration of natural resources and the global impact of human development. Four years later, the WCED published a report titled "Our Common Future," which is also known as the Brundtland Report in recognition of the chair of the WCED, Norway's prime minister Gro Harlem Brundtland.

The Brundtland Report has been viewed as a landmark text in the debates concerning global sustainability. The report examines the role of governments, businesses, and individuals in sustainability, and it provides a comprehensive overview of the major global environmental crises as well as suggestions on how to address these problems. "Our Common Future" is also responsible for a key (and frequently quoted) definition of sustainable development: development that "meets the needs of the present without compromising the ability of future generations to meet their own needs" (par. 11).

As you read this excerpt from "Our Common Future," think about the ways in which sustainability is a global issue and the role that worldwide organizations like the UN and the WCED might play in creating a more sustainable world.

I n the middle of the 20th century, we saw our planet from space for the first time. Historians may eventually find that this vision had a greater impact on thought than did the Copernican revolution° of the 16th century, which upset the human self-image by revealing that the Earth is not the center of the universe. From space, we see a small and fragile ball dominated not by human activity and edifice but by a pattern of clouds, oceans, greenery, and soils. Humanity's inability to fit its activities into that pattern is changing planetary systems, fundamentally. Many such changes are accompanied by life-threatening hazards. This new reality, from which there is no escape, must be recognized — and managed.

Copernican revolution: the now-accepted theory that all planets revolve around the sun as opposed to the earth, proposed by Nicolaus Copernicus (Polish astronomer, 1473–1543).

Fortunately, this new reality coincides with more positive developments new to this century. We can move information and goods faster around the globe than ever before; we can produce more food and more goods with less investment of resources; our technology and science gives us, at least, the potential to look deeper into and better understand natural systems. From space, we can see and study the Earth as an organism whose health depends on the health of all its parts. We have the power to reconcile human affairs with natural laws and to thrive in the process. In this our cultural and spiritual heritages can reinforce our economic interests and survival imperatives.

This Commission believes that people can build a future that is more prosperous, more just, and more secure. Our report, *Our Common Future*, is not a prediction of ever increasing environmental decay, poverty, and hardship in an ever more polluted world among ever decreasing resources. We see instead the possibility for a new era of economic growth, one that must be based on policies that sustain and expand the environmental resource base. And we believe such growth to be absolutely essential to relieve the great poverty that is deepening in much of the developing world.

But the Commission's hope for the future is conditional on decisive political action now to begin managing environmental resources to ensure both sustainable human progress and human survival. We are not forecasting a future; we are serving a notice — an urgent notice based on the latest and best scientific evidence — that the time has come to make the decisions needed to secure the resources to sustain this and coming generations. We do not offer a detailed blueprint for action, but instead a pathway by which the peoples of the world may enlarge their spheres of cooperation.

The Global Challenge

Successes and Failures

Those looking for success and signs of hope can find many: infant 5
mortality is falling; human life expectancy is increasing; the proportion of the world's adults who can read and write is climbing; the proportion of children starting school is rising; and global food production increases faster than the population grows.

But the same processes that have produced these gains have given rise to trends that the planet and its people cannot long bear. These have traditionally been divided into failures of "development" and failures in the management of our human environment. On the development side, in terms of absolute numbers there are more hungry people in the world than ever before, and their numbers are increasing. So are the numbers who cannot read or write, the numbers without safe water or safe and sound homes, and the numbers short of woodfuel with which to cook and warm themselves. The gap between rich and poor nations is widening — not shrinking — and there is little prospect, given present trends and institutional arrangements, that this process will be reversed.

There are also environmental trends that threaten to radically alter the planet, that threaten the lives of many species upon it, including the human species. Each year another 6 million hectares° of productive dryland turns into worthless desert. Over three decades, this would amount to an area roughly as large as Saudi Arabia. More than 11 million hectares of forests are destroyed yearly, and this, over three decades, would equal an area about the size of India. Much of this forest is converted to low-grade farmland unable to support the farmers who settle it. In Europe, acid precipitation kills forests and lakes and damages the artistic and architectural heritage of nations; it may have acidified vast tracts of soil beyond reasonable hope of repair. The burning of fossil fuels puts into the atmosphere carbon dioxide, which is causing gradual global warming.° This "greenhouse effect"° may by early next century[1] have increased average global temperatures enough to shift agricultural production areas, raise sea levels to flood coastal cities, and disrupt national economies. Other industrial gases threaten to deplete the planet's protective ozone shield to such an extent that the number of human and animal cancers would rise sharply and the oceans' food chain would be disrupted, industry and agriculture put toxic substances into the human food chain and into underground water tables beyond reach of cleansing.

There has been a growing realization in national governments and multilateral institutions that it is impossible to separate economic development issues from environment issues; many forms of development erode the environmental resources upon which they must be

---

hectares: a unit of surface, or land, measure equal to 100 acres, or 10,000 square meters.

global warming: an increase in the earth's average atmospheric temperature that causes corresponding changes in climate and that may result from the greenhouse effect.

greenhouse effect: an atmospheric heating phenomenon caused by gases such as carbon dioxide, water vapor, methane, and others, that trap heat within the earth's atmosphere.

[1]This report was written in 1987. — Ed.

based, and environmental degradation can undermine economic development. Poverty is a major cause and effect of global environmental problems. It is therefore futile to attempt to deal with environmental problems without a broader perspective that encompasses the factors underlying world poverty and international inequality.

These concerns were behind the establishment in 1983 of the World Commission on Environment and Development by the UN General Assembly. The Commission is an independent body, linked to but outside the control of governments and the UN system. The Commission's mandate gave it three objectives: to re-examine the critical environment and development issues and to formulate realistic proposals for dealing with them; to propose new forms of international cooperation on these issues that will influence policies and events in the direction of needed changes; and to raise the levels of understanding and commitment to action of individuals, voluntary organizations, businesses, institutes, and governments.

Through our deliberations and the testimony of people at the public hearings we held on five continents, all the commissioners came to focus on one central theme: many present development trends leave increasing numbers of people poor and vulnerable, while at the same time degrading the environment. How can such development serve next century's world of twice as many people relying on the same environment? This realization broadened our view of development. We came to see it not in its restricted context of economic growth in developing countries. We came to see that a new development path was required, one that sustained human progress not just in a few pieces for a few years, but for the entire planet into the distant future. Thus "sustainable development" becomes a goal not just for the "developing" nations, but for industrial ones as well. . . .

Sustainable Development

Humanity has the ability to make development sustainable to ensure that it meets the needs of the present without compromising the ability of future generations to meet their own needs. The concept of sustainable development does imply limits — not absolute limits but limitations imposed by the present state of technology and social organization on environmental resources and by the ability of the biosphere° to absorb the effects of human activities. But technology and social organization can be both managed and improved to make way for a new era of economic growth. The Commission believes that

biosphere: the part of the earth's crust, waters, and atmosphere that supports life.

widespread poverty is no longer inevitable. Poverty is not only an evil in itself, but sustainable development requires meeting the basic needs of all and extending to all the opportunity to fulfill their aspirations for a better life. A world in which poverty is endemic will always be prone to ecological and other catastrophes.

Meeting essential needs requires not only a new era of economic growth for nations in which the majority are poor, but an assurance that those poor get their fair share of the resources required to sustain that growth. Such equity would be aided by political systems that secure effective citizen participation in decision making and by greater democracy in international decision making.

"Sustainable development . . . meets the needs of the present without compromising the ability of future generations to meet their own needs."

Sustainable global development requires that those who are more affluent adopt life-styles within the planet's ecological means — in their use of energy, for example. Further, rapidly growing populations can increase the pressure on resources and slow any rise in living standards; thus sustainable development can only be pursued if population size and growth are in harmony with the changing productive potential of the ecosystem.

Yet in the end, sustainable development is not a fixed state of harmony, but rather a process of change in which the exploitation of resources, the direction of investments, the orientation of technological development, and institutional change are made consistent with future as well as present needs. We do not pretend that the process is easy or straightforward. Painful choices have to be made. Thus, in the final analysis, sustainable development must rest on political will.

The Institutional Gaps

The objective of sustainable development and the integrated nature of the global environment/development challenges pose problems for institutions, national and international, that were established on the basis of narrow preoccupations and compartmentalized concerns. Governments' general response to the speed and scale of global changes has been a reluctance to recognize sufficiently the need to change themselves. The challenges are both interdependent and integrated, requiring comprehensive approaches and popular participation. 15

Yet most of the institutions facing those challenges tend to be independent, fragmented, working to relatively narrow mandates with closed decision processes. Those responsible for managing natural resources and protecting the environment are institutionally separated from those responsible for managing the economy. The real world of interlocked economic and ecological systems will not change; the policies and institutions concerned must.

There is a growing need for effective international cooperation to manage ecological and economic interdependence. Yet at the same time, confidence in international organizations is diminishing and support for them dwindling.

The other great institutional flaw in coping with environment/ development challenges is governments' failure to make the bodies whose policy actions degrade the environment responsible for ensuring that their policies prevent that degradation. Environmental concern arose from damage caused by the rapid economic growth following the Second World War. Governments, pressured by their citizens, saw a need to clean up the mess, and they established environmental ministries and agencies to do this. Many had great success within the limits of their mandates — in improving air and water quality and enhancing other resources. But much of their work has of necessity been after-the-fact repair of damage: reforestation, reclaiming desert lands, rebuilding urban environments, restoring natural habitats, and rehabilitating wild lands.

The existence of such agencies gave many governments and their citizens the false impression that these bodies were by themselves able to protect and enhance the environmental resource base. Yet many industrialized and most developing countries carry huge economic burdens from inherited problems such as air and water pollution, depletion of groundwater, and the proliferation of toxic chemicals and hazardous wastes. These have been joined by more recent problems — erosion, desertification, acidification, new chemicals, and new forms of waste — that are directly related to agricultural, industrial, energy, forestry, and transportation policies and practices.

The mandates of the central economic and sectoral ministries are also often too narrow, too concerned with quantities of production or growth. The mandates of ministries of industry include production targets, while the accompanying pollution is left to ministries of environment. Electricity boards produce power, while the acid pollution they also produce is left to other bodies to clean up. The present challenge is to give the central economic and sectoral ministries the responsibility for the quality of those parts of the human environment affected by their decisions, and to give the environmental agencies more power to cope with the effects of unsustainable development.

The same need for change holds for international agencies concerned with development lending, trade regulation, agricultural development, and so on. These have been slow to take the environmental effects of their work into account, although some are trying to do so.

The ability to anticipate and prevent environmental damage requires that the ecological dimensions of policy be considered at the same time as the economic, trade, energy, agricultural, and other dimensions. They should be considered on the same agendas and in the same national and international institutions.

This reorientation is one of the chief institutional challenges of the 1990s and beyond. Meeting it will require major institutional development and reform. Many countries that are too poor or small or that have limited managerial capacity will find it difficult to do this unaided. They will need financial and technical assistance and training. But the changes required involve all countries, large and small, rich and poor. . . .

A Call for Action

Over the course of this [the twentieth] century, the relationship between the human world and the planet that sustains it has undergone a profound change.

When the century began, neither human numbers nor technology had the power radically to alter planetary systems. As the century closes, not only do vastly increased human numbers and their activities have that power, but major, unintended changes are occurring in the atmosphere, in soils, in waters, among plants and animals, and in the relationships among all of these. The rate of change is outstripping the ability of scientific disciplines and our current capabilities to assess and advise. It is frustrating the attempts of political and economic institutions, which evolved in a different, more fragmented world, to adapt and cope. It deeply worries many people who are seeking ways to place those concerns on the political agendas. 25

The onus lies with no one group of nations. Developing countries face the obvious life-threatening challenges of desertification, deforestation, and pollution, and endure most of the poverty associated with environmental degradation. The entire human family of nations would suffer from the disappearance of rain forests in the tropics, the loss of plant and animal species, and changes in rainfall patterns. Industrial nations face the life-threatening challenges of toxic chemicals, toxic wastes, and acidification. All nations may suffer from the releases by industrialized countries of carbon dioxide and of gases that react with the ozone layer, and from any future war fought with the nuclear arsenals controlled by those nations. All nations will have a role to play in changing trends, and in righting an international economic system that increases rather than decreases inequality, that increases rather than decreases numbers of poor and hungry.

The next few decades are crucial. The time has come to break out of past patterns. Attempts to maintain social and ecological stability through old approaches to development and environmental protection will increase instability. Security must be sought through change. The Commission has noted a number of actions that must be taken to reduce risks to survival and to put future development on paths that are sustainable. Yet we are aware that such a reorientation on a continuing basis is simply beyond the reach of present decision-making structures and institutional arrangements, both national and international.

This Commission has been careful to base our recommendations on the realities of present institutions, on what can and must be accomplished today. But to keep options open for future generations, the present generation must begin now, and begin together.

To achieve the needed changes, we believe that an active follow-up of this report is imperative. It is with this in mind that we call for the UN General Assembly, upon due consideration, to transform this report into a UN Programme on Sustainable Development. Special follow-up conferences could be initiated at the regional level. Within an appropriate period after the presentation of this report to the General Assembly, an international conference could be convened to review progress made, and to promote follow-up arrangements that will be needed to set benchmarks and to maintain human progress.

First and foremost, this Commission has been concerned with people — of all countries and all walks of life. And it is to people that we address our report. The changes in human attitudes that we call for depend on a vast campaign of education, debate, and public participation. This campaign must start now if sustainable human progress is to be achieved.

The members of the World Commission on Environment and Development came from 21 very different nations. In our discussions, we disagreed often on details and priorities. But despite our widely differing backgrounds and varying national and international responsibilities, we were able to agree to the lines along which change must be drawn.

We are unanimous in our conviction that the security, well-being, and very survival of the planet depend on such changes, now.

Understanding the Text

1. Who do you see as the primary audience for this report? How does the report engage that audience? Who are the secondary audiences?

2. This report attempts to balance hope for the future with the current realities of the global environment. Who are some of the primary successes and challenges described here?

3. How does this text describe and define sustainable development? Do you think the definition is accurate and comprehensive? Why or why not?

Reflection and Response

4. The first sentence of this piece reminds us of our accomplishment in seeing our planet from outer space for the first time. Why do you think the authors chose this as an opening sentence?

5. In what ways are poverty and environmental issues connected? Why do the authors address poverty? What problems can poverty cause for natural environments?

6. What is the "Call for Action" identified in the last section of this excerpt? How does it affect you personally?

Making Connections

7. Population growth remains one of the biggest threats to humanity and our ability to maintain a sustainable world. Do you think that governments and international organizations should try to control population growth? What methods should they pursue? What methods should they not pursue?

8. This text is referenced in many other sources throughout this book. Why do you think this is an important piece in the history of sustainability?

9. This document suggests that time is a crucial factor and that efforts toward sustainability must begin immediately. Do some research to determine what steps have been taken toward global sustainability since the report was published in 1987.

Climate of Denial

Al Gore

Al Gore Jr. was the forty-fifth vice president of the United States (1993–2001) under President Bill Clinton. Gore is well-known for his environmental advocacy work as well as for his popular writing about environmental issues. He has founded a number of nonprofit organizations, including the Alliance for Climate Protection, and he has received a Nobel Peace Prize for his work in climate change activism. Gore was the subject of the Academy Award–winning documentary film *An Inconvenient Truth* (2007), which followed Gore's nationwide speaking tour to educate Americans about global climate change.

"Climate of Denial" was published in 2011 in *Rolling Stone* magazine. In the essay, Gore addresses the role of television news media in the debate about global climate change. He argues that business "special interest" groups play an undue role in the debate, at the expense of scientific data. As you read the essay, think about the ways in which debates about climate change and sustainability are portrayed in news broadcasts.

The first time I remember hearing the question "Is it real?" was when I went as a young boy to see a traveling show put on by "professional wrestlers" one summer evening in the gym of the Forks River Elementary School in Elmwood, Tennessee.

The evidence that it was real was palpable: "They're really hurting each other! That's real blood! Look a'there! They can't fake that!" On the other hand, there was clearly a script (or in today's language, a "narrative"), with good guys to cheer and bad guys to boo.

But the most unusual and in some ways most interesting character in these dramas was the referee: Whenever the bad guy committed a gross and obvious violation of the "rules" — such as they were — like using a metal folding chair to smack the good guy in the head, the referee always seemed to be preoccupied with one of the cornermen, or looking the other way. Yet whenever the good guy — after absorbing more abuse and unfairness than any reasonable person could tolerate — committed the slightest infraction, the referee was all over him. The answer to the question "Is it real?" seemed connected to the question of whether the referee was somehow confused about his role: Was he too an entertainer?

That is pretty much the role now being played by most of the news media in refereeing the current wrestling match over whether global warming is "real," and whether it has any connection to the constant dumping of 90 million tons of heat-trapping emissions into the Earth's thin shell of atmosphere every 24 hours.

Admittedly, the contest over global warming is a challenge for the   5
referee because it's a tag-team match, a real free-for-all. In one corner of the ring are Science and Reason. In the other corner: Poisonous
Polluters and Right-wing Ideologues.°

The referee — in this analogy, the news media — seems confused
about whether he is in the news business or the entertainment business. Is he responsible for ensuring a fair match? Or is he part of the
show, selling tickets and building the audience? The referee certainly
seems distracted: by Donald Trump, Charlie Sheen, the latest reality
show — the list of serial obsessions is too long to enumerate here.

But whatever the cause, the referee appears not to notice that the
Polluters and Ideologues are trampling all over the "rules" of democratic discourse. They are financing pseudoscientists whose job is to
manufacture doubt about what is true and what is false; buying
elected officials wholesale with bribes that the politicians themselves
have made "legal" and can now be made in secret; spending hundreds of millions of dollars each year on misleading advertisements
in the mass media; hiring four anti-climate lobbyists for every member of the U.S. Senate and House of Representatives. (Question:
Would Michael Jordan have been a star if he was covered by four de-
fensive players every step he took on the basketball court?)

This script, of course, is not entirely new: A half-century ago,
when Science and Reason established the linkage between cigarettes
and lung diseases, the tobacco industry hired actors, dressed them
up as doctors, and paid them to look into television cameras and tell
people that the linkage revealed in the Surgeon General's Report was
not real at all. The show went on for decades, with more Americans
killed each year by cigarettes than all of the U.S. soldiers killed in all
of World War II.

This time, the scientific consensus is even stronger. It has been
endorsed by every National Academy of science of every major country on the planet, every major professional scientific society related
to the study of global warming and 98 percent of climate scientists
throughout the world. In the latest and most authoritative study by
3,000 of the very best scientific experts in the world, the evidence
was judged "unequivocal."

But wait! The good guys transgressed the rules of decorum, as evi-   10
denced in their private e-mails that were stolen and put on the Internet.

Right-wing Ideologue: a person who zealously advocates an extreme conservative political position.

The referee is all over it: Penalty! Go to your corner! And in their 3,000-page report, the scientists made some mistakes! Another penalty!

And if more of the audience is left confused about whether the climate crisis is real? Well, the show must go on. After all, it's entertainment. There are tickets to be sold, eyeballs to glue to the screen.

Part of the script for this show was leaked to *The New York Times* as early as 1991. In an internal document, a consortium of the largest global-warming polluters spelled out their principal strategy: "Reposition global warming as theory, rather than fact." Ever since, they have been sowing doubt even more effectively than the tobacco companies before them.

To sell their false narrative, the Polluters and Ideologues have found it essential to undermine the public's respect for Science and Reason by attacking the integrity of the climate scientists. That is why the scientists are regularly accused of falsifying evidence and exaggerating its implications in a greedy effort to win more research grants, or secretly pursuing a hidden political agenda to expand the power of government. Such slanderous insults are deeply ironic: extremist ideologues — many financed or employed by carbon polluters — accusing scientists of being greedy extremist ideologues.

After World War II, a philosopher studying the impact of organized propaganda on the quality of democratic debate wrote, "The conversion of all questions of truth into questions of power has attacked the very heart of the distinction between true and false."

Is the climate crisis real? Yes, of course it is. Pause for a moment to consider these events of just the past 12 months: 15

- **Heat.** According to NASA, 2010 was tied with 2005 as the hottest year measured since instruments were first used systematically in the 1880s. Nineteen countries set all-time high temperature records. One city in Pakistan, Mohenjo-Daro, reached 128.3 degrees Fahrenheit, the hottest temperature ever measured in an Asian city. Nine of the 10 hottest years in history have occurred in the last 13 years. The past decade was the hottest ever measured, even though half of that decade represented a "solar minimum" — the low ebb in the natural cycle of solar energy emanating from the sun.

- **Floods.** Megafloods displaced 20 million people in Pakistan, further destabilizing a nuclear-armed country; inundated an area of Australia larger than Germany and France combined; flooded 28 of the 32 districts that make up Colombia, where it has rained almost continuously for the past year; caused a "thousand-year" flood in my home city of Nashville; and led to all-time record flood levels in the Mississippi River Valley. Many places around the world are now experiencing larger and more frequent extreme downpours and snowstorms; last year's "Snowmaggedon" in the northeastern United States is part of the same pattern, notwithstanding the guffaws of deniers.

- **Drought.** Historic drought and fires in Russia killed an estimated 56,000 people and caused wheat and other food crops in Russia, Ukraine and Kazakhstan to be removed from the global market, contributing to a record spike in food prices. "Practically everything is burning," Russian president Dmitry Medvedev declared. "What's happening with the planet's climate right now needs to be a wake-up call to all of us." The drought level in much of Texas has been raised from "extreme" to "exceptional," the highest category. This spring the majority of the counties in Texas were on fire, and Governor Rick Perry requested a major disaster declaration for all but two of the state's 254 counties. Arizona is now fighting the largest fire in its history. Since 1970, the fire season throughout the American West has increased by 78 days. Extreme droughts in central China and northern France are currently drying up reservoirs and killing crops.

- **Melting Ice.** An enormous mass of ice, four times larger than the island of Manhattan, broke off from northern Greenland last year and slipped into the sea. The acceleration of ice loss in both Greenland and Antarctica has caused another upward revision of global sea-level rise and the numbers of refugees expected from low-lying coastal areas. The Arctic ice cap, which reached a record low volume last year, has lost as much as 40 percent of its area during summer in just 30 years.

These extreme events are happening in real time. It is not uncommon for the nightly newscast to resemble a nature hike through the Book of Revelation. Yet most of the news media completely ignore how such events are connected to the climate crisis, or dismiss the connection as controversial; after all, there are scientists on one side of the debate and deniers on the other. A Fox News executive, in an internal e-mail to the network's reporters and editors that later became public, questioned the "veracity of climate change data" and ordered the journalists to "refrain from asserting that the planet has warmed (or cooled) in any given period without IMMEDIATELY pointing out that such theories are based upon data that critics have called into question."

But in the "real" world, the record droughts, fires, floods and mudslides continue to increase in severity and frequency. Leading climate scientists like Jim Hansen and Kevin Trenberth now say that events like these would almost certainly not be occurring without the influence of man-made global warming. And that's a shift in the way they frame these impacts. Scientists used to caution that we were increasing the probability of such extreme events by "loading the dice" — pumping more carbon into the atmosphere. Now the scientists go much further, warning that we are "painting more dots on the dice." We are not only more likely to roll 12s; we are now rolling 13s and 14s. In other words, the biggest storms are not only becoming more frequent, they are getting bigger, stronger and more destructive.

"The only plausible explanation for the rise in weather-related catastrophes is climate change," Munich Re, one of the two largest reinsurance companies in the world, recently stated. "The view that weather extremes are more frequent and intense due to global warming coincides with the current state of scientific knowledge."

Many of the extreme and destructive events are the result of the rapid increase in the amount of heat energy from the sun that is trapped in the atmosphere, which is radically disrupting the planet's water cycle. More heat energy evaporates more water into the air, and the warmer air holds a lot more moisture. This has huge consequences that we now see all around the world.

When a storm unleashes a downpour of rain or snow, the precipitation does not originate just in the part of the sky directly above where it falls. Storms reach out — sometimes as far as 2,000 miles — to suck in water vapor from large areas of the sky, including the skies above oceans, where water vapor has increased by four percent in just the last 30 years. (Scientists often compare this phenomenon to what happens in a bathtub when you open the drain; the water rushing out comes from the whole tub, not just from the part of the tub directly above the drain. And when the tub is filled with more water, more goes down the drain. In the same way, when the warmer sky is filled with a lot more water vapor, there are bigger downpours when a storm cell opens the "drain.")

In many areas, these bigger downpours also mean longer periods between storms — at the same time that the extra heat in the air is also drying out the soil. That is part of the reason so many areas have been experiencing both record floods and deeper, longer-lasting droughts.

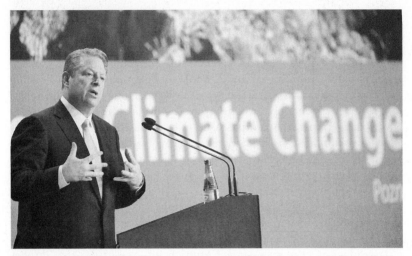

Former U.S. Vice President Al Gore speaking about climate change in December 2008.

Janek Skarzynski/Getty Images

Moreover, the scientists have been warning us for quite some time — in increasingly urgent tones — that things will get much, much worse if we continue the reckless dumping of more and more heat-trapping pollution into the atmosphere. *Drought is projected to spread across significant, highly populated areas of the globe throughout this century.* Look at what the scientists say is in store for the Mediterranean nations. Should we care about the loss of Spain, France, Italy, the Balkans, Turkey, Tunisia? Look at what they say is in store for Mexico. Should we notice? Should we care?

Maybe it's just easier, psychologically, to swallow the lie that these scientists who devote their lives to their work are actually greedy deceivers and left-wing extremists — and that we should instead put our faith in the pseudoscientists financed by large carbon polluters whose business plans depend on their continued use of the atmospheric commons as a place to dump their gaseous, heat-trapping waste without limit or constraint, free of charge.

The truth is this: What we are doing is functionally insane. If we do not change this pattern, we will condemn our children and all future generations to struggle with ecological curses for several millennia to come. Twenty percent of the global-warming pollution we spew into the sky each day will still be there 20,000 years from now!

We do have another choice. Renewable energy sources are coming 25
into their own. Both solar and wind will soon produce power at costs

that are competitive with fossil fuels; indications are that twice as many solar installations were erected worldwide last year as compared to 2009. The reductions in cost and the improvements in efficiency of photovoltaic cells over the past decade appear to be following an exponential curve that resembles a less dramatic but still startling version of what happened with computer chips over the past 50 years.

Enhanced geothermal energy is potentially a nearly limitless source of competitive electricity. Increased energy efficiency is already saving businesses money and reducing emissions significantly. New generations of biomass energy — ones that do not rely on food crops, unlike the mistaken strategy of making ethanol from corn — are extremely promising. Sustainable forestry and agriculture both make economic as well as environmental sense. And all of these options would spread even more rapidly if we stopped subsidizing Big Oil and Coal and put a price on carbon that reflected the true cost of fossil energy — either through the much-maligned cap-and-trade approach, or through a revenue-neutral tax swap.

All over the world, the grassroots movement in favor of changing public policies to confront the climate crisis and build a more prosperous, sustainable future is growing rapidly. But most governments remain paralyzed, unable to take action — even after years of volatile gasoline prices, repeated wars in the Persian Gulf, one energy-related disaster after another, and a seemingly endless stream of unprecedented and lethal weather disasters.

Continuing on our current course would be suicidal for global civilization. But the key question is: How do we drive home that fact in a democratic society when questions of truth have been converted into questions of power? When the distinction between what is true and what is false is being attacked relentlessly, and when the referee in the contest between truth and falsehood has become an entertainer selling tickets to a phony wrestling match?

The "wrestling ring" in this metaphor is the conversation of democracy. It used to be called the "public square." In ancient Athens, it was the Agora. In the Roman Republic, it was the Forum. In the Egypt of the recent Arab Spring, "Tahrir Square" was both real and metaphorical — encompassing Facebook, Twitter, Al-Jazeera and texting.

In the America of the late-18th century, the conversation that led 30 to our own "Spring" took place in printed words: pamphlets, newsprint, books, the "Republic of Letters." It represented the fullest flower of the Enlightenment, during which the oligarchic power of the monarchies, the feudal lords and the Medieval Church was overthrown and replaced with a new sovereign: the Rule of Reason.

The public square that gave birth to the new consciousness of the Enlightenment emerged in the dozen generations following the invention of the printing press — "the Gutenberg Galaxy," the scholar Marshall McLuhan called it — a space in which the conversation of democracy was almost equally accessible to every literate person. Individuals could both find the knowledge that had previously been restricted to elites and contribute their own ideas.

Ideas that found resonance with others rose in prominence much the way Google searches do today, finding an ever larger audience and becoming a source of political power for individuals with neither wealth nor force of arms. Thomas Paine, to take one example, emigrated from England to Philadelphia with no wealth, no family connections and no power other than that which came from his ability to think and write clearly — yet his *Common Sense* became the *Harry Potter* of Revolutionary America. The "public interest" mattered, was actively discussed and pursued.

But the "public square" that gave birth to America has been transformed beyond all recognition. The conversation that matters most to the shaping of the "public mind" now takes place on television. Newspapers and magazines are in decline. The Internet, still in its early days, will one day support business models that make true journalism profitable — but up until now, the only successful news websites aggregate content from struggling print publications. Web versions of the newspapers themselves are, with few exceptions, not yet making money. They bring to mind the classic image of Wile E. Coyote running furiously in midair just beyond the edge of the cliff, before plummeting to the desert floor far beneath him.

The average American, meanwhile, is watching television an astonishing five hours a day. In the average household, at least one television set is turned on more than eight hours a day. Moreover, approximately 75 percent of those using the Internet frequently watch television at the same time that they are online.

Unlike access to the "public square" of early America, access to 35 television requires large amounts of money. Thomas Paine could walk out of his front door in Philadelphia and find a dozen competing, low-cost print shops within blocks of his home. Today, if he traveled to the nearest TV station, or to the headquarters of nearby Comcast — the dominant television provider in America — and tried to deliver his new ideas to the American people, he would be laughed off the premises. The public square that used to be a commons has been refeudalized, and the gatekeepers charge large rents for the privilege of communicating to the American people over the only medium that really affects their thinking. "Citizens" are now referred to more commonly as "consumers" or "the audience."

That is why up to 80 percent of the campaign budgets for candidates in both major political parties is devoted to the purchase of 30-second TV ads. Since the rates charged for these commercials increase each year, the candidates are forced to raise more and more money in each two-year campaign cycle.

Of course, the only reliable sources from which such large sums can be raised continuously are business lobbies. Organized labor, a shadow of its former self, struggles to compete, and individuals are limited by law to making small contributions. During the 2008 campaign, there was a bubble of hope that Internet-based fundraising might even the scales, but in the end, Democrats as well as Republicans relied far more on traditional sources of large contributions. Moreover, the recent deregulation of unlimited — and secret — donations by wealthy corporations has made the imbalance even worse.

In the new ecology of political discourse, special-interest contributors of the large sums of money now required for the privilege of addressing voters on a wholesale basis are not squeamish about asking for the quo they expect in return for their quid. Politicians who don't acquiesce don't get the money they need to be elected and re-elected. And the impact is doubled when special interests make clear — usually bluntly — that the money they are withholding will go instead to opponents who are more than happy to pledge the desired quo. Politicians have been racing to the bottom for some time, and are presently tunneling to new depths. It is now commonplace for congressmen and senators first elected decades ago — as I was — to comment in private that the whole process has become unbelievably crass, degrading and horribly destructive to the core values of American democracy.

Largely as a result, the concerns of the wealthiest individuals and corporations routinely trump the concerns of average Americans and small businesses. There are a ridiculously large number of examples: eliminating the inheritance tax paid by the wealthiest one percent of families is considered a much higher priority than addressing the suffering of the millions of long-term unemployed; Wall Street's interest in legalizing gambling in trillions of dollars of "derivatives" was considered way more important than protecting the integrity of the financial system and the interests of middle-income home buyers. It's a long list. . . .

We haven't gone nuts — but the "conversation of democracy" has 40 become so deeply dysfunctional that our ability to make intelligent collective decisions has been seriously impaired. Throughout American history, we relied on the vibrancy of our public square — and the quality of our democratic discourse — to make better decisions than most nations in the history of the world. But we are now routinely making really bad decisions that completely ignore the best available evidence of what is true and what is false. When the distinction between truth and falsehood is systematically attacked without shame or consequence — when a great nation makes crucially important decisions on the basis of completely false information that is no longer adequately filtered through the fact-checking function of a healthy and honest public discussion — the public interest is severely damaged.

That is exactly what is happening with U.S. decisions regarding the climate crisis. The best available evidence demonstrates beyond any reasonable doubt that the reckless spewing of global-warming pollution in obscene quantities into the atmospheric commons is having exactly the consequences long predicted by scientists who have analyzed the known facts according to the laws of physics.

The emergence of the climate crisis seems sudden only because of a relatively recent discontinuity in the relationship between human civilization and the planet's ecological system. In the past century, we have quadrupled global population while relying on the burning of carbon-based fuels — coal, oil and gas — for 85 percent of the world's energy. We are also cutting and burning forests that would otherwise help remove some of the added CO_2 from the atmosphere, and have converted agriculture to an industrial model that also runs on carbon-based fuels and strip-mines carbon-rich soils.

The cumulative result is a radically new reality — and since human nature makes us vulnerable to confusing the unprecedented with the improbable, it naturally seems difficult to accept. Moreover, since this new reality is painful to contemplate, and requires big changes in policy and behavior that are at the outer limit of our ability, it is all too easy to fall into the psychological state of denial. As with financial issues like subprime mortgages and credit default swaps, the climate crisis can seem too complex to worry about, especially when the shills for the polluters constantly claim it's all a hoax anyway. And since the early impacts of climatic disruption are distributed globally, they masquerade as an abstraction that is safe to ignore.

These vulnerabilities, rooted in our human nature, are being manipulated by the tag-team of Polluters and Ideologues who are trying to deceive us. And the referee — the news media — is once again distracted. As with the invasion of Iraq, some are hyperactive cheerleaders for the deception, while others are intimidated into complicity, timidity and silence by the astonishing vitriol heaped upon those who dare to present the best evidence in a professional manner. Just as TV networks who beat the drums of war prior to the Iraq invasion were rewarded with higher ratings, networks now seem reluctant to present the truth about the link between carbon pollution and global warming out of fear that conservative viewers will change the channel — and fear that they will receive a torrent of flame e-mails from deniers. . . .

All things are not equally true. It is time to face reality. We ignored reality in the marketplace and nearly destroyed the world economic system. We are likewise ignoring reality in the environment, and the consequences could be several orders of magnitude worse. Determining what is real can be a challenge in our culture, but in order to make wise choices in the presence of such grave risks, we must use common sense and the rule of reason in coming to an agreement on what is true. 45

So how can we make it happen? How can we as individuals make a difference? In five basic ways:

First, become a committed advocate for solving the crisis. You can start with something simple: Speak up whenever the subject of climate arises. When a friend or acquaintance expresses doubt that the crisis is real, or that it's some sort of hoax, don't let the opportunity pass to put down your personal marker. The civil rights revolution may have been driven by activists who put their lives on the line, but it was partly won by average Americans who began to challenge racist comments in everyday conversations.

Second, deepen your commitment by making consumer choices that reduce energy use and reduce your impact on the environment. The demand by individuals for change in the marketplace has already led many businesses to take truly significant steps to reduce their global-warming pollution. Some of the corporate changes are more symbolic than real — "green-washing," as it's called — but a surprising amount of real progress is taking place. Walmart, to pick one example, is moving aggressively to cut its carbon footprint by 20 million metric tons, in part by pressuring its suppliers to cut down on wasteful packaging and use lower-carbon transportation alternatives. Reward those companies that are providing leadership.

Third, join an organization committed to action on this issue. The Alliance for Climate Protection (climateprotect.org), which I chair, has grassroots action plans for the summer and fall that spell out lots of ways to fight effectively for the policy changes we need. We can also enable you to host a slide show in your community on solutions to the climate crisis — presented by one of the 4,000 volunteers we have trained. Invite your friends and neighbors to come and then enlist them to join the cause.

Fourth, contact your local newspapers and television stations when they put out claptrap on climate — and let them know you're fed up with their stubborn and cowardly resistance to reporting the facts of this issue. One of the main reasons they are so wimpy and irresponsible about global warming is that they're frightened of the reaction they get from the deniers when they report the science objectively. So let them know that deniers are not the only ones in town with game. Stay on them! Don't let up! It's true that some media outlets are getting instructions from their owners on this issue, and that others are influenced by big advertisers, but many of them are surprisingly responsive to a genuine outpouring of opinion from their viewers and readers. It is way past time for the ref to do his job. 50

Finally, and above all, don't give up on the political system. Even though it is rigged by special interests, it is not so far gone that candidates and elected officials don't have to pay attention to persistent, engaged and committed individuals. President Franklin Roosevelt once told civil rights leaders who were pressing him for change that he agreed with them about the need for greater equality for black Americans. Then, as the story goes, he added with a wry smile, "Now go out and make me do it."

"The climate crisis, in reality, is a struggle for the soul of America."

To make our elected leaders take action to solve the climate crisis, we must forcefully communicate the following message: "I care a lot about global warming; I am paying very careful attention to the way you vote and what you say about it; if you are on the wrong side, I am not only going to vote against you, I will work hard to defeat you — regardless of party. If you are on the right side, I will work hard to elect you."

Why do you think President Obama and Congress changed their game on "don't ask, don't tell"? It happened because enough Americans delivered exactly that tough message to candidates who wanted their votes. When enough people care passionately enough to drive that message home on the climate crisis, politicians will look at their hole cards, and enough of them will change their game to make all the difference we need.

This is not naïve; trust me on this. It may take more individual voters to beat the Polluters and Ideologues now than it once did —

AL GORE Climate of Denial 113

when special-interest money was less dominant. But when enough people speak this way to candidates, and convince them that they are dead serious about it, change will happen — both in Congress and in the White House. As the great abolitionist leader Frederick Douglass once observed, "Power concedes nothing without a demand. It never did, and it never will."

What is now at risk in the climate debate is nothing less than our 55 ability to communicate with one another according to a protocol that binds all participants to seek reason and evaluate facts honestly. The ability to perceive reality is a prerequisite for self-governance. Wishful thinking and denial lead to dead ends. When it works, the democratic process helps clear the way toward reality, by exposing false argumentation to the best available evidence. That is why the Constitution affords such unique protection to freedom of the press and of speech.

The climate crisis, in reality, is a struggle for the soul of America. It is about whether or not we are still capable — given the ill health of our democracy and the current dominance of wealth over reason — of perceiving important and complex realities clearly enough to promote and protect the sustainable well-being of the many. What hangs in the balance is the future of civilization as we know it.

Understanding the Text

1. In the debates about global climate change, Gore compares the news media to referees in professional wrestling. Explain this analogy. Do you believe it is accurate? Why or why not?

2. What are the four main climate events that support the idea that there is a climate crisis?

3. According to Gore, what are the five basic ways that individuals can make a difference in the climate crisis?

Reflection and Response

4. What is the "scientific consensus" about climate change? Why, according to Gore, is this consensus ignored, doubted, and distorted in the news?

5. Gore suggests that climate change deniers are similar to tobacco lobbyists from half a century earlier. Do you agree or disagree? Explain the connection.

6. In what ways has the "public square" for political debates changed throughout history? How do recent changes impact our understanding of climate change?

Making Connections

7. More recently, Gore has compared climate change debates to civil rights debates in America (such as those on race, gender, and sexual equality). Do some research on these issues. Do you see a correlation? Explain.

8. Gore is one of the most visible figures in current environmental and sustainability debates. As a result, he is revered by some and despised by others. Find an example of a "strong opinion" concerning Gore and climate change, and analyze the strengths and weaknesses of that opinion.

9. There are many video interviews of Gore discussing environmental issues and sustainability. Watch one of these on YouTube, and analyze Gore's message, approach, persuasive tactics, and body language, as well as other aspects of the presentation. In your opinion, is Gore a persuasive speaker? Why or why not?

Framing Sustainability

David W. Orr

David W. Orr is a writer, lecturer, and professor of environmental studies at Oberlin College. He is the author of several award-winning books, including *Down to the Wire: Confronting Climate Collapse* (2009). Orr has received numerous accolades for his work on sustainability, including a Lyndhurst Prize, a National Conservation Achievement Award from the National Wildlife Federation, and a Visionary Leadership Award from Second Nature.

In "Framing Sustainability" (2006), Orr makes a historical comparison between the issue of slavery in the 1800s and the issue of sustainability in contemporary society. Orr draws on Abraham Lincoln's framing of slavery to suggest that the issue of sustainability must be properly "framed" in public debates to help address it. As you read the essay, think about the similarities to and differences between these two social issues, as well as the example set by Lincoln.

We are now engaged in a worldwide conversation about the issues of human longevity on Earth, but no national leader has yet framed a satisfactory vision of sustainability. It is still commonly regarded as one of many issues on a long and growing list, not as the linchpin that connects all of the other issues. Relative to the large issues of sustainability, we are virtually everywhere roughly where the United States was, say, in the year 1850 on the matter of slavery. On the art of framing political and moral issues, much of late has been written (Lakoff, 2004). What can be learned from how Lincoln cast the problem of slavery?

First, Lincoln did not equivocate or agonize about the essential nature of slavery. He did not over-think the subject; he regarded slavery as a great wrong and said so plainly and often. "If slavery is not wrong," he wrote in 1864, "nothing is wrong." Moreover, he saw the centrality of the issue to other issues on the national agenda such as the tariff, sectionalism, and national growth. Second, more clearly than any other political figure of his time, he understood the priority of keeping the Constitutional foundation of the nation intact and dealing with slavery within the existing framework of law and philosophy. He did not set out to create something from whole cloth but built a case from sources ready at hand: the Bible, the Declaration of Independence, and the Constitution. Third, he used language and logic with a mastery superior to that of any President before or since. Lincoln was a relentless logician but always spoke with vernacular eloquence in words that could be plainly understood by everyone. Fourth, while the issue of slavery was a great moral wrong, Lincoln did not abuse religion to describe it. While his language was full of Biblical metaphors and allusions, he avoided the temptation to demonize the South and to make the war a religious crusade. Throughout the seven years from the House Divided speech to his assassination in 1865, Lincoln's is one of the masterpieces of political framing that combined shrewdness and sagacity with moral clarity. The result was a progressive clarification of the issues leading to a larger concept of nationhood.

From Lincoln's example we might learn, first, to avoid unnecessary complication and contentiousness. The issues of sustainability are primarily ones of fairness and intergenerational rights, not ones of technology or economics, as important as these may be. Lincoln regarded slavery as wrong because no human had the right to hold property in another human being period, not because it was economically inefficient. This was magnetic North by which he oriented his politics. By a similar logic, ours is in the principle that no human has the right to diminish the life and well-being of another and no generation has the right to inflict harm on generations to come. Lincoln did not equivocate on the issue of slavery, nor should we on the tyranny one generation can now impose on another by leaving it ecologically impoverished. Climate change and biotic impoverishment are prime examples of intergenerational remote tyranny and as such constitute a great and permanent wrong and we should say so. Each generation ought to serve as a Trustee for posterity, a bridge of obligation stretching from the distant past to the far future. In that role each generation is required to act cautiously, carefully, and wisely (Brown, 1994). In Wendell Berry's words this "is a burden that falls with greatest weight on us of the industrial age who have been and are, by any measure, the humans most guilty of desecrating the world and of destroying creation" (Berry, 2005, 67).

Second, Lincoln built his case from sources familiar to his audience — the Declaration of Independence, the Constitution, and the Bible. In doing so, he took Jefferson's views on equality to their logical conclusion and recast the Constitution as the foundation for a truly more perfect union that could protect the dignity of all human beings. In our time we can draw on similar sources but now much enhanced by other constitutions and laws and proclamations of the world community. The Universal Declaration of Human Rights and Earth Charter, for example, describe an inclusive political universe that extends a moral covenant to all the people of Earth and all those yet to be born. It is reasonable to expand this covenant to include the wider community of life, as Aldo Leopold° once proposed.

Third, Lincoln's use of religion is instructive both for its depth and   5
for his restraint. He used Biblical imagery and language frequently, but did not do so to castigate Southerners or to inflate Northern pretensions. His use of religion was cautionary, aimed to heal, not divide. Lincoln oriented the struggle over slavery in a larger vision of an imperfect nation striving to fulfill God's justice on earth. The message for us is to ground the issue of sustainability in higher purposes resonant with what is best in the world's great religions but owned by no one creed.

Fourth, Lincoln understood the power of language to clarify, motivate, and to ennoble. Few, if any leaders have ever used words more powerfully or to better effect in a good cause than did Lincoln. This wasn't what we now call "spin" or manipulation of the gullible, but the art of persuasion at its best. Lincoln did not have speech writers to create his message and calibrate it to the latest polls. He wrote his own addresses and letters and is reported to have agonized sometimes for hours and days to find the right words. He spoke directly, often bluntly but softened by humor and the adroit use of metaphor and home spun stories. The result was to place the horrors of combat and the bitterness of sectional strife into a larger context that motivated many to make heroic sacrifices and a legacy of thought and words that "remade America," as Garry Wills° puts it. Now perhaps more than ever we turn to Lincoln for perspective and inspiration.

The tragedy of the civil war originated in the evasions of the generations prior to 1861. The founders chose not to deal with the problem of slavery in 1787 and it subsequently grew into tragedy the effects of which are still evident. Similarly, without our foresight and action, future generations will attribute the tragedies of climate change and biotic impoverishment to our lies, evasions, and derelictions. But the issue of slavery and that of sustainability also differ in important respects. Slavery was practiced only in a few places and it could be ended by one means or another. The issues comprising the challenge of sustainability, on the other hand, affect everyone on the Earth and for as far into the future as one cares to imagine and they are once and for all time. Never again can we take for granted that the planet will recover from human abuse and insult. For all of its

---

Aldo Leopold: (1887–1948), American author, scientist, and environmental advocate. See the selection "Thinking Like a Mountain" on page 57.
Garry Wills: American author, journalist, and historian.

complications, slavery was a relatively simple issue compared to the complexities of sustainability. Progress toward sustainability, however defined, will require more complicated judgments involving intergenerational ethics, science, economics, politics, and much else as applied to problems of energy, agriculture, forestry, shelter, urban planning, health, livelihood, security and the distribution of wealth within and between generations.

Differences notwithstanding, Lincoln's example is instructive. He understood that the deeper problems of race had not been solved by war which had decided only the Constitutional issues about the right of states to secede. It did nothing to resolve the more volatile problems that created the conflict in the first place. He had the faith that they might someday be solved, but only in a nation in which strife and bitterness were set aside by the better angels of our nature. His aim was to create the framework, including the 13th amendment to the Constitution that prohibited slavery, in which healing and charity might take root. Lincoln continues to inspire in our time because he framed the legalities of Constitution and war in a larger context of history, obligation, human dignity, and fundamental rights.

> "Our role is to frame [the problems of sustainability] in such a way as to create the possibility that they might someday be resolved."

The multiple problems of sustainability will not be solved by this generation or the next. Our role, however, is to frame them in such a way as to create the possibility that they might someday be resolved. Lincoln's example is instructive to us because he understood the importance of preserving the larger framework in which the lesser art of defining particular issues might proceed with adequate deliberation which is to say that he understood that the art of framing issues is a means to reach larger ends. In our time many things that ought to be and must be sustained are in jeopardy, the most important of which are those qualities Lincoln used in defining the specific issue of slavery: clarity, courage, generosity, kindness, wisdom, and humor.

Sources

Brown, P. 1994. *Restoring the Public Trust*. Boston: Beacon Press.

Lakoff, G. 2004. *Don't Think of an Elephant*. White River Junction: Chelsea Green.

Wills, G. 1992. *Lincoln at Gettysburg*. New York: Simon & Schuster.

Understanding the Text

1. Why does so much of this essay focus on Abraham Lincoln and the issue of slavery? What does that have to do with sustainability?

2. What are the four main things the author says we can learn from Lincoln?

3. Orr writes, "For all of its complications, slavery was a relatively simple issue compared to the complexities of sustainability" (par. 7). In what ways is sustainability a more complex issue?

Reflection and Response

4. In what ways does this essay help us in "framing sustainability," as the title indicates?

5. This article uses many quotations from Lincoln. How do these quotations influence your reading of the text? What do they contribute to your understanding of the issues at hand?

6. The first portion of this text focuses on Lincoln's handling of the slavery issue in his time; the second portion focuses more directly on the contemporary issue of sustainability. Do you think the beginning portion is necessary to make the author's point? Why or why not?

Making Connections

7. Orr writes that Lincoln "used language and logic with a mastery superior to that of any president before or since" (par. 2). Find a video of a recent presidential speech. In what ways does the speech demonstrate a mastery of logic and language? In what ways does it fall short? Can you compare it with what you've learned about Lincoln's speeches?

8. Lincoln's use of religious associations and biblical metaphors is addressed in this essay. What could contemporary speakers learn from Lincoln about the use of religion in public debates? How might this translate to current debates about sustainability?

9. How can you use Lincoln's example in framing your own perspective on sustainability? What strategies would you use if you were making a public speech on the subject?

10. What other historical figures could serve as examples for addressing major contemporary issues or problems? How could these figures help us deal with sustainability issues?

Earthcare: Women and the Environment

Carolyn Merchant

Carolyn Merchant is an environmental historian interested in the relationships between humanity and nature, and much of her research focuses on gender and the environment. She is a professor of environmental history, philosophy, and ethics at the University of California, Berkeley. Merchant is a past president of the American Society for Environmental History and has served on the executive and advisory boards for numerous environmental and scientific organizations.

This excerpt from Merchant's book *Earthcare: Women and the Environment* (1995) introduces the concept of ecofeminism and argues for a "partnership ethic," in which humans (men and women) are equal partners with nonhuman nature rather than dominant over it. As you read this excerpt, think about the ways in which our culture constructs nature as feminine. How does this influence our relationship to it?

Ecofeminism emerged in the 1970s with an increasing consciousness of the connections between women and nature. The term, "écoféminisme," was coined in 1974 by French writer Françoise d'Eaubonne who called upon women to lead an ecological revolution to save the planet.[1] Such an ecological revolution would entail new gender relations between women and men and between humans and nature.

Developed by Ynestra King at the Institute for Social Ecology in Vermont about 1976, the concept became a movement in 1980 with a major conference on "Women and Life on Earth" held in Amherst, Massachusetts, and the ensuing Women's Pentagon Action to protest anti-life nuclear war and weapons development.[2] During the 1980s cultural feminists in the United States injected new life into ecofeminism by arguing that both women and nature could be liberated together.

Liberal, cultural, social, and socialist feminism have all been concerned with improving the human/nature relationship, and each has contributed to an ecofeminist perspective in different ways (Table 1).[3] Liberal feminism is consistent with the objectives of reform environmentalism to alter human relations with nature from within existing structures of governance through the passage of new laws and regulations. Cultural ecofeminism analyzes environmental problems from within its critique of patriarchy and offers alternatives that could liberate both women and nature.

Social and socialist ecofeminism, on the other hand, ground their analyses in capitalist patriarchy. They ask how patriarchal relations of reproduction reveal the domination of women by men, and how capitalist relations of production reveal the domination of nature by men. They seek the total restructuring of the market economy's use of both women and nature as resources. Although cultural ecofeminism has delved more deeply into the woman-nature connection, social and socialist ecofeminism have the potential for a more thorough critique of domination and for a liberating social justice.

Ecofeminist actions address the contradiction between production 5 and reproduction. Women attempt to reverse the assaults of production on both biological and social reproduction by making problems visible and proposing solutions. When radioactivity from nuclear powerplant accidents, toxic chemicals, and hazardous wastes threaten the biological reproduction of the human species, women experience this contradiction as assaults on their own bodies and on those of their children and act to halt them. Household products, industrial pollutants, plastics, and packaging wastes invade the homes of First World women threatening the reproduction of daily life, while direct access to food, fuel, and clean water for many Third World women is imperiled by cash cropping on traditional homelands and by pesticides used in agribusiness. First World women combat these assaults by altering consumption habits, recycling wastes, and protesting production and disposal methods, while Third World women act to protect traditional ways of life and reverse ecological damage from multinational corporations and the extractive industries. Women challenge the ways in which mainstream society reproduces itself through socialization and politics by envisioning and enacting alternative gender roles, employment options, and political practices.

"Humans must give nonhuman nature space, time, and care, allowing it to reproduce, evolve, and respond to human actions."

Many ecofeminists advocate some form of an environmental ethic that deals with the twin oppressions of the domination of women and nature through an ethic of care and nurture that arises out of women's culturally constructed experiences. As philosopher Karen Warren conceptualizes it:

An ecofeminist ethic is both a critique of male domination of both women and nature and an attempt to frame an ethic free of male-gender bias about women and nature. It not only recognizes the multiple voices of

Table 1
Feminism and the Environment

	Nature	Human nature	Feminist critique of environmentalism	Image of a feminist environmentalism
Liberal feminism	Atoms Mind/body dualism Domination of nature	Rational agents Individualism Maximization of self-interest	"Man and his environment" leaves out women	Women in natural resources and environmental sciences
Marxist feminism	Transformation of nature by science and technology for human use Domination of nature as a means to human freedom Nature is material basis of life: food, clothing, shelter, energy	Creation of human nature through mode of production, praxis Historically specific — not fixed Species nature of human	Critique of capitalist control of resources and accumulation of goods and profits	Socialist society will use resources for good of all men and women Resources will be controlled by workers Environmental pollution could be minimal since no surpluses would be produced Environmental research by men and women
Cultural feminism	Nature is spiritual and personal Conventional science and technology problematic because of their emphasis on domination	Biology is basic Humans are sexually reproducing bodies Sexed by biology/ gendered by society	Unaware of interconnectedness of male domination of nature and women Male environmentalism retains hierarchy	Woman/Nature both valorized and celebrated Reproductive freedom

Socialist feminism			
Nature is material basis of life: food, clothing, shelter, energy Nature is socially and historically constructed Transformations of nature by production and reproduction	Human nature created through biology and praxis (sex, race, class, age) Historically specific and socially constructed	Insufficient attention to environmental threats to woman's reproduction (chemicals, nuclear war) Leaves out nature as active and responsive Leaves out women's role in reproduction and reproduction as a category Systems approach is mechanistic and not dialectical	Against pornographic depictions of both women and nature Cultural ecofeminism Both nature and human production are active Centrality of biological and social reproduction Dialectic between production and reproduction Multileveled structural analysis Dialectical (not mechanical) systems Socialist ecofeminism

women, located differently by race, class, age, [and] ethnic considerations, it centralizes those voices. Ecofeminism builds on the multiple perspectives of those whose perspectives are typically omitted or undervalued in dominant discourses, for example Chipko women, in developing a global perspective on the role of male domination in the exploitation of women and nature. An ecofeminist perspective is thereby . . . structurally pluralistic, inclusivist, and contextualist, emphasizing through concrete example the crucial role context plays in understanding sexist and naturist practice.[4]

An ecofeminist ethic, she argues, would constrain traditional ethics based on rights, rules, and utilities, with considerations based on care, love, and trust. Yet an ethic of care, as elaborated by some feminists, falls prey to an essentialist critique that women's nature is to nurture.

My own approach is a partnership ethic that treats humans (including male partners and female partners) as equals in personal, household, and political relations and humans as equal partners with (rather than controlled-by or dominant-over) nonhuman nature. Just as human partners, regardless of sex, race, or class, must give each other space, time, and care, allowing each other to grow and develop individually within supportive nondominating relationships, so humans must give nonhuman nature space, time, and care, allowing it to reproduce, evolve, and respond to human actions. In practice, this would mean not cutting forests and damming rivers that make people and wildlife in flood plains more vulnerable to "natural disasters"; curtailing development in areas subject to volcanos, earthquakes, hurricanes, and tornados to allow room for unpredictable, chaotic, natural surprises; and exercising ethical restraint in introducing new technologies such as pesticides, genetically engineered organisms, and biological weapons into ecosystems. Constructing nature as a partner allows for the possibility of a personal or intimate (but not necessarily spiritual) relationship with nature and for feelings of compassion for nonhumans as well as for people who are sexually, racially, or culturally different. It avoids gendering nature as a nurturing mother or a goddess and avoids the ecocentric dilemma that humans are only one of many equal parts of an ecological web and therefore morally equal to a bacterium or a mosquito.

Notes
1. Françoise d'Eaubonne, "Feminism or Death," in Elaine Marks and Isabelle de Courtivron, ed., *New French Feminisms: An Anthology* (Amherst: University of Massachusetts Press, 1980), 64–67, but see especially 25.

2. Ynestra King, "Toward an Ecological Feminism and a Feminist Ecology," in Joan Rothschild, ed., *Machina Ex Dea* (New York: Pergamon Press, 1983), 118–29.

3. Alison Jaggar, *Feminist Politics and Human Nature* (Totowa, N.J.: Rowman and Allanheld, 1983); Karen Warren, "Feminism and Ecology: Making Connections," *Environmental Ethics* 9, no. 1 (1987): 3–10.

4. Karen Warren, "Toward an Ecofeminist Ethic," *Studies in the Humanities* (December 1988): 140–56, quotation on 151.

Understanding the Text

1. What is ecofeminism? How does it differ from other approaches to environmental and ecological thinking?

2. What is the history of ecofeminism? Describe some of the different facets and approaches to feminism that have emerged over the past forty years.

3. In what ways is our culture "patriarchal" when it comes to nature? Why is this attitude a problem?

Reflection and Response

4. Do you think of nature as masculine or feminine? How does this influence your beliefs and actions regarding nature and the environment?

5. In what ways does ecofeminism align with the concept of sustainability?

6. Describe Merchant's "partnership ethic." Do you agree with her perspective? Why or why not?

Making Connections

7. Do some research on the concept of ecofeminism. Does Merchant describe it accurately here? What do you find most interesting and useful in your research?

8. Compare the previous selection, David Orr's "Framing Sustainability," and Merchant's "Earthcare." In what ways do they both equate human equality with sustainability? In your opinion, is sustainability a matter of equality, ethics, and morality?

9. Do you consider yourself to be an ecofeminist? What principles of ecofeminism do you identify with, and which do you oppose? Is it necessary to be a female to be an ecofeminist?

Why Do Conservatives Like to Waste Energy?

Tim McDonnell

Tim McDonnell is the associate producer of *Climate Desk*, a journalistic collaboration designed to explore the human, environmental, and economic impact of global climate change. McDonnell, who lives in New York City, has been a regular writer for *Mother Jones* and *Sierra* magazines. His articles address a range of environmental and political issues, including climate change, fracking, and wildfires.

This 2013 article explores the effects of "green" advertising on politically conservative consumers. As you read the article, think about what this research tells us about environmental messaging. In what ways does your political viewpoint determine the ways you read and react to advertisements?

Back in 2011, Rep. Michele Bachmann (R-Minn.) declared war on energy-efficient light bulbs, calling "sustainability" the gateway into a dystopic, Big Brother–patrolled liberal hellscape. When the lights went off during Beyoncé's halftime set at the last Superbowl [2013], conservative commentators from the Drudge Report to Michelle Malkin pointed blame (erroneously) at new power-saving measures at New Orleans' Superdome. And one recent study found that giving Republican households feedback on their power use actually encourages them to use *more* energy.

Why do conservatives, who should have a natural inclination toward conservation, have a beef with energy efficiency? It could be tied to the political polarization of the climate change debate.

A study out today in the journal *Proceedings of the National Academy of Sciences* examined attitudes about energy efficiency in liberals and conservatives, and found that promoting energy-efficient products and services on the basis of their environmental benefits actually turned conservatives off from picking them. The researchers first quizzed participants on how much they value various benefits of energy efficiency, including reducing carbon emissions, reducing foreign oil dependence, and reducing how much consumers pay for energy; cutting emissions appealed to conservatives the least.

The study then presented participants with a real-world choice: With a fixed amount of money in their wallet, respondents had to "buy" either an old-school light bulb or an efficient compact fluorescent bulb (CFL), the same kind Bachmann railed against. Both bulbs were labeled with basic hard data on their energy use, but without a translation of that into climate pros and cons. When the bulbs cost the same, and even when the CFL cost more, conservatives and liberals were equally likely to buy the efficient bulb. But slap a message on the CFL's packaging that says "Protect the Environment," and "we saw a significant drop-off in more politically moderates and conservatives choosing that option," said study author Dena Gromet, a researcher at the University of Pennsylvania's Wharton School of Business.

The chart below, from the report, shows how much liberals and 5
conservatives value each argument for efficiency: While liberals (gray) valued all three equally, conservatives (white), were significantly less moved by and most at odds with liberals over the carbon-saving argument.

Gromet said she never expected the green message to motivate conservatives, but was surprised to find that it could in fact repel them from making a purchase even while they found other aspects, like saving cash on their power bills, attractive. The reason, she thinks, is that given the

"Why do conservatives, who should have a natural inclination toward conservation, have a beef with energy efficiency?"

political polarization of the climate change debate, environmental activism is so frowned upon by those [on] the right that they'll do anything to keep themselves distanced from it.

"When we're given an option where the choice is made to represent a value that we don't identify with or that our ideological group

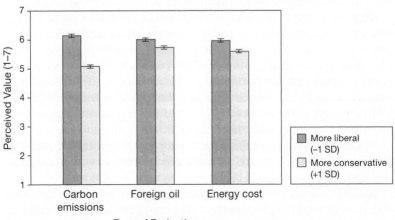

doesn't value," she said, "this can turn the purchase into something undesirable. By making [the environment] part of the choice, even though they might see the economic benefit, they no longer want to put their money toward that option."

This graph, lifted from the report (on the x-axis, −1 is liberal and 1 is conservative), shows the damage the wrong messaging can do: With no messaging, roughly 60 percent of all participants picked the CFL; a pro-environment message boosted support in liberals but cut it sharply in conservatives:

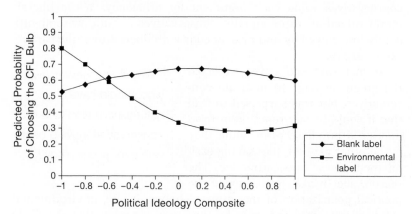

That gap could represent real lost opportunities in the private sector: the EPA's Energy Star label, for example, perhaps the most prominent label for energy-efficient products, puts greenhouse gas savings front and center in its packaging, and proudly boasts that products with the label helps Americans "protect our climate."

This isn't just a problem for businesses trying to push energy-efficient products, but also for environmentalists and policymakers pushing to write efficiency or other climate-friendly policies into law, said Jessica Goodheart, director of RePower LA, which advocates for energy-saving practices in the Los Angeles power utility. Goodheart said while tackling climate change is [the] driving force behind her lobbying, she more often finds herself talking about jobs and the economy, especially when addressing small business owners.

"It's always important to speak to people where they are, and with energy efficiency there are so many positive messages you can use," she said.

And there's no shortage of opportunities to roll those messages out: Last week, Energy Department researchers found that rules requiring utilities to use renewable energy were under attack in over half the states they exist in; such laws might have better luck fending off Bachmann-esque fusillades if they re-focus their rhetoric around their cost-savings, energy independence, or other benefits, Gromet's research suggests, especially in conservative states.

That doesn't necessarily mean green advocates need to somehow cover up the environmental benefits of a policy or product: A study from Stanford psychologists released last December found that re-framing environmental messaging in terms of preserving the "purity" of the natural world resonated morally with conservatives.

"There's not going to be a one-size-fits-all message that will appeal equally," Gromet said. "It's important to know the market you're appealing to; there are some messages you may want to avoid."

Understanding the Text

1. According to this article, how do conservatives react to many environmental messages?
2. What happened in the research study involving lightbulb packaging?
3. Which arguments are effective in persuading liberals concerning lightbulb purchases? Which are effective in persuading conservatives?

Reflection and Response

4. How do liberals and conservatives differ in the messages that motivate them to make environmental purchases?
5. Reread the title of this article. Do you think it makes an accurate statement?

Making Connections

6. Look at some advertisements for CFL lightbulbs. What messages do they use? Based on what you've read in this article, are those advertisements more likely to appeal to liberal or conservative consumers?
7. Compare this article to the essays by Miller and Ross later in this chapter. How do these articles portray the conservative perspective on sustainability? Compare and contrast them.

Yes, It Looks Bad, But . . .

Bjørn Lomborg

Bjørn Lomborg is a Danish author, academic, and public speaker. He is the director of the Copenhagen Consensus Center and an adjunct professor at Copenhagen Business School. Lomborg received international recognition for his controversial 2001 book *The Skeptical Environmentalist*, which questioned much of the data surrounding overpopulation, global warming, and other environmental issues. Lomborg was named one of *Time* magazine's 100 most influential people of 2004, and *The Guardian* listed him in 2006 as one of the "fifty people who could save the planet" in 2006.

This article, first published in *The Guardian* in 2001, argues that many of the reports concerning global environmental crises have been overexaggerated and that, in some ways, the world is getting better. As you read the article, think about how Lomborg's perspective differs from some of the others in this book.

We are all familiar with the litany° of our ever-deteriorating environment. It is the doomsday message endlessly repeated by the media, as when *Time* magazine tells us that "everyone knows the planet is in bad shape," and when the *New Scientist* calls its environmental overview "self-destruct."

We are defiling our Earth, we are told. Our resources are running out. The population is ever-growing, leaving less and less to eat. Our air and water is more and more polluted. The planet's species are becoming extinct in vast numbers — we kill off more than 40,000 each year. Forests are disappearing, fish stocks are collapsing, the coral reefs are dying. The fertile topsoil is vanishing. We are paving over nature, destroying the wilderness, decimating the biosphere, and will end up killing ourselves in the process. The world's ecosystem is breaking down. We are fast approaching the absolute limit of viability.

We have heard the litany so often that yet another repetition is, well, almost reassuring. There is, however, one problem: it does not seem to be backed up by the available evidence. We are not running out of energy or natural resources. There is ever more food, and fewer people are starving. In 1900, we lived for an average of 30 years; today we live for 67. According to the UN, we have reduced poverty more in the last 50 years than we did in the preceding 500, and it has been reduced in practically every country.

litany: a prolonged or tedious account.

Global warming is probably taking place, though future projections are overly pessimistic and the traditional cure of radical fossil-fuel cutbacks is far more damaging than the original affliction. Moreover, its total impact will not pose a devastating problem to our future. Nor will we lose 25–50% of all species in our lifetime — in fact, we are losing probably 0.7%. Acid rain does not kill the forests, and the air and water around us are becoming less and less polluted.

In fact, in terms of practically every measurable indicator, mankind's lot has improved. This does not, however, mean that everything is good enough. We can still do even better. 5

Take, for example, starvation and the population explosion. In 1968, one of the leading environmentalists, Dr. Paul R. Ehrlich, predicted in his bestselling book, *The Population Bomb*, that "the battle to feed humanity is over. In the course of the 1970s, the world will experience starvation of tragic proportions — hundreds of millions of people will starve to death."

This did not happen. Instead, according to the UN, agricultural production in the developing world has increased by 52% per person. The daily food intake in developing countries has increased from 1,932 calories in 1961 — barely enough for survival — to 2,650 calories in 1998, and is expected to rise to 3,020 by 2030. Likewise, the proportion of people going hungry in these countries has dropped from 45% in 1949 to 18% today, and is expected to fall even further, to 12% in 2010 and 6% in 2030. Food, in other words, is becoming not scarcer but ever more abundant. This is reflected in its price. Since 1800, food prices have decreased by more than 90%, and in 2000, according to the World Bank, prices were lower than ever before.

Ehrlich's prediction echoed that made 170 years earlier by Thomas Malthus. Malthus claimed that, unchecked, human population would expand exponentially, while food production could increase only linearly by bringing new land into cultivation. He was wrong. Population growth has turned out to have an internal check: as people grow richer and healthier, they have smaller families. Indeed, the growth rate of the human population reached its peak of more than 2% a year in the early 1960s. The rate of increase has been declining ever since. It is now 1.26%, and is expected to fall to 0.46% by 2050. The UN estimates that most of the world's population growth will be over by 2100, with the population stabilizing at just below 11bn [billion].

Malthus also failed to take account of developments in agricultural technology. These have squeezed ever more food out of each hectare of land. It is this application of human ingenuity that has boosted food production. It has also, incidentally, reduced the need to take new land into cultivation, thus reducing the pressure on biodiversity.

The issues on food, population and air pollution covered here all contradict the litany. Yet opinion polls suggest that many people — in the rich world, at least — nurture the belief that environmental standards are declining. Four factors cause this disjunction between perception and reality. 10

The first is the lopsidedness built into scientific research. Scientific funding goes mainly to areas with many problems. That may be wise policy, but it will also create an impression that many more potential problems exist than is the case.

A second source of misperception is the self-interest of environmental groups. Though these groups are run overwhelmingly by selfless folk, they nevertheless share many of the characteristics of other lobby groups. They need to be noticed by the mass media. They also need to keep the money that sustains them rolling in. The temptation to exaggerate is surely there, and sometimes, indulged in.

In 1997, for example, the World Wide Fund for Nature issued a press release entitled Two-thirds of the World's Forests Lost Forever. The truth turned out to be nearer 20%. This would matter less if people applied the same degree of skepticism to environmental lobbying as they do to other lobby groups. But while a trade organization arguing for, say, weaker pollution controls is instantly seen as self-interested, a green organization opposing such a weakening is seen as altruistic — even if a dispassionate view of the controls might suggest they are doing more harm than good.

A third source of confusion is the attitude of the media. People are clearly more curious about bad news than good, and newspapers and broadcasters give the public what it wants. That can lead to significant distortions of perception: an example was America's encounter with El Niño in 1997 and 1998. This climatic phenomenon was accused of wrecking tourism, causing allergies, melting ski slopes and causing 22 deaths by dumping snow in Ohio. Disney even blamed El Niño for a fall in share prices.

A more balanced view comes from a recent article in the Bulletin of the American Meteorological Society. It estimated the damage caused by the 1997–98 Niño at $4bn, but the benefits amounted to some $19bn. These came from higher winter temperatures (which saved an estimated 850 lives, reduced heating costs and diminished spring floods caused by meltwaters), and from the well-documented connection between past Niños and fewer Atlantic hurricanes. In 1998, America experienced no big Atlantic hurricanes and thus 15 avoided huge losses. These benefits were not reported as widely as the losses.

The fourth factor is poor individual perception. People worry that the endless rise in the amount of stuff everyone throws away will cause the world to run out of places to dispose of waste. Yet even if UK waste production increases at the same rate as that in the US (surely an overestimate, since the British population does not increase as fast), the total landfill area needed for 21st-century UK waste would be a meager 100ft tall and eight miles square — an area equivalent to 28% of the Isle of Man.

Knowing the real state of the world is important because fear of largely imaginary environmental problems can divert political energy from dealing with real ones. The Harvard University center for risk analysis has carried out the world's largest survey of the costs of life-saving public initiatives. Only initiatives whose primary stated political goal is to save human lives are included. Thus, the many environmental interventions which have little or no intention to save human lives, such as raising oxygen levels in rivers, improving wetlands and setting up natural reservations, are not considered here. We only compare those environmental interventions whose primary goal is to save human lives (as in toxin control) with life-saving interventions from other areas.

There are tremendous differences in the price to be paid for extra life-years by means of typical interventions: the health service is quite low-priced, at $19,000 per median price to save a life for one year, but the environment field stands out with a staggeringly high cost of $4.2m.

> "When we fear for our environment, we seem easily to fall victim to short-term, feel-good solutions that spend money on relatively trifling issues."

This method of accounting shows the overall effectiveness of the American public effort to save human life. Overall, information exists about the actual cost of 185 programs that account for an annual expenditure of $21.4bn, which saves around 592,000 life-years. The Harvard study shows that, had the spending been used in the most cost-efficient way, 1,230,000 life-years could have been saved for the same money. Without further costs, it would have been possible to save around 600,000 more life-years or, at 10 years per life, 60,000 more human beings.

When we fear for our environment, we seem easily to fall victim to short-term, feel-good solutions that spend money on relatively trifling issues and thus hold back resources from far more important ones.

When we realize that we can forget about imminent breakdown, we can see that the world is basically heading in the right direction and that we can help to steer this development process by focusing on and insisting on reasonable prioritization. When the Harvard study shows that we forgo saving 60,000 lives every year, this shows us the cost we pay for worrying about the wrong problems — too much for the environment and too little in other areas.

This does not mean that rational environmental management and environmental investment is not often a good idea — only that we should compare the costs and benefits of such investments to similar investments in all the other important areas of human endeavor. And to ensure that sensible, political prioritization, we need to abandon our ingrained belief in a mythical litany and start focusing on the facts — that the world is indeed getting better, though there is still much to do.

Understanding the Text

1. What is Lomborg's opinion about the earth's current living condition?
2. Lomborg writes that "in terms of practically every measurable indicator, mankind's lot has improved" (par. 5). What evidence does he provide to support this?
3. What are the four factors that cause disjunction between perception and reality?

Reflection and Response

4. In paragraph 2, Lomborg lists many reasons why people would think the earth's living condition is deteriorating. Why do you think he does this? Do you think he is serious when listing these problems? Why or why not?
5. What does Lomborg suggest about population? Do some research. Were the predictions by Malthus and Ehrlich flawed?

Making Connections

6. Lomborg states that "since 1800, food prices have decreased by more than 90 percent, and in 2000, according to the World Bank, prices were lower than ever before" (par. 7). Based on your personal experience, do food prices seem to be decreasing? Do some research to determine the validity of Lomborg's statement and your own experience.
7. In what ways does Lomborg's perspective differ from those of many of the other authors in this book? Compare and contrast what Lomborg says with an opposing perspective (such as one by Meadows, Randers, and Meadows; the World Commission; or Gore).
8. Choose one statistic that Lomborg provides in this essay. Research the current statistics for this issue, and determine whether Lomborg's assumptions and perspective were accurate.

Sustainability: The New Holy Grail

Larry Miller

Larry Miller is a social media adviser, Web designer, and chief blogger at Political Christian, a Web site devoted to Christianity and politics in the United States. Miller lives in Clearwater, Florida, and identifies himself as a member of the Tea Party. In this blog entry from 2010, Miller discusses the relationship between sustainability and American innovation. As you read the entry, think about how Miller defines sustainability and how this is similar to and different from other perspectives in this chapter and in the book overall.

It's difficult to watch a newscast on any channel these days where the word "sustainability" is not batted about as the ruling class attempts to tell us what we are, and are not capable of doing. We are told that our lifestyles are not sustainable. We are told that our leadership in the world is not sustainable. We are told that our consumption of resources is not sustainable. We are told these things by members of the party that has been pretty much in charge for the past fifty plus years. One has to wonder how they let us get into this fix in the first place.

The whole argument about whether our path through the world is sustainable or not revolves around the question of whether the American genius that made this country the superpower in the world is capable of maintaining our position. To say that our lifestyle and position in the world is not sustainable is to say that Americans have lost their ability to create new products, concepts and energy sources. To say America is not sustainable, the speaker shows his lack of faith in the American people, the free market system that has carried us to the pinnacle of the global economy and the "divine providence" that guided our nation into existence is unreliable.

These naysayers, even when they recognize the historical significance of these factors, are telling us our time has run out and the individualism that has built our nation and made it prosper must give way to the collective approach driven by leaders with little real world experience who have sheltered themselves behind the ivy covered walls of academia, theorizing about all sorts of things, we, the little people, should be doing.

The American genius that put men on the moon, established the arsenal of democracy and created the prosperity that was the envy of the world has solved most every legitimate problem our nation faced.

Glenn Beck's recommended reading of *The Five Thousand Year Leap* chronicles not only the advances in science, technology, agriculture and society, but the principles that made them possible. These principles revolve around individualism, morality, freedom and recognition of the Creator . . . all of which are denied by the discouraging words questioning our sustainability.

"Whether our path through the world is sustainable or not revolves around the question of whether the American genius that made this country the superpower in the world is capable of maintaining our position."

We are at a fork in the road. We can listen to those who believe our best days are behind us and turn our children's future over to an incapable and uncaring bureaucracy, or we can tell them we will not roll over and play dead while they destroy our economy and freedom. But simply telling them "No!" will not get the job done. Each of us may be called to combat these anti-American, anti-freedom and anti-Christian forces in a different way.

It is essential that we respond to this call and not shrink back. Shrinking back will not help our families, nor will it please our Creator. When we hear from those who tell us they are smarter than we are and that we should do things that are wrong or foolish, we need to give them all the respect they deserve as purveyors of false wisdom. They have no right to run our lives or our country. We need to remember the words of Justice John Marshall, "A legislative act contrary to the Constitution is not law." The same would also apply to regulations by unelected bodies as well.

The sustainability of the United States of America is not determined by the political class. It is determined by the American people. We can choose to believe the ruling class or we can wake up to the fact that the real ruling class is "We the people"! The political class and the formerly mainstream media have been doing their best to make us forget this power that we still have. They are wrong and we have no obligation to believe them.

In some ways, there are some things taking place that really are unsustainable — and that is the debt accumulation of the people inside the beltway. They are not spending their money. They are spending all the money they can beg, steal or borrow from the American taxpayers and the Chinese. The problem is the interest, which if left unchecked, will overshadow our government's annual revenue, so nothing will be left for the legitimate government operations. This is one area where we need to take the concept of sustainability very seriously!

Understanding the Text

1. According to Miller, how are sustainability and innovation tied together?
2. Why does Miller seem to suggest that "American ingenuity" will solve all of our problems? Do you agree with his perspective? Why or why not?
3. What is the "fork in the road" to which Miller refers (par. 5)?

Reflection and Response

4. Is Miller taking a primarily negative or positive approach in this blog entry? In what ways?
5. How is sustainability a "Holy Grail," as Miller suggests through the title?
6. How does Miller tie together Christianity, politics, and sustainability?

Making Connections

7. Miller uses moon landings and the American military as examples of innovation. Are Miller's examples effective? Why or why not? In what ways could innovation address environmental problems?
8. Miller references media personality Glenn Beck, who has been critical of many aspects of the environmental movement and of sustainability. Watch a YouTube video of Beck speaking on some environmental topic. Do you agree or disagree with his perspective? How does Beck attempt to persuade his viewers?

Now Playing: The Sustainability Con

Ron Ross

Ron Ross, Ph.D., is a financial consultant and former professor of economics at Humboldt State University. Ross is a frequent writer and blogger for *The American Spectator*, a conservative U.S. monthly magazine covering news and politics.

This article from 2012 suggests that sustainability is a means for political liberals to expand their control over personal freedoms. Like Lomborg, in his essay earlier in this chapter, Ross questions the impact of environmental degradation, speculating that innovation and new technologies will solve many resource problems. As you read Ross's piece, consider the ways in which Ross and others define the term "resource" and the role that these definitions might play in our vision of the future.

A lthough the issue of "sustainability" has been around a while, recently it has grown in popularity and influence. The way it's happening follows an all too familiar pattern.

There are several common ingredients in how the left° enlarges its control over our lives. The first is the selection of some aspect of reality — global warming, carbon footprints, population growth, inequality, diversity, for example. The second element involves designating the selected aspect of reality as a crisis. The third step is to explain that the only way to avoid Armageddon is by reducing everyone's freedom and by giving more centralized power and control to those who understand the magnitude of the crisis. The rest of us are told that our freedoms are a luxury we simply can no longer afford.

Another common element of the process is defining the crisis as ambiguously as possible. Ordinarily, a desirable characteristic of a definition is that it draws a bright line between what is included and what isn't. Clarity, however, is contrary to the objectives of the crusaders — in regard to defining the problem, the slipperier the better. For example, climate change (or climate disruption) beats global warming. Global warming is too quantifiable in comparison to climate change. No one is quite sure what "climate change" is or isn't or how it can be measured. Sustainability is even more ambiguous than climate change and thus has more sustainability as a ruse.

left: (left-wing), the part of a political or social organization advocating a liberal or radical position.

Ideally the designated crisis is as expansive and open-ended as possible. A vague, loosely defined crisis provides politicians and bureaucrats with what amounts to a blank check or a no-limit credit card, a credit card where someone else gets sent the bill. A problem having no clear definition is a problem without borders.

At Arizona State University you can get a B.S., M.S., or Ph.D. in 5 sustainability. ASU has an entire "School of Sustainability." The school's website offers several answers to the question, "What is sustainability?" Here are four of the answers they offer:

Sustainability is a concept with as much transformative potential as justice, liberty, and equality.
— **MICHAEL CROW,** *president, Arizona State University*

Sustainability is larger than one person, one company, or one country. Its scope, scale and importance demand unprecedented and swift solutions to environmental protection and other complex problems.
— **JULIE ANN WRIGLEY,** president, *Julie Ann Wrigley Foundation*

Sustainability is living in harmony with our social and natural environment, based on a sense of justice and equity.
— **SANDER VAN DER LEEUW,** *dean, School of Sustainability*

Sustainability is a process that engages every discipline to provide dynamic solutions to complex problems.
— **BRIAN MCCOLLOW,** *student, School of Sustainability*

Are you clear now on what sustainability means and why a "School of Sustainability" is of paramount importance?

Academic papers on the topic of sustainability often include such concepts as "intergenerational equity" and "inter-temporal welfare." The left somehow manages to insert its obsession with inequality into every imaginable issue. Inequality is not only a problem at a point in time, but also between time periods.

The Environmental Protection Agency recently spent $700,000 on a study entitled *Sustainability and the U.S. EPA.* The abstract of the report states:

Recognizing the importance of sustainability in its work, the U.S. EPA has been working to create programs and applications in a variety of areas to better incorporate sustainability into decision-making at the agency. . . . This framework provides recommendations for a sustainability approach

*that both incorporates and goes beyond an approach based on assessing
and managing the risks posed by pollutants that have largely shaped environmental policy since the 1980s. . . . EPA should also articulate its vision
for sustainability and develop a set of sustainability principles that would
underlie all agency policies and programs.*

Obviously the EPA sees sustainability as a golden opportunity in its
quest for more power, control, and funding. The EPA's new lease on
life is going to diminish everyone else's lives.

What is sustainability, really? It is actually an old concept that has
once again been warmed over for the umpteenth time. Sustainability
is simply the latest incarnation of Malthusianism. Writing in 1798,
Thomas Malthus warned that England's population growth was going
to outstrip its available endowment of resources such as agricultural
land and coal. The specter that Malthus described was summarized
as population increases geometrically, food increases arithmetically.
Based on that logic, starvation and suffering were seen as inevitable.
Malthus, in other words, was saying that England's economic growth
was not sustainable. It was that profoundly pessimistic theory that
resulted in economics being described as "the dismal science." England, of course, has gone on to experience over 200 years of historically unprecedented economic growth.

As John Maynard Keynes° later observed, "Practical men, who believe themselves to be quite exempt from any intellectual influences,
are usually the slaves of some defunct economist." Although Malthus
certainly ought to be defunct, his diagnosis of the world continues to
have broad appeal.

Obviously, Malthus's predictions did not come to pass. Why not?   10
Malthus's error, in a nutshell, was failing to appreciate the impact of
an increasing stock of knowledge and the resulting technological
revolution. The sustainability crusade is wrong for essentially the
same reasons Malthus was wrong.

● ● ●

A close relative of sustainable is "renewable." An obsession with re-
newability has resulted in many of our silliest and costliest public
policies — subsidies and mandates for ethanol, windmills, and solar
panels, for example. A reflex response has been ingrained in public
policy that renewable is always and everywhere better than non-

John Maynard Keynes: (1883–1946), English economist and writer.

renewable. Buzzwords like *renewable* and *sustainable* act essentially like thought-stoppers.

When in the history of civilization have we actually exhausted or totally depleted any significant resource? The answer is never. What makes us believe we will in the future? Somehow we buy into the notion that something that has never happened in history is going to doom us in the near future. It is another reflection of the inflated self-importance and myopia of the current generation.

The Stone Age did not end because of a stone shortage. It ended because an expanding supply of knowledge created superior alternatives to stones. That dynamic represents a central theme in the history of civilization. Iron ore was around before and during the Stone Age, but the information needed to make it useful did not exist at the time. Petroleum was not even a resource until we knew how to access it and refine it. We also invented new ways to use it, especially for transportation purposes. Sand was not a resource until we learned how to turn it into glass and concrete. As the late Julian Simon observed, "Resources in their raw form are useful and valuable only when found, understood, gathered together and harnessed for human needs. The basic ingredient in the process, along with the raw elements, is human knowledge."

> "Sustainability is even more ambiguous than climate change and thus has more sustainability as a ruse."

In the 19th century lanterns were the main source of illumination and whale oil was the main fuel for lanterns. If that had continued we might have driven some whale species to extinction. Why didn't that happen? (It certainly wasn't because Greenpeace was harassing whaling vessels.) We invented ways to convert coal to kerosene and later, petroleum to kerosene. Kerosene was about a tenth as costly as whale oil and smelled better. Then lanterns as a light source were made obsolete by Edison's invention of the incandescent light bulb.

Copper is an important resource with many uses. It could be categorized as a finite, non-renewable, exhaustible resource. How big a problem is that? To answer that question, consider the numerous ways we have developed superior alternatives for many of the traditional uses of copper. For example, copper wires were once the only alternative for long-distance communication — namely, telephones and telegraph. Now most communication is sent, not through wires, but through the air (cell phone towers and satellites, for example). A single satellite does the job of hundreds of tons of copper. What information is still sent through wires is likely to be done not with copper but rather with fiber-optics (glass). Glass is made with sand or, more specifically, silica. Is sand a non-renewable resource? What's the likelihood we will ever use it all up?

Whether a particular resource is or is not renewable or sustainable is often not what matters. The most important consideration to bear in mind is this: if there are good or even superior substitutes for a resource, its non-renewability is essentially irrelevant and inconsequential.

Another reason we shouldn't worry so much is that all resources are not equally valuable or important. Information is the resource that is far and away the most important in terms of generating human welfare. The foremost reason our current generation is so much better off than previous generations is our access to a greater stock of information and knowledge. We truly are living in the Information Age. In a sense all previous ages have been defined by the amount of information available at the time.

Information is the polar opposite of a non-sustainable resource. Information has the almost magical property of being able to spontaneously generate and expand exponentially. Information gives us the power to create resources and to increase the effectiveness and efficiency of all other resources. The resource that is the most powerful and valuable in regard to human welfare is also the resource that has the most fortuitous characteristics. How lucky could we get?

Coming generations of humans are as likely to be as creative and inventive as the past ones have been. Again to quote Julian Simon, "The ultimate resource is people — skilled, spirited, and hopeful people who will exert their wills and imaginations for their own benefit, and so, inevitably, for the benefit of us all." A necessary ingredient for exercising our wills and imaginations is, of course, a large degree of freedom.

Rather than stressing about hallucinatory anxieties and imaginary problems that are unlikely to ever become real problems, we ought to be celebrating how blessed we are. And we especially should not be giving up our freedoms on the basis of the disproven theories of "some defunct economist." 20

Understanding the Text

1. According to Ross, what are the three steps required by the government to gain control over our lives?
2. What is Ross's opinion regarding sustainability?
3. How does Ross define the term "resource"? Do you agree with his perspective on what a resource is? Why or why not?
4. How are the terms "sustainability" and "resources" similar or different?

Reflection and Response

5. Ross cites several definitions of sustainability from Arizona State University. What is his purpose in presenting these definitions?

6. The author refers to the "left" as the people responsible for the issues discussed in this piece. Who is he talking about? How does this characterization influence your reading of the essay? Does it affect the author's credibility? Explain.

7. In what ways is information a renewable resource?

Making Connections

8. In paragraph 12, Ross claims that we have never "actually exhausted or totally depleted any significant resource." Research the validity of this statement. What did you find?

9. Find other examples of university programs devoted to sustainability and compare their definitions with those from Arizona State University. How are these definitions similar or different? What does this tell you about the concept of sustainability?

Sustainability: Building a Consensus between Liberals and Conservatives

Alex Zorach

Alex Zorach is a blogger, a Web editor, and the owner of Sustainable Computing, a computer consulting company. He holds a master's degree in mathematics from the University of Delaware and a master's degree in statistics from Yale University.

This article, which originally appeared on Zorach's blog in 2010, bridges the gap between the liberal and conservative viewpoints on sustainability. The basic premise is that conservatism and sustainability share much in common and that liberals and conservatives can work together to solve environmental problems. As you read the piece, think about your own political perspective and how you might build a consensus with those whose political views differ from yours on issues involving sustainability and the environment.

Typically, in America, environmentalism is seen as a "liberal" issue. Public perception, especially among liberals, is that liberals care about the environment more than conservatives, and that the solution to environmental problems lies in historically liberal approaches to politics and problem-solving.

However, this couldn't be farther from the truth. There are many ways in which conservative ideals and approaches can be used to preserve, protect, and restore the earth's ecosystems. The term "Conservative" even has the same root as the word "Conserve." Conservatism, at its essence, is an ideology based on resisting change, and, at times, moving back towards an earlier state of things. Conservatism also emphasizes tradition, family, and community.

In many respects, western civilization, particularly the United States, has become less sustainable in recent years, as our society has changed in ways that has destroyed community, weakened family life, and increased our negative impact on the environment. I want to start by presenting skeptics with two powerful concrete examples of how conservatism and sustainability can go hand-in-hand.

Traditionalists and the Natural Foods Movement

Environmentalists, including many self-identified liberals, in working to conserve resources, and to protect and restore the Earth's ecosystems, are actually embodying the very essence of conservatism. Many supposedly novel concepts like organic agriculture and local foods simply represent a move back towards the way agriculture was practiced by humans for thousands of years. [Take for instance], the Central Market in Lancaster, PA. Such markets, integral in supplying people with fresh, local foods, were once common and widespread. Lancaster's market is one of the few that has persisted through the years, and it persisted in large part because Lancaster county residents are so strongly resistant to change — while other communities idly allowed their markets to be replaced by modern supermarkets, people in Lancaster kept shopping at this market and worked through organizations like the Friends of Central Market to keep it vibrant.

> "There are many ways in which conservative ideals and approaches can be used to preserve, protect, and restore the earth's ecosystems."

If you enter this market, you will find a number of stands run by Amish and Mennonites selling fresh 5 produce, baked goods, and even quilts. It is no surprise that the Amish, a group which has been among the staunchest resistors of change in many respects, are leaders in the organic agriculture and natural foods movement. Millers Natural Foods, an Amish-run store in Bird in Hand, PA, was selling a number of natural products years before most people had ever heard of supermarket chains like Whole Foods. The Amish, living a strongly religious, family-centered, and community-centered lifestyle that is among the most conservative of any in the U.S., are not only leaders in the natural foods movement, but have also staunchly resisted the use of automobiles, one of the largest contributors to resource use, pollution, and community fragmentation in the U.S. The Amish are a bold example of conservatism strongly allied to sustainability.

Hunting and Conservation

Another example of conservation coming from a place that liberals often wouldn't want to admit is conservation of land driven by hunters. Hunters, who span a broad range of political views, have a tendency to be more strongly represented among conservatives, and yet hunters are one of the major driving forces behind the conservation movement in the U.S., including the National Wildlife Refuge System and many state and local refuges. The U.S.'s National Wildlife Refuge System, according to their website, currently contains 150 million acres of land, almost twice the 84.6 million acres managed by the National Park Service.

Many more such lands are preserved through state agencies. [Consider] Middle Creek Wildlife Management Area in northern Lancaster County, Pennsylvania. This area is managed by the Pennsylvania Game Commission, which manages over 1.4 million acres of game land.

Serious hunters develop an intimate understanding of ecological relationships, understanding the importance of large, undisturbed tracts of habitat and sustainable hunting practices, both of which protect game populations. These large, intact natural areas have immense ecological value, both for creating clean air and water, for protecting biodiversity, and as every hunter and fisher knows, creating sustainable reserves of meat and fish that is healthy, without the negative environmental impacts of factory farming.

Drawbacks to Liberalism's Approach to Environmentalism

Not only do conservatives have something major to offer to the environmentalist movement, there are a lot of ways in which liberalism's historical approaches are limited in their ability to protect the environment. In the United States, Liberalism has been closely tied to a regulatory and spending-based approach to problem-solving. This approach involves the creation of laws, usually at the federal level, which are enforced by large, complex bureaucracies, many of which have their counterparts at the state level. An example would be the U.S. EPA (Environmental Protection Agency). The problem with this approach is that it avoids the root of the problem, and it is often costly and complex, increasing the size of government and the need for taxes.

In the U.S., most environmental destruction and degradation happens as a result of economic incentives, which reward people for decisions that destroy the environment for personal profit. The regulatory approach, in the eyes of those critical of it, is like sitting next to a pile of gold with a gun and hoping that you keep anyone from taking any of it. It's just a matter of time before someone either sneaks up unnoticed and steals some, or comes along with a bigger gun. (As often happens in the U.S., metaphorically, when big corporations like BP use their massive wealth to influence the political process to convince regulators like the EPA to turn the other way.) The way out of this mess is to remove the gold — changing the economic incentives, many of which are created, conservatives would point out, by government spending.

Conservatives, especially Libertarian-leaning conservatives that constitute much of the base of the Republican party in the United States, prefer a different approach. Conservatives generally want small government and more local control. They also believe in working through creation of simple, natural economic incentives, rather than regulation, whenever possible. Rather than create new laws and restrictions, enforced by bureaucracies, they would rather start by paring down the bad aspects of government and eliminating expenditures that create the wrong incentives.

An Example of a Conservative Approach of Promoting Sustainability by Reducing Expenditures: Targeting Agricultural Subsidies

A good place to start working towards sustainability from a conservative/small government perspective would be elimination or intelligent reduction of agricultural subsidies in the U.S. Agricultural subsidies in the U.S. currently create incentives for large-scale commercial farms (factory farms) whose farming practices are damaging to the environment and which produce food that is less healthy than fresh food grown by small, local farms. The American Enterprise Institute, a conservative think-tank that liberals would be quick to brand as anti-environmentalism, advocates for a complete removal of such subsidies in their 2007 article "Plowing Farm Subsidies Under." I did some of my own research and also found compelling reasons to support such a change. The following chart shows how heavily U.S. agricultural payments are skewed towards supporting factory farms:

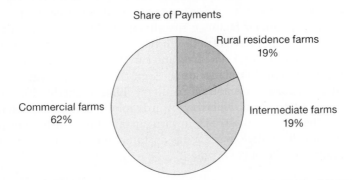

Share of Payments

Rural residence farms
19%

Commercial farms
62%

Intermediate farms
19%

Total government payments received by operator households in 2008 — $10.3 billion

Source: USDA, Economic Research Service.

This chart is from the ERS [Economic Research Service]/USDA Web site's page on Farms Receiving Government Payments, which has more detailed information for those curious. Of the around $10.3 billion in 2008 payments (an amount roughly equal to the EPA's annual budget), 62% of the payments went to commercial farms, with only 19% reaching rural residence farms (and this figure does not take into account abuses such as large corporations setting up sham corporations as subsidiaries, with a resident owner, to qualify as residence farms). In addition, only 30% of all rural residence farms received payments, whereas 70% of commercial farms did. These payments clearly support commercial agriculture more than small farmers.

Our price fixing of various commodities also has devastating human rights and environmental consequences in the third world. An article originally published in the *Philadelphia Inquirer*, "Why U.S. Farm Subsidies are Bad for the World," argued that U.S. agricultural subsidies create poverty in developing countries.

We Could Find More Examples

This issue is just one example: there are many types of government expenditures at the federal, state and even local levels which create bad incentives and have negative impacts on sustainability. Conservatives have an excellent point that it would be prudent, especially when our government is already running a large deficit, to first eliminate expenditures that are having negative environmental impacts, before creating new ones in an attempt to solve environmental problems.

Another example is careless use of highway funding in ways that harm sustainability: Federal highway funding totalled over $40 billion in 2008, and the way these funds are used is closely tied to car and truck use, a major factor in sustainability. Another expenditure which conservatives have often been resistant to touch, but which is a huge portion of federal spending and can have negative impacts on sustainability, is military spending. Even though conservatives are generally supporters of a strong military, liberals might find them more cooperative about working towards intelligent paring down of military spending with an eye toward sustainability, if it were presented as an alternative to achieving sustainability through increased regulation and size of government.

Let's Establish a Consensus between Liberals and Conservatives: We All Care about Sustainability

The constant fighting between liberals and conservatives in America on environmental issues wastes a lot of energy. There is a degree to which liberals' unfair characterization of conservatives as anti-environment has created a form of self-fulfilling prophecy: rather than fight back, conservatives have let liberals own environmentalism, something that in reality should be embraced by all of us.

The bottom line is that each and every American, and indeed, each and every human being in this world, wants clean air and water, and wants a healthy, thriving natural environment that can support us in future generations. We all want safe, affordable food, free of toxins, and produced in a way that is not damaging to the environment or to current or future generations in any way. *We all care about sustainability.* Let us all agree on this.

There are legitimate disagreements between the ideology of liberals and conservatives, and these differences run deep and cannot be glossed over. But let us keep at the forefront of our mind that we are disagreeing on details . . . we agree on where we want to get. We just are having a healthy debate about the best way to get there. Ultimately, the best laws and government are created when we engage in debate and synthesize opposing views to take the best from each side. With this in mind, we can reach better environmental solutions and attain sustainability more quickly and more easily than if either party were able to implement their views unopposed.

What Can You Do?

- Regardless of what your political views are, make a commitment to work toward sustainability in all aspects of your life. 20

- If you identify as liberal, talk to your conservative acquaintances and ask them about their ideas for solutions to environmental problems. Listen, do not argue; you might learn something. Respect differences in viewpoints and ideology, and emphasize to yourself and to others that it is possible for conservatives to disagree with liberal ideology but still be strongly environmentalist.

- If you identify as conservative, call liberals out when they tell you that you do not care about the environment, just because you do not agree with the particular approach or plan that they suggest. Emphasize that you both agree with a common goal and vision of a clean environment, but have very different ideas about how to best realize that vision. When presented with something you disagree with, think about alternative plans and ideas that you can present that fit with your conservative ideology but work toward achieving these goals, so that you have a positive, constructive suggestion to counter each point you disagree with.

• If you are a moderate, independent, or someone who falls outside the normal bounds of the liberal–conservative spectrum, help liberals and conservatives to reach a consensus on caring about sustainability, contribute your own novel ideas to the debate, and help us all hash out the details of how to get where we all want to be.

Understanding the Text

1. How does Zorach define conservatism? How does this definition differ from other definitions of the term? In what ways is conservatism related to sustainability?

2. According to the author, why does the Central Market in Lancaster, Pennsylvania, still exist today? What does that tell us about sustainability and conservatism?

3. In what ways is hunting tied to sustainability? Why is hunting often seen as an anti-environment activity? And hunters as anti-environment? What is your opinion of hunting and its relationship to sustainability?

Reflection and Response

4. In what ways can the Amish be seen as politically active? Has reading this piece altered your perception of the Amish in any way? Explain.

5. What can you do to help bridge the gap between liberals and conservatives on the issue of sustainability?

Making Connections

6. Name something in your area that is controlled by a local government as opposed to the federal government. Explain how this could be beneficial. Explain how it could also be detrimental. Do you agree with the author that more things should be locally controlled? Why or why not?

7. Visit a local food market and learn more about the methods used to grow, gather, or raise the food it provides. In what ways does this contribute to sustainability? Are there any other benefits or drawbacks? Report on your findings to your class.

8. Interview a group of people who hunt or fish to learn their perspective on conservation, sustainability, and other environmental issues. Why do they hold these beliefs?

© Paul Earle Photography/Getty Images

3 How Do Crises and Disasters Create Challenges for Sustainability?

P eople are often drawn to sustainability when they identify a problem, encounter a difficulty, or experience something that makes them change their views about the world. We recognize an unsustainable situation now or in the future, and we look for ways to counteract that predicament. Sometimes this recognition is gradual and subtle — we begin to notice that our communities are not as clean as they used to be, or we are asked to choose "paper or plastic" at the grocery store checkout — and our thinking changes over time. Other times, though, we recognize the need for sustainability when we encounter or perceive a disaster or an emergent critical situation. Drastic changes or disruptions in the world can force us to reconsider our current ways of doing things, and sustainable solutions can help to minimize the impact of catastrophes and crises and to lessen their impact in the future.

This chapter examines several recent crises and disasters and their relationship to sustainability. The reading selections begin with three specific disasters that have affected the United States in the last decade: Hurricane Katrina, Hurricane Sandy, and the BP oil spill in the Gulf of Mexico. Benfield's article addresses sustainable rebuilding efforts in the aftermath of Hurricane Katrina, which made landfall near New Orleans in August 2005. Jervey highlights the need for more resilient, sustainable communities following Hurricane Sandy, which damaged coastal areas in the Northeast in October 2012. Biello's essay focuses on the impact to wildlife following the BP oil spill in April 2010. Other, transnational, disasters are addressed in Chapter 5, most notably the earthquake that devastated Haiti in January 2010 and the tsunami that struck Japan in March 2011. These essays could be read in sequence, though they are separated into chapters based on their relative geographic locations.

The other crises and disasters addressed in this chapter may be less immediate, but they are no less serious or damaging. Essays by Whitty and Diamond examine the crises that emerge from unsustainable human practices, including climate change, species extinction, and degradation of the environment. Mittermeier's article brings the conversation full circle, explaining the ways in which the destruction of biodiverse ecosystems leads to a loss of diversity in human language and culture.

As you read the articles in this chapter, consider the relationship between human activity and recent crises and disasters involving sustainability. Though some of the issues addressed in the chapter are considered "natural" disasters, those disasters are often exacerbated by the choices we make in regard to our world. Think about the ways in which new, different, and more sustainable activities might mitigate or counteract such problems, offering hope for the future.

Sustainable New Orleans: How Katrina Made a City Greener

Kaid Benfield

Kaid Benfield is an author and environmental advocate currently employed as the director of the Sustainable Communities and Growth Program at the Natural Resources Defense Council. He is also the cofounder of Smart Growth America, an environmental advocacy group. In 2010, he was named one of the most influential people in sustainable planning and development by the Partnership for Sustainable Communities.

This article originally appeared in 2011 in *The Atlantic*, a magazine focusing on literature, political science, and foreign affairs. Benfield discusses the importance of maintaining the culture and community of New Orleans while rebuilding after Hurricane Katrina. He also describes the efforts of volunteers and grassroots charities working to make the city more sustainable.

N ew Orleans lost about half its population in 2005 as a result of the devastation wrought by Hurricanes Katrina and Rita, and the failure of the levees built to protect the city from flooding. As of the 2010 census, the population had recovered to 75 percent of its pre-Katrina level.

Most of us know of the tragic failure of multiple levels of government to respond adequately to the disaster, compounding the losses caused by nature and the failure of engineering. But, as David Simon° noted in an interview reported in Part One of this three-part blog series, the city's resilient population has been slowly but surely coming back anyway, in no small part because of the strong sense of belonging that New Orleanians feel for their community.

One of the ways in which this has been manifested is in the rebuilding and re-inhabiting of severely damaged homes. To say the least, this has not been a large-scale and highly coordinated effort, and certainly not a quick one. But it is perhaps even more impressive that it has been happening in small increments, a house at a time, occasionally an enclave at a time, because of determined residents, often with the assistance of grassroots charities and volunteers. I want to stress the "grassroots" part of this: the more locally based the effort, the more likely the product will be true to the character of the city and the people who make it special.

David Simon: (b. 1960), an American author, journalist, and writer/producer of television series.

Following Hurricane Katrina, volunteers from around the country teamed up with Rebuilding Together's Fifty for Five, rebuilding fifty homes in five days in the Gentilly neighborhood of New Orleans.

Cheryl Gerber/AP Images for Rebuilding Together

One of the local organizations that has stepped up big-time is the Preservation Resource Center [PRC], a longstanding group whose mission is to promote the preservation, restoration, and revitalization of New Orleans's historic architecture and neighborhoods. The PRC's web site asserts that, "in post-Katrina New Orleans, it is particularly crucial that we rebuild in a way that is sensitive to our past, or we risk losing everything that makes our city unique." That rings true for me. The PRC says that, since Katrina, it has assisted over 5,000 families in saving their homes and brought over 100 low-income families back to their homes.

One of PRC's programs, Operation Comeback, provides homes for first-time and repeat homebuyers, to serve as a catalyst for the larger-scale rebirth of New Orleans's historic neighborhoods. It was created well before Katrina but has been well-positioned to respond to the needs wrought by the flood damage. In 2008, the program launched an "Adopt a House" program to give prospective volunteers and donors a more structured opportunity to assist the efforts in targeted historic neighborhoods.

"Preserving and restoring historic neighborhoods is inherently green, given the ability to recycle land, infrastructure, and materials, usually in the heart of a region."

Operation Comeback has been active in the neighborhoods hit hard by flood damage. For example, one of the program's newer efforts, Preserving Green, is structured to acquire and restore blighted properties utilizing the highest preservation standards while integrating both passive and active sustainable design elements. I would argue that in most cases preserving and restoring historic neighborhoods is inherently green, given the ability to recycle land, infrastructure, and materials, usually in the heart of a region. But Preserving Green goes further. From the web site:

Preserving Green projects are designed to maintain a building's historic integrity and sense of place while achieving the highest possible comfort levels and energy performance.

Within the still-recovering Lower Ninth Ward, a reconstructed "camelback"-style storefront at 5200 Dauphine Street will serve as the new home of the Holy Cross Neighborhood Association and the Lower 9 Center for Sustainable Engagement and Development. The deteriorated condition of the building called for crews to completely dismantle all structural and interior components including doors and windows. Those salvaged materials are being reused, along with new thermal insulation, photovoltaics, solar water heating, onsite water collection and other environmentally-responsible systems to recreate this historic property as a LEED Platinum° building.

Impressive.

Another particularly impressive PRC program, Rebuilding Together New Orleans [RTNO], is providing assistance at scale, helping low-income residents close the gap between usually inadequate government disaster assistance and the amount necessary to rebuild. The program has been rehabbing over a hundred homes each year, including 29 in the first three months of [2012] (plus three playgrounds). It just recruited over 400 student volunteers to spend their spring

---

LEED Platinum: the best of three levels of LEED certification that is awarded based on the total number of LEED requirements.

breaks working on the houses, which I bet was great fun as well as satisfying for the students. (RTNO is affiliated with, in addition to PRC, the national Rebuilding Together organization, which assists rehabilitation and critical repairs to the homes of low-income Americans.)

Here's a nice description from the local organization's web site:

After Hurricane Katrina, RTNO modified its mission to aid those displaced by the storm. Instead of only smaller projects, RTNO began to focus on the total renovation and rebuilding of storm-damaged homes. By reinvesting in and restoring the existing housing stock of the city, RTNO was able to bring homeowners back to their homes, as well as provide a model for restoring and preserving New Orleans' historic neighborhoods. RTNO's home rehabilitation program targets the urban poor, who are the population in New Orleans most affected by Hurricane Katrina. Families that return to their homes in New Orleans — rather than live in exile or in a trailer — sustain a constant, stable, healthy living environment while building their equity and regaining financial independence.

Four years after the storm, RTNO has quickly grown into the largest home rehabilitation nonprofit organization in New Orleans. By focusing our program in seven target neighborhoods, RTNO meets the needs of the communities we serve quickly and efficiently by leveraging corporate, private and public dollars, volunteer labor and help from the AmeriCorps program. Our staff has grown quickly from only 2 full-time employees in 2005 to 27 full-time employees and 41 AmeriCorps members.

RTNO is also committed to sustainability. The program's rehab standards include measures for energy efficiency, improving indoor air quality, and the use of reclaimed and sustainable building products. Where demolition is involved, the organization salvages the debris, processes it as necessary, and either uses it or makes it available for others to use in future construction projects.

As if all this weren't enough, the organization has also just published a book, *How to Rebuild a City: Field Guide from a Work in Progress*, which takes the most somber of subjects and attempts to help survivors meet big challenges with creativity and energy:

Passionate and funny New Orleans writers and artists share — in essays, short stories, and advice columns — informed but cheeky thoughts on how to restore normalcy in order to rebuild after a disaster.

The book, released in December of 2010, is the brainchild of New Orleans City Councilmember Kristin Gisleson Palmer (who directed Rebuilding Together New Orleans before the election) and her husband Bobby.

Field Guide *is a collection from and for those who, after devastating chaos, chose creative ways to rebuild their families and communities. At times playful, at others sardonic, it is ultimately a book of hard work, perseverance and celebration on the road to New Orleans' recovery. And while the storm is clearly* Field Guide's *framework, the book is applicable to any community or city in need of redemption. . . . It offers simple solutions to complex problems — from how to build bus stop benches to how to educate the city's youth if the schools have closed.*

I haven't seen the book, but I like the idea. It was supported by the Arts Council of New Orleans and the Zeitoun Foundation, which was organized by author Dave Eggers, using proceeds from a book about Hurricane Katrina survivors.

Just looking at the photos begins to tell us what all this has done 10
and is doing for the city and its residents. . . . For me, it is testament not just to the power of the human spirit but also to the power of place. In the first part of this series, David Simon characterized the strong identification of New Orleanians to their city, even through the suffering, as a form of patriotism. I like that description.

Understanding the Text

1. What has the Preservation Resource Center done to make New Orleans a greener city?
2. How does Benfield use the term "grassroots"? What does this term mean, and how is it tied to sustainability?

Reflection and Response

3. Compare the efforts of Operation Comeback and Rebuilding Together New Orleans. Do you think their work has been successful so far? Why or why not? What more could be done to make New Orleans a sustainable city?
4. Describe how this article relates to sustainability.

Making Connections

5. Hurricane Sandy (2012) had a devastating impact on parts of the East Coast. Do some research on the post-Sandy restoration efforts. In what ways were these efforts similar to or different from the Katrina efforts described in this article? The next article in this chapter provides some context on Hurricane Sandy.
6. Do some research on either Operation Comeback or Rebuilding Together New Orleans. What are these programs working on currently?
7. The article mentions student volunteers who spend their spring breaks working on the houses. Find out if your school offers any volunteer programs. If they do, what do they do?

After Sandy, Rebuilding for Storms and Rising Seas

Ben Jervey

Ben Jervey is a New York–based environmental journalist and editor, whose work has appeared in *National Geographic*, *Men's Journal*, the *New York Post*, and other venues. Jervey is the author of *The Big Green Apple: Your Guide to Eco-Friendly Living in New York City*, and he serves on the advisory boards of several New York City sustainability and environmental organizations.

Jervey's article was written in October 2013, a year after Hurricane Sandy struck the Eastern seaboard, causing more than $70 billion in damage and hundreds of deaths. The article describes some of the lessons to be learned about environmental disasters and how local, regional, and national governments might respond to them. As you read the article, think about the best ways to balance recovery from a disaster with planning to avoid future disasters.

When the waters finally receded, Mantoloking, New Jersey, resembled a war zone. All 521 houses in the borough, a seaside enclave on a barrier island about halfway down the state's coast, had suffered damage. Sixty cottages had gone up in flames after natural gas lines ruptured.

A week after Superstorm Sandy struck, when residents were finally bussed back to survey the damage, there was no power or running water. Massive piles of debris filled streets, yards, and patios. Boats from the local yacht club were piled on top of each other like toys.

Now, as the one-year anniversary of Sandy arrives on October 29, [2013], officials in Mantoloking and surrounding Brick Township are finalizing plans to build a massive $40 million sand dune, anchored by a four-mile (6.4-kilometer) steel seawall. . . . The steel will climb 16 feet (5 meters) above the beach and will be piled high with sand, paid for by federal and state dollars.

Brick Township was one of the spots hardest hit by the so-called superstorm, largely because it lacked the beach and dune systems that helped protect other towns along the Jersey Shore.

But the impulse to minimize risk from future superstorms and 5 hurricanes, even amid the rush to rebuild from Sandy, is not unique to Brick or the Jersey Shore. Up and down the eastern seaboard, coastal communities that took Sandy on the chin have transitioned from urgent disaster response to thinking about how to build more resilience into disaster preparedness and infrastructure, especially in the face of increasing threats like climate change and sea level rise. . . .

The efforts stretch from the local to the federal level, and as their implications begin to come into view, they're raising questions about just how much the nation has treated Sandy as an environmental wake-up call.

A Lesson to Be Learned

Days after the storm, as water was still pumping out of New York City's tunnels and while much of Long Island still lacked power, New York Governor Andrew Cuomo was among the chorus of public officials saying that Sandy marked a turning point.

"There is a wake-up call and a lesson to be learned here," he said at the time. "There is a reality that has existed for a long time that we have been blind to. And that is climate change, extreme weather, call it what you will, and our vulnerability to it."

The government's responsibility, Cuomo said, is not to debate climate change's causes, but to prepare for its consequences: "How do you do your best to make sure it doesn't happen again or reduce the damage if it does?"

Cuomo's call to action was echoed by leaders nationwide.   10

"Sandy was a wake-up call, and not just for the Eastern Seaboard but for communities all over the country that we need to start preparing for climate change now," said Brian Holland, Climate Program Director at ICLEI-Local Governments for Sustainability, an environmental association of cities and counties.

While the months immediately following the storm may have been an ideal time to issue such warnings, they were a tough time for action.

"What we learned very quickly is that the first three to six months is not the time to be having those discussions at the local level," said Peter Kasabach, executive director of New Jersey Future, a nonprofit that promotes responsible land-use policies. "Everybody is dealing with relief issues and personal issues."

That means the central challenge for cities and towns, according to Kasabach, "has been to try to get your town back to some kind of normalcy without overinvesting in things that are just going to get wiped out the next time."

Uncle Sam has helped local governments focus on that goal. Indeed,   15
the biggest evolution in disaster-related policymaking post-Sandy isn't

some change to a zoning law or flood insurance plan, but a wholesale shift in how the federal government approaches local planning.

For the first time, the feds are urging local leaders to get serious about climate change planning in very specific ways.

"Sandy was a wake-up call, and not just for the Eastern Seaboard but for communities all over the country that we need to start preparing for climate change now."

In August, the Hurricane Sandy Rebuilding Task Force — convened last year by U.S. President Barack Obama — laid out 69 policy recommendations that would guide recovery. The theme underlying the document: in an age of warmer temperatures and rising seas, plan for a future with stronger, more frequent storms.

"Decision-makers at all levels," the report said, "must recognize that climate change and the resulting increase in risks from extreme weather have eliminated the option of simply building back to outdated standards and expecting better outcomes after the next extreme event."

The Brookings Institute's Robert Puentes says that the strategy laid out in the task force's report "emphasizes a bottom-up approach" that breaks with 100 years of top-down managing.

"It understands that there's a different role for the federal government, that not all decisions will be dictated," says Puentes, who directs Brookings' Metropolitan Infrastructure Initiative. "Local leaders and local communities are the ones who are going to be leading in the rebuilding."   20

Secretary of the U.S. Department of Housing and Urban Development Shaun Donovan said as much in a letter introducing the report from the federal task force, which he chaired.

"Local governments and community leaders are the front lines of disaster recovery," he wrote in the August letter, "and it is the job of the Federal Government to have their back by supporting their efforts, providing guidance when necessary and delivering resources to help them fulfill their needs."

New Model in Action

The battered seaside borough of Mantoloking provides a glimpse of this new model. Local leaders learned the value of dunes from data shared by state and federal sources, which showed that towns with dunes fared much better in the storm.

After many community meetings, Mantoloking authorities decided to work with Brick Township leaders to build a dune of their own.

The legwork — hosting meetings, selling the plan, securing ease-   25
ments, wrestling through eminent domain proceedings — has been led by locals. But when it's time to bury the massive steel wall into the beach, the U.S. Army Corps of Engineers will step in, and the federal government will pick up the bill.

In New York, Governor Cuomo is using federal money for an innovative local program, also illustrating the bottom-up approach to Sandy rebuilding. In January, the governor made headlines by offering to buy flood-ravaged properties in particularly high-risk locations from homeowners at prestorm market prices.

With funding from the federal Community Development Block Grant Disaster Recovery Program, the first offers were sent to homeowners in the Oakwood Beach section of Staten Island.

Roughly 185 homeowners have opted for the buyout, and the first sale went through a few weeks ago. A new set of offers landed in 600 Long Island mailboxes this month. Once the property of the State of New York, the houses — or what's left of them — will be demolished.

The land, Cuomo says, will be "given back to Mother Nature."

Design Competitions and Sea Level Calculators

Other aspects of the federal task force's recommendations may be get-   30
ting close to reality. The group organized a Rebuild By Design competition that selected ten teams to propose planning that makes coastal areas more resilient.

The teams have been at work for months, and on October 28 each team will unveil a single design concept to focus on for the rest of the process, which will be their official entry into the contest. All ten teams will then go to work with the Municipal Art Society, Regional Plan Association, and Van Alen Institute, all nonprofits that advocate for smarter urban planning and design solutions in New York City and the surrounding areas, to connect with potential partners within Sandy-impacted communities and further shape the projects to local needs and site specifics. Next year, a handful of the designs will be selected as winners, and will be implemented in local communities, all courtesy of federal funds.

The task force also set into motion a free, map-based sea level rise planning tool, built by the National Oceanic and Atmospheric Administration (NOAA) with help from FEMA and the Army Corps of Engineers, to facilitate smarter long-term decision-making at the local level.

The new maps show expansions of coastal floodplain boundaries that could be used by local planners, and a sea level change calculator that gives site-specific details on projected flood elevations from 2010 through the turn of the next century, which is useful in determining how tall to cut the stilts for a rebuilt beachfront house.

The most lasting impacts of the task force's recommendations are likely to come from guidelines that the federal government is now hashing out for new development and rebuilding along the coast. Many guidelines dovetail with those laid out in President Obama's Climate Action Plan, announced in June.

That includes the minimum flood risk standard that will ensure that all rebuilding projects relying on federal funds must be elevated or flood-proofed in accordance with FEMA's latest flood mapping guidance. 35

The task force is recommending that all infrastructure projects in coastal areas be held to new resiliency guidelines, though so far the guidelines are only applicable to projects that take federal Sandy relief funds.

The federal government is also working to restore some natural resiliency measures to the coastal landscape. Just this week, Department of the Interior Secretary Sally Jewell announced an additional $162 million in federal funding to pay for the restoration of marshes and wetlands along the coast, and to rebuild shorelines to better protect coastal communities.

"What we witnessed during Hurricane Sandy was that our public lands and other natural areas are often the best defense against Mother Nature," Jewell said before her visit to the Forsythe National Wildlife Refuge in Galloway, New Jersey, where she made the announcement.

A Slow Process

Of course, big announcements and sweeping recommendations have come after other big disasters. Think of the lofty Gulf Coast plans after Katrina, which aside from the reinforcement of levees, have largely been left to languish. How much the Sandy recovery winds up changing disaster preparedness and infrastructure is yet to be seen.

Some argue that the federal government has already been too slow to turn recommendations into action. 40

"It's been a slow process," said Holland of ICLEI-Local Governments for Sustainability, "partially because federal agencies have been hamstrung by Congress. From the sequester to the shutdown, the federal agencies haven't been empowered to implement these things as quickly as they've needed to."

Some task force recommendations, like mapping tools, can be implemented with relative ease (NOAA's sea level rise tool is now readily available and state-specific models have already been released in New Jersey and Massachusetts), and executive orders can ensure that taxpayer dollars don't pay for wrecked homes and roads that could be flooded anew.

But beyond projects funded by Sandy-related relief funds, there are no enforceable guidelines yet. "Rutgers put out a flood mapping project," said Kasabach, referring to a project called NJ Floodmapper, "but nobody is compelled to use it at this point."

Back in Mantoloking, it's easy to see how federal resiliency guidelines could play out. Homeowners who do choose to rebuild, if they take federal relief funds, will have to elevate their homes and utility boxes in accordance with FEMA's flood projections.

Still, most cities and towns across the country are still ill prepared 45 to deal with the worsening impacts of climate change. JoAnn Carmin, a Professor of Environmental Policy and Planning at MIT, has studied climate planning on the local government level.

In a recently published report, Carmin found that only about half of the 298 American cities she surveyed has any climate planning underway, and that just 13 percent had completed an assessment of local vulnerabilities and had approved long-term plans.

Carmin's survey started in 2011, and she hasn't secured funding for a follow-up, so she can't say whether there had been an increase in such planning since Sandy. But she says the views of local planners and officials she talks to have been impacted by the storm. After Sandy, she said, "there has been a much greater awareness on 'preparedness' than on 'adaptation.'" Communities are far less likely to do anything to "adapt" to a new climate normal that may be perceived as decades away, explained Carmin. But "storms and disasters are imminent," so governments are motivated to be prepared for extreme weather events.

While cities and towns wait for federal guidance, many are taking matters into their own hands, signing onto a Resilient Communities for America campaign organized by ICLEI, which invites collaboration between communities and offers planning resources to help local leaders make smarter decisions. The campaign also advocates for stronger standards and guidelines, and for better support from federal and state governments.

On paper, the White House and the task force are pushing for the same things. A year after Sandy, it remains to be seen whether these proposals are put into action or back on the shelf.

Understanding the Text

1. Based on what you read in the article, what areas were most affected by Hurricane Sandy?
2. What role did local and national governments play in the recovery efforts?
3. Why is building design addressed in an article about a hurricane?
4. What role might sea levels play in future hurricanes and their impact on coastal areas?

Reflection and Response

5. What is the underlying premise about climate change in this article? How do the various people mentioned in the article refer to climate change?
6. Why is it difficult to address disaster preparation efforts immediately following a disaster? When is the ideal time to discuss preparation and future planning?
7. What is the "new model" for disaster response that is referred to in the article? How is this different from older models? How does it change the way government organizations often operate?

Making Connections

8. Read a portion of the Hurricane Sandy Rebuilding Report. What does it address? How does it consider sustainable solutions? You can find the report through the U.S. Department of Housing and Urban Development here: http://portal.hud.gov/hudportal/HUD?src=/sandyrebuilding.

9. Do some research on sustainability and construction design, focusing specifically on efforts in coastal areas. What are some sustainable design solutions that seem useful in coastal locations? How are the challenges different along the coast than they might be inland?

10. What are the similarities and differences between the Hurricane Katrina disaster and the Hurricane Sandy disaster? Most sources suggest that the response and recovery was much more effective for Sandy, and slower and less effective for Katrina. Why do you think this was the case? What are the various factors that led to this difference?

How Did the BP Oil Spill Affect Gulf Coast Wildlife?

David Biello

David Biello is a writer who focuses on environmental and energy-related topics. He also is an associate editor at *Scientific American* and a host of *Scientific American*'s news podcast *60-Second Earth*. He is currently working on a documentary with Detroit Public Television about the future of electricity.

This article from 2011 deals with the BP oil spill, which occurred in the Gulf of Mexico in April 2010. Biello describes some of the short-term and long-term effects of the spill, particularly focusing on the wildlife of the Gulf Coast. Although scientists are certain that marine and bird life has been affected, the consequences may also be more profound than they know.

Cocodrie, La. — The tendrils of coastline here were some of the first shores to see oil after BP's Macondo well blowout last year. On May 7, 2010 — two days before the start of the annual fishing season — oil bounced off Grand Isle and flowed into Terrebonne Bay, remembers Michel Claudet, Terrebonne Parish president. In fact, oil fouled 35 percent of the U.S. Gulf Coast's 2,625 kilometers of shoreline before the spill was done.

"The people of Terrebonne are still trying to recover from the spill," Claudet says. "No one knew and we still do not know what might be the long-term effects."

The murky waters of the Mississippi River Delta obscure a profusion of life, hence the abundant local commercial and sport fishing. They also do an excellent job of hiding the long-term impacts of last year's oil spill. The oil that reached shore has been absorbed into the sponge-like wetlands or drifted to the sediment bottom, impacting shoreline that serves as a nursery for sealife, coastal habitat and a stopover for migrating birds.

"This spill is significant and, in all likelihood, will affect fish and wildlife across the Gulf, if not all of North America, for years, if not decades," warned Rowan Gould, then acting director of the U.S. Fish and Wildlife Service last May. "We will recover a small number of oil-covered birds. The concern is what we can't see. . . . We may never know the spill's impacts on many species of birds and marine life, given how far offshore they are found."

Six years after Hurricane Katrina, the storm's impact is still visible throughout New Orleans, as evidenced by the emptied neighborhoods 5 or the new houses in the Ninth Ward that resemble fresh scar tissue, easily distinguished from the former housing stock. One year after BP's oil spill, however, its impacts are largely invisible, hidden by the deep, cold waters of the Gulf and dispersed in that vast volume of water or tucked away into the endless marshes of the Louisiana coast.

A massive scientific effort is ongoing to precisely quantify the environmental damage caused by the oil spill — whether measured in oily sediments or missing generations of sealife. This is part of the National Oceanic and Atmospheric Administration (NOAA) Natural Resource Damage Assessment Process to determine what and how much BP will have to pay as well as an undertaking to understand

> "We may never know the spill's impacts on many species of birds and marine life, given how far offshore they are found."

a unique oil spill: one that happened more than 1,500 meters beneath the sea surface, spewing roughly five million barrels of oil before it was plugged.

As a result of this looming legal fight, much of what could be known about ecological impacts remains hidden. "Free and open access to scientific information concerning oil spills is not a given," noted the authors of a Congressional Research Service report on the oil spill's ecosystem impacts last October. For example, dead dolphins that washed ashore earlier this spring have been seized by the U.S. government. "NOAA and other federal agencies came into every lab with a dolphin in the fridge and confiscated it," says Casi Callaway, baykeeper for Mobile Bay in Alabama. "All data, all studies, all work on dolphins was sequestered."

Known Unknowns

Long-term impacts of the oil spill will not be known for years: After the *Exxon Valdez* spill in Alaska, it took three years before the local herring fishery collapsed. "A lot of species were spawning during the Deepwater Horizon [spill]," notes biological oceanographer Edward Chesney of the Louisiana Universities Marine Consortium (LUMCON). "We undoubtedly lost a lot of those fish and egg larvae — they can't move and are highly vulnerable to oil toxicity." The loss of entire generations of young marine life may also propagate up the food chain — over time. Already, scientists have found evidence of oil passing into plankton, which serve as the broad base of the food web.

A large plume of smoke rises from fires on BP's Deepwater Horizon offshore oil rig on April 21, 2010.

AP Photo/Gerald Herbert

Impacts to marine life range from outright death to reduced reproduction, altered development, impaired feeding as well as compromised immune systems. Even exposure to low concentrations of oil that fish embryos survive can alter the shape of their hearts as adults and reduce their ability to swim, according to research published April 11 in *Proceedings of the National Academy of Sciences*.

And simply because scientists had little information on certain   10
species before the spill — such as the denizens of the deep that bore the brunt of the dispersed oil — its impacts may prove impossible to measure, although research continues into the array of nematodes, fungi, mollusks and other organisms that thrive on the seafloor. "We don't have a lot of information on deep water species in general," Chesney notes.

Known Knowns

What is clear, however, is that the approximately five million barrels of Lousiana sweet (low-sulfur) crude that spewed into the Gulf of Mexico was toxic — a toxicity exacerbated by the use of 1.8 million gallons of dispersant both in the deep sea and at the surface. The oil itself sports an array of so-called polycyclic aromatic hydrocarbons (PAHs) — benzene, toluene and the like that are known to cause cancer. NOAA testing found more than 800 oil-related compounds in the water during the spill. "Those components are very toxic," says toxicologist Scott Miles of Louisiana State University. "Those are the ones you're sniffing when filling up the gas tank."

At the same time, they are compounds that fish and other organisms are efficient at not taking up into their tissues. "Accumulation of PAH is very difficult," notes toxicologist Joe Griffitt of the University of Southern Mississippi, who is studying how oil exposures that do not kill an animal can affect its reproductive success.

And these different compounds have different effects, some of which cancel each other out. "You have a very complex situation, very quickly," says Griffitt. PAH can have impacts that don't kill the marine organism directly but reduce its reproductive success or promote tumors — even interfere with the process of copying the genetic code. "There is some evidence that PAH can affect methylation patterns," Griffitt says. "You stick a methyl group on DNA somewhere and then effect gene transcription. It's theoretically heritable."

Further, it is difficult to tell whether a decline in reproduction or an increase in cancer is a direct result of the BP oil spill, a natural oil seep, some combination of causes or another cause entirely — in addition to being difficult to detect in the first place. "We are starting to see some tumors and lesions in fish exposed to Deepwater Horizon [spilled oil]," Chesney notes. In fact, fish caught in the Gulf, such as red snapper, are showing signs of weakened immune systems that have allowed opportunistic infections. The cause may or may not be BP's oil spill.

Evidence from prior spills, such as the *Exxon Valdez* suggests fur- 15 ther long-term effects. "Salmon embryos exposed to oil, when they grow up, their babies are compromised, through mechanisms such as messing with the [hormonal] system," says biologist Andrew Whitehead of Louisiana State University, who studied Louisiana marshes both before and after the oil spill. Alaskan shorebirds also did not breed as much, had smaller eggs when they did breed, and those chicks that did hatch died more frequently.

In addition, BP's Macondo well oil itself smothered birds; more than 8,000 such birds representing 102 different species were collected — 2,263 of them already dead — by government workers. Of course, this is likely just a fraction of the birds impacted because an oil-coated bird at sea sinks. "It is this phenomenon that makes an accurate estimate of bird deaths extremely difficult," wrote the Congressional Research Service in an October report on oil spill ecosystem impacts. The Center for Biological Diversity estimates that the oil spill killed or harmed approximately 82,000 birds as well as more than 6,000 sea turtles and 25,000 marine mammals, such as various species of dolphins.

And, unfortunately, the oil that did reach the coast — nearly 700 kilometers of marshland and 235 kilometers of beach was oiled, according to the government's Shoreline Cleanup Assessment Teams — "is very persistent once it gets up in the marsh grass," Miles says. "We still have a lot of oil in the Louisiana marshlands." That oil killed the spartina marsh grass at times, reducing coastal wetlands and, ultimately, exacerbating coastal erosion. "If it does kill the grass in high enough concentrations and a big storm comes up, it's going to start eroding," Miles adds.

Deep Clean?

At the same time, the closure of Gulf fisheries during the oil spill last year removed the enormous pressure from commercial fishing on populations ranging from shrimp to the tiny fish known as menhaden, the latter of which is caught to be ground up into meal. As a result, fishing this year is some of the best ever. "There are some fish species that are not as prolific as they have been. Others, there are millions, because we didn't fish them last year," Mobile Bay's Callaway says. "The food web has been touched and changed. We just don't know what that means."

And the fact that the spill occurred at sea — and beneath 1,500 meters of water — spared some of the most productive fisheries and spawning grounds in the world. "What is arriving at shore is much less toxic, much less difficult to deal with than what is coming out of the wellhead," says biologist Christopher D'Elia, dean of the School of the Coast and Environment at Louisiana State University. "If [the spill] had been closer, we would have been in much more trouble."

In the meantime, the Gulf shores enjoy a profusion of tarballs and 20 tar mats in excess of the ones that are always present as a result of natural seeps. "I have spent every summer of my life in Gulf Shores

[Alabama], and I have never seen anything that is remotely close to what we have here now," Callaway says. "You just run your fingers through the sand and you've got hundreds, depending on when the last time they did a deep clean."

Such "deep cleans" have their own impacts. "There weren't sand crab holes anywhere — those are a major chunk of the food web," Callaway adds. "I didn't see periwinkles or clams along the shoreline. I'm hoping that is temporary and not long-lasting."

But evidence from prior oil spills suggests that Macondo well oil will be a part of the Gulf Coast for a very long time. "Oil persisted for much longer in the environment than anyone expected," Whitehead notes of the *Exxon Valdez* spill. "The oil was gone from the surface pretty quickly but sediment-associated organisms were persistently exposed to oil over long periods of time — we're talking five to 10 years after the spill."

Only that kind of time will tell what the abundance of life in the Mississippi Delta and the Gulf of Mexico reveals about the long-term impacts of the oil that spewed from BP's Macondo well in 2010. "We are trying to link exposure to effect," Whitehead says. "We are asking the organisms themselves to tell us: 'Has there been a relevant exposure?'"

Understanding the Text

1. How was Terrebonne Bay affected by the BP oil spill?
2. This article was written one year after the disaster. What effects remained from the spill at that time?
3. What are some of the plants and animals that have been affected by the spill?

Reflection and Response

4. How did the National Oceanic and Atmospheric Administration work to quantify the environmental damage caused by the oil spill?
5. What are the "known knowns" and the "known unknowns" concerning the oil spill?

Making Connections

6. This article was written a year after the BP disaster occurred. Do some research to find out how Terrebonne Bay and other affected areas along the Gulf of Mexico have recovered since this article was published.
7. Tourism is a major economic factor in the Gulf Coast region affected by the oil spill. Do some research on how the tourism industry has addressed these problems.

Animal Extinction: The Greatest Threat to Mankind

Julia Whitty

Julia Whitty is an award-winning author and former documentary filmmaker. Born in Bogota, Colombia, Whitty went on to write environmental books such as *Deep Blue Home*, *The Fragile Edge*, and *A Tortoise for the Queen of Tonga*. She has worked on more than seventy nature documentaries, which have aired on PBS, *Nature*, the Discovery Channel, and *National Geographic*. She is currently an environmental correspondent at *Mother Jones* magazine.

This article first appeared in 2007 in *The Independent*, a British national morning newspaper. Whitty uses statistics to shed light on the rates of extinction and endangerment of animal and plant species. She describes certain species that are overlooked by humanity and explains the chain reaction caused by extinctions.

In the final stages of dehydration the body shrinks, robbing youth from the young as the skin puckers, eyes recede into orbits, and the tongue swells and cracks. Brain cells shrivel and muscles seize. The kidneys shut down. Blood volume drops, triggering hypovolemic shock, with its attendant respiratory and cardiac failures. These combined assaults disrupt the chemical and electrical pathways of the body until all systems cascade toward death.

Such is also the path of a dying species. Beyond a critical point, the collective body of a unique kind of mammal or bird or amphibian or tree cannot be salvaged, no matter the first aid rendered. Too few individuals spread too far apart, or too genetically weakened, are susceptible to even small natural disasters: a passing thunderstorm; an unexpected freeze; drought. At fewer than 50 members, populations experience increasingly random fluctuations until a kind of fatal arrhythmia takes hold. Eventually, an entire genetic legacy, born in the beginnings of life on earth, is removed from the future.

Scientists recognize that species continually disappear at a background extinction rate° estimated at about one species per million per year, with new species replacing the lost in a sustainable fashion. Occasional mass extinctions convulse this orderly norm, followed by excruciatingly slow recoveries as new species emerge from the re-

---

background extinction rate: the standard rate of extinction in earth's geological and biological history before humans became a primary contributor to extinctions.

maining gene-pool, until the world is once again repopulated by a different catalogue of flora and fauna.

From what we understand so far, five great extinction events have reshaped earth in cataclysmic ways in the past 439 million years, each one wiping out between 50 and 95 percent of the life of the day, including the dominant life forms; the most recent event killing off the non-avian dinosaurs. Speciations followed, but an analysis published in *Nature* showed that it takes 10 million years before biological diversity even begins to approach what existed before a die-off.

Today we're living through the sixth great extinction, sometimes   5
known as the Holocene extinction event.° We carried its seeds with us 50,000 years ago as we migrated beyond Africa with Stone Age blades, darts, and harpoons, entering pristine Ice Age ecosystems and changing them forever by wiping out at least some of the unique megafauna of the times, including, perhaps, the saber-toothed cats and woolly mammoths. When the ice retreated, we terminated the long and biologically rich epoch sometimes called the Edenic period with assaults from our newest weapons: hoes, scythes, cattle, goats, and pigs.

But, as harmful as our forebears may have been, nothing compares to what's under way today. Throughout the 20th century the causes of extinction — habitat degradation, overexploitation, agricultural monocultures, human-borne invasive species, human-induced climate-change — increased exponentially, until now in the 21st century the rate is nothing short of explosive. The World Conservation Union's Red List — a database measuring the global status of Earth's 1.5 million scientifically named species — tells a haunting tale of unchecked, unaddressed, and accelerating biocide.

When we hear of extinction, most of us think of the plight of the rhino, tiger, panda or blue whale. But these sad sagas are only small pieces of the extinction puzzle. The overall numbers are terrifying. Of the 40,168 species that the 10,000 scientists in the World Conservation Union have assessed, one in four mammals, one in eight birds, one in three amphibians, one in three conifers and other gymnosperms are at risk of extinction. The peril faced by other classes of organisms is less thoroughly analyzed, but fully 40 percent of the examined species of planet earth are in danger, including perhaps 51 percent of reptiles, 52 percent of insects, and 73 percent of flowering plants.

By the most conservative measure — based on the last century's recorded extinctions — the current rate of extinction is 100 times the

---

Holocene extinction event: the extinction of species during the present Holocene epoch (since around 10,000 BCE).

background rate. But the eminent Harvard biologist Edward O. Wilson, and other scientists, estimate that the true rate is more like 1,000 to 10,000 times the background rate. The actual annual sum is only an educated guess, because no scientist believes that the tally of life ends at the 1.5 million species already discovered; estimates range as high as 100 million species on earth, with 10 million as the median guess. Bracketed between best- and worst-case scenarios, then, somewhere between 2.7 and 270 species are erased from existence every day. Including today.

We now understand that the majority of life on Earth has never been — and will never be — known to us. In a staggering forecast, Wilson predicts that our present course will lead to the extinction of half of all plant and animal species by 2100.

You probably had no idea. Few do. A poll by the American Museum 10 of Natural History finds that seven in 10 biologists believe that mass extinction poses a colossal threat to human existence, a more serious environmental problem than even its contributor, global warming; and that the dangers of mass extinction are woefully underestimated by almost everyone outside science. In the 200 years since French naturalist Georges Cuvier first floated the concept of extinction, after examining fossil bones and concluding "the existence of a world previous to ours, destroyed by some sort of catastrophe," we have only slowly recognized and attempted to correct our own catastrophic behavior.

Some nations move more slowly than others. In 1992, an international summit produced a treaty called the Convention on Biological Diversity that was subsequently ratified by 190 nations — all except the unlikely coalition of the United States, Iraq, the Vatican, Somalia, Andorra and Brunei. The European Union later called on the world to arrest the decline of species and ecosystems by 2010. Last year, worried biodiversity experts called for the establishment of a scientific body akin to the Intergovernmental Panel on Climate Change to provide a united voice on the extinction crisis and urge governments to action.

"Our present course will lead to the extinction of half of all plant and animal species by 2100."

Yet, despite these efforts, the Red List, updated every two years, continues to show metastatic growth. There are a few heartening examples of so-called Lazarus species lost and then found: the wollemi pine and the mahogany glider in Australia, the Jerdon's courser in India, the takahe in New Zealand, and, maybe, the ivory-billed

The giant panda, native to China, is a conservation-reliant endangered species.
John Giustina/Getty Images

woodpecker in the United States. But for virtually all others, the Red List is a dry country with little hope of rain, as species ratchet down the listings from secure to vulnerable, to endangered, to critically endangered, to extinct.

All these disappearing species are part of a fragile membrane of organisms wrapped around the Earth so thinly, writes Wilson, that it "cannot be seen edgewise from a space shuttle, yet so internally complex that most species composing it remain undiscovered." We owe everything to this membrane of life. Literally everything. The air we breathe. The food we eat. The materials of our homes, clothes, books, computers, medicines. Goods and services that we can't even imagine we'll someday need will come from species we have yet to identify. The proverbial cure for cancer. The genetic fountain of youth. Immortality. Mortality. The living membrane we so recklessly destroy is existence itself.

Biodiversity is defined as the sum of an area's genes (the building blocks of inheritance), species (organisms that can interbreed), and ecosystems (amalgamations of species in their geological and chemical landscapes). The richer an area's biodiversity, the tougher its immune system, since biodiversity includes not only the number of species but also the number of individuals within that species, and all the inherent genetic variations — life's only army against the diseases of oblivion.

Yet it's a mistake to think that critical genetic pools exist only in 15 the gaudy show of the coral reefs, or the cacophony of the rainforest. Although a hallmark of the desert is the sparseness of its garden, the orderly progression of plants and the understated camouflage of its animals, this is only an illusion. Turn the desert inside out and upside down and you'll discover its true nature. Escaping drought and heat, life goes underground in a tangled overexuberance of roots and burrows reminiscent of a rainforest canopy, competing for moisture, not light. Animal trails criss-cross this subterranean realm in private burrows engineered, inhabited, stolen, shared and fought over by ants, beetles, wasps, cicadas, tarantulas, spiders, lizards, snakes, mice, squirrels, rats, foxes, tortoises, badgers and coyotes.

To survive the heat and drought, desert life pioneers ingenious solutions. Coyotes dig and maintain wells in arroyos, probing deep for water. White-winged doves use their bodies as canteens, drinking enough when the opportunity arises to increase their bodyweight by more than 15 percent. Black-tailed jack rabbits tolerate internal temperatures of 111°F. Western box turtles store water in their oversized bladders and urinate on themselves to stay cool. Mesquite grows taproots more than 160ft deep in search of moisture.

These life-forms and their life strategies compose what we might think of as the "body" of the desert, with some species the lungs and others the liver, the blood, the skin. The trend in scientific investigation in recent decades has been toward understanding the interconnectedness of the bodily components, i.e. the effect one species has on the others. The loss of even one species irrevocably changes the desert (or the tundra, rainforest, prairie, coastal estuary, coral reef, and so on) as we know it, just as the loss of each human being changes his or her family forever.

Nowhere is this better proven than in a 12-year study conducted in the Chihuahuan desert by James H. Brown and Edward Heske of the University of New Mexico. When a kangaroo-rat guild composed of three closely related species was removed, shrublands quickly converted to grasslands, which supported fewer annual plants, which in turn supported fewer birds. Even humble players mediate stability. So when you and I hear of this year's extinction of the Yangtze river dolphin, and think, "how sad," we're not calculating the deepest cost: that extinctions lead to co-extinctions because most living things on Earth support a few symbionts, while keystone species influence and support myriad plants and animals. Army ants, for example, are known to support 100 known species, from beetles to birds. A European study finds steep declines in honeybee diversity in the past 25 years but also significant attendant declines in plants that depend on bees for pollination — a job estimated to be worth £50bn [about $80 billion] worldwide. Meanwhile, beekeepers in 24 American states report that perhaps 70 percent of their colonies have recently died off, threatening £7bn [about $11 billion] in U.S. agriculture. And bees are only a small part of the pollinator crisis.

One of the most alarming developments is the rapid decline not just of species but of higher taxa, such as the class Amphibia, the 300-million-year-old group of frogs, salamanders, newts and toads hardy enough to have preceded and then outlived most dinosaurs. Biologists first noticed die-offs two decades ago, and, since then, have watched as seemingly robust amphibian species vanished in as little as six months. The causes cover the spectrum of human environmental assaults, including rising ultraviolet radiation from a thinning ozone layer, increases in pollutants and pesticides, habitat loss from agriculture and urbanization, invasions of exotic species, the wildlife trade, light pollution, and fungal diseases. Sometimes stressors merge to form an unwholesome synergy;° an African frog brought to the West in the 1950s for use in human pregnancy tests likely introduced a fungus deadly to native frogs. Meanwhile, a recent analysis in *Nature* estimated that, in the past 20 years, at least 70 species of South American frogs had gone extinct as a result of climate change.

In a 2004 analysis published in *Science*, Lian Pin Koh and his colleagues predict that an initially modest co-extinction rate will climb alarmingly as host extinctions rise in the near future. Graphed out, the forecast mirrors the rising curve of an infectious disease, with the human species acting all the parts: the pathogen, the vector, the Typhoid Mary who refuses culpability, and, ultimately, one of up to 100 million victims.

"Rewilding" is bigger, broader, and bolder than humans have thought before. Many conservation biologists believe it's our best hope for arresting the sixth great extinction. Wilson calls it "mainstream conservation writ large for future generations." This is because more of what we've done until now — protecting pretty landscapes, attempts at sustainable development, community-based conservation and ecosystem management — will not preserve biodiversity through

synergy: the interaction of elements that when combined produce a total effect that is greater than the sum of the individual elements and contributions, and so on.

the critical next century. By then, half of all species will be lost, by Wilson's calculation.

To save Earth's living membrane, we must put its shattered pieces back together. Only "megapreserves" modelled on a deep scientific understanding of continent-wide ecosystem needs hold that promise. "What I have been preparing to say is this," wrote Thoreau more than 150 years ago, "in wildness is the preservation of the world." This, science finally understands.

The Wildlands Project, the conservation group spearheading the drive to rewild North America — by reconnecting remaining wildernesses (parks, refuges, national forests, and local land trust holdings) through corridors — calls for reconnecting wild North America in four broad "megalinkages": along the Rocky Mountain spine of the continent from Alaska to Mexico; across the arctic/boreal from Alaska to Labrador; along the Atlantic via the Appalachians; and along the Pacific via the Sierra Nevada into the Baja peninsula. Within each megalinkage, core protected areas would be connected by mosaics of public and private lands providing safe passage for wildlife to travel freely. Broad, vegetated overpasses would link wilderness areas split by roads. Private landowners would be enticed to either donate land or adopt policies of good stewardship along critical pathways.

It's a radical vision, one the Wildlands Project expects will take 100 years or more to complete, and one that has won the project a special enmity from those who view environmentalists with suspicion. Yet the core brainchild of the Wildlands Project — that true conservation must happen on an ecosystem-wide scale — is now widely accepted. Many conservation organizations are already collaborating on the project, including international players such as Naturalia in Mexico, US national heavyweights like Defenders of Wildlife, and regional experts from the Southern Rockies Ecosystem Project to the Grand Canyon Wildlands Council. Kim Vacariu, the South-west director of the US's Wildlands Project, reports that ranchers are coming round, one town meeting at a time, and that there is interest, if not yet support, from the insurance industry and others who "face the reality of car–wildlife collisions daily."

At its heart, rewilding is based on living with the monster under the bed, since the big, scary animals that frightened us in childhood, and still do, are the fierce guardians of biodiversity. Without wolves, wolverines, grizzlies, black bears, mountain lions and jaguars, wild populations shift toward the herbivores, who proceed to eat plants into extinction, taking birds, bees, reptiles, amphibians and rodents with them. A tenet of ecology states that the world is green because carnivores eat herbivores. Yet the big carnivores continue to die out because we fear and hunt them and because they need more room than we preserve and connect. Male wolverines, for instance, can possess home ranges of 600 sq m. Translated, Greater London would have room for only one.

The first campaign out of the Wildlands Project's starting gate is the "spine of the continent," along the mountains from Alaska to Mexico, today fractured by roads, logging, oil and gas development, grazing, ski resorts, motorized back-country recreation and sprawl.

The spine already contains dozens of core wildlands, including wilderness areas, national parks, national monuments, wildlife refuges, and private holdings. On the map, these scattered fragments look like debris falls from meteorite strikes. Some are already partially buffered by surrounding protected areas such as national forests. But all need interconnecting linkages across public and private lands — farms, ranches, suburbia — to facilitate the travels of big carnivores and the net of biodiversity that they tow behind them.

The Wildlands Project has also identified the five most critically endangered wildlife linkages along the spine, each associated with a keystone species. Grizzlies already pinched at Crowsnest Pass on Highway Three, between Alberta and British Columbia, will be entirely cut off from the bigger gene pool to the north if a larger road is built. Greater sage grouse, Canada lynx, black bears and jaguars face their own lethal obstacles further south.

But by far the most endangered wildlife-linkage is the borderland between the US and Mexico. The Sky Islands straddle this boundary, and some of North America's most threatened wildlife — jaguars, bison, Sonoran pronghorn, Mexican wolves — cross, or need to cross, here in the course of their life's travels. Unfortunately for wildlife, Mexican workers cross here too. Men, women, and children, running at night, one-gallon water jugs in hand.

The problem for wildlife is not so much the intrusions of illegal 30 Mexican workers but the 700-mile border fence proposed to keep them out. From an ecological perspective, it will sever the spine at the lumbar, paralyzing the lower continent.

Here, in a nutshell, is all that's wrong with our treatment of nature. Amid all the moral, practical, and legal issues with the border fence, the biological catastrophe has barely been noted. It's as if extinction is not contagious and we won't catch it.

If, as some indigenous people believe, the jaguar was sent to the world to test the will and integrity of human beings, then surely we need to reassess. Border fences have terrible consequences. One between India and Pakistan forces starving bears and leopards, which can no longer traverse their feeding territories, to attack villagers.

The truth is that wilderness is more dangerous to us caged than free — and has far more value to us wild than consumed. Wilson suggests the time has come to rename the "environmentalist view" the "rear-world view," and to replace the gross national product with the more comprehensive "genuine progress indicator," which estimates the true environmental costs of farming, fishing, grazing, mining, smelting, driving, flying, building, paving, computing, medicating and so on. Until then, it's like keeping a ledger recording income but not expenses. Like us, the Earth has a finite budget.

Understanding the Text

1. According to Whitty, what are the causes of extinction?
2. What is Whitty's main argument in this piece? What does she hope to accomplish?
3. Describe the Wildlands Project that is discussed in this article. Why is this project an important enterprise?

Reflection and Response

4. Why does the author begin this piece by talking about dehydration? What is the analogy here? What effect does it have on you as a reader?
5. Whitty writes that mass extinction is a "more serious environmental problem than even its contributor, global warming" (par. 10). Explain her argument.
6. How does the extinction of one species affect other species? How does animal extinction relate to sustainability?

Making Connections

7. Do some research and find out how many native U.S. species have become extinct in the past one hundred years. Which extinctions are most significant? Is it possible to assess the impact of one species extinction over another?
8. This article quotes Henry David Thoreau, "In wildness is the preservation of the world" (par. 22). Find a connection between this article and the excerpt by Thoreau on page 22 of this book, and explain the connection.

The Last Americans: Environmental Collapse and the End of Civilization

Jared Diamond

Jared Diamond is a scientist and an author of thirteen books, including *The Third Chimpanzee*; the Pulitzer Prize–winning *Guns, Germs, and Steel*; and *Collapse: How Societies Choose to Fail or Succeed.* He earned a B.A. in biochemistry from Harvard University and a Ph.D. in physiology and membrane biophysics from the University of Cambridge. He is currently a professor of geography and physiology at University of California, Los Angeles. Diamond is equally renowned for his work in the fields of ecology and evolutionary biology as for his groundbreaking studies of the birds of Papua New Guinea.

Diamond begins this article by comparing today's society with those of previous civilizations that have crumbled. He relates overpopulation and environmental stress to governmental collapse. Diamond specifically compares our modern society to that of the Mayans, examining their lifestyles and technology regarding sustaining population. As you read the article, think about the similarities to and differences between our own society and those that have collapsed.

I met a traveler from an antique land
Who said: Two vast and trunkless legs of stone
Stand in the desert . . . Near them, on the sand,
Half sunk, a shattered visage lies, whose frown,
And wrinkled lip, and sneer of cold command,
Tell that its sculptor well those passions read
Which yet survive, stamped on these lifeless things,
The hand that mocked them, and the heart that fed.
And on the pedestal these words appear:
"My name is Ozymandias, king of kings:
Look on my works, ye Mighty, and despair!"
Nothing beside remains. Round the decay
Of that colossal wreck, boundless and bare
The lone and level sands stretch far away.

—PERCY BYSSHE SHELLEY, "OZYMANDIAS"

One of the disturbing facts of history is that so many civilizations collapse. Few people, however, least of all our politicians, realize that a primary cause of the collapse of those societies has been the destruction of the environmental resources on which they depended. Fewer still appreciate that many of those civilizations share a sharp curve of decline. Indeed, a society's demise may begin only a decade or two after it reaches its peak population, wealth, and power.

Recent archaeological discoveries have revealed similar courses of collapse in such otherwise dissimilar ancient societies as the Maya in the Yucatán, the Anasazi in the American Southwest, the Cahokia mound builders outside St. Louis, the Greenland Norse, the statue builders of Easter Island, ancient Mesopotamia in the Fertile Crescent, Great Zimbabwe in Africa, and Angkor Wat in Cambodia. These civilizations, and many others, succumbed to various combinations of environmental degradation and climate change, aggression from enemies taking advantage of their resulting weakness, and declining trade with neighbors who faced their own environmental problems. Because peak population, wealth, resource consumption, and waste production are accompanied by peak environmental impact — approaching the limit at which impact outstrips resources — we can now understand why declines of societies tend to follow swiftly on their peaks.

These combinations of undermining factors were compounded by cultural attitudes preventing those in power from perceiving or resolving the crisis. That's a familiar problem today. Some of us are inclined to dismiss the importance of a healthy environment, or at least to suggest that it's just one of many problems facing us — an "issue." That dismissal is based on three dangerous misconceptions.

> "Few people . . . realize that a primary cause of the collapse of those societies has been the destruction of the environmental resources on which they depended."

Foremost among these misconceptions is that we must balance the environment against human needs. That reasoning is exactly upside-down. Human needs and a healthy environment are not opposing claims that must be balanced; instead, they are inexorably linked by chains of cause and effect. We need a healthy environment because we need clean water, clean air, wood, and food from the ocean, plus soil and sunlight to grow crops. We need functioning natural ecosystems, with their native species of earthworms, bees, plants, and microbes, to generate and aerate our soils, pollinate our crops, decompose our wastes, and produce our oxygen. We need to prevent toxic substances from accumulating in our water and air and soil. We need to prevent weeds, germs, and other pest species from becoming established in places where they aren't native and where they cause economic damage. Our strongest arguments for a healthy environment are selfish: we want it for ourselves, not for threatened species like snail darters, spotted owls, and Furbish louseworts.

Another popular misconception is that we can trust in technology 5 to solve our problems. Whatever environmental problem you name, you can also name some hoped-for technological solution under discussion. Some of us have faith that we shall solve our dependence on fossil fuels by developing new technologies for hydrogen engines, wind energy, or solar energy. Some of us have faith that we shall solve our food problems with new or soon-to-be-developed genetically modified crops. Some of us have faith that new technologies will succeed in cleaning up the toxic materials in our air, water, soil, and foods without the horrendous cleanup expenses that we now incur.

Those with such faith assume that the new technologies will ultimately succeed, but in fact some of them may succeed and others may not. They assume that the new technologies will succeed quickly enough to make a big difference soon, but all of these major technological changes will actually take five to thirty years to develop and implement — if they catch on at all. Most of all, those with faith assume that new technology won't cause any new problems. In fact, technology merely constitutes increased power, which produces changes that can be either for the better or for the worse. All of our current environmental problems are unanticipated harmful consequences of our existing technology. There is no basis for believing that technology will miraculously stop causing new and unanticipated problems while it is solving the problems that it previously produced.

The final misconception holds that environmentalists are fearmongering, overreacting extremists whose predictions of impending disaster have been proved wrong before and will be proved wrong again. Behold, say the optimists: water still flows from our faucets, the grass is still green, and the supermarkets are full of food. We are more prosperous than ever before, and that's the final proof that our system works.

Well, for a few billion of the world's people who are causing us increasing trouble, there isn't any clean water, there is less and less green grass, and there are no supermarkets full of food. To appreciate what the environmental problems of those billions of people mean for us Americans, compare the following two lists of countries. First ask some ivory-tower academic ecologist who knows a lot about the environment but never reads a newspaper and has no interest in politics to list the overseas countries facing some of the worst problems of environmental stress, overpopulation, or both. The ecologist would answer, "That's a no-brainer, it's obvious. Your list of environmentally stressed or overpopulated countries should surely include Afghanistan, Bangladesh, Burundi, Haiti, Indonesia, Iraq, Nepal, Pakistan, the Philippines, Rwanda, the Solomon Islands, and Somalia, plus others." Then ask a First World politician who knows nothing, and cares less, about the environment and population problems to list the world's worst trouble spots: countries where state government has already been overwhelmed and has collapsed, or is now at risk of collapsing, or has been wracked by recent civil wars; and countries that, as a result of their problems, are also creating problems for us rich First World countries, which may be deluged by illegal immigrants, or have to provide foreign aid to those countries, or may decide to provide them with military assistance to deal with rebellions and terrorists, or may even (God forbid) have to send in our own troops. The politician would answer, "That's a no-brainer, it's obvious. Your list of political trouble spots should surely include Afghanistan, Bangladesh, Burundi, Haiti, Indonesia, Iraq, Nepal, Pakistan, the Philippines, Rwanda, the Solomon Islands, and Somalia, plus others."

The connection between the two lists is transparent. Today, just as in the past, countries that are environmentally stressed, overpopulated, or both are at risk of becoming politically stressed, and of seeing their governments collapse. When people are desperate and undernourished, they blame their government, which they see as responsible for failing to solve their problems. They try to emigrate at any cost. They start civil wars. They kill one another. They figure that they have nothing to lose, so they become terrorists, or they support or tolerate terrorism. The results are genocides such as the ones that already have exploded in Burundi, Indonesia, and Rwanda; civil wars, as in Afghanistan, Indonesia, Nepal, the Philippines, and the Solomon Islands; calls for the dispatch of First World troops, as to Afghanistan, Indonesia, Iraq, the Philippines, Rwanda, the Solomon Islands, and Somalia; the collapse of central government, as has already happened in Somalia; and overwhelming poverty, as in all of the countries on these lists.

But what about the United States? Some might argue that the environmental collapse of ancient societies is relevant to the modern decline of weak, far-off, overpopulated Rwanda and environmentally devastated Somalia, but isn't it ridiculous to suggest any possible relevance to the fate of our own society? After all, we might reason, those ancients didn't enjoy the wonders of modern environment-friendly technologies. Those ancients had the misfortune to suffer from the effects of climate change. They behaved stupidly and ruined their own environment by doing obviously dumb things, like cutting down their forests, watching their topsoil erode, and building cities in dry areas likely to run short of water. They had foolish leaders who didn't have books and so couldn't learn from history, and who embroiled them in destabilizing wars and didn't pay attention to problems at home. They were overwhelmed by desperate immigrants, as one society after another collapsed, sending floods of economic refugees to tax the resources of the societies that weren't collapsing. In all those respects, we modern Americans are fundamentally different from those primitive ancients, and there is nothing that we could learn from them.

Or so the argument goes. It's an argument so ingrained both in our subconscious and in public discourse that it has assumed the status of objective reality. We think we are different. In fact, of course, all of those powerful societies of the past thought that they too were unique, right up to the moment of their collapse. It's sobering to consider the swift decline of the ancient Maya, who 1,200 years ago were themselves the most advanced society in the Western Hemisphere, and who, like us now, were then at the apex of their own power and numbers. Two excellent recent books, David Webster's *The Fall of the Ancient Maya* and Richardson Gill's *The Great Maya Droughts*, help bring the trajectory of Maya civilization back to life for us. Their studies illustrate how even sophisticated societies like that of the Maya (and ours) can be undermined by details of rainfall, farming methods, and motives of leaders.

• • •

By now, millions of modern Americans have visited Maya ruins. To do so, one need only take a direct flight from the United States to the Yucatán capital of Mérida, jump into a rental car or minibus, and drive an hour on a paved highway. Most Maya ruins, with their great temples and monuments, lie surrounded by jungles (seasonal tropical forests), far from current human settlement. They are "pure" archaeological sites. That is, their locations became depopulated, so they were not covered up by later buildings as were so many other ancient cities, like the Aztec capital of Tenochtitlán — now buried under modern Mexico City — and Rome.

One of the reasons few people live there now is that the Maya homeland poses serious environmental challenges to would-be farmers.

Although it has a somewhat unpredictable rainy season from May to October, it also has a dry season from January through April. Indeed, if one focuses on the dry months, one could describe the Yucatán as a "seasonal desert."

Complicating things, from a farmer's perspective, is that the part of the Yucatán with the most rain, the south, is also the part at the highest elevation above the water table. Most of the Yucatán consists of karst — a porous, sponge-like, limestone terrain — and so rain runs straight into the ground, leaving little or no surface water. The Maya in the lower-elevation regions of the north were able to reach the water table by way of deep sinkholes called *cenotes*, and the Maya in low coastal areas without sink holes could reach it by digging wells up to 75 feet deep. Most Maya, however, lived in the south. How did they deal with their resulting water problem?

Technology provided an answer. The Maya plugged up leaks on   15
karst promontories by plastering the bottoms of depressions to create reservoirs, which collected rain and stored it for use in the dry season. The reservoirs at the Maya city of Tikal, for example, held enough water to meet the needs of about 10,000 people for eighteen months. If a drought lasted longer than that, though, the inhabitants of Tikal were in deep trouble.

Maya farmers grew mostly corn, which constituted the astonishingly high proportion of about 70 percent of their diet, as deduced from isotope analyses of ancient Maya skeletons. They grew corn by means of a modified version of swidden slash-and-burn agriculture, in which forest is cleared, crops are grown in the resulting clearing for a few years until the soil is exhausted, and then the field is abandoned for fifteen to twenty years until regrowth of wild vegetation restores the soil's fertility. Because most of the land under a swidden agricultural system is fallow at any given time, it can support only modest population densities. Thus, it was a surprise for archaeologists to discover that ancient Maya population densities, judging from numbers of stone foundations of farmhouses, were often far higher than what unmodified swidden agriculture could support: often 250 to 750 people per square mile. The Maya probably achieved those high populations by such means as shortening the fallow period and tilling the soil to restore soil fertility, or omitting the fallow period entirely and growing crops every year, or, in especially moist areas, growing two crops per year.

Socially stratified societies, ours included, consist of farmers who produce food, plus nonfarmers such as bureaucrats and soldiers who do not produce food and are in effect parasites on farmers. The farmers must grow enough food to meet not only their own needs but also those of everybody else. The number of nonproducing consumers who can be supported depends on the society's agricultural productivity. In the United States today, with its highly efficient agriculture, farmers make up only 2 percent of our population, and each farmer can feed, on the average, 129 other people. Ancient Egyptian agriculture was efficient enough for an Egyptian peasant to produce five times the food required for himself and his family. But a Maya peasant could produce only twice the needs of himself and his family.

Fully 80 percent of Maya society consisted of peasants. Their inability to support many nonfarmers resulted from several limitations of their agriculture. It produced little protein, because corn has a much lower protein content than wheat, and because the few edible domestic animals kept by the Maya (turkeys, ducks, and dogs) included no large animals like our cows and sheep. There was little use of terracing or irrigation to increase production. In the Maya area's humid climate, stored corn would rot or become infested after a year, so the Maya couldn't get through a longer drought by eating surplus corn accumulated in good years. And unlike Old World peoples with their horses, oxen, donkeys, and camels, the Maya had no animal-powered transport. Indeed, the Maya lacked not only pack animals and animal-drawn plows but also metal tools, wheels, and boats with sails. All of those great Maya temples were built by stone and wooden tools and human muscle power alone, and all overland transport went on the backs of human porters. Those limitations on food supply and food transport may in part explain why Maya society remained politically organized in small kingdoms that were perpetually at war with one another and that never became unified into large empires like the Aztec empire of the Valley of Mexico (fed by highly productive agriculture) or the Inca empire of the Andes (fed by diverse crops carried on llamas). Maya armies were small and unable to mount lengthy campaigns over long distances. The typical Maya kingdom held a population of only up to 50,000 people, within a radius of two or three days' walk from the king's palace. From the top of the temple of some Maya kingdoms, one could see the tops of the temples of other kingdoms.

Presiding over the temple was the king himself, who functioned both as head priest and as political leader. It was his responsibility to pray to the gods, to perform astronomical and calendrical rituals, to ensure the timely arrival of the rains on which agriculture depended, and thereby to bring prosperity. The king claimed to have the supernatural power to deliver those good things because of his asserted family relationship to the gods. Of course, that exposed him to the risk that his subjects would become disillusioned if he couldn't fulfill his boast of being able to deliver rains and prosperity. . . .

• • •

We can identify increasingly familiar strands in the Classic Maya col-   20
lapse. One consisted of population growth outstripping available resources: the dilemma foreseen by Thomas Malthus in 1798. As Webster succinctly puts it in *The Fall of the Ancient Maya*, "Too many
farmers grew too many crops on too much of the landscape." While
population was increasing, the area of usable farmland paradoxically
was decreasing from the effects of deforestation and hillside erosion.

The next strand consisted of increased fighting as more and more
people fought over fewer resources. Maya warfare, already endemic,
peaked just before the collapse. That is not surprising when one reflects that at least 5 million people, most of them farmers, were
crammed into an area smaller than the state of Colorado. That's a
high population by the standards of ancient farming societies, even if
it wouldn't strike modern Manhattan-dwellers as crowded.

Bringing matters to a head was a drought that, although not the first
one the Maya had been through, was the most severe. At the time of
previous droughts, there were still uninhabited parts of the Maya
landscape, and people in a drought area or dust bowl could save themselves by moving to another site. By the time of the Classic collapse,
however, there was no useful unoccupied land in the vicinity on which
to begin anew, and the whole population could not be accommodated
in the few areas that continued to have reliable water supplies.

The final strand is political. Why did the kings and nobles not recognize and solve these problems? A major reason was that their attention was evidently focused on the short-term concerns of enrich-
ing themselves, waging wars, erecting monuments, competing with
one another, and extracting enough food from the peasants to support all those activities. Like most leaders throughout human history,
the Maya kings and nobles did not have the leisure to focus on long-
term problems, insofar as they perceived them.

• • •

What about those same strands today? The United States is also at the
peak of its power, and it is also suffering from many environmental

problems. Most of us have become aware of more crowding and stress. Most of us living in large American cities are encountering increased commuting delays, because the number of people and hence of cars is increasing faster than the number of freeway lanes. I know plenty of people who in the abstract doubt that the world has a population problem, but almost all of those same people complain to me about crowding, space issues, and traffic experienced in their personal lives.

Many parts of the United States face locally severe problems of   25 water restriction (especially southern California, Arizona, the Everglades, and, increasingly, the Northeast); forest fires resulting from logging and forest-management practices throughout the intermontane West; and losses of farmlands to salinization, drought, and climate change in the northern Great Plains. Many of us frequently experience problems of air quality, and some of us also experience problems of water quality and taste. We are losing economically valuable natural resources. We have already lost American chestnut trees, the Grand Banks cod fishery, and the Monterey sardine fishery; we are in the process of losing swordfish and tuna and Chesapeake Bay oysters and elm trees; and we are losing topsoil.

The list goes on: All of us are experiencing personal consequences of our national dependence on imported energy, which affects us not only through higher gas prices but also through the current contraction of the national economy, itself the partial result of political problems associated with our oil dependence. We are saddled with expensive toxic cleanups at many locations, most notoriously near Montana mines, on the Hudson River, and in the Chesapeake Bay. We also face expensive eradication problems resulting from hundreds of introduced pest species — including zebra mussels, Mediterranean fruit flies, Asian longhorn beetles, water hyacinth, and spotted knapweed — that now affect our agriculture, forests, waterways, and pastures.

These particular environmental problems, and many others, are enormously expensive in terms of resources lost, cleanup and restoration costs, and the cost of finding substitutes for lost resources: a billion dollars here, 10 billion there, in dozens and dozens of cases. Some of the problems, especially those of air quality and toxic substances, also exact health costs that are large, whether measured in dollars or in lost years or in quality of life. The cost of our homegrown environmental problems adds up to a large fraction of our gross national product, even without mentioning the costs that we incur from environmental problems overseas, such as the military operations that they inspire. Even the mildest of bad scenarios for our future include a gradual economic decline, as happened to the Roman and British empires. Actually, in case you didn't notice it, our economic decline is already well under way. Just check the numbers for our national debt, yearly government budget deficit, unemployment statistics, and the value of your investment and pension funds.

* * *

The environmental problems of the United States are still modest compared with those of the rest of the world. But the problems of environmentally devastated, overpopulated, distant countries are now our problems as well. We are accustomed to thinking of globalization in terms of us rich, advanced First Worlders sending our good things, such as the Internet and Coca-Cola, to those poor backward Third Worlders. Globalization, however, means nothing more than improved worldwide communication and transportation, which can convey many things in either direction; it is not restricted to good things carried only from the First to the Third World. They in the Third World can now, intentionally or unintentionally, send us their bad things: terrorists; diseases such as AIDS, SARS, cholera, and West Nile fever, carried inadvertently by passengers on transcontinental airplanes; unstoppable numbers of immigrants, both legal and illegal, arriving by boat, truck, train, plane, and on foot; and other consequences of their Third World problems. We in the United States are no longer the isolated Fortress America to which some of us aspired in the 1930s; instead, we are tightly and irreversibly connected to overseas countries. The United States is the world's leading importer, and it is also the world's leading exporter. Our own society opted long ago to become interlocked with the rest of the world.

That's why political stability anywhere in the world now affects us, our trade routes, and our overseas markets and suppliers. We are so dependent on the rest of the world that if a decade ago you had asked a politician to name the countries most geopolitically irrelevant to U.S. interests because of their being so remote, poor, and weak, the list would have begun with Afghanistan and Somalia, yet these countries were subsequently considered important enough to warrant our dispatching U.S. troops. The Maya were "globalized" only within the Yucatán: the southern Yucatán Maya affected the northern Yucatán Maya and may have had some effects on the Valley of Mexico, but they had no contact with Somalia. That's because Maya transportation was slow, short-distance, on foot or else in canoes, and had low cargo capacity. Our transport today is much more rapid and has much higher cargo capacity. The Maya lived in a globalized Yucatán; we live in a globalized world.

● ● ●

If all of this reasoning seems straightforward when expressed so 30
bluntly, one has to wonder: Why don't those in power today get the message? Why didn't the leaders of the Maya, Anasazi, and those other societies also recognize and solve their problems? What were the Maya thinking while they watched loggers clearing the last pine forests on the hills above Copán? Here, the past really is a useful guide to the present. It turns out that there are at least a dozen reasons why past societies failed to anticipate some problems before they developed, or failed to *perceive* problems that had already developed, or failed even to try to solve problems that they did perceive. All of those dozen reasons still can be seen operating today. Let me mention just three of them.

First, it's difficult to recognize a slow trend in some quantity that fluctuates widely up and down anyway, such as seasonal temperature, annual rainfall, or economic indicators. That's surely why the Maya didn't recognize the oncoming drought until it was too late, given that rainfall in the Yucatán varies several-fold from year to year. Natural fluctuations also explain why it's only within the last few years that all climatologists have become convinced of the reality of climate change, and why our president still isn't convinced but thinks that we need more research to test for it.

Second, when a problem is recognized, those in power may not attempt to solve it because of a clash between their short-term interests and the interests of the rest of us. Pumping that oil, cutting down those trees, and catching those fish may benefit the elite by bringing them money or prestige and yet be bad for society as a whole (including the children of the elite) in the long run. Maya kings were consumed by immediate concerns for their prestige (requiring more and bigger temples) and their success in the next war (requiring more followers), rather than for the happiness of commoners or of the next generation. Those people with the greatest power to make decisions in our own society today regularly make money from activities that may be bad for society as a whole and for their own children; those decision-makers include Enron executives, many land developers, and advocates of tax cuts for the rich.

Finally, it's difficult for us to acknowledge the wisdom of policies that clash with strongly held values. For example, a belief in individual freedom and a distrust of big government are deeply ingrained in Americans, and they make sense under some circumstances and up to a certain point. But they also make it hard for us to accept big government's legitimate role in ensuring that each individual's freedom to maximize the value of his or her land holdings doesn't decrease the value of the collective land of all Americans.

• • •

Not all societies make fatal mistakes. There are parts of the world where societies have unfolded for thousands of years without any collapse, such as Java, Tonga, and (until 1945) Japan. Today, Germany and Japan are successfully managing their forests, which are even expanding in area rather than shrinking. The Alaskan salmon fishery and the Australian lobster fishery are being managed sustainably. The Dominican Republic, hardly a rich country, nevertheless has set aside a comprehensive system of protected areas encompassing most of the country's natural habitats.

Is there any secret to explain why some societies acquire good environmental sense while others don't? Naturally, part of the answer depends on accidents of individual leaders' wisdom (or lack thereof). But part also depends upon whether a society is organized so as to minimize built-in clashes of interest between its decision-making elites and its masses. Given how our society is organized, the executives of Enron, Tyco, and Adelphi correctly calculated that their own interests would be best promoted by looting the company coffers, and that they would probably get away with most of their loot. A good example of a society that minimizes such clashes of interest is the Netherlands, whose citizens have perhaps the world's highest level of environmental awareness and of membership in environmental organizations. I never understood why, until on a recent trip to the Netherlands I posed the question to three of my Dutch friends while driving through their countryside.

Just look around you, they said. All of this farmland that you see lies below sea level. One fifth of the total area of the Netherlands is below sea level, as much as 22 feet below, because it used to be shallow bays, and we reclaimed it from the sea by surrounding the bays with dikes and then gradually pumping out the water. We call these reclaimed lands "polders." We began draining our polders nearly a thousand years ago. Today, we still have to keep pumping out the water that gradually seeps in. That's what our windmills used to be for, to drive the pumps to pump out the polders. Now we use steam, diesel, and electric pumps instead. In each polder there are lines of them, starting with those farthest from the sea, pumping the water in sequence until the last pump finally deposits it into a river or the ocean. And all of us, rich or poor, live down in the polders. It's not the case that rich people live safely up on top of the dikes while poor people live in the polder bottoms below sea level. If the dikes and pumps fail, we'll all drown together.

Throughout human history, all peoples have been connected to some other peoples, living together in virtual polders. For the ancient Maya, their polder consisted of most of the Yucatán and neighboring areas. When the Classic Maya cities collapsed in the southern Yucatán, refugees may have reached the northern Yucatán, but probably not the Valley of Mexico, and certainly not Florida. Today, our whole world has become one polder, such that events in even Afghanistan and Somalia affect Americans. We do indeed differ from the Maya, but not in ways we might like: we have a much larger population, we have more potent destructive technology, and we face the risk of a worldwide rather than a local decline. Fortunately, we also differ from the Maya in that we know their fate, and they did not. Perhaps we can learn.

Understanding the Text

1. What are the three "dangerous misconceptions" the author refers to regarding the lack of seriousness about a healthy environment?

2. What were some factors that influenced the Mayans' success? What were some of their downfalls?

3. According to Diamond, why is it important that we concern ourselves with the problems of third-world countries as well as our own?

4. Near the end of the article, Diamond lists several reasons why past societies failed to anticipate problems (pars. 30–34). What are these reasons? Which seems most damaging to a society? In what ways is our own society failing to anticipate such problems?

Reflection and Response

5. Describe the tone Diamond uses and the effect it has on your opinions.

6. This article discusses overpopulation as a major problem. Do you agree with Diamond's perspective? Do you think something should be done about the problem? Why or why not?

7. World leaders are often blamed for the problems of a society. People say, "Well, I would have done things differently." If you were a world leader, how would you address some of the problems Diamond describes in the article?

8. In what ways is Diamond's article about sustainability? How can an understanding of history help us to make more sustainable decisions for the future?

Making Connections

9. Diamond writes that "those with faith assume that new technology won't cause any new problems" (par. 6). In what ways does technology help us advance as a society? In what ways does it cause problems that might affect future sustainability and our environment?

10. In 1979, China passed a law that couples were allowed to have only one child. Research this law and its current state today. Did it work? Would a law like this work in the United States? Should such a law be enforced nationally or even globally?

Language Diversity Is Highest in Biodiversity Hotspots

Russell Mittermeier

Russell Mittermeier is a prominent environmentalist; he also studies primates and amphibians. He holds a Ph.D. from Harvard University in biological anthropology and has served as president of Conservation International since 1989. He was named a "Hero for the Planet" by *Time* magazine in 1998. Mittermeier has conducted environmental research studies in more than twenty countries, focusing specifically on Madagascar and the Atlantic forest region of Brazil. He has published hundreds of articles and more than a dozen books, including *Hotspots* (2000) and *Wilderness* (2012).

In this article for the *Huffington Post* from 2012, Mittermeier draws from his extensive travels to explain the link between biodiversity and human cultural diversity. He addresses the ways in which a culture's language affects the individuals in that culture, as well as the relationship between languages and ecosystems. As you read the article, think about the connections between linguistic and biological diversity. How are these two things connected?

In my decades of traveling the world, I've gotten to see firsthand many of the fascinating human cultures inhabiting our planet, from the Kayapó of the Brazilian Amazon to the San people of the Kalahari to the multitude of cultures of Melanesia.

Many people from these cultures, including a wide variety of indigenous peoples, live in the most biologically rich regions of our planet — regions that hold the key to maintaining global biodiversity and ensuring the continued flow of ecosystem services — such as fresh water, pollination and clean air — that are essential to the more than 7 billion of us now living on Earth.

Yet as globalization moves forward, many of these traditional and indigenous communities seem to be forgotten or cheated out of the equitable distribution of benefits derived from the ecosystem services they steward. Even worse, as many of these vital habitats and territories bow to the pressures of economic development, so too does our unique cultural heritage, which is ever more endangered.

As conservation scientists, we have always assumed a strong linkage between biodiversity and human cultural diversity, but it's never been quantified in a way that demonstrates how strongly the two go hand in hand. To remedy this, I and several colleagues recently published a paper in the journal *Proceedings of the National Academy of*

Sciences[1] on the strong and fundamental connections between biodiversity and the diversity of human languages.

There is some discussion regarding the extent to which languages 5 are a good surrogate for human cultural diversity, but it would be hard to find a better indicator. Languages distinguish one cultural group from another, they derive from and reflect the world view of each group of people, and they are a source of pride and a record of history that sets each community apart from even its closest neighbors. Consequently, when we decided to look at the linkages between biodiversity and human cultural diversity, we chose languages as the best manifestation of the diversity of the world's peoples.

The results of our study — carried out by Larry Gorenflo from Penn State University, Suzanne Romaine from Oxford University, and Kristen Walker-Painemilla and myself from Conservation International (CI) — were quite remarkable. We began with the best available database on human linguistic diversity from SIL International, which recognizes some 6,900 languages still spoken on our planet. We looked to see how these were distributed globally, especially in relation to the highest priority areas for terrestrial biodiversity — the 35 biodiversity hotspots and the five high biodiversity wilderness areas that have been central to CI's conservation strategy for the past quarter century.

The biodiversity hotspots are the places on our planet — such as Madagascar, the Philippines, the Tropical Andes and South Africa's Cape Region — that have lost more than 70 percent of their original natural vegetation and yet still contain high concentrations of endemic species found nowhere else on Earth. Collectively, at least 50 percent of plants and more than 42 percent of vertebrates found in the hotspots are endemics found nowhere else. The planet's high biodiversity wilderness areas — places like Amazonia, the Congo Forests and the Island of New Guinea — are also rich in biodiversity, but are distinguished by still being 70 percent or more intact.

Together, hotspots and high biodiversity wilderness areas are home to at least 67.1 percent of all plants and 50.2 percent of all vertebrate animals. They once covered about 24 percent of Earth's land surface, but today that coverage has dwindled to an alarming 8.1 percent. What's more, if one looks at the endangered species — those at

---

[1]L.J. Gorenflo, Suzanne Romaine, Russell A. Mittermeier, and Kristen Walker-Painemilla. (2012). "Co-occurrence of linguistic and biological diversity in biodiversity hotspots and high biodiversity wilderness areas." *PNAS 109*(21): 8032–8037.

greatest risk of disappearing in the next few decades — we find that between 82–90 percent of the three groups of vertebrates (birds, mammals and amphibians) for which we have the best information are restricted to these priority areas.

Yes, that's a lot of numbers, but the bottom line is: These biodiversity hotspots and wilderness areas must be among our top priorities for terrestrial conservation if we hope to preserve Earth's natural ecosystem services and biodiversity for future generations of people.

Now consider the correlations and added benefits to language diversity. In our research, we found to our great surprise that these areas of exceptionally high biodiversity are also home to an amazing 70 percent (4,824) of the world's known languages. What is more, many of these languages are also in danger of extinction; other research indicates that 50–90 percent of known languages will have disappeared before the end of the century. 10

If we look at the languages — and the cultures they represent — that are most at risk of disappearing this century, we find that more than 30 percent of languages spoken by fewer than 10,000 people and almost 28 percent of those spoken by fewer than 1,000 people are found in the hotspots and high biodiversity wilderness areas. This means that nearly two-thirds of languages spoken by fewer than 10,000 people are found only in these priority regions for biodiversity, a large portion of them indigenous groups that are still highly dependent on natural ecosystems for their daily needs.

There are numerous theories about why this connection between species and language diversity exists. One possibility is that access to plentiful, diverse resources in places like biodiversity hotspots reduces the likelihood of distinct groups of people needing to communicate and share resources with other groups. Another theory suggests that during the time of colonization, European countries mostly focused on expanding into regions with temperate climates, therefore limiting contact with people in tropical areas where most of the high biological and linguistic diversity still occurs. For example, the highlands of New Guinea — the island with the highest linguistic diversity on Earth — were not explored by the outside world until the early 1930s.

Regardless of the reason behind it, at its most basic level this finding further reinforces an ethos that we have at CI: "People need nature to

> "To prevent language extinctions, we must redouble our efforts to prevent biodiversity hotspots and wilderness areas from being converted for short-term gain."

thrive." It also shows that we can have real win-win approaches in which efforts to conserve nature and ensure the integrity of human cultures can go hand in hand.

At the Rio+20 conference next month [July 2013], discussions about the development of healthy sustainable economies will be in the global spotlight. The key message at the heart of these discussions should be that integrating conservation of nature and development initiatives is absolutely essential to maintain the full range of life on Earth, including the amazing diversity, traditions and values of human cultures.

To prevent language extinctions, we must redouble our efforts to   15
prevent biodiversity hotspots and wilderness areas from being converted for short-term gain. If we can do this, I believe that we'll have a much better chance of saving the language diversity and cultural heritage of our own species.

Understanding the Text

1. According to Mittermeier, what are the consequences of globalization on indigenous peoples?
2. Why are languages such an important part of culture?
3. What are biodiversity hotspots?
4. What were some of the findings of the Conservation International study?

Reflection and Response

5. Why is it important to preserve lesser-used languages?
6. What does Mittermeier hope to achieve in the future?
7. What is the connection between species and language diversity? Discuss some of the theories that explain this connection that are found in Mittermeier's article.
8. In what ways is language preservation a sustainability issue?

Making Connections

9. How is language an important part of your own culture? How are your beliefs and ideas tied to the language you speak?
10. Do some research on an indigenous tribal language. How does this language reflect the culture's belief system? How is it tied to the natural environment?

4 | How Is Sustainability Connected to Local and Urban Environments?

Sustainability often addresses the need for preserving the natural world, recognizing the value of forests, oceans, wildlife, and natural ecosystems. As the introduction to this book explains, our current definitions of sustainability are closely tied to our historical and cultural relationship with nature. However, sustainability also focuses on creating and implementing sustainable practices in cities, suburbs, and other urban or industrial areas. Sustainability is about preserving resources and maintaining processes that are cyclical, repeatable, and enduring — the concept remains the same whether the focus is on the long-term biodiversity of a wetland or on the development of a shopping mall. Natural and urban environments are all part of the same global system; in fact, as should be clear by now, all environments are deeply enmeshed and interrelated in one way or another.

This chapter focuses on the ways sustainability is connected to local, urban, and industrial environments and processes. Many of the reading selections deal with things you encounter in your everyday life, including the food you eat, the products you use, the communities and spaces you inhabit, and even the profession you may choose. These selections draw attention to the three pillars of sustainability (social equity, environmental preservation, and economic viability) as vital interlocking components; all three factors must be considered in a sustainable human society. The People, Planet, Profit model is central to sustainability in developed cultural settings, and it can serve as a useful guide in your personal choices and decisions about your role in the world.

Kaplan helps to contextualize this subject by addressing the history of consumer culture in America. Westervelt extends this examination of society and sustainability by examining recycling. Pollan and Capra explore the important interrelations among food, health, and environments. MacMillan and Handwerk examine sustainable jobs, and Newport addresses sustainability on college campuses. The last two essays in the chapter (Heimbuch and Goleman/Norris) focus on personal electronics and their negative and positive impacts on sustainability, the environment, and our culture.

As you read the selections in this chapter, think about how sustainability affects your local environment and the ways in which you operate on a personal level. Other chapters in this book address sustainability in terms of national and global issues, but this chapter can help you consider sustainability as a subject that impacts you personally, immediately, and locally. Consequently, the reading selections have the potential to influence the choices you make in your everyday life.

The Gospel of Consumption

Jeffrey Kaplan

Jeffrey Kaplan is an activist and a writer who lives in the San Francisco Bay area. Kaplan writes regularly for *Orion* magazine, in which this article first appeared, as well as for the *Chicago Tribune* and *Yes!* magazine.

This article (2008) describes consumption in the early twentieth century, particularly the rapid rate at which goods were being produced. It goes on to explain how American consumption has changed since then in the light of consumerism. As you read, think about the idea of consumerism and what it means in modern society.

Private cars were relatively scarce in 1919 and horse-drawn conveyances were still common. In residential districts, electric streetlights had not yet replaced many of the old gaslights. And within the home, electricity remained largely a luxury item for the wealthy.

Just ten years later things looked very different. Cars dominated the streets and most urban homes had electric lights, electric flat irons, and vacuum cleaners. In upper-middle-class houses, washing machines, refrigerators, toasters, curling irons, percolators, heating pads, and popcorn poppers were becoming commonplace. And although the first commercial radio station didn't begin broadcasting until 1920, the American public, with an adult population of about 122 million people, bought 4,438,000 radios in the year 1929 alone.

But despite the apparent tidal wave of new consumer goods and what appeared to be a healthy appetite for their consumption among the well-to-do, industrialists were worried. They feared that the frugal habits maintained by most American families would be difficult to break. Perhaps even more threatening was the fact that the industrial capacity for turning out goods seemed to be increasing at a pace greater than people's sense that they needed them.

It was this latter concern that led Charles Kettering, director of General Motors Research, to write a 1929 magazine article called "Keep the Consumer Dissatisfied." He wasn't suggesting that manufacturers produce shoddy products. Along with many of his corporate cohorts, he was defining a strategic shift for American industry — from fulfilling basic human needs to creating new ones.

In a 1927 interview with the magazine *Nation's Business*, Secretary of Labor James J. Davis provided some numbers to illustrate a problem that the *New York Times* called "need saturation." Davis noted that "the textile mills of this country can produce all the cloth needed in six months' operation each year" and that 14 percent of the American shoe factories could produce a year's supply of footwear. The magazine went on to suggest, "It may be that the world's needs ultimately will be produced by three days' work a week."

Business leaders were less than enthusiastic about the prospect of a society no longer centered on the production of goods. For them, the new "labor-saving" machinery presented not a vision of liberation but a threat to their position at the center of power. John E. Edgerton, president of the National Association of Manufacturers, typified their response when he declared: "I am for everything that will make work happier but against everything that will further subordinate its importance. The emphasis should be put on work — more work and better work." "Nothing," he claimed, "breeds radicalism more than unhappiness unless it is leisure."

By the late 1920s, America's business and political elite had found a way to defuse the dual threat of stagnating economic growth and a radicalized working class in what one industrial consultant called "the gospel of consumption"— the notion that people could be convinced that however much they have, it isn't enough. President Herbert Hoover's 1929 Committee on Recent Economic Changes observed in glowing terms the results: "By advertising and other promotional devices . . . a measurable pull on production has been created which releases capital otherwise tied up." They celebrated the conceptual breakthrough: "Economically we have a boundless field before us; that there are new wants which will make way endlessly for newer wants, as fast as they are satisfied."

Today "work and more work" is the accepted way of doing things. If anything, improvements to the labor-saving machinery since the 1920s have intensified the trend. Machines *can* save labor, but only if they go idle when we possess enough of what they can produce. In other words, the machinery offers us an opportunity to work less, an opportunity that as a society we have chosen not to take. Instead, we have allowed the owners of those machines to define their purpose: not reduction of labor, but "higher productivity"— and with it the imperative to consume virtually everything that the machinery can possibly produce.

● ● ●

From the earliest days of the Age of Consumerism there were critics. One of the most influential was Arthur Dahlberg, whose 1932 book *Jobs, Machines, and Capitalism* was well known to policymakers and elected officials in Washington. Dahlberg declared that "failure to shorten the length of the working day . . . is the primary cause of our rationing of opportunity, our excess industrial plant, our enormous wastes of competition, our high pressure advertising, [and] our economic imperialism." Since much of what industry produced was no longer aimed at satisfying human physical needs, a four-hour workday, he claimed, was necessary to prevent society from becoming disastrously materialistic. "By not shortening the working day when all the wood is in," he suggested, the profit motive becomes "both the creator and satisfier of spiritual needs." For when the profit motive can turn nowhere else, "it wraps our soap in pretty boxes and tries to convince us that that is solace to our souls."

There was, for a time, a visionary alternative. In 1930 Kellogg Company, the world's leading producer of ready-to-eat cereal, announced that all of its nearly fifteen hundred workers would move from an eight-hour to a six-hour workday. Company president Lewis Brown and owner W. K. Kellogg noted that if the company ran "Four six-hour shifts . . . instead of three eight-hour shifts, this will give work and paychecks to the heads of three hundred more families in Battle Creek." 10

This was welcome news to workers at a time when the country was rapidly descending into the Great Depression. But as Benjamin Hunnicutt explains in his book *Kellogg's Six-Hour Day*, Brown and Kellogg wanted to do more than save jobs. They hoped to show that the "free exchange of goods, services, and labor in the free market would not have to mean mindless consumerism or eternal exploitation of people and natural resources." Instead "workers would be liberated by increasingly higher wages and shorter hours for the final freedom promised by the Declaration of Independence — the pursuit of happiness."

To be sure, Kellogg did not intend to stop making a profit. But the company leaders argued that men and women would work more efficiently on shorter shifts, and with more people employed, the overall purchasing power of the community would increase, thus allowing for more purchases of goods, including cereals.

A shorter workday did entail a cut in overall pay for workers. But Kellogg raised the hourly rate to partially offset the loss and provided for production bonuses to encourage people to work hard. The company eliminated time off for lunch, assuming that workers would rather work their shorter shift and leave as soon as possible. In a "personal letter" to employees, Brown pointed to the "mental income" of "the enjoyment of the surroundings of your home, the place you work, your neighbors, the other pleasures you have [that are] harder to translate into dollars and cents." Greater leisure, he hoped, would lead to "higher standards in school and civic . . . life" that would benefit the company by allowing it to "draw its workers from a community where good homes predominate."

It was an attractive vision, and it worked. Not only did Kellogg prosper, but journalists from magazines such as *Forbes* and *BusinessWeek* reported that the great majority of company employees embraced the shorter workday. One reporter described "a lot of gardening and community beautification, athletics and hobbies . . . libraries well patronized and the mental background of these fortunate workers . . . becoming richer."

A U.S. Department of Labor survey taken at the time, as well as   15
interviews Hunnicutt conducted with former workers, confirm this picture. The government interviewers noted that "little dissatisfaction with lower earnings resulting from the decrease in hours was expressed, although in the majority of cases very real decreases had resulted." One man spoke of "more time at home with the family." Another remembered: "I could go home and have time to work in my garden." A woman noted that the six-hour shift allowed her husband to "be with 4 boys at ages it was important."

Those extra hours away from work also enabled some people to accomplish things that they might never

"If we want to save the Earth, we must also save ourselves from ourselves."

have been able to do otherwise. Hunnicutt describes how at the end of her interview an eighty-year-old woman began talking about ping-pong. "We'd get together. We had a ping-pong table and all my relatives would come for dinner and things and we'd all play ping-pong by the hour." Eventually she went on to win the state championship.

Many women used the extra time for housework. But even then, they often chose work that drew in the entire family, such as canning. One recalled how canning food at home became "a family project" that "we all enjoyed," including her sons, who "opened up to talk freely." As Hunnicutt puts it, canning became the "medium for something more important than preserving food. Stories, jokes, teasing, quarreling, practical instruction, songs, griefs, and problems were shared. The modern discipline of alienated work was left behind for an older . . . more convivial kind of working together."

This was the stuff of a human ecology in which thousands of small, almost invisible, interactions between family members, friends, and neighbors create an intricate structure that supports social life in much the same way as topsoil supports our biological existence. When we allow either one to become impoverished, whether out of greed or intemperance, we put our long-term survival at risk.

Our modern predicament is a case in point. By 2005 per capita household spending (in inflation-adjusted dollars) was twelve times what it had been in 1929, while per capita spending for durable goods — the big stuff such as cars and appliances — was thirty-two times higher. Meanwhile, by 2000 the average married couple with children was working almost five hundred hours a year more than in 1979. And according to reports by the Federal Reserve Bank in 2004 and 2005, over 40 percent of American families spend more than they earn. The average household carries $18,654 in debt, not including home-mortgage debt, and the ratio of household debt to income is at record levels, having roughly doubled over the last two decades. We are quite literally working ourselves into a frenzy just so we can consume all that our machines can produce.

Yet we could work and spend a lot less and still live quite comfort-   20
ably. By 1991 the amount of goods and services produced for each hour of labor was double what it had been in 1948. By 2006 that figure had risen another 30 percent. In other words, if as a society we made a collective decision to get by on the amount we produced and consumed seventeen years ago, we could cut back from the standard forty-hour week to 5.3 hours per day — or 2.7 hours if we were willing to return to the 1948 level. We were already the richest country on the planet in 1948 and most of the world has not yet caught up to where we were then.

Rather than realizing the enriched social life that Kellogg's vision offered us, we have impoverished our human communities with a form of materialism that leaves us in relative isolation from family, friends, and neighbors. We simply don't have time for them. Unlike our great-grandparents who passed the time, we spend it. An outside observer might conclude that we are in the grip of some strange curse, like a modern-day King Midas whose touch turns everything into a product built around a microchip.

Of course not everybody has been able to take part in the buying spree on equal terms. Millions of Americans work long hours at poverty wages while many others can find no work at all. However, as advertisers well know, poverty does not render one immune to the gospel of consumption.

Meanwhile, the influence of the gospel has spread far beyond the land of its origin. Most of the clothes, video players, furniture, toys, and other goods Americans buy today are made in distant countries, often by underpaid people working in sweatshop conditions. The raw material for many of those products comes from clearcutting or strip mining or other disastrous means of extraction. Here at home, business activity is centered on designing those products, financing their manufacture, marketing them — and counting the profits.

• • •

Kellogg's vision, despite its popularity with his employees, had little support among his fellow business leaders. But Dahlberg's book had a major influence on Senator (and future Supreme Court justice) Hugo Black who, in 1933, introduced legislation requiring a thirty-hour workweek. Although Roosevelt at first appeared to support Black's bill, he soon sided with the majority of businessmen who opposed it. Instead, Roosevelt went on to launch a series of policy initiatives that led to the forty-hour standard that we more or less observe today.

By the time the Black bill came before Congress, the prophets of   25 the gospel of consumption had been developing their tactics and techniques for at least a decade. However, as the Great Depression deepened, the public mood was uncertain, at best, about the proper role of the large corporation. Labor unions were gaining in both public support and legal legitimacy, and the Roosevelt administration, under its New Deal° program, was implementing government regulation of industry on an unprecedented scale. Many corporate leaders saw the New Deal as a serious threat. James A. Emery, general counsel for the National Association of Manufacturers (NAM), issued a "call to arms" against the "shackles of irrational regulation" and the "back-breaking burdens of taxation," characterizing the New Deal doctrines as "alien invaders of our national thought."

In response, the industrial elite represented by NAM, including General Motors, the big steel companies, General Foods, DuPont, and others, decided to create their own propaganda. An internal NAM memo called for "re-selling all of the individual Joe Doakes on the advantages and benefits he enjoys under a competitive economy." NAM launched a massive public relations campaign it called the "American Way." As the minutes of a NAM meeting described it, the

---

New Deal: a recovery program enacted by the U.S. government from 1933 to 1938, designed to provide jobs and stimulate the economy during the Great Depression.

purpose of the campaign was to link "free enterprise in the public consciousness with free speech, free press and free religion as integral parts of democracy."

Consumption was not only the linchpin of the campaign; it was also recast in political terms. A campaign booklet put out by the J. Walter Thompson advertising agency told readers that under "private capitalism, the *Consumer,* the *Citizen* is boss," and "he doesn't have to wait for election day to vote or for the Court to convene before handing down his verdict. The consumer 'votes' each time he buys one article and rejects another."

According to Edward Bernays, one of the founders of the field of public relations and a principal architect of the American Way, the choices available in the polling booth are akin to those at the department store; both should consist of a limited set of offerings that are carefully determined by what Bernays called an "invisible government" of public-relations experts and advertisers working on behalf of business leaders. Bernays claimed that in a "democratic society" we are and should be "governed, our minds . . . molded, our tastes formed, our ideas suggested, largely by men we have never heard of."

NAM formed a national network of groups to ensure that the booklet from J. Walter Thompson and similar material appeared in libraries and school curricula across the country. The campaign also placed favorable articles in newspapers (often citing "independent" scholars who were paid secretly) and created popular magazines and film shorts directed to children and adults with such titles as "Building Better Americans," "The Business of America's People Is Selling," and "America Marching On."

Perhaps the biggest public relations success for the American Way 30 campaign was the 1939 New York World's Fair. The fair's director of public relations called it "the greatest public relations program in industrial history," one that would battle what he called the "New Deal propaganda." The fair's motto was "Building the World of Tomorrow," and it was indeed a forum in which American corporations literally modeled the future they were determined to create. The most famous of the exhibits was General Motors' 35,000-square-foot Futurama, where visitors toured Democracity, a metropolis of multilane highways that took its citizens from their countryside homes to their jobs in the skyscraper-packed central city.

For all of its intensity and spectacle, the campaign for the American Way did not create immediate, widespread, enthusiastic support for American corporations or the corporate vision of the future. But it did lay the ideological groundwork for changes that came after the Second World War, changes that established what is still commonly called our post-war society.

The war had put people back to work in numbers that the New Deal had never approached, and there was considerable fear that unemployment would return when the war ended. Kellogg workers had been working forty-eight-hour weeks during the war and the majority of them were ready to return to a six-hour day and thirty-hour week. Most of them were able to do so, for a while. But W. K. Kellogg and Lewis Brown had turned the company over to new managers in 1937.

The new managers saw only costs and no benefits to the six-hour day, and almost immediately after the end of the war they began a campaign to undermine shorter hours. Management offered workers a tempting set of financial incentives if they would accept an eight-hour day. Yet in a vote taken in 1946, 77 percent of the men and 87 percent of the women wanted to return to a thirty-hour week rather than a forty-hour one. In making that choice, they also chose a fairly dramatic drop in earnings from artificially high wartime levels.

The company responded with a strategy of attrition, offering special deals on a department-by-department basis where eight hours had pockets of support, typically among highly skilled male workers. In the culture of a post-war, post-Depression U.S., that strategy was largely successful. But not everyone went along. Within Kellogg there was a substantial, albeit slowly dwindling group of people Hunnicutt calls the "mavericks," who resisted longer work hours. They clustered in a few departments that had managed to preserve the six-hour day until the company eliminated it once and for all in 1985.

The mavericks rejected the claims made by the company, the 35 union, and many of their co-workers that the extra money they could earn on an eight-hour shift was worth it. Despite the enormous difference in societal wealth between the 1930s and the 1980s, the language the mavericks used to explain their preference for a six-hour workday was almost identical to that used by Kellogg workers fifty years earlier. One woman, worried about the long hours worked by her son, said, "He has no time to live, to visit and spend time with his family, and to do the other things he really loves to do."

Several people commented on the link between longer work hours and consumerism. One man said, "I was getting along real good, so there was no use in me working any more time than I had to." He added, "Everybody thought they were going to get rich when they got that eight-hour deal and it really didn't make a big difference. . . . Some went out and bought automobiles right quick and they didn't gain much on that because the car took the extra money they had."

The mavericks, well aware that longer work hours meant fewer jobs, called those who wanted eight-hour shifts plus overtime "work hogs." "Kellogg's was laying off people," one woman commented, "while some of the men were working really fantastic amounts of overtime — that's just not fair." Another quoted the historian Arnold Toynbee, who said, "We will either share the work, or take care of people who don't have work."

• • •

People in the Depression-wracked 1930s, with what seems to us today to be a very low level of material goods, readily chose fewer work hours for the same reasons as some of their children and grandchildren did in the 1980s: to have more time for themselves and their families. We could, as a society, make a similar choice today.

But we cannot do it as individuals. The mavericks at Kellogg held out against company and social pressure for years, but in the end the marketplace didn't offer them a choice to work less and consume less. The reason is simple: that choice is at odds with the foundations of the marketplace itself — at least as it is currently constructed. The men and women who masterminded the creation of the consumerist society understood that theirs was a political undertaking, and it will take a powerful political movement to change course today.

Bernays's version of a "democratic society," in which political deci- 40 sions are marketed to consumers, has many modern proponents. Consider a comment by Andrew Card, George W. Bush's former chief of staff. When asked why the administration waited several months before making its case for war against Iraq, Card replied, "You don't roll out a new product in August." And in 2004, one of the leading legal theorists in the United States, federal judge Richard Posner, declared that "representative democracy . . . involves a division between rulers and ruled," with the former being "a governing class," and the rest of us exercising a form of "consumer sovereignty" in the political sphere with "the power not to buy a particular product, a power to choose though not to create."

Sometimes an even more blatant antidemocratic stance appears in the working papers of elite think tanks. One such example is the prominent Harvard political scientist Samuel Huntington's 1975 contribution to a Trilateral Commission report on "The Crisis of Democracy." Huntington warns against an "excess of democracy," declaring that "a democratic political system usually requires some measure of apathy and noninvolvement on the part of some individuals and groups." Huntington notes that "marginal social groups, as in the case of the blacks, are now becoming full participants in the political system" and thus present the "danger of overloading the political system" and undermining its authority.

According to this elite view, the people are too unstable and ignorant for self-rule. "Commoners," who are viewed as factors of production at work and as consumers at home, must adhere to their proper roles in order to maintain social stability. Posner, for example, disparaged a proposal for a national day of deliberation as "a small but not trivial reduction in the amount of productive work." Thus he appears to be an ideological descendant of the business leader who warned that relaxing the imperative for "more work and better work" breeds "radicalism."

As far back as 1835, Boston workingmen striking for shorter hours declared that they needed time away from work to be good citizens: "We have rights, and we have duties to perform as American citizens and members of society." As those workers well understood, any meaningful democracy requires citizens who are empowered to create and re-create their government, rather than a mass of marginalized voters who merely choose from what is offered by an "invisible" government. Citizenship requires a commitment of time and attention, a commitment people cannot make if they are lost to themselves in an ever-accelerating cycle of work and consumption.

We can break that cycle by turning off our machines when they have created enough of what we need. Doing so will give us an opportunity to re-create the kind of healthy communities that were beginning to emerge with Kellogg's six-hour day, communities in which human welfare is the overriding concern rather than subservience to machines and those who own them. We can create a society where people have time to play together as well as work together, time to act politically in their common interests, and time even to argue over what those common interests might be. That fertile mix of human relationships is necessary for healthy human societies, which in turn are necessary for sustaining a healthy planet.

If we want to save the Earth, we must also save ourselves from ourselves. We can start by sharing the work *and* the wealth. We may just find that there is plenty of both to go around. 45

Understanding the Text

1. Why did some 1920s industrialists view saving and frugality as threats? What did they do to change this?
2. What happened when the Kellogg Company shortened the work day in 1930? Why and how did this practice stop?
3. What is the "gospel of consumption" that Kaplan refers to in the title of this essay?

Reflection and Response

4. This article suggests that people would be happier with a shorter work schedule. Do you agree? What are the arguments for and against a six-hour work day?
5. What is the relationship between working and democracy? Do you think that Americans would be more involved in politics if they spent less time working and spending money? Would this be a good thing or a bad thing?
6. How are working and consumption tied to issues of sustainability?

Making Connections

7. Do some research on the debates surrounding a shorter work week. Is this debate still active today? What are the arguments for and against it?
8. In what ways is consumption tied to the other concerns in this chapter? For instance, how are recycling, green jobs, personal electronics, and other issues essentially based on the ways in which we produce and consume things? How is consumption a sustainability issue? Compare and contrast the articles in this chapter based on the notion of consumption.

Can Recycling Be Bad for the Environment?

Amy Westervelt

Amy Westervelt is a freelance journalist based in Oakland, California, who writes about environmental issues. She is a contributing editor to *Forbes* magazine and won the prestigious Folio Eddie award in 2007.

Westervelt has written for *Condé Nast Traveler, BusinessWeek, Travel + Leisure* magazine, *Sustainable Industries,* and other publications.

This article, first published in *Forbes* in 2012, discusses the potential ramifications of recycling. Westervelt explains how public opinion about recycling has changed over the past decades and how that is tied to government recycling programs. As you read, think about how recycling is perceived in today's culture and whether you think this will change in the coming years.

It could be argued that the U.S. environmental movement started with recycling. For old-school environmentalists, recycling is such an integral part of the movement that it's difficult to separate the two. And in those early days, back in the 1980s, the cause was noble and pure: Why throw away products that could be new again? Why not turn trash into raw materials?

At a certain point, though, recycling developed something of a dark side from an environmental perspective. On the surface, it's still a good idea both to recycle waste and to design products and packaging with the idea of recycling them in a closed loop. Unfortunately, in its modern-day incarnation, recycling has also given the manufacturers of disposable items a way to essentially market overconsumption as environmentalism. Every year, reports come out touting rising recycling rates and neglecting to mention the soaring consumption that goes along with them. American consumers assuage any guilt they might feel about consuming mass quantities of unnecessary, disposable goods by dutifully tossing those items into their recycling bins and hauling them out to the curb each week.

Trade groups representing various packaging interests — plastic, paper, glass — have become the largest proponents and financial

A recycling station in Quebec, Canada.
© David Chapman/Design Pics/Corbis

sponsors of recycling. If you go to the Environmental Protection Agency's° website looking for statistics on packaging recycling, the stats on plastics recycling come from the American Plastics Council and the Society of the Plastics Industries, Inc. (SPI), both trade associations representing the plastics industry.

The plastics industry's interest in recycling is two-fold of course — on the one hand, by supporting recycling and helping to establish infrastructure for plastic recycling, the industry ensures a steady supply of new materials. On the other, it helps consumers to justify the consumption of more disposable plastic goods and packaged items if they can comfort themselves with the idea that whatever they toss in the bin will be recycled.

Environmental Protection Agency: an agency of the U.S. government that protects human health and the environment by writing and enforcing laws.

The thing is, recycling isn't the small operation it once was, it's   5
a commodity business that fluctuates with supply and demand. It's
also a global market, with recyclables collected in the United States
being shipped to wherever demand is highest (often China). A few
years ago, when demand for recycled paper products dropped, recyclers all over the country were warehousing stacks of cardboard,
waiting for the prices to turn around. "The hope is that eventually
the markets turn around and that the material is sold, but I have
heard of instances where it gets land-
filled, because a community doesn't
have the demand or the space or the
company to deal with it," says Gene
Jones, executive director of Southern
Waste Information Exchange — a nonprofit center for information about recycling waste.

> "Recycling has . . . given the manufacturers of disposable items a way to essentially market overconsumption as environmentalism."

Moreover, not everything that's "recyclable" actually gets recycled.
Even when you're dealing with easily recycled items like PET or
HDPE plastic (the plastics commonly used for bottles), or glass or
cardboard, first you've got to get consumers to dispose of the items
properly, then you've got to have a collection system in place (just
over half of U.S. cities have curbside recycling, keep in mind), and
then recyclers typically need to have a buyer lined up to justify recycling anything.

"There's a difference between things being recyclable and actually
being recycled," says Gerry Fishbeck, vice president of United Resource
Recovery Corporation (URRC), one of the largest recyclers in the
country. "It's centered around critical mass — is there enough of the
material out there? And even if there is, is it worth it for recyclers to
create a whole separate stream?"

Fishbeck cites PVC as a perfect example: Technically it's recyclable, but most recyclers don't handle the stuff. It can mimic PET
and thus easily get into a PET recycling stream, but when it's melted
down it will create brown particles in the resin, creating color problems with the resulting material. "So even though it's recyclable, that
material will get separated out and disposed of as waste at the recycling facility," Fishbeck explains.

Bioplastics° are another example. With the exception of bio-based
PET and HDPE, bioplastics fall into the recyclable but not recycled

bioplastics: a form of plastics made from renewable biomass sources, such as vegetable
fats and oils.

category. They are treated as contaminants of the recycling stream by most recyclers and separated out as waste. "If PLA (polylactic acid, the most common bioplastic today) gets into the recycling stream, it will cause contamination, it will be a defect, and that means we'll do everything we can to keep it out of the stream and it will become waste," Fishbeck says. "There's just not enough of it around to have the critical mass to justify getting it separated and recycled. It can be done, but it isn't."

Emissions are another sticky subject for recycling. In the case of   10
some materials — aluminum, corrugated cardboard, newspaper, dimensional lumber, and medium-density fiberboard — the net greenhouse gas emissions reductions enabled by recycling are actually greater than they would be if the waste source was simply reduced, according to the EPA. For others — glass, plastic — while in some cases the energy required to recycle versus making virgin material is lower, there are concerns about the particulates emitted by recycling factories. In recent studies of air quality in Oakland [California], recycling centers were, perhaps surprisingly, included amongst the city's polluters.

One metal recycling plant in West Oakland has been protested so much by local residents that it was set to close its doors and move out of the city until a local group came up with the idea of helping the plant move to a more industrial part of town. The city wanted to keep the plant within its limits not just to maintain its tax base and keep jobs, but to support the so-called hidden economy, wherein some local residents make a living collecting and redeeming recyclable materials.

It's a perfect illustration of the state of recycling today: Like any other business, it's neither altruistic nor completely self-serving; it comes with clear societal and environmental benefits — perhaps more so than many other businesses — but it also comes with some costs and cannot be considered a perfect solution to the United States' large and ever-growing consumption and waste problems.

Understanding the Text

1. What are the downsides to recycling as described in this article?
2. Why is the plastics industry so interested in recycling?
3. Are bioplastics and emissions recyclable or nonrecyclable? Why or why not?

Reflection and Response

4. Do you believe that recycling could have a negative impact on the environment? Back up your opinion with examples from the text or from other sources.

5. How do you think recycling will continue to change over the next decade?

6. Do you believe that recycling is an important sustainability issue? In what ways does the recycling debate depend on the concept and philosophy of sustainability?

Making Connections

7. Westervelt begins the article by describing the "early days" of recycling in the 1980s. Do some research to find out the similarities and differences between recycling then and now. What do we do differently today?

8. What sort of recycling efforts are taking place on your campus or in your community? Do you think that these efforts are entirely beneficial, or do you see negative impacts that are not accounted for? Explain your response.

Wendell Berry's Wisdom

Michael Pollan

Michael Pollan is an author, a journalist, an activist, and a journalism professor at the UC Berkeley Graduate School of Journalism. He studied English at Bennington College and Columbia University and has written six books about the importance of food to human society and the environment. Many of his essays have been published in the *New York Times*.

This article, which first appeared in 2009 in *The Nation*, a weekly newspaper focused on politics and culture, examines the "food movement" in the United States. Pollan identifies Wendell Berry as one of the first writers to begin the food conversation in this country. As you read, think about the role of politics in the food movement in the United States.

A few days after Michelle Obama broke ground on an organic vegetable garden on the South Lawn of the White House in March, the business section of the Sunday *New York Times* published a cover story bearing the headline "Is a Food Revolution Now in Season?" The article, written by the paper's agriculture reporter, said that "after being largely ignored for years by Washington, advocates of organic and locally grown food have found a receptive ear in the White House."

Certainly these are heady days for people who have been working to reform the way Americans grow food and feed themselves — the "food movement," as it is now often called. Markets for alternative kinds of food — local and organic and pastured — are thriving, farmers' markets are popping up like mushrooms and for the first time in many years the number of farms tallied in the Department of Agriculture's° census has gone up rather than down. The new secretary of agriculture has dedicated his department to "sustainability" and holds meetings with the sorts of farmers and activists who not many years ago stood outside the limestone walls of the USDA holding signs of protest and snarling traffic with their tractors. Cheap words, you might say; and it is true that, so far at least, there have been more words than deeds — but some of those words are astonishing. Like these: shortly before his election, Barack Obama told a reporter for *Time* that "our entire agricultural system is built on cheap oil"; he

---

Department of Agriculture: also known as the USDA; the U.S. federal executive department that is responsible for developing and carrying out government policy on farming, agriculture, forestry, and food.

went on to connect the dots between the sprawling monocultures of industrial agriculture and, on the one side, the energy crisis and, on the other, the healthcare crisis.

Americans today are having a national conversation about food and agriculture that would have been impossible to imagine even a few short years ago. To many Americans it must sound like a brand-new conversation, with its bracing talk about the high price of cheap food, or the links between soil and health, or the impossibility of a society eating well and being in good health unless it also farms well.

But the national conversation unfolding around the subject of food and farming really began in the 1970s, with the work of writers like Wendell Berry,° Frances Moore Lappé, Barry Commoner and Joan Gussow. All four of these writers are supreme dot-connectors, deeply skeptical of reductive science and far ahead not only in their grasp of the science of ecology but in their ability to think ecologically: to draw lines of connection between a hamburger and the price of oil, or between the vibrancy of life in the soil and the health of the plants, animals and people eating from that soil.

> "Americans today are having a national conversation about food and agriculture that would have been impossible to imagine even a few short years ago."

I would argue that the conversation got under way in earnest in 1971, when Berry published an article in *The Last Whole Earth Catalogue* introducing Americans to the work of Sir Albert Howard, the British agronomist whose thinking had deeply influenced Berry's own since he first came upon it in 1964. Indeed, much of Berry's thinking about agriculture can be read as an extended elaboration of Howard's master idea that farming should model itself on natural systems like forests and prairies, and that scientists, farmers and medical researchers need to reconceive "the whole problem of health in soil, plant, animal and man as one great subject." No single quotation appears more often in Berry's writing than that one, and with good reason: it is manifestly true (as even the most reductive scientists are coming to recognize) and, as a guide to thinking through so many of our problems, it is inexhaustible. 5

That same year, 1971, Lappé published *Diet for a Small Planet*, which linked modern meat production (and in particular the feeding

---

Wendell Berry: (b. 1934), an American academic; economic critic; farmer; and author of multiple novels, short stories, poems, and essays.

of grain to cattle) to the problems of world hunger and the environment. Later in the decade, Commoner implicated industrial agriculture in the energy crisis, showing us just how much oil we were eating when we ate from the industrial food chain; and Gussow explained
to her nutritionist colleagues that the problem of dietary health could
not be understood without reference to the problem of agriculture.

Looking back on this remarkably fertile body of work, which told
us all we needed to know about the true cost of cheap food and the
value of good farming, is to register two pangs of regret, one personal, the other more political: first, that as a young writer coming to
these subjects a couple of decades later, I was rather less original
than I had thought; and second, that as a society we failed to heed a
warning that might have averted or at least mitigated the terrible
predicament in which we now find ourselves.

For what would we give today to have back the "environmental
crisis" that Berry wrote about so prophetically in the 1970s, a time
still innocent of the problem of climate change? Or to have back the
comparatively manageable public health problems of that period, before obesity and type 2 diabetes became "epidemic"? (Most experts
date the obesity epidemic to the early 1980s.)

But history will show that we failed to take up the invitation to
begin thinking ecologically. As soon as oil prices subsided and Jimmy
Carter was rusticated to Plains, Georgia (along with his cardigan,
thermostat and solar panels), we went back to business — and agribusiness — as usual. In the mid-1980s Ronald Reagan removed
Carter's solar panels from the roof of the White House, and the issues
that the early wave of ecologically conscious food writers had raised
were pushed to the margins of national politics and culture.

When I began writing about agriculture in the late 1980s and   10
1990s, I quickly figured out that no editor in Manhattan thought the
subject timely or worthy of his or her attention, and that I would be
better off avoiding the word entirely and talking instead about food,
something people then still had some use for and cared about, yet
oddly never thought to connect to the soil or the work of farmers.

It was during this period that I began reading Berry's work
closely — avidly, in fact, because I found in it practical answers to
questions I was struggling with in my garden. I had begun growing a
little of my own food, not on a farm but in the backyard of a second
home in the exurbs of New York, and had found myself completely ill
prepared, especially when it came to the challenges posed by critters
and weeds. An obedient child of Thoreau and Emerson (both of
whom mistakenly regarded weeds as emblems of wildness and

gardens as declensions from nature), I honored the wild and didn't fence off my vegetables from the encroaching forest. I don't have to tell you how well that turned out. Thoreau did plant a bean field at Walden, but he couldn't square his love of nature with the need to defend his crop from weeds and birds, and eventually he gave up on agriculture. Thoreau went on to declare that "if it were proposed to me to dwell in the neighborhood of the most beautiful garden that ever human art contrived, or else of a dismal swamp, I should certainly decide for the swamp." With that slightly obnoxious declaration, American writing about nature all but turned its back on the domestic landscape. It's not at all surprising that we got better at conserving wilderness than at farming and gardening.

It was Wendell Berry who helped me solve my Thoreau problem, providing a sturdy bridge over the deep American divide between nature and culture. Using the farm rather than the wilderness as his text, Berry taught me I had a legitimate quarrel with nature — a lover's quarrel — and showed me how to conduct it without reaching for the heavy artillery. He relocated wildness from the woods "out there" (beyond the fence) to a handful of garden soil or the green shoot of a germinating pea, a necessary quality that could be not just conserved but cultivated. He marked out a path that led us back into nature, no longer as spectators but as full-fledged participants.

Obviously much more is at stake here than a garden fence. My Thoreau problem is another name for the problem of American environmentalism, which historically has had much more to say about leaving nature alone than about how we might use it well. To the extent that we're finally beginning to hear a new, more neighborly conversation between American environmentalists and American farmers, not to mention between urban eaters and rural food producers, Berry deserves much of the credit for getting it started with sentences like these:

Why should conservationists have a positive interest in . . . farming? There are lots of reasons, but the plainest is: Conservationists eat. To be interested in food but not in food production is clearly absurd. Urban conservationists may feel entitled to be unconcerned about food production because they are not farmers. But they can't be let off so easily, for they are all farming by proxy. They can eat only if land is farmed on their behalf by somebody somewhere in some fashion. If conservationists will attempt to resume responsibility for their need to eat, they will be led back fairly directly to all their previous concerns for the welfare of nature.
— *"Conservationist and Agrarian," 2002.*

That we are all implicated in farming — that, in Berry's now-famous formulation, "eating is an agricultural act" — is perhaps his signal contribution to the rethinking of food and farming under way today. All those taking part in that conversation, whether in the White House or at the farmers' market, are deep in his debt.

Understanding the Text

1. What is the "food movement" and what are its goals?
2. What lessons did Pollan learn from Wendell Berry? How were those lessons connected to Henry David Thoreau?
3. What is Pollan's main point about food consumption and food production?

Reflection and Response

4. In what ways are many Americans "detached" from the foods they eat? Why is this a problem?
5. What is the relationship between American environmentalism and American farming? What does Pollan see happening today between environmentalists and farmers?
6. How is food tied to sustainability? Why would an article about food be included in a sustainability textbook like this one?

Making Connections

7. Do some research on the food movement in the United States. What are the central issues? What changes are taking place? What do you find most compelling or important?
8. What sort of food-related debates or changes are taking place on your campus or in your community? Where do you stand on these issues?
9. Pollan points to Michelle Obama's efforts to highlight food issues in America. Do some research on food as a political and social issue, drawing on Obama's work or some other source.

Ecology and Community

Fritjof Capra

Fritjof Capra is an Austrian-born physicist, writer, and systems theorist. He is a founding director of the Center for Ecoliteracy in Berkeley, California, and is on the faculty of Schumacher College, an international center for ecological studies in London, England. Capra is the author of several best-selling books, including *The Tao of Physics*, *Steering Business toward Sustainability*, edited with Gunter Pauli, and *The Web of Life*.

Capra's work focuses on the networked relationships of living systems, and he speaks regularly on holistic and systems thinking to professional and academic audiences. The following essay was first delivered to a group of school administrators in 1994, and it provides an overview of the basic principles of ecology. As you read the essay, think about what Capra is saying about life, communities, and the ways we think about our place in the world.

The understanding of community is extremely important today, not only for our emotional and spiritual well-being, but for the future of our children and, in fact, for the survival of humanity.

As you well know, we are faced with a whole series of global environmental problems which are harming the biosphere and human life in alarming ways that may soon become irreversible. The great challenge of our time is to create sustainable communities; that is, social and cultural environments in which we can satisfy our needs without diminishing the chances of future generations.

In our attempts to build and nurture sustainable communities we can learn valuable lessons from ecosystems, which *are* sustainable communities of plants, animals, and microorganisms. In over four billion years of evolution, ecosystems have developed the most intricate and subtle ways of organizing themselves so as to maximize sustainability.

There are laws of sustainability which are natural laws, just as the law of gravity is a natural law. In our science in past centuries, we have learned a lot about the law of gravity and similar laws of physics, but we have not learned very much about the laws of sustainability. If you go up to a high cliff and step off it, disregarding the laws of gravity, you will surely die. If we live in a community, disregarding the laws of sustainability, as a community we will just as surely die in the long run. These laws are just as stringent as the laws of physics, but until recently they have not been studied.

The law of gravity, as you know, was formalized by Galileo° and 5
Newton°, but people knew about stepping off cliffs long before Galileo and Newton. Similarly, people knew about the laws of sustainability long before ecologists in the twentieth century began to discover them. In fact, what I'm going to talk about today is nothing that
a ten-year-old Navajo boy or Hopi girl who grew up in a traditional
Native American community would not understand and know. In
preparing this presentation, I discov-
ered that if you really try to distill the
essence of the laws of sustainability,
it's very simple. The more you go to
the essence, the simpler it is.

"The great challenge of our
time is to create sustainable
communities; that is, social
and cultural environments in
which we can satisfy our
needs without diminishing
the chances of future
generations."

What I want you to understand is
the essence of how ecosystems organize themselves. You can abstract certain principles of organization and call
them the principles of ecology; but it
is not a list of principles that I want
you to learn. It's a pattern of organiza-
tion I want you to understand. You will see that whenever you for-
malize it and say, "This is a key principle, and this is a key principle,"
you don't really know where to start, because they all hang together.
You have to understand all of them at the same time. So, when you
teach the principles of ecology in school, you can't say, "In third
grade we do interdependence and then in fourth grade we do diversity." One cannot be taught or practiced without the others.

What I'm going to do, then, is describe how ecosystems organize
themselves. I'll present to you the very essence of their principles of
organization.

Relationships

When you look at an ecosystem — say at a meadow or a forest — and
you try to understand what it is, the first thing you recognize is that
there are many species there. There are many plants, many animals,
many microorganisms. And they're not just an assemblage or collection of species. They are a community, which means that they are
interdependent; they depend on one another. They depend on one
another in many ways, but the most important way in which they

Galileo: (1564–1642), Italian physicist and astronomer.
Newton: Sir Isaac Newton (1642–1727), English philosopher and mathematician; formu-
lator of the law of gravity.

depend on one another is a very existential way — they eat one another. That's the most existential interdependence you can imagine.

Indeed, when ecology was developed in the 1920s, one of the first things people studied were feeding relationships. At first, ecologists formulated the concept of food chains. They studied big fish eating smaller fish, which eat still smaller fish, and so on. Soon these scientists discovered that these are not linear chains but cycles, because when the big animals die, they in turn are eaten by insects and bacteria. The concept shifted from food chains to food cycles.

And then they found that various food cycles are actually inter- 10
linked, so the focus again shifted, from food cycles to food webs or networks. In ecology, this is what people are now talking about. They're talking about food webs, networks of feeding relationships.

These are not the only examples of interdependence. The members of an ecological community, for example, also give shelter to one another. Birds nest in trees and fleas nest in dogs and bacteria attach themselves to the roots of plants. Shelter is another important kind of interdependent relationship.

To understand ecosystems, then, we need to understand relationships. That's a key aspect of the new thinking. Also, always keep in the back of your minds that when I talk about ecosystems I'm talking about communities. The reason we're studying ecosystems here is so that we can learn about building sustainable human communities.

So we need to understand relationships, and this is something that runs counter to the traditional scientific enterprise in Western culture. Traditionally in science, we have tried to measure and weigh things, but relationships cannot be measured and weighed. Relationships need to be mapped. You can draw a map of relationships that shows the connections between different elements or different members of the community. When you do that, you discover that certain configurations of relationships appear again and again. These are what we call patterns. The study of relationships leads us to the study of patterns. A pattern is a configuration of relationships appearing repeatedly.

The Study of Form and Pattern

So this study of ecosystems leads us to the study of relationships, which leads us to the notion of pattern. And here we discover a tension that has been characteristic in Western science and philosophy throughout the ages. It is a tension between the study of substance and the study of form. The study of substance starts with the question,

What is it made of? The study of form starts with the question, What is its pattern? Those are two very different approaches. Both of them have existed throughout our scientific and philosophical tradition. The study of pattern began with the Pythagoreans° in Greek antiquity, and the study of substance began at the same time with Parmenides, Democritus, and with various philosophers who asked: What is matter made of? What is reality made of? What are its ultimate constituents? What is its essence?

In asking this question, the Greeks came up with the idea of four 15 fundamental elements: earth, fire, air, and water. In modern times, these were recast into the chemical elements; many more than four, but still the basic elements of which all matter consists. In the nineteenth century, Dalton° identified the chemical elements with atoms, and with the rise of atomic physics in our century the atoms were reduced to nuclei and electrons, and the nuclei to other subatomic particles.

Similarly, in biology the basic elements first were organisms, or species. In the eighteenth and nineteenth centuries there were very complex classification schemes of species. Then, with the discovery of cells as the common elements in all organisms, the focus shifted from organisms to cells. Cellular biology was at the forefront of biology. Then the cell was broken down into its macromolecules, into the enzymes and proteins and amino acids and so on, and molecular biology was the new frontier. In all of this endeavor, the question always was: What is it made of? What is its ultimate substance?

At the same time, throughout the same history of science, the study of pattern was always there, and at various times it came to the forefront, but most times it was neglected, suppressed, or sidelined by the study of substance. As I said, when you study pattern, you need to map the pattern, whereas the study of substance is the study of quantities that can be measured. The study of pattern, or of form, is the study of quality, which requires visualizing and mapping. Form and pattern must be visualized.

This is a very important aspect of studying patterns, and it is the reason why, every time the study of pattern was in the forefront, artists contributed significantly to the advancement of science. Perhaps the two most famous examples are Leonardo da Vinci, whose scientific life was a study of pattern, and the German poet Goethe in the

Pythagoreans: pertaining to Pythagoras (c. 570–490 BCE), an ancient Greek philosopher and mathematician.
Dalton: John Dalton (1766–1844), English chemist and physicist.

eighteenth century, who made significant contributions to biology through his study of pattern.

This is very important to us as parents and educators, because the study of pattern comes naturally to children; to visualize pattern, to draw pattern, is natural. In traditional schooling this has not been encouraged. Art has been sort of on the side. We can make this a central feature of ecoliteracy: the visualization and study of pattern through the arts.

Now, recognizing that the study of pattern is central to ecology, we can then ask the crucial question: What is the pattern of life? At all levels of life — organisms, parts of organisms, and communities of organisms — we have patterns, and we can ask: What is the characteristic pattern of life? . . . I could give you a fairly technical description of the characteristics of the pattern of life; but here I want to concentrate on its very essence.

Networks

The first step in answering this question, and perhaps the most important step, is a very easy and obvious one: the pattern of life is a network pattern. Wherever you see the phenomenon of life, you observe networks. Again, this was brought into science with ecology in the 1920s when people studied food webs — networks of feeding relationships. They began to concentrate on the network pattern. Later on, in mathematics, a whole set of tools was developed to study networks. Then scientists realized that the network pattern is not only characteristic of ecological communities as a whole, but of every member of that community. Every organism is a network of organs, of cells, of various components; and every cell is a network of similar components. So what you have is networks within networks. Whenever you look at life you look at networks.

Then you can ask: What is a network and what can we say about networks? The first thing you see when you draw a network is that it is nonlinear; it goes in all directions. So the relationships in a network pattern are nonlinear relationships. Because of this nonlinearity, an influence or message may travel around a cyclical path and come back to its origin.

In a network you have cycles and you have closed loops; these loops are feedback loops. The important concept of feedback, which was discovered in the 1940s, in cybernetics, is intimately connected with the network pattern. Because you have feedback in networks, because an influence travels around a loop and comes back, you can have self-regulation; and not only self-regulation but self-organization. When you have a network — for instance, a community — it can regulate itself. The community can learn from its mistakes, because the mistakes travel and come back along these feedback loops. Then you can learn, and next time around you can do it differently. Then the effect will come back again and you can learn again, in steps.

So the community can organize itself and can learn. It does not need an outside authority to tell it "You guys did something wrong." A community has its own intelligence, its own learning capability. In fact, every living community is always a learning community. Development and learning are always part of the very essence of life because of this network pattern.

Self-Organization

As soon as you understand that life is networks, you understand that   25
the key characteristic of life is self-organization, so if somebody asks you, "What is the essence of life? What is a living organism all about?" you could say, "It is a network and because it is a network it can organize itself." This answer is simple, but it's at the very forefront of science today. And it is not generally known. When you go around in academic departments, this is not the answer you will hear. What you will hear is "Amino Acids," "Enzymes," and things like that; very complex information, because that is the inquiry into substance: What is it made of?

It is important to understand that, in spite of the great triumphs of molecular biology, biologists still know very little about how we breathe or how a wound heals or how an embryo develops into an organism. All of the coordinating activities of life can only be grasped when life is understood as a self-organizing network. So self-organization is the very essence of life, and it's connected with the network pattern.

When you look at the network of an ecosystem, at all these feedback loops, another way of seeing it, of course, is as recycling. Energy and matter are passed along in cyclical flows. The cyclical flows of energy and matter — that's another principle of ecology. In fact, you can define an ecosystem as a community where there is no waste.

Of course, this is an extremely important lesson we must learn from nature. This is what I focus on when I talk to business people about introducing ecoliteracy into business. Our businesses are now designed in a linear way — to consume resources, produce goods, and throw them away. We need to redesign our businesses to imitate the cyclical processes of nature rather than to create waste. Paul Hawken° has recently written about this very eloquently in his book *The Ecology of Commerce.*

So we have interdependence, network relationships, feedback loops; we have cyclical flows; and we have many species in a community. All of this together implies cooperation and partnership. As various nutrients are passed along through the ecosystem, the relationships we observe are many forms of partnership, of cooperation. In the nineteenth century, the Darwinists and Social Darwinists talked about the competition in nature, the fight — "Nature, red in tooth and claw." In the twentieth century ecologists have discovered that in the self-organization of ecosystems cooperation is actually much more important than competition. We constantly observe partnerships, linkages, associations, species living inside one another depending on one another for survival. Partnership is a key characteristic of life. Self-organization is a collective enterprise.

We see that these principles — interdependence, network patterns, feedback loops, the cyclical flows of energy and matter, recycling, cooperation, partnership — are all different aspects, different perspectives on one and the same phenomenon. This is how ecosystems organize themselves in a sustainable way.

30

Paul Hawken: (b. 1946), environmentalist, entrepreneur, journalist, and best-selling author.

Understanding the Text

1. In paragraph 2, Capra offers a short definition of *sustainable communities*. What is this definition? Do you agree with how he's defined the concept?

2. How does Capra compare ecosystems in nature to human communities? Why does he make this comparison? In what ways are the ecosystems and the human communities connected?

3. Capra uses four subheads in the article: "Relationships," "The Study of Form and Pattern," "Networks," and "Self-Organization." How do these four sections explain the essence of ecosystems?

Reflection and Response

4. What is Capra's goal with this essay? How does his writing style help him accomplish this goal? Who is his audience?

5. In paragraph 23, under Networks, Capra talks about self-regulation and self-organization. How do these two terms relate to sustainability?

6. What does Capra suggest about Western culture and Western ways of thinking? In what ways would Capra suggest we change our conceptions of life and communities?

Making Connections

7. Find other definitions of sustainability, either in this book or through online research. How are these definitions similar to or different from what Capra presents?

8. Capra mentions two artists who contributed significantly to the advancement of science: Leonardo da Vinci and Johann Wolfgang von Goethe. Do a little research on one or both of these men. How did they combine art and science? What can we learn about the patterns of life through their work?

9. This essay argues for a nontraditional approach to education — one focusing on ecology, interconnections, and sustainable thinking. What do you think about such an approach? Can you find examples of it being used in education today?

Switching to Green-Collar Jobs

Douglas MacMillan

Douglas MacMillan is a reporter for Bloomberg News and Bloomberg Businessweek in San Francisco. Previously, he was a staff writer for *Businessweek*, covering technology, careers, and lifestyle. Prior to working at *Businessweek*, MacMillan was an intern at *Rolling Stone* and for the advertising trade publication Adotas.com. He is a graduate of Vanderbilt University.

This article (2008) examines the lives of people who have changed their careers to be more environmentally friendly. MacMillan writes that many people are making mid-career changes from office jobs to environmentally based ones. As you read, think about some reasons these career changes may be occurring.

On December 6, Berkeley (Calif.) nonprofit Avoided Deforestation° Partners hosted a panel at the United Nations Climate Change Conference in Bali on the topic of REDD (reducing emissions from deforestation and forest degradation). The group's 55-year-old founder, Jeff Horowitz, took the stage and addressed a crowded room of environmental movers and shakers on his vision for the protection of rainforests. Horowitz describes the moment as a career milestone. But he is no lifelong activist; only a year before, he was a highly paid, sought-after architect in San Francisco.

A growing number of midlife career-changers like Horowitz are trading in their nine-to-fives for jobs more in line with their convictions and concerns for Mother Earth. So-called "green-collar jobs" are on the rise — the current tally of 8.5 million U.S. jobs in renewable-energy and energy-efficiency industries could grow to as many as 40 million by 2030, according to a November report commissioned by the American Solar Energy Society.

> "So-called 'green-collar jobs' are on the rise — the current tally of 8.5 million jobs . . . could grow to as many as 40 million by 2030."

And the burgeoning industry is claiming scores of experienced workers who can put to use the skills they've acquired in more established fields such as construction, finance, and marketing. In some cases, the high demand for green career-changers translates into a

---

Avoided Deforestation: reducing greenhouse gas emissions by not clearing forests.

larger paycheck. But more often, the satisfaction of making a positive difference in the world is enough of a boost.

Put Your Skills in a Green Context

Many people are tired of their jobs and know they want to give back to the environment, but have no idea where to look for a green-collar job. That's where consultants such as Marie Kerpan can help out. Weary of her own job as a career adviser at New York outplacement firm Drake Beam Morin (DKBMF), and anticipating the looming trend of green career-changers, Kerpan in 2000, positioned herself as an environmental career consultant — the first, she claims, of her kind.

Since then, her company, Green Careers, has helped thousands of 5 people assess what cause their skills and interests are best suited to — which could be anything from renewable energy to water conservation — and has helped them get hired. Most of her clients come from middle management or higher, and are seeking what she calls a path-of-least-resistance move, "doing something you already know how to do and putting it in the context of the green agenda," she explains.

One former human resources manager at General Electric (GE),° for example, had "a whole kitbag of tools, and just had to figure out how to use them" in a green job. The solution was simple enough: She landed a post as human resources manager at an organic foods company.

Awakening an Inner Passion

But if someone prefers his green second career to be a completely new experience, that's okay too, says Kerpan, "This is a new frontier, and there's also a lot more latitude to make a more radical change."

Such was the case with architect-turned-activist Horowitz. As partner in San Francisco's KMD Architects, he seemed to have it all: a central role in high-profile commercial projects such as Two Rodeo Drive in Los Angeles, frequent travel to exotic destinations, and enough downtime to mind his own Sonoma Valley vineyard. But through his involvement with Equator Environmental, a for-profit group he helped to found with nephew Gerrity Lansing, Horowitz awakened an inner passion for the environment. The creation and

---

General Electric: an American corporation best known for generating and transmitting electric power.

sale of carbon credits, he realized, could make conserving rainforests a profitable enterprise.

A Different Kind of Bonus

So last year he left behind architecture altogether and started Avoided Deforestation Partners, a think tank aimed at realizing this goal through new international policy. While his day-to-day routine has changed dramatically — instead of leading a large internal team, he networks with contacts all over the world — some of his skills have carried over into his new career. Just as architect-Horowitz "was never satisfied unless [I] saw the project built and completed," activist-Horowitz strives toward real-world results, such as a plot of forest saved from the bulldozer.

Horowitz says his salary doesn't come close to what he used to   10
make as an architect. But he doesn't care — he'll take a menial paycheck if it means bringing about positive change in the world. And the way he describes his experience speaking at the UN Climate Change Conference —"It felt like we were at a rock-and-roll concert with 20,000 people and we were backstage with the lead singer"— makes it sound as if he had a better year-end bonus than most.

Understanding the Text

1. Why are people making mid-career changes from office jobs to environmentally based ones? List a few reasons.

2. What does Green Careers do? How is the organization tied to sustainability and the environment?

3. What are the benefits and disadvantages of a green job? Make a list of pros and cons and discuss them.

Reflection and Response

4. Would you ever consider taking a "green" job? What do you think you could gain from the experience? Would you take a green job over a higher-paying job that does not focus on the environment? How much of a pay cut would you be willing to consider to take such a job?

5. As we progress into the next decade, do you think green jobs will become more common? Explain why or why not.

Making Connections

6. Find the Web site for Green Careers or some other green company. List some things you find on the Web site that would encourage you to work for them. How do they market and promote their "green" perspective?

7. Research a particular type of "green job" that is related to your future career. Is this a growing area of employment? Would you pursue a specialization in a "green" area of your field? Why or why not?

"Blue Jobs" Key to Future Fisheries

Brian Handwerk

Brian Handwerk is a graduate of Bucknell University. A former National Geographic producer, he now lives in Amherst, New Hampshire, and works as a freelance writer for several publications, including *National Geographic News*. He wrote *Safe Drinking Water Is Essential* for the National Academy of Sciences; it can be found at drinking-water.org.

In this article, first published on the National Geographic Newswatch Web site in 2012, Handwerk defines "blue job" fisheries and how they are becoming increasingly necessary in order to protect our food supply. He also explains the methods used in sustainable fisheries to catch fish. As you read, consider the importance of consuming sustainably caught fish.

There are a lot of fish in the sea. But their numbers are no match for growing human appetites and the ultra-efficient fisheries° that have sprung up to feed our hunger. A shift towards "blue job" fisheries is urgently needed, experts say, if the oceans are to nourish future generations as they have in the past.

(Discussions are ongoing at Rio+20° on making international oceans policy more sustainable.)

About three billion people count on fish and other marine species as their primary source of protein, and about 8 percent of the world's population are fishermen. Until recently, many people believed that the ocean held so much marine life that even such huge numbers of humans could not deplete its bounty.

But since the mid 20th century industrial fishing operations have used ever-improving technology to fish farther, faster, and longer—rapidly emptying waters of seafood to satisfy the swelling hunger of Earth's growing population. Many fisheries have shown steep declines for decades and some studies estimate that populations of large ocean fish are just 10 percent of their pre-industrial levels.

Sustainability is the key concept for successful management of both 5 fish stocks and fisheries jobs themselves, said Rashid Sumaila, director of the Fisheries Center at the University of British Columbia. "Sustainable jobs, to me, are based on taking what the resource can withstand year in

---

fisheries: corporations or businesses engaged in raising or harvesting fish.
Rio+20: the third international conference on sustainable development aimed at reconciling the economic and environmental goals of the global community; hosted by Brazil in Rio de Janeiro, June 13–22, 2012.

The movement to make fisheries sustainable is creating "blue jobs."

B. Anthony Stewart/National Geographic Creative

and year out. That's crucial because right now at the moment we are kill-ing future jobs for current ones. That's not sustainable. That's not green jobs. You want the jobs you create today not to prevent future generations from having these jobs but we're front loading jobs because it's politi-cally more convenient."

Blue jobs fishermen use science-based stock management programs and only harvest sustainable levels of fish.

"Based on stock assessments we can estimate how much fish can be taken out safely, that's the total allowable catch," Sumaila said. "To me a green fishery is one that takes only the additional growth from a re-source, so that we don't eat up all the capital or the biomass base."

Blue fishermen also use environmentally friendly methods and gear rather than less enlightened techniques that not only harvest too many fish but destroy the habitat they need to survive and reproduce. Using long lines to hook-catch fish, for example, is a blue alternative to bottom-trawling with enormous drag nets.

"The nets just plow up the bottom of the entire ocean, which is crazy," said Sumaila. "It destroys the homes of the fish, the places where they can grow and live. Long lines are more selective and they are also good in the market — because those fish are caught nicely they fetch higher prices."

Fisheries managers can employ tools like marine reserves and pro- 10 tected areas and strict catch limits to achieve sustainability while providing blue jobs for generations to come. But they can only succeed if they can overcome pressures that continue to support unsustainable practices — like simply allowing too much fishing.

"Politics come into it, economics come into it. And most of the time we overdo it and that's why we have this fishing problem," Sumaila said.

Compounding this quandary is the international nature of the resource, which leads national fisheries to compete for their own interests — sometimes to the detriment of all. "The ocean is essentially one big global ocean," Sumaila said. "What you do on one side affects the other. The interests of nations do come into play but it's necessary to deal with this as a global problem."

Global factors are also growing the problem. Earth's surging population is putting increased strain on marine resources. And it's not just a matter of more mouths to feed, Sumaila said, but also a matter of changing tastes and the increasing ability to finance them. "In many parts of the world, Asia is a big one, incomes are rising so people have the money to buy more fish," Sumaila said. "So it's an increase in the total number of people but also an increase in consumption per capita of fish. And there just aren't enough fish in the sea."

> "A shift toward 'blue job' fisheries is urgently needed, experts say, if the oceans are to nourish future generations as they have in the past."

Aquaculture, also known as fish farming, can help to fill the gap. In fact today half of the world's fish supply isn't caught by anyone — it's farmed. As wild stocks decline and demand grows the role of aquaculture is sure to surge in the future, but it can't save us, Sumaila cautioned, because the practice has sustainability issues of its own. Blue fish farmers are needed.

Fish farms often pollute coastal waters and lakes with waste, some- 15 times creating ecological havoc, causing dead zones or unleashing disease on native populations. And many fish are raised on fish meal, which means someone has to catch and grind up countless wild fish, resulting in a zero sum or perhaps a net loss for the ocean resources consumed to produce "sustainable" farmed fish. Better, bluer methods are needed and some are already being developed. A few species, tilapia for example, can be raised primarily on renewable vegetarian feed.

But no matter how blue we can make fish farms, Sumaila cautioned, they can't take the place of our oceans.

"One thing I worry about with aquaculture is this feeling you get sometimes when you kind of read between the lines that we can let wild fish go because there is aquaculture," he said. "That scares me a lot, especially for poor and developing countries (where people depend on catching their own food). Whatever we do with aquaculture it should be complimentary to wild fisheries."

What can be done? Sumaila said consumers can make a big difference by choosing sustainably caught fish, identified by resources like the Monterey Bay Aquarium's Seafood Watch° program, and even by choosing to eat fish less often.

"Personally, I've been limiting how much fish I eat," he said. "I gave a talk at an AAAS meeting entitled 'Whose Fish Are You Eating — Yours or Your Grandchildren's?' And I often quote Adam Smith in these lectures, from his own 1766 Lecture on Jurisprudence. 'The Earth and the fullness of it belongs to every generation, and the preceding one can have no right to bind it up from posterity.' I think when it comes to our fish we have to weigh that and ultimately begin to think that way."

Monterey Bay Aquarium's Seafood Watch program: a program created by California's Monterey Bay Aquarium to help raise awareness of conservation of ocean resources.

Understanding the Text

1. Define "blue job." How are "blue" jobs similar to "green" jobs?
2. Why are blue-job fisheries so important?
3. What makes a blue-job fishery different from a regular fishery?

Reflection and Response

4. Do you think more people will choose careers in "blue" fishing in the coming decade? Why or why not?
5. How can consumers help protect the fish in our oceans?
6. In what ways is sustainability an important issue for the commercial fishing industry? What strategies is the industry using to become more sustainable? What are the challenges of becoming more sustainable?

Making Connections

7. Research other environmentally sustainable careers. How do they compare to blue fisheries?
8. Compare blue fisheries to other nonsustainable forms of commercial fishing. How could blue fisheries compete against them? What could be done to move toward a more sustainable fishing industry worldwide?

Campus Sustainability: It's About People

Dave Newport

Dave Newport is the director of the Environmental Center at the University of Colorado Boulder. He is also the secretary of the board of directors of the Association for the Advancement of Sustainability in Higher Education. He previously served as director of the University of Florida's Office of Sustainability, where he researched and published higher education's first sustainability report that met global business standards.

This article originally appeared in 2012 in *The Chronicle of Higher Education*, a magazine and Web site for college faculty, staff, and administrators. The article explains the importance of sustainable college campuses and the movement intended to increase awareness of sustainability issues. Newport explains what some colleges are doing to increase sustainability on campus. As you read, think about sustainability on your own college campus and what improvements or changes could be made.

In 2004, Michael Shellenberger and Ted Nordhaus, two prominent environmentalists, published an article that was part eulogy and part warning for the green movement. In the essay, "The Death of Environmentalism," they asserted that if environmentalists are to survive, they must create the "I have a dream" eco-vision of the future, not the "I have a nightmare" version, and must connect it to people, not just bunnies and trees. A lack of focus on people and their needs, the authors said, would marginalize environmentalism, perhaps fatally.

Now the budding campus-sustainability movement, which was born of the same impulses and sentiments as the environmental movement, may be at risk of falling victim to the same problems that Shellenberger and Nordhaus described: eco-centricity.

Campus sustainability has long been premised on the "three legs of the stool": environmental protection, fiscal equity, and social justice. It aspires to merge the natural world with man's world — to envision a future devoid of natural-resource depletion, an equitable distribution of wealth, and social systems that promote justice and peace. Just as environmental harm ultimately affects people worldwide (climate change, for example), sustainable solutions require all populations to benefit.

Some people could argue that this vision of sustainability is taking root in higher education. The Association for the Advancement of

Sustainability in Higher Education,° known as Aashe, has tracked remarkable growth in campus-sustainability programs — the group's membership has gone from a handful of campuses in 2006 to about 1,000 today. The American College & University Presidents' Climate Commitment, a landmark carbon-neutrality effort, has committed almost 700 college presidents to zeroing out greenhouse-gas emissions and increasing climate-literacy efforts. The Princeton Review° and others now routinely assess greenness in their annual campus ratings.

> "The Association for the Advancement of Sustainability in Higher Education . . . has tracked remarkable growth in campus-sustainability programs . . . from a handful of campuses in 2006 to about 1,000 today."

Those facts may suggest that campus sustainability is alive and well — but is it also devoutly eco-centric?   5

Aashe's recent survey of sustainability-staff members found that 92 percent of them are white. That raises a question: If sustainability is such a powerful and integrative theme, marrying environmental, economic, and social concerns, where are all the people of color in the sustainability field? Aashe has tried to highlight social-justice imperatives in its calls for presentations and in the theme of its conferences (for example, "Aashe 2010: Campus Initiatives to Catalyze a Just and Sustainable World"). Yet few such papers show up.

Julian Agyeman, a professor of urban and environmental policy and planning at Tufts University, has been critical of environmental groups that espouse social-justice ends but whose actions are overwhelmingly eco-centric. In his keynote speech at Aashe's 2010 conference, he noted the eco-centric focus of the organization's 2009 digest of campus-sustainability activity: "Three hundred eighty pages, over 1,250 stories and initiatives from nearly 600 institutions, 24 chapters, and the word 'justice' appears 13 times."

Agyeman argues that to fully integrate sustainability's three legs, we need to begin by focusing on people — people at risk, people who bear the brunt of societal problems. "Think about your institutional definition of sustainability," he said in his talk. "Broaden it to include social equity and justice and mean it."

Association for the Advancement of Sustainability in Higher Education: an organization that provides administrators, faculty, staff, and students with resources for achieving sustainability.
The Princeton Review: a standardized test preparation and admissions consulting company based in Framingham, Massachusetts.

Indeed, some data indicate that higher education uses sustainability as an incentive for conservation efforts that save money but stop short of fully integrating the movement's strategic vision or social-justice ideals.

For instance, Aashe's survey reports a low number of executive-level campus-sustainability leaders. Of 473 leaders who responded, only 28 reported directly to the president. Thirty reported to a provost. Most sustainability positions were defined as managers or coordinators, a lower level in the hierarchy.

That indicates that higher education does not see sustainability efforts as having a standing equivalent to, say, managing computers. Many campuses have established chief information officers, but chief sustainability officers are rare. Higher education has generally eschewed such a job title in favor of expanded roles for the campus business officer.

A recent cover story on these repurposed campus CSO's in *Business Officer Magazine* showed many trying to do good things, albeit standing almost entirely on the environmental and economic legs of the sustainability stool. There is nothing wrong with cost savings and conservation, but who in the boardroom is speaking exclusively for integrating the other element of sustainability: social justice?

Yet in the corporate world, chief sustainability officers are growing like global carbon-dioxide levels. *The New York Times* reported that the most important thing about corporate CSO's is "that the position—which generally includes responsibility for human rights and work-force diversity as well as environmental issues—reports directly to the chief executive."

Campus sustainability needs its own voice—and brand. Despite many individual campus-sustainability activities that benefit people, the planet, and the bottom line, we are tagged as simply "green." I'm not sure why. Perhaps the three legs of the stool are seen as too complicated or idealistic or unrealistic—or just wrong.

Perhaps there's only one leg: people.

Consider Adam Werbach's metamorphosis from president of the Sierra Club, one of the largest environmental organizations in the country, to a consultant for Xerox, Nike, Wal-Mart, and other big companies. "Focusing solely on saving the environment did not suffice—did not save lives, livelihoods, or neighborhoods," he wrote in his book, *Strategy for Sustainability: A Business Manifesto.* "We needed to fight for a larger kind of sustainability: one that took into account our social, economic, and cultural sustainability as well as our ecological surroundings. I could not be just an environmentalist."

Yet even social progressives and cultural groups — natural allies in the fight for a just society — see campus sustainability as an environment-only movement. I have been told by leaders in various social and cultural arenas that this sustainability thing is nice, but that it's "a white-people issue." They are more concerned about their own day-to-day survival on the social-justice front.

Is campus sustainability similarly fighting for its survival?

Aashe's survey showed that creation of new sustainability positions peaked in 2008, then dropped 31 percent in 2009. Clearly, we are at a critical point. Depending on our steps in the next few years, we either flower into fullness or hit the green wall, doomed to irrelevance or a patronizing tolerance. Eco-centricity is a fatal toxin, but it has an antidote: people. For campus sustainability to escape a death sentence, we must put people first.

Understanding the Text

1. What do Shellenberger and Nordhaus argue in their article "The Death of Environmentalism"? Why does Newport cite this article in paragraph 1?

2. How has sustainability begun to change on college campuses? Have these changes been happening quickly enough, and are they positive, according to Newport?

3. What does Professor Julian Agyeman believe should be done to make campuses more sustainable?

Reflection and Response

4. Why is the "budding campus-sustainability movement" (par. 2) so important? What is its main goal?

5. What are some things colleges could do to become more environmentally friendly?

Making Connections

6. Do some research on your own school's sustainability. Are there any clubs or organizations that work to make the school more environmentally friendly? How could your school improve its sustainability efforts? How could you get involved?

7. Take a walk around your campus and take note of how environmentally friendly it appears. For example, do you see recycling bins, parking areas for energy-efficient cars, information about sustainable building, and so on? Do you think there are sustainability efforts that aren't visible? How could you find out more about them?

How Cell Phones Are Changing the Face of Green Activism

Jaymi Heimbuch

Jaymi Heimbuch graduated from California Polytechnic State University with a degree in English and creative writing. She previously worked as managing editor for EcoGeek.org and is currently employed as a writer and photographer for TreeHugger.com.

In this article from 2009, Heimbuch offers facts about cell phone use and how these devices are rarely recycled. She also describes how cell phones can be powerful tools for activism and lists helpful apps for environmental activism. As you read, consider how cell phones and other mobile communication devices could affect sustainability in the coming years.

Today, mobile phones are ubiquitous. The sheer volume of the devices on this planet is staggering — in the United States alone, 450,000 cell phones are *discarded* every day. Over half of the world's population has quick, easy access to cell phones and wireless technology. For example, 97 percent of people surveyed in Tanzania had access to a mobile phone, while just 27 percent could access a land line phone. In Kenya, only 19 percent of the country's 36 million people are reached by traditional banking methods . . . but virtually all have access to mobile phones. Knowing these facts, it isn't surprising that the devices are being used as a key tool for environmental change. Here's a look at successful projects using cell phones and mobile devices for eco-activism, the apps that help us go green, and some how-to ideas for eco-activism via mobile phones.

The Ubiquitous Cell Phone

Practically Everyone Has a Cell Phone, or Can Get One

MobileActive is an organization dedicated to helping people use mobile devices as a tool for change. According to a report by the group, more than 3.5 billion people carry mobile phones today. And according to the EPA, just in 2005 there were 140 million cell phones put out into the market, with 126.3 million cell phones disposed of, and only 14 million recycled. That means there is a huge surplus of phones that could be put to good use through donations or a used cell phone market.

The widespread use of mobile phones has helped spur social activism.
© Tristan Spinski/Corbis

Mobile Phones Are Used Everywhere, Even More Than Internet

We may think that mobile phones are secondary to Internet access, but TechSoup reports that mobile phone usage vastly exceeds Internet usage. They note, "In China in 2005, there were 350 million mobile phone users, and 100 million Internet users. In sub-Saharan Africa in 2004, there were 52 million mobile phone users and approximately 5 to 8 million Internet users." The International Telecommunications Union tells us that the United States had over 40 million active users of the mobile web, and a survey by CTIA, The Wireless Association® and Harris Interactive states that 78 percent of teens — that ever increasingly important demographic for environmental change — have a cell phone, and 15 percent have a smart phone with Internet access. More importantly, 57 percent of those teens with Internet access use it for checking email and 48 percent use it for accessing social networking sites. That means mobile activism just among teens in the United States has incredible potential.

Also according to TechSoup, in the Middle East, sub-Saharan Africa, and South and South-East Asia, where mobile phone use is growing most rapidly, mobile technology is leapfrogging land lines. Residents are going from no phone communication at all, to mobile phone communication. The technology that exists today can go directly into the hands of people who haven't had access to anything like it before.

The Power of Mobile Phones for Activism

Mobile Phones Make Fast, Effective Action Possible

We have seen repeatedly how the use of mobile phones has helped   5
spur rapid social activism around politics. Smart mobs° can be brought together through text messages, such as bringing thousands of Ukraine activists to the streets of Kiev in 2004 to protest election fraud, and people can be spurred to action through using networks like Twitter via mobile phones, as we just saw happen in the Iranian election protests [2009–2010].

MobileActive reports that mobile phones seem to spur people to action more effectively than other media, including email. And while response metrics for text messaging are difficult to obtain, anecdotal evidence shows that text campaigns have a response rate of 20–40%. Greenpeace Argentina has reported that 15–25% of their mobile activists give feedback to the organization that they took action on a particular message campaign.

In addition, mobile messaging can change how people view a product or shop, with one study concluding that the likelihood of a person buying a product after receiving mobile communication about it can be an average of 35% higher. This same effort, and so much more, can go toward specifically environmental causes, not just as a way to gather people but as a way to gather information that can impact species and ecosystems.

Mobile Phones Are Great for Gathering Environmental Information

As pointed out by MobileActive, cell phones are a great device for gathering information, and researchers are noticing. For example, by embedding sensors in cell phones, researchers could gather real-time, location-specific information on things like air quality, weather

---

smart mob: a group that behaves intelligently or efficiently because of its exponentially increasing network links, enabling people to connect to information and others and allowing a form of social coordination.

conditions, or traffic conditions. It would make users passive citizen scientists. While there are currently privacy issues about this kind of participatory urbanism,° the possibility for sensory capabilities in cell phones for environmental monitoring is there.

Platforms that make users active participants are also possibilities, and tools exist for helping people everywhere, including in developing nations, be active information gatherers. For example, DataDyne is a company committed to making data collection and mobile communication available to everyone. One of their open source products is EpiSurveyor, a data collection form generator. It allows people to create a handheld data entry form, gather data on their mobile device, and send it back in to a laptop or desktop for analyzation. Another of their projects, called MIP, allows any group to start an RSS feed to communicate information rapidly to an audience via mobile devices. More apps are on their way from countless companies that will allow mobile phone users to capture and upload information to larger scientific databases for analysis, and communicate with one another.

> "The fact is, mobile phones are being used in some amazing ways for environmental activism right now."

These uses seem like they're close but still in the future in terms   10
of applying them to projects. But the fact is, mobile phones are being used in some amazing ways for environmental activism right now.

Environmental Activism Projects That Use Mobile Phones

Using Mobile Devices to Help Wildlife

Mobile phones are already assisting wildlife conservation efforts on a wide range of projects. Save the Elephants in Kenya is using GPS/GSM collars to track elephants in the area in order to help keep humans and elephants from clashing. Tensions between farmers and elephants are often high and mobile devices — specifically push-to-talk technology — allows communication among people to tell farmers and ranchers to take proactive steps against possible damage to their crops from the animals.

---

urbanism: the characteristic way of interaction of inhabitants of urban areas with the built environment.

The Okapi Wildlife Reserve patrols in the Democratic Republic of Congo use SMS° to text the GPS their locations to a central operator, who is then able to mobilize them if there is an emergency threat to the reserve. In a country with so much political upheaval, that kind of fast reaction time and mobilization is important.

Using Mobile Devices to Save Forests

Greenpeace Argentina showed the power of cell phone networking when they utilized it for advocating for The Forest Law, Argentina's first federal forest protection act, in 2007. The group was able to collect 3,000 signatures for the petition via text messaging, as well as asked the 350,000 people in their mobile phone network list to call specific legislators. The effort helped the law to pass, providing a one-year moratorium on cutting down native forests.

Helveta is a company that is deploying bar coding technology to prevent illegal logging. Forestry companies hammer in bar codes into stumps and felled trees, then use mobile devices to scan the codes and upload them via satellite or wifi to a central database. The idea is any tree that doesn't have a bar code with tracked scans is considered illegal when it reaches mills.

Using Cell Phones to Green Consumer Behavior

Using mobile technology to make consumer behavior more eco-friendly is already highly popular. When it comes to food, for instance, FishMS helps consumers make on-the-spot purchasing decisions, and also tracks trends in consumer behavior regarding fish selections. For instance, the service often sees spikes in SMS inquiries about certain fish species after that species has been in the news. airTEXT does a similar thing for Londonites who want to receive updates about air pollution levels in [the] city. Access to this information can shift to what parts of the city people travel, and the method they use to get from one place to another. Many more examples will be discussed later when we talk about all the apps available to shoppers.

15

SMS: Short Message Service, a standard text-messaging component.

Using Cell Phones to Affect Green Politics

Crowdsourcing° is a big aspect of using mobile technology to affect people's behavior. It's a way of getting a massive group of people involved in tackling an issue, rather than one or a few organizations bearing the burden. Americans for Informed Democracy's Richard Graves pointed out in last year's Bioneers conference the idea of bird-dogging. The group asks people with video on their cell phones, or with Flip cameras, to ask political leaders tough questions on camera, committing them to a certain action on a certain issue. It creates an instantly uploadable video of a political leader making, for example, promises to help the environment that they can then be held to.

Using mobile devices for things like live-blogging environmental events or reporting on actions as they roll out — especially via platforms like Twitter that help information go viral — huge numbers of people can be made aware of eco-issues, all thanks to cell phones and similar devices. MobileActive is a great resource for seeing, and using, mobile devices for social change like this.

How to Use Mobile Phones for Your Environmental Activism

Guides and Tips for Getting Started with Mobile Activism

SocialBright has a great how-to guide for getting started in mobile activism. If you're looking to utilize mobile devices for your cause, this is a great starting point for learning the technology and steps you'll need to take for an effective campaign. It even has screenshots to illustrate how texting is used for various campaigns.

The site also has a top notch tips guide that walks you through effective ways of using the technology of texting. It walks you through what to do — such as to know your constituency, be relevant, and be action oriented — and what not to do — such as avoid sending too many messages, and be aware of the time of day you're sending messages.

Organizations Helping to Get Phones and Information to People

Hope Phones takes used phones and puts them in the hands of community health care workers in developing countries. It's an excellent way to give new life to the millions upon millions of used cell phones getting replaced each year in the US alone. The phone being sent in 20

crowdsourcing: the practice of obtaining needed services, ideas, or content by soliciting contributions from a large group of people, and especially from an online community, rather than from more-traditional sources such as employees or suppliers.

doesn't even need to be usable. Donors can print a free shipping label and send their old phone in to The Wireless Source, a global leader in wireless device recycling. The phone's value in selling it to recyclers allows FrontlineSMS:Medic to purchase usable, recycled cell phones for health care workers.

Mobile Database [is] still a somewhat small database but it is set up to grow infinitely as more and more projects are created and added to it. It is searchable by several filters, including article, report or project, or by location, category, or keyword. Searching just *conservation*, 41 entries came up, from 3rdWhale Mobile and Nokia's Eco Sensor Concept, to Rare Bird Alert and GPS/GSM Animal Collars. The database seeks to compile all the information on the social and environmental impact of mobile technology globally. If you start up a project using mobile technology for environmental good, be sure to suggest its addition to this database.

Top Apps That Help You Use Your Phone for Environmental Activism

There are some great applications on the market and coming down the pipes that will allow for some interesting possibilities in citizen science. For example, one possibility is eventually having pollution detectors built into phones so anyone can help record atmospheric conditions and potentially contribute to climate activism. Also, a future iPhone app for snapping photos of flora and fauna, then uploading the information to a database can help scientists identify and monitor changes in species.

Google Earth on the phone also works for a few tricks, from checking out the potential of renewable energy to "visiting" the farm where your grocery store produce comes from before purchasing it. Ecorio helps people not only calculate carbon footprints but also encourage one another through social networking to green up even more. A plethora of iPhone apps support green living, from driving to public transportation, from shopping to home automation.

Speaking of green shopping, voting with your dollar is a big way to make an impact, and mobile devices are becoming an increasingly more active component of shopping. 3rd Whale has an app out that helps you pick which businesses to patronize and Good Guide helps you hone in on [the] greenest products. Greenpeace has a specific app for picking out which toilet paper to use. And there's even an app that keeps your coupons for you so you can ditch paper where possible.

While these last couple seem a little overly specific, the fact is every purchase decision is a form of activism. With 40 million people in the US accessing the mobile web, having immediate access via mobile phone can make a significant impact on consumer behavior.

From elephants to toilet paper, mobile phones are truly changing the face of environmental activism and green living.

Understanding the Text

1. According to Heimbuch, how many cell phones are discarded each day in the United States?
2. Describe how cell phones can be used for activism. Had you previously considered such use — or used your own cell phone in a similar way?
3. List a few environmental organizations that use cell phones in their work.

Reflection and Response

4. This article was published in 2009 and, since then, technology has progressed even further. What additions would you make to this article in light of these technological advancements?
5. What do you think about Heimbuch's suggestions for using your cell phone for activism? Do you think this is an important use for communication technology? What are the benefits and drawbacks?

Making Connections

6. Research some cell phone apps that have to do with sustainability and conservation. How could these apps be used by environmental organizations?
7. Choose one of the organizations listed in this article and visit its Web site. Find out how the organization continues to use technology in its activism.

How Green Is My iPad?

Daniel Goleman and Gregory Norris

Daniel Goleman codirects the Consortium for Research on Emotional Intelligence in Organizations at Rutgers University, and he is also an award-winning author and science journalist. Gregory Norris is a lecturer in public health at Harvard University and the founder of New Earth, a nonprofit organization for sustainable development.

This article, which originally appeared in 2010 in the *New York Times*, raises the question of whether e-readers or books are more environmentally friendly. Goleman and Norris examine the evidence in five steps: materials, manufacturing, transportation, reading, and disposal. As you read, consider the environmental benefits of both e-readers and "old-fashioned" books.

W ith e-readers like Apple's new iPad and Amazon's Kindle touting their vast libraries of digital titles, some bookworms are bound to wonder if tomes-on-paper will one day become quaint relics. But the question also arises, which is more environmentally friendly: an e-reader or an old-fashioned book?

To find the answer, we turned to life-cycle assessment, which evaluates the ecological impact of any product, at every stage of its existence, from the first tree cut down for paper to the day that hardcover decomposes in the dump. With this method, we can determine the greenest way to read.

"Which is more environmentally friendly: an e-reader or an old-fashioned book?"

(A note about e-readers: some technical details — for instance, how those special screens are manufactured — are not publicly available and these products vary in their exact composition. We've based our estimates on a composite derived from available information. It's also important to keep in mind that we're focusing on the e-reader aspect of these devices, not any other functions they may offer.)

Step One: Materials

One e-reader requires the extraction of 33 pounds of minerals. That includes trace amounts of exotic metals like columbite-tantalite, often mined in war-torn regions of Africa. But it's mostly sand and gravel to build landfills; they hold all the waste from manufacturing wafer boards for the integrated circuits. An e-reader also requires 79 gallons of water to produce its batteries and printed wiring boards, and in refining metals like the gold used in trace quantities in the circuits.

A book made with recycled paper consumes about two-thirds of a 5
pound of minerals. (Here again, the greatest mineral use is actually gravel, mainly for the roads used to transport materials throughout the supply chain.) And it requires just 2 gallons of water to make the pulp slurry that is then pressed and heat-dried to make paper.

Step Two: Manufacture

Fossil Fuels°

The e-reader's manufacture, along a vast supply chain of consumer electronics, is relatively energy-hungry, using 100 kilowatt hours of fossil fuels and resulting in 66 pounds of carbon dioxide. For a single book, which, recycled or not, requires energy to form and dry the sheets, it's just two kilowatt hours, and 100 times fewer greenhouse gases.°

Health

The unit for comparison here is a "disability adjusted life-year," the length of time someone loses to disability because of exposure to, say, toxic material released into the air, water and soil, anywhere along the line.

For both the book and the e-reader, the main health impacts come from particulate emissions like nitrogen and sulfur oxides, which travel deep into our lungs, worsening asthma and chronic coughing and increasing the risk of premature death. The adverse health

---

fossil fuels: fuels formed by natural processes such as decomposition of buried dead organisms. Fossil fuels include coal, petroleum, and natural gas.
greenhouse gas: a gas in an atmosphere that absorbs and emits radiation within the thermal infrared range. This process is the fundamental cause of the greenhouse effect.

impacts from making one e-reader are estimated to be 70 times greater than those from making a single book.

Step Three: Transportation

If you order a book online and have it shipped 500 miles by air, that creates roughly the same pollution and waste as making the book in the first place. Driving five miles to the bookstore and back causes about 10 times the pollution and resource depletion as producing it. You'd need to drive to a store 300 miles away to create the equivalent in toxic impacts on health of making one e-reader — but you might do that and more if you drive to the mall every time you buy a new book.

Step Four: Reading

If you like to read a book in bed at night for an hour or two, the   10 light bulb will use more energy than it takes to charge an e-reader, which has a highly energy-efficient screen. But if you read in daylight, the advantage tips to a book.

Step Five: Disposal

If your e-reader ends up being "recycled" illegally so that workers, including children, in developing countries dismantle it by hand, they will be exposed to a range of toxic substances. If it goes through state-of-the-art procedures — for example, high-temperature incineration with the best emissions controls and metals recovery — the "disability adjusted life-year" count will be far less for workers.

If your book ends up in a landfill, its decomposition generates double the global warming emissions and toxic impacts on local water systems as its manufacture.

• • •

Some of this math is improving. More and more books are being printed with soy-based inks, rather than petroleum-based ones, on paper that is recycled or sourced from well-managed forests and that was produced at pulp mills that don't use poisons like chlorine to whiten it. The electronics industry, too, is trying to reduce the use of toxic chemicals, and to improve working conditions and worker safety throughout its far-flung supply chains.

So, how many volumes do you need to read on your e-reader to break even?

With respect to fossil fuels, water use and mineral consumption, the impact of one e-reader payback equals roughly 40 to 50 books. When it comes to global warming, though, it's 100 books; with human health consequences, it's somewhere in between.

All in all, the most ecologically virtuous way to read a book starts by walking to your local library.

Understanding the Text

1. What kinds of materials make up iPads and e-readers? Where do these materials come from?
2. How does the transportation of e-books impact the environment?
3. What is the most ecologically virtuous way to read books? Why? How might this change in the future?

Reflection and Response

4. What are some ways to use an iPad or another e-reader in a more environmentally friendly way?
5. Assuming that e-readers become more popular in the coming decade, how do you think companies will alter production to better serve the environment?
6. Do you think the convenience of an e-reader is worth the environmental impact? Explain why or why not.

Making Connections

7. Interview a few people (roommates, classmates, family) and find out whether they prefer e-readers or physical books. What are their reasons for their choices? If they were aware of the environmental factors described in this article, would they choose one format over the other?
8. This article and the one that precedes it (Heimbuch) address the relationship between mobile technologies and sustainability. In what ways are technology and sustainability interconnected? How does technology simultaneously create and help solve environmental problems?

How Is Sustainability a Transnational Issue?

S ustainability is a global, transnational issue, although that may not be obvious to readers of this textbook who live in the United States. The world we live in is increasingly interconnected, and the challenges of sustainability are not limited by geographic, cultural, or political boundaries. Choices about how to manage resources, facilitate social equity, and address environmental degradation affect all of us, no matter where those choices and the resulting actions originate or are centralized. Though some of the subjects addressed in this chapter may seem far removed from your daily life, it is important to remember that we are all part of the same global system. Sustainability is not just a local, regional, and a national issue — it is a global issue as well.

This chapter highlights sustainability and environmental challenges as global, transnational subjects. It begins with a *National Geographic* news article describing how the United States compares to other countries in terms of sustainable behavior, beliefs, and attitudes. The next excerpt, written by the UN Panel on Global Sustainability, has been described as "a second Brundtland report" because it provides a twenty-five-year update on progress toward international sustainability. You may wish to read the two UN reports together — see Chapter 2 for the first report. The next four articles look at challenges and opportunities of sustainability across the globe: in the world's oceans (Smith), in the aftermath of the Japanese tsunami of 2011 (Biggs and Myhrvold), and through the recovery efforts from the earthquake in Haiti in 2010 (Interlandi). The last two pieces in the chapter look at global challenges to sustainability in the future, focusing on alternative energy sources (Rifkin) and the limits of Earth's various resources (Moyer and Storrs).

These eight readings provide just a glimpse into the many transnational issues involving sustainability. Many other sustainability-related topics are worth considering, and you may encounter some of them through your research and writing. As you read the selections in this chapter, consider the ways in which the issues they address transcend various borders, the ways in which these seemingly remote topics influence and affect you, and the degree to which your choices can impact global sustainability.

Americans Least Green—And Feel Least Guilt, Survey Suggests

Ker Than

Ker Than is a science writer and editor based in New York City. He has written for *National Geographic*, *Popular Science*, *COSMOS*, *New Scientist*, and other publications. Than holds a master's degree from New York University's Science, Health and Environmental Reporting Program.

This article appeared in 2012 in *National Geographic News*, an online news outlet owned and operated by the National Geographic Society. The article presents the findings of a global study examining different attitudes toward environmentally friendly living. The article also describes how the United States compares to other countries when it comes to green transportation, recycling, and purchasing goods. As you read, think about what this article reveals about American culture and sustainability.

Americans are the least likely to suffer from "green guilt" about their environmental impact, despite trailing the rest of the world in sustainable behavior, according to a new National Geographic survey.

This year's Greendex° report, conducted by the National Geographic Society° and the research consultancy GlobeScan,° also found that Americans are the most confident that their individual actions can help the environment. (*National Geographic News* is a division of the Society.)

"There's a disconnect there, and we hope the Greendex helps shed light on it," said Eric Whan, GlobeScan's director of sustainability.

"In our culture of consumption, we've sort of been indoctrinated to believe that we can buy ourselves out of environmental problems," said Whan, who's based in Toronto, Canada, another country ranked low in the survey.

"But what people need to realize is that the sheer volume of con- 5 sumption is relevant as well."

Greendex: a survey of sustainable consumption conducted by the National Geographic Society.
National Geographic Society: one of the largest nonprofit scientific and educational institutions in the world; based in Washington, D.C.
GlobeScan: a public opinion research organization that handles reputation, brand, sustainability, engagement, and trends research.

Conducted by the National Geographic Society and GlobeScan since 2008, the Greendex report explored environmental attitudes and behaviors among 17,000 consumers in 17 countries through an online survey that asks questions relating to housing, transportation, food, and consumer goods.

"Americans are the least likely to suffer from 'green guilt' about their environmental impact, despite trailing the rest of the world in sustainable behavior."

This year Americans ranked last in sustainable behavior, as they have every year since 2008. Just 21 percent of Americans reported feeling guilty about the impact they have on the environment, among the lowest of those surveyed.

Yet they had the most faith in an individual's ability to protect the environment, at 47 percent.

Consumers in India, China, and Brazil led the pack, with Greendex scores in the high fifties. Paradoxically, many Indians, Chinese, and Brazilians reported feeling the most guilt about their environmental impact and had the least confidence that their individual actions can help the environment.

Green Guilt

Taken together, the findings suggest that those with the lightest environmental footprint are also the most likely to feel both guilty and disempowered, Whan said. 10

"Despite their relatively light footprints as consumers, there seems to have been some internalization and a sensitization to environmental issues in places like China, India, and Brazil," he added.

"There's a more widespread sense that environmental issues are affecting people's health in those countries. Concern is higher about things like water and air pollution, and there's also a real sensitivity to global warming."

Nicole Darnall, a researcher at the School of Sustainability at Arizona State University (ASU), called the association between guilt and Greendex scores "intriguing."

"In order to feel guilty, you have to accept that some sort of problem exists," said Darnall, who was not involved in the survey.

"And in looking at the countries that don't feel guilty, they're the ones that I would suggest are not necessarily accepting that a problem exists. These are countries in which there's still a lot of political de- 15 bate about whether certain problems" — such as climate change — "exist or not."

Moving Forward

Americans also ranked last in the area of transportation. According to the Greendex report, Americans were the most likely to report regularly driving alone in a car or truck (56 percent) and the least likely to use public transportation (7 percent).

They were also the least likely to bike or walk to their destination, while Chinese consumers were the most likely to do so.

This could just be a reflection of the fewer number of people who own cars in the country, GlobeScan's Whan noted, and China's Greendex transportation score could decrease as the use of cars in the country rises.

ASU's Darnall noted that China, and other countries where cycling rates are high, have cultures that are more accepting of bikes on the road in the first place.

Residents commute on bicycles, electric bikes, and mopeds in Shanghai, China.
AP Photo/Gerald Herbert

"In Phoenix and most other U.S. cities, you're often taking your life   20
in your own hands when you get on a bicycle," she said.

What's Really Green?

One area where Americans scored well was in the area of purchased
goods, with U.S. respondents (31 percent) saying that they prefer to
buy "used" or "pre-owned" products over new ones.

Americans are also above average when it comes to recycling
(69 percent) but are surpassed by Canadian, British, German, and
Australian consumers. Despite ranking second in the subcategory
relating to consumption of goods, South Koreans are the least likely
(29 percent) to recycle, according to the survey.

One common trend revealed by the survey is that many consumers find it difficult to justify the price premium often associated with
environmentally friendly products. Russians, Brazilians, Americans,
and Indians were the most likely to respond that the extra cost does
not justify the value.

Part of the problem is that in the U.S. and many countries, there is a
lack of good information and trusted sources regarding green products
that consumers can turn to, said Thomas Dean, of Colorado State
University's College of Business, who did not participate in the survey.

ASU's Darnall agreed. "How do we know that one product is   25
greener than another? Right now, in our current marketplace, we
can't," Darnall said. "This is one area where the government can step
in and play a stronger leadership role."

Dean thinks setting up a third-party certification system for green
products like the one that exists for organic foods would be helpful.

"In the United States we know a food is organic because there's a
certification process in place that is set out by the U.S. Department of
Agriculture to define what organic foods are," he said.

"And that results in a label that is considered legitimate by
consumers."

Green Eating

On the topic of food, more than half of all consumers in almost all
the countries surveyed reported eating beef — one of the most environmentally intensive food sources — once or more per week. Ar-
gentines reported eating the most beef (61 percent), as opposed to
35 percent of Americans and 9 percent of Indians.

Chinese consumers eat the most vegetables: 63 percent eat them 30
every day, versus just 37 percent of Americans.

Other interesting food findings: Germans are the biggest consumers of bottled water, with two-thirds reporting that they drink it daily. And Spaniards are now the biggest consumers of seafood, while the Japanese are eating less — probably a consequence of the 2011 tsunami and Fukushima nuclear power plant disaster, Whan said.

"There's some evidence of some fisheries being closed in [Japan] because of radioactive contamination," he added. "We also know that the capacity of the fishing fleet was severely affected [by the tsunami]."

Green Self-Delusion?

One puzzling and potentially worrisome trend observed among respondents in all of the countries surveyed was that consumers tended to report being greener than they actually may be.

When asked what proportion of their fellow citizens were green, most people responded 20 to 40 percent. Yet when asked if they themselves were green, more than half said they are.

"This might be a form of green self-delusion on the part of consumers, but it might also be due to a well-known effect in sociology called the social desirability bias, in which respondents often say what is socially desirable [rather] than stating their true feelings and actions," said Darnall.

"It's not a surprise that consumers believed they were environmentally responsible," she said. "Consumers want to respond in a socially desirable way, and there is a lot of research that suggests they're not going to respond very honestly about their less socially acceptable behaviors."

GlobeScan's Whan said he hopes the Greendex survey will make people take a closer look at their own consumption patterns and their effects on the environment.

"The first step is to be aware," he said. "We hope that the Greendex helps people keep in mind the implications of not only the choices they make as consumers but also how *much* they consume."

Understanding the Text

1. What is "green guilt"? Why is it so low among Americans? Is this a good thing or a bad thing?

2. What is the "disconnect" displayed by Americans as described in this article? What is the relationship between sustainable behavior and beliefs and attitudes about environmental issues?

3. Which countries appear to be the most sustainability-minded? What issues are they concerned about?

Reflection and Response

4. Are the findings in this article surprising to you? Why or why not?

5. In which ways is the United States ahead of other countries in terms of sustainable practices and policies?

6. In what ways are transportation, consumer goods, and food parts of the sustainability equation?

Making Connections

7. Do you try to be environmentally friendly in your daily life? If yes, what do you do? If not, what do you think you could do to improve? Does this article make you think differently about your practices or beliefs?

8. This article explains the environmental impact of transportation, particularly in the United States. How do you think this problem will change in the future?

9. This article addresses consumption, recycling, transportation, and food — issues that are discussed in other articles in this chapter. Compare and contrast the ways in which one or more of the other articles treat these topics.

Resilient People, Resilient Planet: A Future Worth Choosing

The United Nations Panel on Global Sustainability

In January 2012, the United Nations Panel on Global Sustainability released a report containing recommendations for world leaders to put sustainable development into practice and to mainstream sustainability into global economic policy. The report, titled *Resilient People, Resilient Planet: A Future Worth Choosing*, was coauthored by more than twenty global political figures led by Tarja Halonen, president of the Republic of Finland, and Jacob Zuma, president of the Republic of South Africa.

The report has been referred to as "a second Brundtland report," designed to be visionary and describe a future twenty years from now. This excerpt serves as the panel's introduction to the ninety-five-page report. As you read this introduction, consider what it suggests about our future and what world leaders could do to shape it.

The Panel's Vision

Today our planet and our world are experiencing the best of times, and the worst of times. The world is experiencing unprecedented prosperity, while the planet is under unprecedented stress. Inequality between the world's rich and poor is growing, and more than a billion people still live in poverty. In many countries, there are rising waves of protest reflecting universal aspirations for a more prosperous, just and sustainable world.

Every day, millions of choices are made by individuals, businesses and governments. Our common future lies in all those choices. Because of the array of overlapping challenges the world faces, it is more urgent than ever that we take action to embrace the principles of the sustainable development agenda. It is time that genuine global action is taken to enable people, markets and governments to make sustainable choices.

The need to integrate the economic, social and environmental dimensions of development so as to achieve sustainability was clearly defined a quarter of a century ago. It is time to make it happen. The opportunities for change are vast. We are not passive, helpless victims of the impersonal, determinist forces of history. And the exciting thing is that we can choose our future.

The challenges we face are great, but so too are the new possibilities that appear when we look at old problems with new and fresh eyes. These possibilities include technologies capable of pulling us back from the planetary brink; new markets, new growth and new jobs emanating from game-changing products and services; and new approaches to public and private finance that can truly lift people out of the poverty trap.

The truth is that sustainable development is fundamentally a question of people's opportunities to influence their future, claim their rights and voice their concerns. Democratic governance and full respect for human rights are key prerequisites for empowering people to make sustainable choices. The peoples of the world will simply not tolerate continued environmental devastation or the persistent inequality which offends deeply held universal principles of social justice. Citizens will no longer accept governments and corporations breaching their compact with them as custodians of a sustainable future for all. More generally, international, national and local governance across the world must fully embrace the requirements of a sustainable development future, as must civil society and the private sector. At the same time, local communities must be encouraged to participate actively and consistently in conceptualizing, planning and executing sustainability policies. Central to this is including young people in society, in politics and in the economy.

> "Sustainable development is fundamentally a question of people's opportunities to influence their future, claim their rights and voice their concerns."

Therefore, the long-term vision of the High-level Panel on Global Sustainability is to eradicate poverty, reduce inequality and make growth inclusive, and production and consumption more sustainable, while combating climate change and respecting a range of other planetary boundaries. This reaffirms the landmark 1987 report by the World Commission on Environment and Development, "Our Common Future" (United Nations document A/42/427, annex), known to all as the Brundtland° report.

But what, then, is to be done if we are to make a real difference for the world's people and the planet? We must grasp the dimensions of the challenge. We must recognize that the drivers of that challenge

Brundtland: the Brundtland Commission, a UN organization of world leaders formed in 1983 whose mission was to unite countries to pursue sustainable development together. See the Brundtland report in Chapter 2, page 92.

include unsustainable lifestyles, production and consumption patterns and the impact of population growth. As the global population grows from 7 billion to almost 9 billion by 2040, and the number of middle-class consumers increases by 3 billion over the next 20 years, the demand for resources will rise exponentially. By 2030, the world will need at least 50 percent more food, 45 percent more energy and 30 percent more water — all at a time when environmental boundaries are throwing up new limits to supply. This is true not least for climate change, which affects all aspects of human and planetary health.

The current global development model is unsustainable. We can no longer assume that our collective actions will not trigger tipping points as environmental thresholds are breached, risking irreversible damage to both ecosystems and human communities. At the same time, such thresholds should not be used to impose arbitrary growth ceilings on developing countries seeking to lift their people out of poverty. Indeed, if we fail to resolve the sustainable development dilemma, we run the risk of condemning up to 3 billion members of our human family to a life of endemic poverty. Neither of these outcomes is acceptable, and we must find a new way forward.

A quarter of a century ago, the Brundtland report introduced the concept of sustainable development to the international community as a new paradigm for economic growth, social equality and environmental sustainability. The report argued that sustainable development could be achieved by an integrated policy framework embracing all three of those pillars. The Brundtland report was right then, and it remains right today. The problem is that, 25 years later, sustainable development remains a generally agreed concept, rather than a day-to-day, on-the-ground, practical reality. The Panel has asked itself why this is the case, and what can now be done to change that.

The Panel has concluded that there are two possible answers. They are both correct, and they are interrelated. Sustainable development has undoubtedly suffered from a failure of political will. It is difficult to argue against the principle of sustainable development, but there are few incentives to put it into practice when our policies, politics and institutions disproportionately reward the short term. In other words, the policy dividend is long-term, often intergenerational, but the political challenge is often immediate.

There is another answer to this question of why sustainable development has not been put into practice. It is an answer that we argue with real passion: the concept of sustainable development has not yet been incorporated into the mainstream national and international economic policy debate. Most economic decision makers still regard sustainable development as extraneous to their core responsibilities for macroeconomic management and other branches of economic policy. Yet integrating environmental and social issues into economic decisions is vital to success.

For too long, economists, social activists and environmental scientists have simply talked past each other — almost speaking different languages, or at least different dialects. The time has come to unify the disciplines, to develop a common language for sustainable development that transcends the warring camps; in other words, to bring the sustainable development paradigm into mainstream economics. That way, politicians and policymakers will find it much harder to ignore.

That is why the Panel argues that the international community needs what some have called "a new political economy" for sustainable development. This means, for example: radically improving the interface between environmental science and policy; recognizing that in certain environmental domains, such as climate change, there is "market failure," which requires both regulation and what the economists would recognize as the pricing of "environmental externalities," while making explicit the economic, social and environmental costs of action and inaction; recognizing the importance of innovation, new technologies, international cooperation and investments responding to these problems and generating further prosperity; recognizing that an approach should be agreed [on] to quantify the economic cost of sustained social exclusion — for example, the cost of excluding women from the workforce; recognizing that private markets alone may be incapable of generating at the scale necessary to bring about a proper response to the food security crisis; and requiring international agencies, national governments and private corporations to report on their annual sustainable development performance against agreed sustainability measures. We must also recognize that this is a core challenge for politics itself. Unless the political process is equally capable of embracing the sustainable development paradigm, there can be no progress.

The scale of investment, innovation, technological development and employment creation required for sustainable development and poverty eradication is beyond the range of the public sector. The Panel therefore argues for using the power of the economy to forge inclusive and sustainable growth and create value beyond narrow concepts of wealth. Markets and entrepreneurship will be a prime driver of decision-making and economic change. And the Panel lays down a challenge for our governments and international institutions: to work better together in solving common problems and advancing shared interests. Quantum change is possible when willing actors join hands in forward-looking coalitions and take the lead in contributing to sustainable development.

The Panel argues that by embracing a new approach to the political economy of sustainable development, we will bring the sustainable development paradigm from the margins to the mainstream of the global economic debate. Thus, both the cost of action and the cost of inaction will become transparent. Only then will the political process be able to summon both the arguments and the political will necessary to act for a sustainable future. 15

The Panel calls for this new approach to the political economy of sustainable development so as to address the sustainable development challenge in a fresh and operational way. That sustainable development is right is self-evident. Our challenge is to demonstrate that it is also rational — and that the cost of inaction far outweighs the cost of action.

The Panel's report makes a range of concrete recommendations to take forward our vision for a sustainable planet, a just society and a growing economy:

- It is critical that we embrace a new nexus between food, water and energy rather than treating them in different "silos." All three need to be fully integrated, not treated separately if we are to deal with the global food security crisis. It is time to embrace a second green revolution — an "ever-green revolution" — that doubles yields but builds on sustainability principles;
- It is time for bold global efforts, including launching a major global scientific initiative, to strengthen the interface between science and policy. We must define, through science, what scientists refer to as "planetary boundaries," "environmental thresholds" and "tipping points." Priority should be given to challenges now facing the marine environment and the "blue economy";
- Most goods and services sold today fail to bear the full environmental and social cost of production and consumption. Based on the science, we need to reach consensus, over time, on methodologies to price them properly. Costing environmental externalities could open new opportunities for green growth and green jobs;
- Addressing social exclusion and widening social inequity, too, requires measuring them, costing them and taking responsibility for them. The next step is exploring how we can deal with these critical issues to bring about better outcomes for all;

- Equity needs to be at the forefront. Developing countries need time, as well as financial and technological support, to transition to sustainable development. We must empower all of society — especially women, young people, the unemployed and the most vulnerable and weakest sections of society. Properly reaping the demographic dividend calls on us to include young people in society, in politics, in the labor market and in business development;
- Any serious shift towards sustainable development requires gender equality. Half of humankind's collective intelligence and capacity is a resource we must nurture and develop, for the sake of multiple generations to come. The next increment of global growth could well come from the full economic empowerment of women;
- Many argue that if it cannot be measured, it cannot be managed. The international community should measure development beyond gross domestic product (GDP) and develop a new sustainable development index or set of indicators;
- Financing sustainable development requires vast new sources of capital from both private and public sources. It requires both mobilizing more public funds and using global and national capital to leverage global private capital through the development of incentives. Official development assistance will also remain critical for the sustainable development needs of low-income countries;
- Governments at all levels must move from a silo mentality to integrated thinking and policymaking. They must bring sustainable development to the forefront of their agendas and budgets and look at innovative models of international cooperation. Cities and local communities have a major role to play in advancing a real sustainable development agenda on the ground;
- International institutions have a critical role. International governance for sustainable development must be strengthened by using existing institutions more dynamically and by considering the creation of a global sustainable development council and the adoption of sustainable development goals;
- Governments and international organizations should increase the resources allocated to adaptation and disaster risk reduction and integrate resilience planning into their development budgets and strategies;
- Governments, markets and people need to look beyond short-term transactional agendas and short-term political cycles.

Incentives that currently favor short-termism in decision-making should be changed. Sustainable choices often have higher up-front costs than business as usual. They need to become more easily available, affordable and attractive to both poor consumers and low-income countries.

This Panel believes it is within the wit and will of our common humanity to choose for the future. This Panel therefore is on the side of hope. All great achievements in human history began as a vision before becoming a reality. The vision for global sustainability, producing both a resilient people and a resilient planet, is no different.

In 2030, a child born in 2012 — the year our report is published — will turn 18. Will we have done enough in the intervening years to give her the sustainable, fair and resilient future that all of our children deserve? This report is an effort to give her an answer.

Understanding the Text

1. What are the key issues identified in this report?
2. What is the relationship between this report and the Brundtland report, published twenty-five years earlier? See the excerpt on page 92.
3. How does this excerpt from "Resilient People, Resilient Planet" define "sustainable development"?

Reflection and Response

4. Who do you see as the primary audience for this report? Who are the secondary audiences?
5. In what ways does this selection portray sustainability as a social issue, involving human rights and social justice? Do you think this is an important aspect of sustainability?
6. What is the relationship between science and policy? Why is there often a breakdown between these two arenas? What can be done to bring them closer together?

Making Connections

7. This report ties racial and gender equality into sustainability. Do some research on race, gender, and sustainability, and report on your findings.
8. Find the complete report online by searching for "Resilient People, Resilient Planet: A Future Worth Choosing." Choose one excerpt from the report and analyze it.
9. Compare and contrast the focus, tone, recommendations, or any other aspect of this report with its predecessor, the Brundtland report (page 92). What similarities and differences do you see?

The Coming Green Wave: Ocean Farming to Fight Climate Change

Brendan Smith

Brendan Smith is an oysterman and the cofounder of Voices for a Sustainable Future, a group that promotes sustainable living. Smith is also a senior fellow at the Progressive Technology Project. He has written for the *Los Angeles Times*, *The Guardian*, CBS News, and other publications.

This article originally appeared in 2011 in *The Atlantic*, a magazine that offers commentary on contemporary issues. In the article, Smith raises an important question: how can we use the oceans to save us from environmental problems? Smith also introduces the idea of seaweed farms and how they can grow large amounts of nutrient-rich food. As you read, think about the benefits of ocean farming and how this practice could impact climate change in the future.

For decades environmentalists have fought to save our oceans from the perils of overfishing,° climate change, and pollution. All noble efforts — but what if environmentalists have it backward? What if the question is not how to save the oceans, but how the oceans can save us?

That is what a growing network of scientists, ocean farmers, and environmentalists around the world is trying to figure out. With nearly 90 percent of large fish stocks threatened by over-fishing and 3.5 billion people dependent on the seas as their primary food source, these ocean farming advocates have concluded that aquaculture is here to stay.

But rather than monolithic factory fish farms, they see the oceans as the home of small-scale farms where complementary species are cultivated to provide food and fuel — and to clean up the environment and fight climate change. Governed by an ethic of sustainability, they are re-imagining our oceans with the hope of saving us from the grip of the ever-escalating climate, energy, and food crises.

The Death and Rebirth of the Ocean Farm

Ocean farming is not a modern innovation. For thousands of years cultures as diverse as the ancient Egyptians, Romans, Aztecs, and Chinese have farmed finfish, shellfish, and aquatic plants. Atlantic

---

overfishing: depleting fish stocks to unacceptable levels, regardless of water body size.

salmon have been farmed in Scotland since the early 1600s; seaweed was a staple food for American settlers.

Unfortunately, what was once a sustainable fishery has been mod- 5 ernized into large-scale industrial-style farming. Modeled on land-based factory livestock farms, aquaculture operations are infamous for their low-quality, tasteless fish pumped full of antibiotics and polluting local waterways. According to a recent *New York Times* editorial, aquaculture "has repeated too many of the mistakes of industrial farming—including the shrinking of genetic diversity, a disregard for conservation, and the global spread of intensive farming methods before their consequences are completely understood."

> "Governed by an ethic of sustainability, [ocean farmers] are re-imagining our oceans with the hope of saving us from the grip of the ever-escalating climate, energy, and food crises."

Unsurprisingly, once information got out among the general public, "aquaculture" quickly became a dirty word. Industry responded with a strategy of mislabeling seafood and upping their marketing budgets, rather than investing in more sustainable and environmentally benign farming techniques.

But a small group of ocean farmers and scientists decided to chart a different course. Rather than relying on mono-aquaculture operations, these new ocean farms are pioneering multi-trophic° and sea-vegetable aquaculture, whereby ocean farmers grow abundant, high-quality seafood while improving, rather than damaging, the environment.

One example is Ocean Approved° in Maine, which cultivates seaweed that doubles as a nutrient-rich food source and a sponge for organic pollutants. Farmers in Long Island Sound are exploring diversifying small-scale organic shellfish farms with various species of seaweed to filter out the pollutants, mitigate oxygen depletion, and develop a sustainable source for fertilizer and fish meal. In southern Spain Veta La Palma designed its farm to restore wetlands, and in the process created the largest bird sanctuary in Spain, with over 220 species of birds.

Seaweed farms alone have the capacity to grow massive amounts of nutrient-rich food. Professor Ronald Osinga at Wageningen University

---

multi-trophic: multi-trophic aquaculture is a form of marine farming in which different plants and animals are raised together in a mutually beneficial environment.
Ocean Approved: an organization that produces vegetables from the sea with minimal impact to the environment.

Seaweed farms have the capacity to grow large amounts of nutrient-rich food, and oysters can act as an efficient carbon and nitrogen sink.

Vladislav Gajic/Shutterstock

in the Netherlands has calculated that a global network of "sea-vegetable" farms totaling 180,000 square kilometers — roughly the size of Washington state — could provide enough protein for the entire world population.

The goal, according to chef Dan Barber — named one of the world's most influential people by *Time* and a hero of the organic food movement — is to create a world where "farms restore instead of deplete" and allow "every community to feed itself."

But here is the real kicker: Because they require no fresh water, no deforestation, and no fertilizer — all significant downsides to land-based farming — these ocean farms promise to be more sustainable than even the most environmentally sensitive traditional farms.

Ramping up food production without increasing greenhouse gas emissions is vital if we are to survive the coming decades. But land-based food production is entering an era of crisis. The UN estimates that global grain production will plummet by 63 million metric tons this year alone mainly because of weather-related calamities like the Russian heat wave and the floods in Pakistan.

Bun Lai, world-renowned sustainable seafood chef, believes that:

If done right, this new generation of green aquaculture is poised to become the most sustainable form of farming on the planet. We need healthy food that protects rather than harms our climate and Earth. It is a key piece of the puzzle for building a sustainable future.

Nature's Climate Warriors: Seaweed and Shellfish

Rather than finfish, the anchor crops of the emerging green ocean farms are seaweed and shellfish — two gifted organisms that might well be mother nature's secret weapons to fight climate change.

Considered the "tree" of coastal ecosystems, seaweed uses photo- 15 synthesis to pull massive amounts of carbon from the atmosphere — with some varieties capable of absorbing five times more carbon dioxide than land-based plants.

Seaweed is one of the fastest growing plants in the world; kelp, for example, grows up to 9–12 feet long in a mere three months. This turbo-charged growth cycle enables farmers to scale up their carbon sinks quickly. Of course, the seaweed grown to mitigate emissions would need to be harvested to produce carbon-neutral biofuels to ensure that the carbon is not simply recycled back into the air as it would be if the seaweed is eaten. The Philippines, China, and other Asian countries, which have long farmed seaweed as a staple food source, now view seaweed farms as an essential ingredient for reducing their carbon emissions.

Oysters also absorb carbon, but their real talent is filtering nitrogen out of the water column. Nitrogen is the greenhouse gas you don't pay attention to — it is nearly 300 times as potent as carbon dioxide, and according to the journal *Nature*, the second worst in terms of having already exceeded a maximum "planetary boundary." Like carbon, nitrogen is an essential part of life — plants, animals, and bacteria all need it to survive — but too much has a devastating effect on our land and ocean ecosystems.

The main nitrogen polluter is agricultural fertilizer runoff. All told, the production of synthetic fertilizers and pesticides contributes more than one trillion pounds of greenhouse gas emissions to the atmosphere globally each year. That's the same amount of emissions that are generated by 88 million passenger cars each year.

Much of this nitrogen from fertilizers ends up in our oceans, where nitrogen is now 50 percent above normal levels. According to the journal *Science*, excess nitrogen "depletes essential oxygen levels in the water and has significant effects on climate, food production, and ecosystems all over the world."

Oysters to the rescue. One oyster filters 30–50 gallons of water a 20 day — and in the process filters nitrogen out of the water column. Recent work done by Roger Newell of the University of Maryland shows that a healthy oyster habitat can reduce total added nitrogen by up to 20 percent. A three-acre oyster farm filters out the equivalent nitrogen load produced by 35 coastal inhabitants.

There is an array of projects sprouting up that use a mix of seaweed and shellfish to clean up polluted urban waterways and help communities prepare for the effects of climate change. One initiative, spearheaded by Dr. Charles Yarish of the University of Connecticut, is growing kelp and shellfish on floating lines in New York's Bronx River to filter nitrogen, mercury, and other pollutants out of the city's toxic waterways, with the goal of making them healthier, more productive, and more economically viable.

Then there is the emerging field of "oyster-tecture," dedicated to building artificial oyster reefs and floating gardens to help protect coastal communities from future hurricanes, sea level rise, and storm surges. Architect Kate Orff from the design firm SCAPE is developing urban aquaculture parks that use floating rafts and suspended shellfish long-lines to build more urban green space while improving the environment. She envisions the new urban ocean farmer as part shell fisherman tending to oyster reefs, and part landscaper, tending the above-surface floating parks.

In Connecticut, advocates are pushing for an expansion of the state's existing nitrogen credit trading program to include shellfish farms, thereby reimbursing oystermen for the nitrogen they filter from Long Island Sound each year. With new oyster operations sprouting up all around the country, rewarding "green fishermen" for the positive effect their farms have on the environment could be a model for how to stimulate job growth while saving the planet.

Farm Your Fuel, Power the Planet

Finding a clean replacement for existing biofuels is becoming increasingly urgent. A report commissioned by the European Union found biofuels from soy beans can create up to four times more climate-warming emissions than equivalent fossil fuels. Biofuels have also forced global food prices up by 75 percent — far more than previously estimated — according to a confidential World Bank study. And a recent report from the International Food Policy and Research Institute warned that U.S. government support for corn ethanol was a major factor behind this year's food price spikes.

Seaweed and other algae is increasingly looking like a viable sub- 25 stitute. About 50 percent of seaweed's weight is oil, which can be used to make biodiesel for cars, trucks, and airplanes. Scientists at the University of Indiana recently figured out how to turn seaweed into biodiesel four times faster than other biofuels, and researchers at the Georgia Institute of Technology have discovered a way to use alginate extracted from kelp to ramp up the storage power of lithium-ion batteries by a factor of ten.

But unlike land-based biofuel crops, seaweed farming does not require fertilizers, forest clearing, water, or heavy use of fuel-burning machinery — and, as a result, according to the World Bank, has a negative carbon footprint. While the technology is still in development, farmers are eager to begin growing their own fuel and create some of the first closed energy loop farms on the planet.

The U.S. Navy has already developed the Riverine Combat ship and Seahawk helicopters powered by seaweed-based bio-diesel. The Pentagon views seaweed and other algae as a key component in their efforts to reduce their carbon footprint. According to Alan Shaffer, the Pentagon's principal deputy director of defense research and engineering:

The beauty with algae is that you can grow it anywhere and to grow it needs to absorb carbon dioxide, so it's not only a very effective fuel, in theory it's also a carbon sink. That's a pretty good deal.

The DOE estimates that seaweed biofuel can yield up to 30 times more energy per acre than land crops such as soybeans. According to *Biofuels Digest,*

Given the high oil yield from algae, some 10 million acres would be sufficient . . . to replace the total petro-diesel fuel in the United States today. This is about 1 percent of the total amount of acreage used in the United States today for grazing and farming.

The world's energy needs could be met by setting aside 3 percent of the world's oceans for seaweed farming. "I guess it's the equivalent of striking oil," says University of California, Berkeley, microbial biology professor Tasios Melis.

The Bitter Reality of Climate Change

These are urgent times, demanding creative and bold solutions. In his best-selling book *Eaarth: Making Life on a Tough New Planet*, Bill McKibben breaks the news that climate change is no longer a future threat — it is here and now and we had better get our affairs in order.

Our oceans are already locked in a death spiral. According to the International Program on the State of the Ocean (IPSO) — a consortium of 27 of the top ocean experts in the world — the effects of climate change, ocean acidification, and oxygen depletion have already triggered a "phase of extinction of marine species unprecedented in human history." Simultaneously, greenhouse gas emissions are breaking records, exceeding even the worst-case scenario envisioned by scientists four years ago.

We face a bitter new reality: Mitigating the effects of climate change may force us to develop our seas to save them — and [our] planet. This re-imaging of the oceans will be heart-wrenching and controversial. Our waters are revered as some of the last wild spaces on Earth — ungoverned and untouched by human hands. If we develop our oceans, farms will some day dot coastlines, mirroring our agricultural landscape. But in the face of the escalating climate crisis, we have little choice but to explore new ways of sustaining humanity while protecting the planet.

As we search for new solutions, we cannot afford to repeat the errors made on land, subsidizing industrial-scale factory farms at the expense of environmental and food quality. Simply substituting destructive fishing fleets with destructive fish farms will only hasten the demise of our oceans.

Instead, we can learn from our mistakes and chart a new course guided by principles of sustainability and meeting social needs. This means dedicating portions of ocean to farming — while reserving large swaths for marine conservation parks. And rather than building sprawling ocean factories, we need [to] create decentralized networks of small-scale food and energy farms growing food, generating power, and creating jobs for local communities. While no panacea, ocean farming — carefully conceived — could be a vital part of reversing course and building a greener future.

All of us who hold dear the deep blue sea need to confront the brutal reality that if we ignore the largest environmental crisis of our generation, our wild oceans will be dead oceans.

Understanding the Text

1. What are some ways environmentalists suggest that the ocean could help us?
2. Which other cultures have used ocean farming? Why is it important to recognize its history?
3. How can seaweed farms help the environment? What is seaweed's relationship to atmospheric carbon?

Reflection and Response

4. Do you think ocean farming is a good way to combat environmental problems and protect our oceans? Explain why or why not.
5. This article makes some comparisons between industrial land-based farming and aquaculture. What are the negative aspects of these two methods of food production? How could they be improved?

Making Connections

6. This article mentions "overfishing." Do some research to find out exactly what this is and why it is detrimental to the environment. What are the major problems caused by overfishing?
7. Do some research on ocean farms. What are the possibilities and challenges of ocean farming? Which type of ocean farming seems most logical or beneficial?

Tsunami Cities Fight Nuclear Elites to Create Green Jobs

Stuart Biggs

Stuart Biggs, a journalist from Rugby, England, studied history and politics at Trinity College in Dublin, Ireland, and journalism at the University of Hong Kong. He worked as a business reporter for the *South China Morning Post* in Hong Kong. He is currently based in Tokyo, Japan, as a reporter for Bloomberg News, where he covers Asian environmental and clean-energy issues.

This article was written in July 2012 about the aftereffects of the tsunami in Japan. Biggs focuses specifically on the city of Rikuzentakata and its gradual decline. He also addresses ways to deal with environmental issues that have arisen, such as making Rikuzentakata into an ecocity. As you read, think about the term "ecocity" and whether it seems like a viable option for the future.

Rikuzentakata,° like many cities on Japan's rugged northeast Pacific coast, was in decline even before last year's tsunami killed 1,700 of its 24,000 inhabitants and destroyed most of its downtown buildings.

With two-thirds of the remaining residents homeless, Mayor Futoshi Toba questioned whether the city could recover, *Bloomberg Markets* magazine reports in its August issue. Damage to infrastructure and the economy, he said, would force people to move away to find jobs.

Sixteen months later, the city is trying to rebuild in a way that Toba says would reinvent the region and provide a model to overcome obstacles that have hobbled the Japanese economy for more than 20 years: the fastest-aging population in the developed world, loss of manufacturing competitiveness to China and South Korea and reliance on imported fossil fuels.

Rikuzentakata is part of a government program to create one of the country's first so-called ecocities.°

They would be smaller and more self-sufficient and would lower 5 costs through technology and create new jobs in renewable energy to replace those lost to the decline of agriculture and fisheries.

Toba says Japan must address the depopulation of rural areas that has coincided with agriculture's shrinking role in the broader

---

Rikuzentakata: a city in Iwate, Japan, which contained Lake Furukawanuma until the 2011 tsunami destroyed it.
ecocity: a city designed with consideration of environmental impact, inhabited by people dedicated to minimization of required inputs of energy, water, and food, and waste output of heat, air pollution, and water pollution.

economy — from about 6 percent in the 1970s to 1.4 percent today — and it must do so as soon as possible.

"It's a race against time," he says.

"Super-Aging Society"

Ecocities can lead the way, says Hideaki Miyata, an engineering professor at the University of Tokyo who's advising local officials on the project.

"We can provide a solution for Japan's super-aging society," he says. "Younger people were already leaving these cities, but what we're planning to do here will provide new jobs and factories."

That's essential, says Kiyoshi Murakami, an executive at BNY Mellon Asset Management Japan Ltd. who grew up in Rikuzentakata and also advises Toba. 10

"For the ecocity, its impact on employment is the most important thing," he says.

After the tsunami, which reached as high as the fourth story on the city's seafront hospital, Rikuzentakata joined

"Rikuzentakata is part of a government program to create one of [Japan's] first so-called ecocities."

forces with neighboring Ofunato and Sumita in the Kesen district.

They applied for aid under the national government's FutureCity program, which has an annual budget of about 1 billion yen ($12.5 million) to create blueprints for urban development that promotes environmental protection and clean-energy use.

Clean Energy

The goal of the Kesen project is to generate at least 50 percent of the region's electricity through solar and other renewable-energy sources, reducing Kesen's near-total dependence on Tohoku Electric Power Co. (9506), Japan's fifth-largest utility, and lowering electricity costs for the area's 67,000 residents.

Planners say they hope to attract clean-energy companies, including makers of lithium-ion batteries used to store power before it is fed to the grid. 15

They also envision using electric buses to ferry residents around town and rebuilding schools to double as community centers and evacuation shelters, thereby streamlining public infrastructure.

Making the Kesen project a reality hinges on how much of the central government's 19 trillion yen in reconstruction spending goes to the three cities, as well as alternative-energy subsidies, says another project adviser, Kimikazu Uemura, chief executive officer of Index Consulting Inc., a project management firm.

Anti-Nuclear Zeitgeist

"It's important that whatever is built brings new business and is sustainable," [Uemura] says. "If the government focuses only on rebuilding existing infrastructure, we'll have areas with new roads and buildings but nobody living there."

The regeneration ideas swirling around Kesen fit the current anti-nuclear Japanese Zeitgeist.

After the March 2011 tsunami° damaged the Fukushima Daiichi   20
nuclear power plant, and radiation spread across the area, polling by the Asahi newspaper found that 74 percent of those surveyed were in favor of decommissioning all of Japan's reactors.

The sour mood is deepening long-standing public disaffection with the economic and political malaise that has gripped Japan since the asset-bubble collapse of the early 1990s, says Andrew DeWit, a professor of the politics of public finance at Tokyo's Rikkyo University.

Quadrillion Yen

The economy has contracted in three of the past four years. As of June 11, the Nikkei 225 Stock Average had fallen 78 percent from its peak in December 1989.

In May, Fitch Ratings cut Japan's yen sovereign rating by two levels, to A+ from AA, as the country struggled to rein in the biggest public debt burden — both in absolute terms and as a percentage of gross domestic product — in the world. The amount of debt is expected to exceed a quadrillion yen for the first time this year.

In rejecting nuclear, DeWit says, the Japanese are rejecting the web of cozy ties at the very top of society, forming what's commonly called "the nuclear village" — the politicians, utilities, bureaucrats and academics that promoted Japan's reliance on atomic energy in the first place.

2011 tsunami: caused by an earthquake off the Pacific coast of Tōhoku, Japan. The tsunami caused nuclear accidents, primarily the level 7 meltdowns at three reactors in the Fukushima Daiichi Nuclear Power Plant complex.

A wave approaches Miyako City, Japan, after an earthquake struck on March 11, 2011. The powerful earthquake, combined with the massive tsunami, killed more than 15,800, devastated many eastern coastline communities, and triggered a nuclear catastrophe at the Fukushima Daiichi nuclear power station.

Reuters/Mainichi Shimbun

Energy shortages risk making things worse. Nuclear power has 25 been the linchpin of the resource-poor country's economic planning since the 1960s.

Zero Nuclear

It has fed industrial giants such as Toyota Motor Corp. and Sony Corp. that helped Japan recover from the devastation of World War II to become the world's second-largest economy by 1967.

Before the disaster, Japan depended on atomic power for 30 percent of its energy needs.

That share had fallen to zero by May 5 this year as nuclear plants taken offline for regular maintenance weren't restarted while the government and regulators scrambled to reassure a doubting public of their safety.

The impasse ended in June when Prime Minister Yoshihiko Noda approved the restart of two reactors in western Japan, a measure he says is necessary for the economy. The first was running at full capacity by July 9.

Still, the long-term policy remains to reduce dependency on nuclear and move toward renewables such as wind and solar. 30

That's good news for nontraditional energy companies, as well as Kesen-like smart-city projects.

FutureCity Program

To help the upstarts, the government is introducing so-called feed-in tariffs that force utilities to pay a higher price for renewable power over the next 20 years: 42 yen per kilowatt-hour compared with the 13.65 yen rate charged to industrial and commercial users.

This allows new, alternative-energy operators, who face high startup costs, to enter the market on a more competitive footing.

Out of 11 cities in the government's FutureCity program, six are in the tsunami-hit northeastern region, which Jun Iio of Japan's Reconstruction Design Council says is "a microcosm of the problems being faced by all of Japan."

About a third of Rikuzentakata's population is over the age of 35 65. Japan's population, which peaked in 2005, is poised to shrink to 125.2 million in 2014 from 127.7 million last year, according to data compiled by Bloomberg.

People over the age of 65 make up about 23 percent of the population, a proportion that may increase to 40 percent by 2050, government estimates show.

Rural Decline

Smart cities can help reverse rural decline, DeWit says. There's an economic rationale for converting land to renewable-energy use.

Rice paddies that were inundated with seawater in March 2011 can yield more profit if they're covered with solar panels than if they're rehabilitated as agricultural land.

"When you're sitting on land, or an old factory, rather than clear it up, you can cover it with solar panels," says Penn Bowers, a utility and trading-company analyst at CLSA Asia-Pacific Markets in Tokyo.

That's what Masayoshi Son, Japan's second-richest person, would   40
like to do on irradiated farmland around the Fukushima plant, including the strict no-go area that can't be used for crops or grazing.

The CEO of mobile-phone-service provider Softbank Corp. (9984)
is eager to press ahead with a vast array of solar plants producing
more than 200 megawatts, enough to power about 48,600 homes. He's
awaiting passage of government legislation that would guarantee projects such as his access to the electricity grid.

New Opportunities

The spread of new energy sources could create opportunities for
players other than utilities, says Ali Izadi-Najafabadi, an energy technologies analyst at Bloomberg New Energy Finance.

Wind and sunshine aren't constant, and the energy they produce
needs to be stored in batteries so that it can be released in such a way
as to meet the ebb and flow of peak and off-peak consumption.

By the end of the year, Japan may have more lithium-ion batteries
installed on the power grid than any other country, Izadi-Najafabadi
says.

"That wouldn't have happened without Fukushima," he says. "The   45
utilities weren't considering these so-called smart-grid technologies.
They operate in a different world now."

Hitachi Ltd. (6501) and NEC Corp. (6701), both makers of industrial-
grade batteries, are among thirty companies in the Kesen ecocity
consortium.

Consumer Electronics

Creating demand in northeast Japan may help battery makers compete against global rivals, the University of Tokyo's Miyata says.

"Japan led the development of lithium-ion batteries for use in consumer electronics and then with cars," Miyata says. "Each time, Korea
and China caught up rapidly, and now, everyone is trying to be first
to develop the next generation of batteries, which is industrial, large
scale."

In Rikuzentakata, Mayor Toba has a personal stake in regeneration.

His wife was killed when the tsunami engulfed their seaside home.   50
He was at city hall and survived, as did their two children, who were
at school.

Reborn, Rikuzentakata would be a fitting legacy to those who perished.

"We have to do more than simply rebuild houses," Toba says. "If we do that but don't provide people with jobs, their lives won't get better."

Understanding the Text

1. What was the condition of the Japanese city Rikuzentakata before the 2011 tsunami?

2. How did the tsunami affect the city? How did this tragedy create some new opportunities?

3. How is the city trying to rebuild? In what ways are the rebuilding efforts tied to sustainability?

Reflection and Response

4. Why do you think the city's mayor Futoshi Toba described the environmental situation as "a race against time" (par. 7)?

5. What is the goal of the Kesen project? Do you think this goal can be achieved in the near future?

Making Connections

6. Research other Japanese cities that were impacted by the 2011 tsunami. How are they rebuilding? Are they using environmentally friendly practices?

7. This article mentions the FutureCity program. Visit futurecity.org to learn more. What exactly does FutureCity do? How is the organization trying to help Japanese cities?

8. This article was published in July 2012. Do some research to find out how Rikuzentakata is doing today.

After Fukushima: Now, More Than Ever

Nathan Myhrvold

Nathan Myhrvold is a former chief technology officer at Microsoft and a cofounder of Intellectual Ventures, a patent portfolio holding company. He held a postdoctoral fellowship at the University of Cambridge, working under physicist Stephen Hawking, and he assisted Microsoft cofounder Bill Gates in writing *The Road Ahead*, a *New York Times* bestseller. In addition, he has written for *Fortune*, *Time*, *Scientific American*, and *National Geographic Traveler*.

This article, originally published in December 2011 in the *New York Times*, describes the Fukushima Daiichi nuclear power plant accidents. Myhrvold highlights the lessons that can be learned from this disaster, including the dangers of tsunamis and the growing need for reliable energy. He also describes what other countries have learned from this disaster. As you read, think about the Fukushima accident and how it impacts the future of nuclear energy.

After the accidents at the Fukushima Daiichi° nuclear power plant in Japan, the role of nuclear energy is again at a turning point—the third since the birth of the industry in the 1950s. Views about its future are pulled between the fear of nuclear destruction and the need for energy. Memories of Hiroshima and the Cold War, while fading, can still induce anxiety. The accident at Fukushima° also brought the Soviet-era disaster of Chernobyl back to mind.

The primary lesson from Japan's recent trauma, however, is that a tsunami is dangerous to everything in its path, nuclear plants included. Consider the growing needs for reliable energy, the fact that nuclear is probably the safest form of power that can meet those needs, and the unfortunate truth that fossil-fueled alternatives emit so much pollution that they arguably pose a much greater threat than the darkest nuclear accident scenario.

A logician would see no reason for ambivalence, but most people are not logical when it comes to scary events. That's why people worry

---

Fukushima Daiichi: a nuclear power plant (now disabled) located on a 3.5-square-kilometer (860-acre) site in the towns of Okuma and Futaba in Japan.
accident at Fukushima: a series of equipment failures, nuclear meltdowns, and releases of radioactive materials at the Fukushima Daiichi Nuclear Power Plant, following the Tōhoku earthquake and tsunami on March 11, 2011; the largest nuclear disaster since the Chernobyl disaster of 1986.

about dying in a plane crash while driving to the airport, even though the drive is more dangerous than the flight.

So even as countries like Germany, Switzerland and — to a lesser extent — Japan swerve away from nuclear energy, many faster-growing economies are staying on course. They see an urgent need for vast amounts of electricity, and see no cleaner, safer, more reliable way to make it.

The first major transformation in nuclear technology was from atomic bombs to commercial electricity generators. The public and politicians were fascinated by the idea of electricity that, they were told, would be too cheap to meter. Although the promise of free energy never came true, the technology pretty much worked as advertised — reliable and safe. 5

> "After the accidents at the Fukushima Daiichi nuclear power plant in Japan, the role of nuclear energy is again at a turning point — the third since the birth of the industry in the 1950s."

Despite nuclear power's impeccable safety record, fears of leaks and meltdowns grew through the late 1960s as the environmental movement came of age. Having cleaned up the atmosphere and public waters, many environmentalists trained their sights on eliminating nuclear power. That set the stage for the second turning point — a move away from nuclear energy.

That transition got a shove in 1979 from two events: The release of *The China Syndrome*, a fictional movie starring Jane Fonda, and the accident at the Three Mile Island nuclear power plant in Pennsylvania, in the eastern United States. Public support of nuclear power flagged, and the industry was buffeted by strong economic headwinds, including a prolonged recession and a collapse in natural gas prices.

Nuclear fears and doubts trumped the perceived need. Environmental groups lobbied for safe, "clean" power plants — often, plants that burned coal. The logic must have seemed sound then. Nuclear plants could, under improbable but not impossible circumstances, cause large-scale environmental disaster. Chernobyl was a case in point.

Why take the risk? What similar harm could come from burning coal? Quite a bit. As we now know, coal power plants emit enormous amounts of carbon dioxide — the main greenhouse gas° that is changing

---

greenhouse gas: a gas in the atmosphere that absorbs infrared radiation, trapping and holding heat. This process is the primary cause of the greenhouse effect.

the earth's climate. Nuclear plants do not. Today, environmental activists point to plausible scenarios in which runaway global warming causes far worse damage to the Earth than if every nuclear plant — more than 400 of them as of 2010 — were to melt down. At the most extreme, James Hansen, head of NASA's Goddard Institute for Space Studies, offers the "Venus syndrome": as warming accelerates, oceans evaporate faster, pushing more water vapor into the atmosphere. Water vapor is itself a powerful greenhouse gas, so a vicious cycle could set in until "the ocean boils into the atmosphere, and life is extinguished."

Now the world has focused on the danger of global warming and the need for technologies that can supply large amounts of power all day, every day, without emitting CO_2. Nuclear plants are the only proven technology that fits that bill; they actually deliver 90 percent of rated capacity. That means a reactor rated at 1,000 megawatts pumps a full 900 megawatts onto the grid, averaged over a decade or so. In contrast, the vicissitudes of sunlight and wind mean that, over a similar period, a solar plant delivers less than 20 percent of its rated peak capacity even if it is in a sunny desert, and a wind farm generates less than 30 percent of its potential. With no good technology to store large amounts of energy, power companies must add baseload generators (nuclear, gas or coal) as backup for every wind and solar facility.

The need for low-emissions power is particularly acute in emerging economies like India and China. Electricity use in China, the Middle East and Africa is growing rapidly — and so far that's been a good thing. Electricity is displacing dirty sources of heat and light, like home coal or wood fires, which sicken and kill hundreds of thousands every year with their soot.

The energy problem for the 21st century is giving every citizen of Earth enough energy to support a modern standard of living — that probably means quadrupling the output of electrical plants. Advances in efficiency could, in principle, lower that number, but more likely other factors will raise it. Today, for example, only about 1,500 watts of the approximately 6,700 watts of power a typical American uses comes in the form of electricity, based on figures from the International Energy Agency. But if we continue to use more electricity to power cars, trains and other vehicles, demand for electrical power will probably soar.

Where is all that electricity going to come from? We call earthquake-induced waves tsunami — a Japanese word — because these giant sea swells have pounded Japan with some regularity for millennia. Living near the seashore in Japan is wonderful in many ways,

10

but it carries an unavoidable danger of inundation. Although the people of Japan understand that risk, their engineers and planners made some tragic decisions.

The reactors at Fukushima Daiichi, which were designed in the slide rule era and are far less safe than modern reactors, were part of a plant created to survive a 5.7-meter tsunami even though Japan had been hit by a 29-meter tsunami as recently as 1933. When the waves of the March tsunami, thought to have exceeded 14 meters at Fukushima, swept through the plant and disabled the reactor cooling systems, reactions by operators and officials compounded the damage. Fukushima teaches us that nuclear plants — like hospitals, schools and other structures that are hard to evacuate safely — should not be built where tsunamis are likely to reach.

Germans apparently took away a different lesson. Although Germany is not prone to tsunamis, the government decided this summer to shut down seven reactors immediately and to turn off the rest by 2022. It's not clear whether this policy will stick; the country decided more than 10 years ago to get rid of nuclear power, but that phaseout never happened.

Nor is it clear how the country will meet commitments to make steep reductions in national CO_2 emissions if it turns off all its reactors. Germans have heavily subsidized solar power and bet big on wind power, both of which are backed up, when the sun doesn't shine or the wind doesn't blow, by electricity imported mainly from nuclear plants in France, Poland and Russia. Is it fair to call yourself nuclear-free if you effectively outsource the plants?

Germany is prosperous, and perhaps its taxpayers can afford to subsidize solar power, bail out Greece and wind down nuclear power. But money is just one thing at risk. If Germany turns away from nuclear power, its CO_2 emissions will inevitably increase. And that will harm the environment everywhere. One hopes that, in the land of Faust, Germans understand the relevance that the bargain he struck has to their current choices.

The future of nuclear energy hinges on how we reconcile fears with needs. For Germans, the emission of CO_2 appears to be the lesser evil, at least at the moment.

In just the past few months, Brazil, South Africa and Saudi Arabia announced plans to move ahead with the construction of nuclear plants — 16 of them, in Saudi Arabia's case. In those nations and in India, China and other parts of the world where nuclear reactors are scheduled to go up by the dozens, the complex calculus of risk may yield a different result.

Understanding the Text

1. What happened at the Fukushima nuclear power plant?

2. What is Myhrvold's perspective on nuclear power? How would you summarize his point of view?

3. How does Germany react to the Fukushima disaster? What lessons could be learned from Germany's decisions?

Reflection and Response

4. How high is the demand for electrical power across the world? Explain.

5. What are some of the stages or phases of energy production described in this article? Where does nuclear power fit into those stages?

6. What lessons can be learned from the Fukushima disaster?

7. In what ways is this disaster tied to sustainability? How is nuclear power a sustainability issue?

Making Connections

8. The article describes two previous nuclear accidents: the Three Mile Island accident in Pennsylvania and the Chernobyl disaster in Ukraine. How were these accidents similar to or different from the Fukushima disaster? Based on your research, do you believe nuclear power is safe or unsafe? Explain your answer.

9. Like most energy sources, nuclear power has strengths and weaknesses. Do some research on the major energy sources in use today, as well as those that might play a major role in the future. If it were your decision, what energy sources would the world depend on in the coming decades?

A Tree Grows in Haiti: Recovery Efforts May Hinge on Something Green

Jeneen Interlandi

Jeneen Interlandi is a science writer who contributes to *Scientific American* and *The New York Times Magazine.* She spent four years as a staff writer for *Newsweek,* where she covered health, science, and the environment. Interlandi has worked as a researcher at both Harvard Medical School and Lamont Doherty Earth Observatory. She holds master's degrees in environmental science and journalism, both from Columbia University in New York.

This article originally appeared in *Newsweek* in July 2010, six months after a devastating earthquake in Haiti. Interlandi focuses on the Haitian city of Gonaïves and, in particular, on methods of recovery, including planting trees to combat deforestation. As you read, consider other possible solutions to deal with the ramifications of a major natural disaster.

Surrounded as it is by an amphitheater of treeless mountains, the city of Gonaïves° has long been defenseless against the onslaught of hurricanes that pound Haiti every summer. Unencumbered by trunks or roots or shrubs, the water sloshes freely downward, gathering into apocalyptic mudslides that destroy homes, crops, and livelihoods. In 2004 a single storm claimed 2,000 lives from this one city.

Like the rest of Haiti, Gonaïves is bracing for another punishing hurricane season, even as earthquake°-recovery efforts falter and the city struggles to absorb thousands of refugees from Port-au-Prince, 100 miles to the south. Amid a host of competing priorities, the seemingly least urgent task may prove to be the most significant: planting as many trees as possible. "Almost all of the country's problems —

Gonaïves: a coastal city in northern Haiti, the fifth largest in the county by population (300,000). The city, also known as Haiti's "independence city," was founded in 1422.
earthquake: the 2010 Haiti earthquake, a magnitude 7.0 earthquake that impacted parts of Haiti and other Caribbean islands on January 12, 2010.

natural disasters, food shortages, poverty — can be traced back to rampant deforestation,"° says Ethan Budiansky, the Caribbean-programs officer at Trees for the Future, a nonprofit group that is planting thousands of trees in the mountains around Gonaïves. "So if we want to fix the country, we have to start there." While there are no panaceas in Haiti, successful reforestation might come close. By absorbing water and holding soil in place, trees can minimize the impact of natural disasters and repair nutrient-poor agricultural lands. An aggressive reforestation campaign would also bring much-needed jobs to the region and, if done correctly, could solve the energy conundrum that led Haitians to cull their forests in the first place. "Planting trees is not just some quaint side project," says UN Development Group chair Helen Clark. "It's the key to rebuilding the country."

Haitian deforestation has many culprits — from French colonizers' coffee and sugar plantations to the swaggering timber industry of the 19th and 20th centuries — but most experts agree that the biggest modern contributors are the food and fuel needs of Haitians themselves. As the population grew — from 3 million in 1940 to 9 million in 2000 — rural Haitians were forced to clear ever-larger swaths of mountainside for subsistence crops. The trees themselves doubled as a source of fuel and cash for families who not only used the wood to cook with but also sold it as charcoal in energy-starved Port-au-Prince. (Charcoal is made by burning wood and other carbon-rich substances in an oxygen-proof furnace.) In time, the charcoal trade grew to account for 20 percent of the rural economy and 80 percent of the country's energy supply. Before long, 98 percent of the country's forests had been chopped down, and Haitians were burning 30 million trees' worth of charcoal annually. Soil eroded, crop yields shrank, and floods became more severe. Eventually, everyone who could abandoned the countryside for the capital city.

That's saying a lot. Six months after the earthquake, collapsed buildings still addle the landscape; millions of Haitians continue to live in makeshift tent cities. And with February elections still waiting to be held, the country's government has all but dissolved. Meanwhile, torrential rains have begun to lash Haiti daily. According to

> "Six months after a devastating earthquake, the nation is still struggling to regain its footing. The best recovery efforts may hinge on something green."

deforestation: the removal of a forest or stand of trees where the land is thereafter converted to a nonforest use.

forecasts by Columbia University's International Research Institute for Climate and Society, the country faces a 55 percent chance of above-average rainfall this season, and a slightly higher-than-average chance of being hit by a tropical storm. And thanks to the January earthquake that disturbed massive amounts of rock and soil, landslides are almost certain to be worse.

And as Port-au-Prince grew populous, economic development took 5 a decidedly urban bent. Haitian entrepreneurs invested millions of dollars in hotels and restaurants, and the international community focused on promoting tourism and attracting manufacturers from the U.S. and Brazil. In 2009 former president Bill Clinton, the U.S. special envoy to Haiti, secured Haitian-based textile companies duty-free access to U.S. markets, and persuaded Royal Caribbean Cruise Lines to invest $55 million in an expansion project on Haiti's northern coast. Those efforts brought some welcome attention and investment dollars to the beleaguered country, but did little for the 6.5 million rural Haitians who earn their living off the land. And as the agricultural sector continued to wither, farmers turned increasingly to the charcoal markets.

In 2008 the economic toll of such environmental degradation became apparent. That year's hurricane season — the worst to hit Haiti in decades — cost the country tens of millions of dollars in export crops and infrastructure. And the economic consequences of deforestation stretch well beyond those losses. Without trees to protect the soil, rains have washed it down into rivers and streams at a rate of 36 million tons per year. Sediment buildup has polluted drinking water and choked the life out of once bountiful fisheries. And without soil to absorb the rain, water tables have dwindled precipitously, adding a string of droughts to the country's woes.

These days, "decentralization" — refocusing economic-development efforts from dense urban centers like Port-au-Prince to rural outposts like the mountains around Gonaïves — has become a buzzword among relief workers and legislators. They say that if the recent rash of natural disasters has taught them anything, it's that in Haiti there can be no economic growth without environmental restoration. "The land is so degraded that just one storm or quake can undo a decade's worth of progress," says Budiansky. "And with people pouring into the countryside now, it's only going to get worse." Since the earthquake, more than 600,000 Haitians have fled Port-au-Prince searching for food, shelter, and work among their rural kin. With no other recourse, they will soon be forced to convert the remaining 330 square miles of forests into subsistence farms and charcoal for sale.

Understanding the Text

1. What environmental situation does the city of Gonaïves continue to face?
2. What are some methods Gonaïves is using to recover?
3. What happened to the country's government after the earthquake?
4. What is agroforestry? How could this help to solve Haiti's problems?

Reflection and Response

5. What effect has deforestation had on Haiti? How did it impact many of the country's other problems?
6. What happened as the population of Port-au-Prince grew?
7. In what ways are Haiti's problems tied to sustainability? How could sustainable development and planning help Haiti to improve in the future?

Making Connections

8. Research the impact of deforestation on other countries. Are they similar to or different from what has happened in Haiti? What are other countries doing to address the problem?
9. Several articles in this chapter seem to suggest that natural disasters can create new opportunities to implement sustainable development plans. Do some research on the types of "green" initiatives that have followed natural disasters like floods, hurricanes, earthquakes, and fires.
10. Do a Google search using terms like "Haiti Earthquake." What impacts do you see? What did Haiti look like before and after the earthquake? In what ways do the before images reveal a landscape particularly susceptible to destruction? What do the images reveal about the recovery efforts, and how do they reflect more sustainable development?

The Third Industrial Revolution: Toward a New Economic Paradigm

Jeremy Rifkin

Jeremy Rifkin is a writer, a public speaker, a political adviser, and an activist from Denver, Colorado. Rifkin is the founder and president of the Foundation on Economic Trends. He is also the founder of The Third Industrial Revolution Global CEO Business Roundtable, which works to transition the economy into a new infrastructure. Rifkin's work explores the potential impact of scientific and technological changes on the economy, the workforce, society, and the environment.

This is an excerpt from *The Third Industrial Revolution: How Lateral Power Is Transforming Energy, the Economy, and the World*, published in 2011. Rifkin explains the changes faced by our industrial civilization, including the depletion of oil resources and the threat of hunger and starvation. As you read, think about the idea of a third industrial revolution and how it has developed over the past three decades.

O ur industrial civilization is at a crossroads. Oil and the other fossil fuel energies that make up the industrial way of life are sunsetting, and the technologies made from and propelled by these energies are antiquated. The entire industrial infrastructure built off of fossil fuels is aging and in disrepair. The result is that unemployment is rising to dangerous levels all over the world. Governments, businesses and consumers are awash in debt and living standards are plummeting everywhere. A record one billion human beings — nearly one seventh of the human race — face hunger and starvation.

Worse, climate change from fossil fuel–based industrial activity looms on the horizon. Our scientists warn that we face a potentially cataclysmic change in the temperature and chemistry of the planet, which threatens to destabilize ecosystems around the world. Scientists worry that we may be on the brink of a mass extinction of plant and animal life by the end of the century, imperiling our own species' ability to survive. It is becoming increasingly clear that we need a new economic narrative that can take us into a more equitable and sustainable future.

By the 1980s the evidence was mounting that the fossil fuel–driven industrial revolution was peaking and that human-induced climate change was forcing a planetary crisis of untold proportions. For the past 30 years I have been searching for a new paradigm that could usher in a post-carbon era. In my explorations, I came to realize that the great economic revolutions in history occur when new communication technologies converge with new energy systems. New energy regimes make possible the creation of more interdependent economic activity and expanded commercial exchange as well as facilitate more dense and inclusive social relationships. The accompanying communication revolutions become the means to organize and manage the new temporal and spatial dynamics that arise from new energy systems.

In the 19th century, steam-powered print technology became the communication medium to manage the coal-fired rail infrastructure and the incipient national markets of the First Industrial Revolution. In the 20th century, electronic communications — the telephone and later, radio and television — became the communication medium to manage and market the oil-powered auto age and the mass consumer culture of the Second Industrial Revolution.

In the mid-1990s, it dawned on me that a new convergence of communication and energy was in the offing. Internet technology and renewable energies were about to merge to create a powerful new infrastructure for a Third Industrial Revolution (TIR) that would change the world. In the coming era, hundreds of millions of people will produce their own green energy in their homes, offices, and factories and share it with each other in an "energy Internet," just like we now create and share information online. The democratization of energy will bring with it a fundamental reordering of human relationships, impacting the very way we conduct business, govern society, educate our children, and engage in civic life.

I introduced the Third Industrial Revolution vision at the Wharton School's Advanced Management Program (AMP), at the University of Pennsylvania, where I have been a senior lecturer for the past sixteen years on new trends in science, technology, the economy, and society. The five-week program exposes CEOs and business executives from around the world to the emerging issues and challenges they will face in the 21st century. The idea soon found its way into corporate suites and became part of the political lexicon among heads of state in the European Union.

By the year 2000, the European Union was aggressively pursuing policies to significantly reduce its carbon footprint and transition into a sustainable economic era. Europeans were readying targets and benchmarks, resetting research and development priorities, and putting into place codes, regulations, and standards for a new economic journey. By contrast, America was preoccupied with the newest gizmos and "killer apps" coming out of Silicon Valley, and homeowners were flush with excitement over a bullish real estate market pumped up by subprime mortgages.

Few Americans were interested in sobering peak oil forecasts, dire climate change warnings, and the growing signs that beneath the surface, our economy was not well. There was an air of contentment, even complacency, across the country, confirming once again the belief that our good fortune demonstrated our superiority over other nations.

Feeling a little like an outsider in my own country, I chose to ignore Horace Greeley's sage advice to every malcontent in 1850 to "Go West, young man, go West," and decided to travel in the opposite direction, across the ocean to old Europe, where new ideas about the future prospects of the human race were being seriously entertained.

> "It is becoming increasingly clear that we need a new economic narrative that can take us into a more equitable and sustainable future."

I know at this point, many of my 10 American readers are rolling their eyes and saying, "Give me a break! Europe is falling apart and living in the past. The whole place is one big museum. It may be a nice destination for a holiday but is no longer a serious contender on the world scene."

I'm not naïve to Europe's many problems, failings, and contradictions. But pejorative slurs could just as easily be leveled at the United States and other governments for their many limitations. And before we Americans become too puffed up about our own importance, we should take note that the European Union, not the United States or China, is the biggest economy in the world. The gross domestic product (GDP) of its twenty-seven member states exceeds the GDP of our fifty states. While the European Union doesn't field much of a global military presence, it is a formidable force on the international stage. More to the point, the European Union is virtually alone among the governments of the world in asking the big questions about our future viability as a species on Earth.

So I went east. For the past ten years, I have spent more than 40 percent of my time in the European Union, sometimes commuting weekly back and forth across the Atlantic, working with governments, the business community, and civil society organizations to advance the Third Industrial Revolution.

In 2006, I began working with the leadership of the European Parliament in drafting a Third Industrial Revolution economic development plan. Then, in May 2007, the European Parliament issued a formal written declaration endorsing the Third Industrial Revolution as the long-term economic vision and road map for the European Union. The Third Industrial Revolution is now being implemented by the various agencies within the European Commission as well as in the member states.

A year later, in October 2008, just weeks after the global economic collapse, my office hurriedly assembled a meeting in Washington, D.C., of eighty CEOs and senior executives from the world's leading companies in renewable energy, construction, architecture, real estate, IT, power and utilities, and transport and logistics to discuss how we might turn the crisis into an opportunity.

Business leaders and trade associations attending the gathering agreed that they could no longer go it alone and committed to creating a Third Industrial Revolution network that could work with governments, local businesses, and civil society organizations toward the goal of transitioning the global economy into a distributed postcarbon era. The economic development group — which includes Philips, Schneider Electric, IBM, Cisco Systems, Acciona, CH2M Hill, Arup, Adrian Smith + Gordon Gill Architecture, and Q-Cells, among others — is the largest of its kind in the world and is currently working with cities, regions, and national governments to develop master plans to transform their economies into Third Industrial Revolution infrastructures. 15

The Third Industrial Revolution vision is quickly spreading to countries in Asia, Africa, and the Americas. On May 24, 2011, I presented the five pillar TIR economic plan in a keynote address at the fiftieth anniversary conference of the Organization for Economic Cooperation and Development (OECD) in Paris, attended by heads of state and ministers from the thirty-four participating member nations. The presentation accompanied the rollout of an OECD green growth economic plan which will serve as a template to begin preparing the nations of the world for a post carbon industrial future.

In designing the EU blueprint for the Third Industrial Revolution, I have been privileged to work with many of Europe's leading heads of state, including Chancellor Angela Merkel of Germany; Prime Minister Romano Prodi of Italy; Prime Minister José Luis Rodríguez Zapatero of Spain; Manuel Barroso, the president of the European Commission; and five of the presidents of the European Council.

Is there anything we Americans can learn from what's happening in Europe? I believe so. We need to begin by taking a careful look at what our European friends are saying and attempting to do. However falteringly, Europeans are at least coming to grips with the reality that the fossil fuel era is dying, and they are beginning to chart a course into a green future. Unfortunately, Americans, for the most part, continue to be in a state of denial, not wishing to acknowledge that the economic system that served us so well in the past is now on life support. Like Europe, we need to own up and pony up.

But what can we bring to the party? While Europe has come up with a compelling narrative, no one can tell a story better than America. Madison Avenue, Hollywood, and Silicon Valley excel at this. What has distinguished America is not so much our manufacturing acumen or military prowess, but our uncanny ability to envision the future with such vividness and clarity that people feel as if they've arrived even before they've left the station. If and when Americans truly "get" the new Third Industrial Revolution narrative, we have the unequalled ability to move quickly to make that dream a reality.

The Third Industrial Revolution is the last of the great Industrial 20 Revolutions and will lay the foundational infrastructure for an emerging collaborative age. The forty year build-out of the TIR infrastructure will create hundreds of thousands of new businesses and hundreds of millions of new jobs. Its completion will signal the end of a two-hundred-year commercial saga characterized by industrious thinking, entrepreneurial markets, and mass labor workforces and the beginning of a new era marked by collaborative behavior, social networks and boutique professional and technical workforces. In the coming half century, the conventional, centralized business operations of the First and Second Industrial Revolutions will increasingly be subsumed by the distributed business practices of the Third Industrial Revolution; and the traditional, hierarchical organization of economic and political power will give way to lateral power organized nodally across society.

At first blush, the very notion of lateral power seems so contradictory to how we have experienced power relations through much of history. Power, after all, has traditionally been organized pyramidically from top to bottom. Today, however, the collaborative power unleashed by the coming together of Internet technology and renewable energies fundamentally restructures human relationships, from top to bottom to side to side, with profound implications for the future of society.

The music companies didn't understand distributed power until millions of young people began sharing music online, and corporate revenues tumbled in less than a decade. Encyclopedia Britannica did not appreciate the distributed and collaborative power that made

Wikipedia the leading reference source in the world. Nor did the newspapers take seriously the distributed power of the blogosphere; now many publications are either going out of business or transferring much of their activities online. The implications of people sharing distributed energy in an open commons are even more far-reaching.

Like every other communication and energy infrastructure in history, the various pillars of a Third Industrial Revolution must be laid down simultaneously or the foundation will not hold. That's because each pillar can only function in relationship to the others. The five pillars of the Third Industrial Revolution are (1) shifting to renewable energy; (2) transforming the building stock of every continent into micro-power plants to collect renewable energies on-site; (3) deploying hydrogen and other storage technologies in every building and throughout the infrastructure to store intermittent energies; (4) using Internet technology to transform the power grid of every continent into an energy-sharing intergrid that acts just like the Internet (when millions of buildings are generating a small amount of energy locally, on-site, they can sell surplus back to the grid and share electricity with their continental neighbors); and (5) transitioning the transport fleet to electric plug-in and fuel cell vehicles that can buy and sell electricity on a smart, continental, interactive power grid.

The critical need to integrate and harmonize these five pillars at every level and stage of development became clear to the European Union in the fall of 2010. A leaked European Commission document warned that the European Union would need to spend €1 trillion [approx. 725 billion USD] between 2010 and 2020 on updating its electricity grid to accommodate an influx of renewable energy. The internal document noted that "Europe is still lacking the infrastructure to enable renewables to develop and compete on an equal footing with traditional sources."

The European Union is expected to draw one-third of its electricity from green sources by 2020. This means that the power grid must be digitized and made intelligent to handle the intermittent renewable energies being fed to the grid from tens of thousands of local producers of energy.

Of course, it will also be essential to quickly develop and deploy hydrogen and other storage technologies across the European Union's infrastructure when the amount of intermittent renewable energy exceeds 15 percent of the electricity generation, or much of that electricity will be lost. Similarly, it is important to incentivize the construction and real estate sectors with low interest green loans and mortgages to encourage the conversion of millions of buildings in the European Union to mini power plants that can harness renewable energies on-site and send surpluses back to the smart grid. And unless these other considerations are met, the European Union won't be able to provide enough green electricity to power millions of electric plug-in and hydrogen fuel cell vehicles being readied for the market. If any of the five pillars fall behind the rest in their development, the others will be stymied and the infrastructure itself will be compromised.

The creation of a renewable energy regime, loaded by buildings, partially stored in the form of hydrogen, distributed via smart intergrids, and connected to plug-in, zero-emission transport, opens the door to a Third Industrial Revolution. The entire system is interactive, integrated, and seamless. When these five pillars come together, they make up an indivisible technological platform — an emergent system whose properties and functions are qualitatively different from the sum of its parts. In other words, the synergies between the pillars create a new economic paradigm that can transform the world.

To appreciate how disruptive the Third Industrial Revolution is to the existing way we organize economic life, consider the profound changes that have taken place in just the past twenty years with the introduction of the Internet revolution. The democratization of information and communication has altered the very nature of global commerce and social relations as significantly as the print revolution in the early modern era. Now, imagine the impact that the democratization of energy across all of society is likely to have when managed by Internet technology.

The Third Industrial Revolution build-out is particularly relevant for the poorer countries in the developing world. We need to keep in mind that 40 percent of the human race still lives on two dollars a day or less, in dire poverty, and the vast majority have no electricity. Without access to electricity they remain "powerless," literally and figuratively. The single most important factor in raising hundreds of millions of people out of poverty is having reliable and affordable access to green electricity. All other economic development is impossible in its absence. The democratization of energy and universal access to electricity is the indispensable starting point for improving the lives of the poorest populations of the world. The extension of micro credit to generate micro power is already beginning to transform life across the developing nations, giving potentially millions of people hope of improving their economic situation.

There is no inevitability to the human sojourn. History is riddled with examples of great societies that collapsed, promising social experiments that withered, and visions of the future that never saw the light of day. This time, however, the situation is different. The stakes are higher. The possibility of utter extinction is not something the human race ever had to consider before the past half-century. The prospect of proliferation of weapons of mass destruction, coupled now with the looming climate crisis, has tipped the odds dangerously in favor of an endgame, not only for civilization as we know it, but for our very species.

The Third Industrial Revolution offers the hope that we can arrive at a sustainable post-carbon era by mid-century. We have the science, the technology, and the game plan to make it happen. Now it is a question of whether we will recognize the economic possibilities that lie ahead and muster the will to get there in time.

Understanding the Text

1. What is the "third industrial revolution" as defined by Rifkin?
2. What environmental changes did the European Union make in the early 2000s?

Reflection and Response

3. How can Europe contribute to this movement toward sustainability?
4. How can the United States contribute?
5. How does the third industrial revolution impact third-world countries?

Making Connections

6. This article touches on the effects of the "Internet Age" on the environment. How do you think you could adjust your technological use to be more sustainable? What connections do you see between this article and those by Heimbuch (page 243) and Goleman/Norris (page 251) in Chapter 4?
7. Do some research on the idea of a "third industrial revolution." Has the idea become more widespread? Are there other similar visions for energy production in the future? If so, what are they?

How Much Is Left? The Limits of Earth's Resources

Michael Moyer and Carina Storrs

Michael Moyer is a technology editor for *Scientific American*. In addition, he writes about digital culture, energy, and environmental issues, and he has appeared on CNN Headline News, Discovery Channel, and National Geographic Channel. Carina Storrs is a freelance writer based in New York City. She studied environmental reporting at New York University and later received her Ph.D. in microbiology from Columbia University. She has written and edited for Health.com, *Scientific American*, *Popular Science*, and ScienceLine.org.

This article outlines the limits to resources on the planet. It also provides a list of potential environmental events and corresponding dates (for example, the peak of oil and species extinction). As you read, think about the ways in which limited resources affect our quality of life and how this pattern could continue in the future.

If the twentieth century was an expansive era seemingly without boundaries — a time of jet planes, space travel and the Internet — the early years of the twenty-first have showed us the limits of our small world. Regional blackouts remind us that the flow of energy we used to take for granted may be in tight supply. The once mighty Colorado River, tapped by thirsty metropolises of the desert West, no longer reaches the ocean. Oil is so hard to find that new wells extend many kilometers underneath the seafloor. The boundless atmosphere is now reeling from two centuries' worth of greenhouse gas emissions. Even life itself seems to be running out, as biologists warn that we are in the midst of a global extinction event comparable to the last throes of the dinosaurs.

The constraints on our resources and environment — compounded by the rise of the middle class in nations such as China and India — will shape the rest of this century and beyond. Here is a visual accounting of what we have left to work with, a map of our resources plotted against time.

1976–2005: Glacier Melt Accelerates

Glaciers have been losing their mass at an accelerating rate in recent decades. In some regions such as Europe and the Americas, glaciers now lose more than half a meter each year.

2014: The Peak of Oil

The most common answer to "how much oil is left" is "depends on how hard you want to look." As easy-to-reach fields run dry, new technologies allow oil companies to tap harder-to-reach places (such as 5,500 meters under the Gulf of Mexico). Traditional statistical models of oil supply do not account for these advances, but a new approach to production forecasting explicitly incorporates multiple waves of technological improvement. Though still controversial, this multicyclic approach predicts that global oil production is set to peak in four years and that by the 2050s we will have pulled all but 10 percent of the world's oil from the ground.

> "If the twentieth century was an expansive era seemingly without boundaries — a time of jet planes, space travel and the Internet — the early years of the twenty-first have showed us the limits of our small world."

2025: Battle Over Water

In many parts of the world, one major river supplies water to multiple countries. Climate change, pollution and population growth are putting a significant strain on supplies. In some areas renewable water reserves are in danger of dropping below the 500 cubic meters per person per year considered a minimum for a functioning society.

Potential Hot Spots

Egypt: A coalition of countries led by Ethiopia is challenging old agreements that allow Egypt to use more than 50 percent of the Nile's flow. Without the river, all of Egypt would be desert.

Eastern Europe: Decades of pollution have fouled the Danube, leaving downstream countries, such as Hungary and the Republic of Moldova, scrambling to find new sources of water.

Middle East: The Jordan River, racked by drought and diverted by Israeli, Syrian and Jordanian dams, has lost 95 percent of its former flow.

Former Soviet Union: The Aral Sea, at one time the world's fourth-largest inland sea, has lost 75 percent of its water because of agricultural diversion programs begun in the 1960s.

2028: Indium

Indium is a [soft, silvery metal that sits between cadmium and tin on the periodic table.] Indium tin oxide is a thin-film conductor used in flat-panel televisions. At current production levels, known indium reserves contain an 18-year world supply.

2029: Silver

Because silver naturally kills microbes, it is increasingly used in bandages and as coatings for consumer products. At current production levels, about 19 years' worth of silver remains in the ground, but recycling should extend that supply by decades.

2030: Gold

The global financial crisis has boosted demand for gold, which is seen by many as a tangible (and therefore lower-risk) investment. According to Julian Phillips, editor of the Gold Forecaster newsletter, probably about 20 years are left of gold that can be easily mined.

Fewer Fish

Fish are our last truly wild food, but the rise in demand for seafood has pushed many species to the brink of extinction. Here are five of the most vulnerable.

Hammerhead sharks have declined by 89 percent since 1986. The animals are sought for their fins, which are a delicacy in soup.

Russian sturgeon have lost spawning grounds because of exploitation for caviar. Numbers are down 90 percent since 1965.

Yellowmouth grouper may exist only in pockets of its former range, from Florida to Brazil.

European eel populations have declined by 80 percent since 1968; because the fish reproduces late in life, recovery could take 200 years.

Orange roughy off the coast of New Zealand have declined by 80 percent since the 1970s because of overfishing by huge bottom trawlers.

Our Mass Extinction

Biologists warn that we are living in the midst of a mass extinction 10
on par with the other five great events in Earth's history, including
the Permian-Triassic extinction (also known as the Great Dying; it
knocked out up to 96 percent of all life on Earth) and the Cretaceous-
Tertiary extinction that killed the dinosaurs. The cause of our
troubles? Us. Human mastery over the planet has pushed many species
out of their native habitats; others have succumbed to hunting or environmental pollutants. If trends continue — and unfortunately, species
loss is accelerating — the world will soon be a far less diverse place.

2044: Copper

Copper is in just about everything in infrastructure, from pipes to
electrical equipment. Known reserves currently stand at 540 million
metric tons, but recent geologic work in South America indicates
there may be an additional 1.3 billion metric tons of copper hidden in
the Andes Mountains.

2050: Feeding a Warming World

Researchers have recently started to untangle the complex ways rising temperatures will affect global agriculture. They expect climate
change to lead to longer growing seasons in some countries; in others
the heat will increase the frequency of extreme weather events or
the prevalence of pests. In the United States, productivity is expected
to rise in the Plains states but fall further in the already struggling
Southwest. Russia and China will gain; India and Mexico will lose. In
general, developing nations will take the biggest hits. By 2050 coun-
teracting the ill effects of climate change on nutrition will cost more
than $7 billion a year.

Mortal Threats

As the total number of species declines, some have fared worse than
others. Here are five life-forms, the estimated percentage of species
thought to be endangered, and an example of the threats they face.

Mammals
18 percent endangered
The Iberian lynx feeds on rabbits, a prey in short supply in the
.lynx's habitat ever since a pediatrician introduced the disease
myxomatosis from Australia to France in 1952 to kill the
rabbits in his garden.

Plants
8 percent endangered
The St. Helena redwood is native to the island in the South
Atlantic where Napoleon lived his last years. Its excellent
timber led to exploitation; by the 20th century only one
remained in the wild.

Lizards
20 percent endangered
The blue spiny lizard must retreat from the sun before it over-
heats; higher temperatures have cut down on the time it can
forage for food.

Birds
10 percent endangered
The black-necked crane suffers from habitat loss in the wetlands
of the Tibetan plateau.

Amphibians
30 percent endangered
Archey's frog has been devastated by a fungal disease in its
native New Zealand.

2060: Changing the Course of a River

Climate change will shift weather patterns, leading to big changes in
the amount of rain that falls in any given region, as well as the
amount of water flowing through streams and rivers. Scientists at the
U.S. Geological Survey averaged the results of twelve climate models
to predict how streamflow will alter over the next fifty years. While
East Africa, Argentina and other regions benefit from more water,
southern Europe and the western United States will suffer.

2070: Himalayan Ice

Snow melt from the Himalayas is a prime source of water for Asia's   15
major river valleys, including the Yellow, Yangtze, Mekong and Ganges.

By 2070 ice-covered landmass in the Himalayas could decrease by 43 percent.

2072: Limits of Coal

Unlike oil, coal is widely thought to be virtually inexhaustible. Not so, says David Rutledge of the California Institute of Technology. Governments routinely overestimate their reserves by a factor of four or more on the assumption that hard-to-reach seams will one day open up to new technology. Mature coal mines show that this has not been the case. The U.K. — the birthplace of coal mining — offers an example. Production grew through the 19th and early 20th centuries, then fell as supplies were depleted. Cumulative production curves in the U.K. and other mature regions have followed a predictable S shape. By extrapolating to the rest of the world's coal fields, Rutledge concludes that the world will extract 90 percent of available coal by 2072.

2100: The Alps

Parts of the Alps are warming so quickly that the Rhone Glacier is expected to have disappeared by the end of the century.

2560: Lithium

Because lithium is an essential component of the batteries in electric cars, many industry analysts have worried publicly that supplies won't keep up with growing demand for the metal. Still, known lithium reserves are big enough to keep us supplied for more than five centuries, even ignoring the vast supply of lithium in seawater.

Understanding the Text

1. How long do the authors think it will take for the world to run out of oil?
2. Which countries could be most severely impacted by a water shortage?
3. Which species of fish are at the greatest risk of endangerment?

Reflection and Response

4. Do you agree that our "mass extinction" is imminent? Why or why not?
5. How do you react to the information in this article? How does it make you think about your future?

6. Which of the limits addressed in this article do you believe to have the most impact on you, your family, or your region?

Making Connections

7. Choose one event on this timeline that interests you and write about it. Do you think that event is likely to occur? Why or why not?

8. The authors write that if weather patterns shift because of climate change, rainfall will be affected. Do some research to find out what else could be affected by changing weather patterns.

6   How Are Tourism and Recreation Connected to Sustainability?

Y ou may think that sustainability is serious business — and it is. Sustainability involves difficult decisions and complex thinking in business, political, and social spheres. However, sustainability is also connected to the things we do in our free time. Most of us are lucky enough to have some time to travel, to attend and participate in leisure activities, and to enjoy various forms of recreation. These activities are serious business in themselves, and they have a significant impact on sustainability. The travel, recreation, and sports industries are trillion-dollar businesses, and they are also responsible for massive usages of resources like fuel, raw materials, and space. However, many people are drawn to sustainability out of a desire to protect and preserve resources that they use for recreation — most travelers, adventurers, and sports enthusiasts recognize the need for sustainability to ensure that their favorite activities can continue. The industries surrounding travel, leisure, and tourism have begun to notice the public interest in sustainability, and many have adopted more-sustainable practices and policies in response to public demand.

This chapter examines the role of tourism, leisure activities, and recreation in creating and engaging with a more sustainably minded public. The chapter begins with a focus on ecotourism, which involves low-impact, education-based travel to natural areas. Lindsay's article explains the benefits and dangers of ecotourism for fragile or endangered ecosystems. The excerpt from O'Brien's book explains the importance of natural parks as sites for ecotourism, proposing solutions for more-sustainable management of protected natural sites in the future. Bowen's article examines the role of zoos and aquariums in educating people about sustainability. Bass's essay addresses the subject of hunting, drawing on Bass's own experiences as a hunter to explain how it shaped his environmental ethic.

The next essay, by Patagonia CEO Yvon Chouinard, explains how and why Chouinard transformed his outdoor clothing company to more-sustainable practices. In the final essay in the book, Schendler, of the Aspen Skiing Company, explores the relationship among sustainability, religion, and the role of humans in shaping the future.

Consider the ways in which recreational activities relate to sustainability. Do the articles in this chapter make you reconsider the impact of tourism and recreation on our shared resources? Do you engage in sustainable recreation, or do you plan to change your recreational activities to become more sustainable? In what ways are tourism and leisure activities both detrimental and beneficial to sustainability?

Ecotourism: The Promise and Perils of Environmentally Oriented Travel

Heather E. Lindsay

Heather Lindsay is a senior editor with the Center for Ecotourism Science, a division of Cambridge Information Group. Heather holds a master's degree in sustainable development and conservation biology from the University of Maryland.

This article defines ecotourism and explains its benefits and dangers. As you read, think about how a sustainably oriented practice can both help and hurt a natural environment.

Ecotourism,° defined as responsible tourism focused on the natural world, has emerged as a concept that unites the interests of environmentalists and developers. Proponents of ecotourism see it as potential salvation of some of the world's most endangered ecosystems, and an opportunity for communities that possess biological resources to develop sustainable economic strategies, instead of pursuing environmentally damaging patterns of resource use. However, finding a compromise between preservation and development is often challenging, and ecotourism can generate additional environmental problems for the very regions it is intended to protect.

Ecotourism is intended to be sustainable, focused on the natural world, and beneficial to local communities. The IUCN (World Conservation Union) defines it as environmentally responsible travel and visitation to relatively undisturbed natural areas, in order to enjoy and appreciate nature that promotes conservation, has low negative visitor impact, and provides for beneficially active socio-economic involvement of local populations [Ceballos-Lascuráin].

Practically speaking, ecotourism includes activities in which visitors enjoy hands-on experiences, such as bird-watching in the Brazilian rainforest, hiking in the mountains of Nepal, participating in a traditional village celebration, or taking a canoe trip down a river.

---

ecotourism: a form of tourism involving visiting fragile, pristine, and relatively undisturbed natural areas; intended as a low-impact and often small-scale alternative to standard mass tourism.

Local guides usually accompany small groups of tourists on expeditions, teaching them about the local flora, fauna, and culture of the region. Ecotourism is characterized by small-scale outfits in remote locations where commercialization and mass-tourism outfits have not yet penetrated. Tourists typically stay with local families, or at small, environmentally friendly hotels called ecolodges. These opportunities for personal contact with members of the host community facilitate cross-cultural exchange and add greatly to the value of ecotourism experiences for some people. Ecotourism is rooted in a conservation ethic and has a mission to support the biological and cultural resources of the community. Revenues from safari expeditions, for instance, may go to protecting the animals from poaching, while the entry fees from visiting a village may go to supporting education and health care for the local children. Prime locations where ecotourism has become popular include Latin America, Southeast Asia, and Australia.

Participants in the Sustainable Ecotourism in North America Online Conference in May 2000, organized by ecotourism consultant Ron Mader, developed a number of standards that characterize ecotourism:

1. tourism activity in relatively undisturbed natural settings
2. minimal negative impacts on the environment
3. conservation of natural and cultural heritage
4. active involvement with and benefit to local community
5. tourism-generated profits contribute to sustainable development
6. educational experience for visitors that incorporates both natural and cultural heritage [Ceballos-Lascuráin]

Worldwide, tourism generates annual revenues of nearly 3 trillion   5
dollars and contributes nearly 11 percent of the global GNP (gross national product), making it the world's largest industry. Although the events of September 11th rocked the tourism industry and made it difficult to predict long-term trends, ecotourism is a growing component of the larger tourism industry, and several factors indicate that it is likely to thrive over time. These factors include increased awareness of environmental problems among tourist populations, willingness of tourists to engage in socially aware travel, and interest in visiting lesser-known countries like Thailand and Belize rather than traditional vacation getaways.

Benefits of Ecotourism

Ecotourism has been described as "one of the most potent tools in the arsenal of the contemporary conservationists" [Downs]. It presents an environmentally friendlier and potentially more sustainable alternative to extractive activities, such as farming, logging, mining, or harvesting of wildlife. It offers local people the chance to escape a cycle of poverty and, by sharing their knowledge of the local terrain and ecology with visitors, to develop a stronger sense of community pride and a broader, more global perspective that recognizes the value of biodiversity to all people.

Businesses initiated through ecotourism ventures can become self-sufficient within a short time and can enhance the long-term economic prospects of a community. The Eco-Escuela school in the Maya Biosphere Reserve in the Petén region of Guatemala, for example, was developed in cooperation with Conservation International, an international nonprofit organization, and became financially independent within three years. The school, which provides employment to 56 local families, offers a week-long program to tourists including Spanish classes and lodgings in the Petén community [Ecomaya]. Ecotourism also encourages the development of markets in native handicrafts and artwork for souvenirs, and thus contributes to the preservation of cultural heritage.

For foreign visitors, tourism provides an educational glimpse of a world not their own, often a world of striking natural beauty and rich cultural heritage. Educational and spiritually satisfying, ecotourism appeals to the desire to "get back to nature." A more subtle benefit is the opportunity to engage in an international dialogue with people from different backgrounds. This cross-cultural exchange can form a healthy bridge between industrialized and developing countries.

For environmentalists, ecotourism provides an opportunity for long-term protection of the land and its resources. This is particularly valuable considering that the hot spots of biological diversity are generally the poorest regions of the world, where economic necessity is most likely to drive people to pursue environmentally damaging options. Ecotourism is an opportunity to preserve ecosystems and biological diversity that would otherwise be lost. It is also a chance to generate revenue to support research efforts. Entry fees for an ecotourism attraction can be channeled into programs that further scientific knowledge about the area's ecology; that support captive breeding, rehabilitation, or reforestation; or that monitor human impact to ensure that visitation does not degrade the resource. The Kakum canopy walkway in Kakum National Park, Ghana, for example, is a rainforest walkway designed and built by Conservation International. The walkway is used both by tourists and scientists and is a source of revenue for conservation efforts in the park. It was credited with boosting visitation levels from 2,000 in 1992 to 70,000 in 1999 [Conservation International].

Ecotourism can play an important role in raising awareness of the 10 problems facing a particular locale or its people. Tourism drew attention to the at-risk Everglades ecosystem in Florida, motivated the preservation of the Everglades National Park, funded a program to save the highly endangered Bahama parrot, and assisted many more conservation activities [META]. Marine Ecotourism for the Atlantic Area (META), a transnational program led by a team of UK researchers, expects that marine ecotourism will raise the profile of marine resources in the planning process and will provide "an economic rationale for ecological stewardship" [Davies].

> "Ecotourism, defined as responsible tourism focused on the natural world, has emerged as a concept that unites the interests of environmentalists and developers."

A well-known ecotourism success story is the Maquipucuna Reserve in Ecuador. The reserve is a 15,000 acre property in the cloud forest region that is owned and managed by a private foundation. Visitors stay at an ecolodge that employs staff and tour guides from the local community, and enjoy local attractions including a project to rehabilitate wild bears that had become dependent on handouts from humans, a sustainably harvested orchid collection, a pre-Incan archaeological site, and the popular annual Bear Festival. The lodge is adjacent to a scientific research station. Thanks to the ecotourism development efforts in this region, local people have been inspired to see bears as symbols of their heritage that they proudly show off to visitors, instead of as pests or threats.

The Dangers of Ecotourism

However, not all efforts that bill themselves as ecotourism are beneficial to local people and ecosystems. Tourism writer Deborah McLaren notes, "At its worst, ecotravel is environmentally destructive, economically exploitative, culturally insensitive, 'greenwashed' travel."

Tourists photograph a Galapagos tortoise.
© Tristan Spinski/Corbis

"Greenwashing," or environmental claims by outfits that are not necessarily environmentally responsible, is prevalent throughout the tourism industry. Because of their location in environmentally sensitive
areas, ecotourism operations that fail to live up to conservation ideals
can have very serious environmental consequences. Tourists represent an increase in population, however temporary, and their demands on local resources can require the installation of additional
infrastructure, produce large amounts of waste and pollution, and further the degradation of fragile ecosystems. Even a harmless-sounding
activity like a nature hike can be destructive, as hikers can contribute
to soil erosion and damage plant roots. In the Annapurna Circuit in
Nepal, the presence of 60,000 tourists annually has worn deep ruts in
the trail [McLaren]. Tourists who go to view wildlife can scare animals
away from their feeding and nesting sites, while those who opt for air-
plane or boat tours contribute pollution and noise to the environment.
Tourists may even encourage the development of destructive economies, such as markets in wildlife souvenirs (skins, bones, etc.). Tourist
overcrowding is causing severe environmental damage to the Galapagos Islands, with inadequate enforcement of visitor limits by the
government of Ecuador [McLaren]. Tourism in a region that boasts op-

portunities to view endangered species can cause the further endangerment or extinction of these species.

Such failures can occur both because of lack of organization and lack of commitment to conservation goals. Many governments and states do not have adequate tourism departments and are unable to finance responsible development efforts. Others are unwilling to limit the flow of tourist money into the country, so they encourage development past sustainable levels. Simple lack of regulation — too many people, too much water, too much waste — causes what was originally a sustainable effort to mushroom out of proportion.

A primary value of ecotourism is the employment opportunities it provides to local people, yet many tourism operations are owned and run by foreign corporations, providing little or no benefit for locals. Revenues are siphoned off to foreign investors instead of being reinvested in the community, environmental resources are degraded, and the needs of the local population are marginalized. In Surinam, a thriving ecotourism business focused around a marine turtle reserve benefits the reserve and one indigenous community, but provides no income for the larger community that surrounds the reserve. To get to the reserve, visitors must first pass through a coastal village characterized by trash, boat debris, and low-income housing. Because the locals receive no benefit from tourists, they have no incentive to protect the reserve, and a significant portion of the reserve's budget must go to guarding the reserve from poachers.

A related problem is that not all operations that claim to be "green" 15 actually participate in conservation efforts. It is tempting for some outfits to claim to be green whether or not they engage in ecologically responsible activities, since they know tourists will make a special effort to patronize environmentally responsible establishments. Others may have good intentions but find that due to financial and organizational limitations, they are unable to live up to their goals. One not-so-green business is Ecodesarrollo Papagayo in Costa Rica, a development project that includes housing, hotels, and a shopping center, and promotes itself as an ecotourism destination, but has been accused of not following the principles of ecotourism [McLaren]. Another example, a profitable ecotourism theme park in Quintana Roo, Mexico, which advertises itself as Natures Sacred Paradise, is responsible for displacing local Mayan communities and illegally keeps endangered species in captivity to attract visitors [Barkin].

Tourist needs can take priority over those of wildlife and native people, and can lead to the monopoly of regional resources. In Kenya, a spring in the Shaba National Reserve provided fresh water for wildlife and for the local Samburu people and their livestock. When the Sarova Shaba Hotel was built, its water needs took priority and the spring was blocked off from public access. Deprived of water, wildlife and livestock are dying and the Samburu are close to famine [McLaren].

In some places, locals have resisted tourism development efforts, including ecotourism, because of the potential for disruption to their lives. Because past visitors were considered disrespectful, today's visitors to the Hopi Nation reservation in Arizona are no longer permitted to take pictures, enter the residential portion of the village, or participate in hiking and off-road travel [McLaren]. Local people may also oppose tourism because they resent policies they view as beneficial to others, but not to them; for instance, fishing limits may be enforced to protect the populations of reef fishes for tourist viewing expeditions. Tourism can bring new restrictions or more rigorous enforcement of existing legislation that protects species and their habitats, and unaccustomed government interference in local activities may breed widespread resentment among residents. Tourism may also bring about social changes, such as the exchange of traditional roles for unconventional ones, that disrupt the social hierarchy in the community.

The Need for Standards

There is no standard set of guidelines for ecotourism, and no formal system of accreditation by which green businesses may be rated. The two largest programs for certification, the Certificate of Sustainable Tourism (CST) in Costa Rica and the Nature Ecotourism Accreditation Program (NEAP) sponsored by the Ecotourism Association of Australia, have only local authority, though the latter has developed an International Ecotourism Standard that will be released soon. Condé Nast offers an Ecotourism Award for which organizations must apply, but does not check applicants' claims before choosing a winner. The Rainforest Alliance is sponsoring a study to examine the feasibility of international certification through the Sustainable Stewardship Council, but it may be years before standards go into effect.

Problems with certification include the difficulty with applying broad standards to local situations, the need to enforce standards through regular inspections from some higher authority, and the expense and organization that regulation entails. Small outfits may not be able to afford certification even if a recognized and scientifically sound program becomes available [Rome].

The lack of certification poses a significant problem, for it means 20 that ecolodges and other establishments are not answerable as far as the extent and success of their environmental efforts. Recycling programs, promotion of low-impact tourist activities, and support for conservation efforts are entirely voluntary once minimum existing environmental standards have been met. Most travelers plan their ecotourism trips using the Internet and are dependent on an outfit's own advertising and on the advice of friends, so they are unable to make a truly informed choice.

Best Practices for Ecotourism

Sound ecotourism activities contribute long-term benefits to both the environment and the host community. Pam Wight's guiding principles for ecotourism include the following provisions:

1. tourist activities must not degrade the resource
2. visitors should be offered educational first-hand experiences
3. all stakeholders (host community, government, non-governmental organizations, industry, and tourists) must be involved
4. tourism must respect the intrinsic value of natural resources°
5. tourism cannot overtax the resource supplies of the local region
6. stakeholders must be encouraged to develop partnerships
7. tourist revenue must provide conservation, scientific, or cultural benefits to the resource, local community, and industry as a whole
8. these benefits must be long-term [Wight 1993].

Achieving these principles depends in large part upon the scale of the operation. The cardinal rule of ecotourism is: keep things small. A region that can absorb the impact of a few dozen visitors over the course of a month, including the infrastructure to support their presence (such as plumbing, sewage wastewater, electricity generators, and transportation facilities), may suffer under the influence of more visitors. Small-scale grass-roots development that incorporates the

natural resources: resources that exist in the environment in a natural form and are relatively undisturbed by humans.

desires and opinions of local people tends to be the best policy. Following this principle requires managers to reject the growth-oriented philosophy that has typically characterized economic policy in ecotourism hotspots. Wight notes that sustainable development does not imply absolute limits on the number of visitors, but limits based on present technology and organization and on the capacity of the biosphere to absorb present forms of damage; thus, thoughtful evaluation of tourist behaviors can reveal ways to reduce the impacts of visitors on the environment, without reducing the total number of visitors [Wight 2002].

One conservation objective is to ensure that construction and maintenance of ecolodges follow environmental protocols to avoid degrading the very areas that tourists value for their pristine qualities. Low consumption, efficient use, and strict recycling of resources are key. While a hotel in an industrialized nation might be able to throw away large amounts of garbage, an ecolodge in a remote rainforest location has no place to get rid of trash, and must find ways to recycle it instead. Modern-day tourists are used to having clean sheets in their bedrooms daily. In order to conserve water, power, and labor, an ecolodge might have to adopt a weekly schedule of linen-changing. Tourists are also used to throwing away large amounts of packaging and other trash in the course of their daily activities. Binna Burra, an ecolodge in Australia, provides visitors with biodegradable toiletries and offers boxed lunches for hikers in reusable containers, generating no trash [Rome].

In addition to keeping the enterprise to a manageable scale, ecotourism developers must demonstrate an upfront commitment to environmental objectives, provide quality leadership, and exploit small market niches where personalized service and unique experiences are favored over large-scale operations [Kirstges].

Education for host communities and for the tourists who plan to visit them is key to providing both with a good experience. Guides need to have the social skills, familiarity with English (or other languages), basic knowledge about the region, and capacity for authority to lead well-organized tours. More than one tourism operation has foundered due to lack of human resources in the host community. At the same time, tourists must be prepared for what they will encounter, and must have the proper attitude and maturity to appreciate their experiences. Most ecotravelers are well-educated, respectful of local traditions, and eager to contribute to conservation efforts, though some arrive with ill-conceived expectations that result in less-than-ideal experiences both for the tourists and for the host community.

Prioritizing conservation over short-term profit lies at the heart of the ecotourism challenge. Conservation provides the moral authority for ecotourism efforts and the basis for long-term economic stability, but it can be difficult to preach a philosophy of preservation to people used to surviving in a short-term, unstable economy. A local resident who can expect to receive large sums on the black market for an animal skin may be unwilling to believe that the long-term benefit of not killing the animal will be greater. Indeed, his personal benefit may be lower, given that revenues from tourism aren't distributed equally throughout the community, and that even if he stops poaching, his neighbors may well continue. The World Resources Institute suggests that the key to gaining local enthusiasm for a project is to do as much as possible to ensure that benefits are shared fairly and that no one shoulders a disproportionate share of the cost [WRI].

Another rule for successful ecotourism is to develop an economy that does not rely on tourism as the sole source of income for the community. Because it is a seasonal business that is influenced by far-off political, social, and financial trends, and that is easily damaged by natural disasters, disease outbreaks, and political unrest, tourism can dry up without warning.

In addition, a good ecotourism site must follow principles of common sense. Blazing trails through the forest to allow tourists to take nature hikes and look for wildlife will be pointless if the presence of humans on the trail scares away wildlife. Instead, offering visitors a guided tour that focuses on the natural history of the area and a visit to a captive breeding° or rehabilitation facility may be more effective in terms of satisfying visitor expectations.

Government support is necessary to provide financial backing for rural and indigenous people who lack the resources to acquire education or start up business initiatives, to provide organization and coordination of ecotourism efforts, to give small communities access to knowledge about sustainable development, and to prevent abuses. If governments or agencies do not empower rural guides and tourism operations, the absence of local participation betrays one of the main components of ecotourism, Ron Mader warns [Mader].

---

captive breeding: the process of breeding animals in human-controlled environments with restricted settings, such as wildlife reserves, zoos, and other conservation facilities.

However, government control cannot be allowed to overshadow local interests. Since much of the decision-making power for land-use rests with local authorities, gaining their endorsement for an ecotourism project can go a long way toward meeting conservation goals. Certainly, bringing in outsiders to run all aspects of the project is undesirable, since it not only divorces the community from the effort, reducing their interest in supporting it, but ensures that they will not profit from it, limiting their ability to survive without turning to unsustainable industries. Ecotourism consultant Abi Rome suggests that guidelines for certification of ecotourism businesses ought to include local ownership and 80 percent local staffing [Rome].

Ecotourism can live up to its promise if it follows the principles of wise development, adequately monitors and protects its resources, and ensures fair distribution of profits within the host community. Awareness of the pitfalls of unsustainable or unregulated tourism can guide communities that are struggling to take their place in a global economy without damaging the resources we all value. 30

References

1. Barkin, David. Ecotourism for Sustainable Regional Development. *Current Issues in Tourism* 5(3–4), 252.

2. Ceballos-Lascuráin, Hector. Preface, *Current Issues in Tourism* 5(3–4), 169.

3. Conservation International. Washington, D.C. http://www.ecotour.org/destinations/kakum.html.

4. Davies, Terry, and Sarah Cahill. Environmental Implications of the Tourism Industry (discussion paper). Resources for the Future (RFF), Washington, D.C. http://www.rff.org/CFDOCS/disc_papers/PDF_files/0014.pdf.

5. Downs, J. (1994) Protecting Paradise Is a Priority. *Wildlife Conservation* 97(2), 2.

6. Ecomaya. Petén, Guatemala. http://www.ecomaya.com/introduction.asp.

7. Kirstges, Torsten. Basic Questions of Sustainable Tourism. *Current Issues in Tourism* 5(3–4), 184.

8. Mader, Ron. Latin American Ecotourism: What Is It? *Current Issues in Tourism* 5(3–4), 272.

9. McLaren, Deborah. *Rethinking Tourism and Ecotravel: The Paving of Paradise and What You Can Do to Stop It.* West Hartford, Connecticut: Kumarian Press, Inc., 1998.

10. Marine Ecotourism for the Atlantic Area (META), Bristol, UK. http://www.tourism-research.org/project_Introduction.html.

11. Rome, Abi. Ecotourism Explained workshop, sponsored by the Institute for Policy Studies, Washington, D.C., November 6, 2002.

12. Wight, Pamela A. Supporting the Principles of Sustainable Development. *Current Issues in Tourism* 5(3–4), 237.

13. Wight, Pamela A. Ecotourism: Ethics or Eco-Sell. *Journal of Travel Research* 31(3), 3–9.

14. World Resources Institute, 10 G Street, Suite 180, Washington, D.C.

Understanding the Text

1. What is ecotourism? How does the author define it in paragraphs 2–5?
2. What are the benefits of ecotourism? In what ways is it better than other forms of tourism?
3. What are the dangers of ecotourism? In what ways can it be harmful or exploitative to local people and ecosystems?
4. What is "greenwashing," and how can it be a problem for ecotourism?

Reflection and Response

5. Do you think ecotourism is a good idea? Explain your answer.
6. What role should a governmental tourism department play in a country's ecotourism programs? Should there be international standards, or do you believe a country should create its own standards for ecotourism? Explain your answer.
7. In what ways is ecotourism connected to sustainability? How is it "rooted in a conservation ethic"?

Making Connections

8. Have you ever been an "ecotourist"? If not, where would you like to visit? Is it important to you to travel in an environmentally sensitive way? Why or why not?
9. Research some other places affected by ecotourism. How do these places and situations compare to the one described in this article?

Our National Parks and the Search for Sustainability

Bob O'Brien

Bob O'Brien was a professor of geography at San Diego State University. He taught courses on national parks, outdoor recreation, and ecotourism. An avid traveler, Bob explored all seven continents and twice completed the 222-mile John Muir Trail.

This excerpt from O'Brien's book *Our National Parks and the Search for Sustainability* examines the history of national parks and explains their importance to society. In the book, O'Brien suggests that national parks are good for environmental preservation and simultaneously provide enjoyment for visitors. He also proposes some solutions for how national parks could be preserved. As you read, think about the importance of national parks. What role do they play in our culture?

W hen we complain about lack of political concern with the environment we should think back 125 years, to the time when the first national park was established, and be thankful for what we have. Then, there were no environmental legislation, no environmental organizations, and almost no ecological concern. There were of course far fewer people in the United States, only about 40 million in 1872, but they were capable of immense destruction with no environmental laws or ethics to stop them. Most of the big game animals in America, such as bison, elk, and antelope, were in danger of becoming extinct, and landscapes from forests to grasslands were losing their productivity. The entire natural landscape had little value for most people, and without the environmental consciousness that came with the national parks movement, the nation would be far bleaker than it is today.

I consider the establishment of Yellowstone National Park° one of the real miracles of American history. In the midst of one of the most rapacious eras in our history, we quietly set aside an area the size of one of the original states to be preserved in perpetuity. The establishment of national parks has probably been the most copied of American institutions, emulated by over a hundred nations today.

Yellowstone National Park: a national park located primarily in Wyoming. It was established in 1872 as the first U.S. national park and has many geothermal features, including the popular Old Faithful Geyser.

President Grant° signed the Yellowstone National Park Act on March 1, 1872. The key words in this act of only six hundred words were: "[Yellowstone Park] . . . is hereby reserved and withdrawn from settlement, occupancy, or sale under the laws of the United States, and dedicated and set apart as a public park or pleasuring-ground for the benefit and enjoyment of the people . . . [and] such regulations shall provide for the preservation from injury or spoliation of all timber, mineral deposits, natural curiosities, or wonders within said park, and their retention in their natural condition."

Here we have an act that breaks new ground in two major fields: it gave to the *people* of the United States — not individuals, not states — a large parcel of land to enjoy as a park, and it called for the preservation of that landscape in its natural state, in perpetuity. We have then the forerunner of thousands of areas throughout the world preserved as parks, wilderness areas, game refuges, and other areas for the enjoyment of the people. We also have, in reality, one of the first attempts at a sustainable use of a landscape.

Sustainability is the key word for environmentalists today, or for 5 that matter anyone who cares about the future of this planet. At one time it may have been possible to live off the capital of the land, to leave the world a little less able to support those who came afterwards; now we *have* to find a sustainable lifestyle to have any hope at all for the future. Yet, with so many people of the world living in grinding poverty, sustainability becomes an almost impossible dream. The rainforest and its priceless contribution to world biodiversity° and climatic stability count for less than the few years' survival it can promise to those who slash and burn. On a different level, even in the United States and Canada it is hard to preserve the small amount of ancient forest left when jobs in lumbering are at stake. Here, and through much of the world where remnants of the natural landscape exist, ecotourism offers almost the only hope of saving those landscapes.

Ecotourism is a form of tourism that offers economic support to attractive tourist destinations that would otherwise be exploited for timber, minerals, agriculture, or water resources. Classic ecotourism locations — Costa Rica, Nepal, Africa — are relatively poor areas where the influx of foreign travel dollars offers the alternative to cutting the rainforest, farming steep hillsides, or killing elephants. The same

President Grant: Ulysses S. Grant (1822–1885), the eighteenth president of the United States (1869–1877).
biodiversity: diversity among and within plant and animal species in an environment.

principles, however, can be applied to raft trips through the Grand Canyon, which helped keep dams out of the canyon, or making a tourist destination out of a historic village where a shopping center is planned.

The basic idea of national parks, from the beginning, was to preserve the parks for the people's enjoyment. It became obvious, however, that if a person's enjoyment consisted of breaking off pieces of one of Yellowstone's geyser cones for souvenirs or catching hundreds of trout in an afternoon, this brand of ecotourism was not going to work. The use must be sustainable. Protecting the parks meant preserving the park from commercial exploitation, *and* preserving it from the tourists. The first goal was the most important in the early years of the national parks, while the second has been the most important in recent years.

> "We must be proud of our wisdom in setting aside national parks."

The national parks have been highly successful in achieving their earliest goals: to preserve the parks from commercial exploitation and to make easily accessible the most scenic portions of the United States. The preservation question is the subject of this book, but let's look at the geographic question: are the most scenic portions of the United States in the National Park System? One has only to flip through any travel brochure or picture book of the United States to answer in the affirmative, but listing superlatives also hints at the attractiveness of the national parks. Here are a few: tallest mountain in North America and one of tallest in the world from base to top (Mount McKinley in Denali National Park); most active volcanic area in United States (Hawaii Volcanoes National Park); most recent volcano in the conterminous United States (Mount Saint Helens Volcanic National Monument, run by the U.S. Forest Service); largest canyon in the world (Grand Canyon); tallest waterfalls in the United States (Yosemite); deepest lake in the United States (Crater Lake); tallest, largest, and oldest trees in the world (Redwood, Sequoia, and Great Basin National Parks); highest temperature in the United States (Death Valley); and greatest annual snowfall in the world (Mount Rainier).

Focusing on the unique and spectacular might cause us to ignore what ultimately will be the most important factor in park management: preserving habitat and ecosystems. The value of park areas has climbed sharply in the last few decades as the acreage of natural areas in the United States has been reduced. Rocky Mountain

National Park was probably not the most beautiful section of the Colorado Rocky Mountains that could have been preserved in a park, but as the years go by it is becoming increasingly unique as ski resorts and backcountry vehicles scar the rest of the Colorado backcountry. It is becoming evident that we should have paid more attention to the "ordinary" landscapes such as prairie, coastal lagoons, marshlands, and hardwood forests, which might be ecologically more important than spectacular landscapes like mountains.

Other benefits seemed even more obscure when the national parks were first established. Wildlife, for example, was not particularly abundant in Yellowstone National Park compared to areas outside the park in the 1870s. Animals, like humans, prefer rich, warm lowlands to high, cold plateaus. The animals will live, however, where they need to live to survive, and in the days when game laws were virtually nonexistent they found safety inside park boundaries. Because it was protected, Yellowstone National Park became the home of the last wild buffalo herd in the United States, some of the last elk, and some of the last trumpeter swans. National parks gave breathing room to many species in the days before game laws had a chance to protect wildlife.

Watershed protection is an added bonus in having national parks. Many rivers, such as the Snake, Yellowstone, and Missouri, flow out of our parks pure and naturally regulated by uncut vegetation and undisturbed soil that absorbs the often copious rainfall. How many dams and water treatment plants would be necessary to replace what we get for free in the parks? The sight of a free-flowing stream, undammed and unpolluted, is a sight rare enough to thrill many park visitors.

Wilderness travel has become a major form of outdoor recreation. More and more people are discovering the ultimate delight in the out-of-doors, where the landscape is unmarred by roads, buildings, and the crush of people. In the national parks, wilderness begins just beyond the shoulder of the road and can be enjoyed by visitors the minute they enter park boundaries. Outside the national parks, roads invariably mean development, whether cutover forests, mined hillsides, or dammed streams. To the park motorist, roads seem numerous, but by far the greatest acreage in most national parks is roadless. Of course, the best wilderness experience comes when you leave roads far behind, and set out on foot to discover land affected only by nature.

Most visitors want only to escape the urban environment, and even the most crowded areas of the parks can fill that need. Visitors are apt to feel they are back in the city in the area surrounding Old Faithful, where thousands of people mingle for food, lodging, and parking. Then they catch a glimpse of a buffalo in the distance and can look miles beyond into pristine wilderness.

The first attention given to outdoor recreation by the federal government centered on the national parks, although it was not intended as a primary purpose of the parks. Recreational travel by car, bicycle, or on foot; recreational living in tent, trailer, cabin, or resort; boating, swimming, fishing, nature study, cross-country skiing, and mountaineering can reach their qualitative peak in the national parks. The escalation of these pursuits has worried many who feel that they could take place just as easily outside the parks, but most of the pursuits mentioned above can, with care, continue to be enjoyed at their present level, and some, like hiking, can be much expanded.

In a situation that makes local chambers of commerce happy and   15
fills environmentalists with foreboding, the National Park System has become one of the top tourist attractions in the world. It would be hard to think of a way to extract a greater monetary benefit from developing the resources of any park than the tourist dollars that flow into it now. Even cutting back development within the parks would not stem the flow of tourist income into the surrounding areas, because the more beautiful the parks become, the more people are going to want to see them.

Finally, the educational value of the national parks is immense. People come to the Grand Canyon primarily to see one of the great natural wonders in the world. Many of them will also just look awhile, take a picture, and leave. But most will wonder how the canyon was formed and stand in awe at the unimaginable duration represented by one of the greatest exposures of geologic time in the world. They might also wonder how the area is being preserved by the National Park Service (NPS) for future generations and what is being done about current problems such as the noise from overflights and overcrowding. The answers are available there from rangers, in visitor centers, and in an extensive literature on the canyon and the park, although lack of funds has reduced the educational potential of this and other national parks.

We must be proud of our wisdom in setting aside national parks. We all sometimes look at our past and think of ourselves as heartless exploiters of the country's natural wealth. Thanks to the national parks, however, and other forms of preservation that have followed, we have probably saved more of the country's outstanding scenic, historic, and scientific areas than we have lost. Furthermore, there is every expectation that the national parks might someday represent one of the largest areas of sustainable use in the world.

Understanding the Text

1. Which national park does O'Brien consider "one of the real miracles of American history"? Why was its establishment important?

2. What are some benefits of national parks as described in this article? How do economics and education factor in to these benefits?

Reflection and Response

3. How do you think environmentalism has changed over the past century?

4. Why do you think national parks are important?

5. What is the danger in focusing only on the "unique and spectacular" in national parks? Why should we have more "ordinary" places preserved?

Making Connections

6. Have you ever visited a national park? Describe the experience. If you haven't, research the nearest one and describe it.

7. This article also discusses ecotourism. How does O'Brien's opinion compare to Lindsay's in the previous article?

8. John Muir's article in Chapter 1 of this book (page 37) addresses a similar topic and location. Imagine a conversation between O'Brien and Muir. What would they have to say to each other? Would Muir agree with (or be surprised by) the things that O'Brien mentions?

The Wildlife Conservation Society Makes Zoos Sustainable

Ted Bowen

Ted Bowen is a freelance writer from the Boston area whose work focuses on culture, technology, and environmental issues. His work has appeared in *The Economist*, the *New York Times*, *Wired* magazine, *Fast Company*, NationalGeographic.com, and other publications.

This article appeared in *Grist*, a nonprofit environmental news magazine. As you read, think about the role that zoos and aquariums can play in educating people about sustainability. Do zoos have an obligation to act sustainably?

Is it better to compost elephant dung or tap its energy with a methane generator? Will a ring-tailed lemur feel at home under energy-efficient lights?

The Wildlife Conservation Society [WCS], which runs New York City's zoos and aquarium, is increasingly turning its attention to these and other environmental quandaries. In addition to managing what it describes as the largest urban wildlife park system in the world, the Bronx Zoo–based WCS, formerly the New York Zoological Society, is a major international conservation group with extensive research and education programs. Having recently dodged a budgetary bullet from the city government that might have put an end to the Brooklyn and Queens zoos, WCS is in the midst of revising its master plan for the first time since the 1960s, with the goal of incorporating sustainable practices throughout its facilities.

"We spend a lot of money overseas working toward wildlife conservation, and if we're going to do that, we had better be living our mission at home," says Sue Chin, director of planning and design for WCS.

Such eco-friendly concerns may not top the agenda at most zoos and aquariums, where attendance usually trumps sustainability in the hierarchy of goals. Still, the industry's main trade group, the American Zoo and Aquarium Association (AZA), is promoting ecological responsibility, and WCS and other zoo operators are putting the theory into practice.

The Wildlife Conservation Society, which runs the Bronx Zoo and other zoos and aquariums in New York City, is incorporating sustainable practices throughout its facilities.

© dbimages/Alamy

How Do You Zoo?

Among environmentalists, zoos have always generated, at best, 5 mixed reactions; for some, they are synonymous with cruelty and imprisonment, while others see them as progressive outposts of research and conservation. In reality, it's tough to generalize about zoos and aquariums, since they run the gamut from unlicensed roadside menageries to professionally staffed institutions with international conservation programs and education divisions. But whatever their role in society, zoos encompass major operations with considerable resource needs and often sprawling campuses. They may or may not preach ecological awareness, but their ecological footprints are substantial.

Through its Animal and Plant Health Inspection Service [APHIS], the U.S. Department of Agriculture licenses zoos, aquariums, and other animal exhibitors — around 2,500 at present. The AZA claims to have more stringent criteria than APHIS in the areas of animal welfare, conservation, professional conduct, ethics, and education; it currently counts 212 North American institutions as members.

While the AZA members represent just a fraction of all animal operations in North America, they collectively occupy a sizeable chunk of real estate and do a high volume of business, with last year's attendance at their facilities topping 134 million visitors. Member organizations typically sit on dozens (and sometimes hundreds or thousands) of developed acres; annual operating budgets can exceed $100 million. Although 85 percent are nonprofit, AZA institutions are big business.

The AZA may represent a step up from basic zoo licensing, but groups like the Humane Society charge that even some of the AZA's more progressive members maintain outdated and unhealthy facilities. "There are some facilities doing some fairly innovative things, and we don't want to discourage them," says Richard Farinato, director of the captive wild animal protection program for the Humane Society of the United States. But at the same time, he notes, there are notable lapses in animal care, including an incident earlier this year in which two endangered red pandas at Washington, D.C.'s National Zoo were accidentally poisoned with rat bait. Yet even in high-profile cases like that one, institutions can be slow to reform, according to Farinato. "They've done lots on paper, shuffled people around, assembled a commission from the National Academy of Sciences to examine the situation, but so far, they've just paid lip service to the problems," he says.

"Sustainability at zoos is a tall order."

Farinato also argues that zoos' definition of animal welfare needs to be expanded. "To them, it means a clean cage and a good diet, but those are just the minimum responsibilities. An animal's welfare also means its psychological well-being, choices, and the ability to express itself in a species-appropriate way," he says. "Then you get into the question of which animals are not suited to captivity. The issue is quite large."

And if zoos' treatment of animals has been uneven, as a group their environmental practices have historically been even less impressive. 10

"You can't overlook the impact of your institution and staff on the local environment," says Christine Sheppard, curator of ornithology and green team leader at the Bronx Zoo. "You can't just think about your animals, but zoos did."

In recent years, though, there have been signs of change, from water conservation practices to renewable energy use to green building design. In a 2001 AZA member survey, about 40 percent of institutions reported composting, 40 percent said they had environmentally sensitive procurement policies, and 11 percent said they treated gray water onsite.

Regional differences in environmental politics can dictate the pace of change, according to Sheppard. Some zoos — notably those in Toronto and Portland, Ore. — have "absolutely tremendous" environmental programs, she says, while others are resistant to change and worried about the bottom line: "You're starting to see things happen within the context of local environmentalism. The more the local communities are involved in [the environmental movement], like in California and Oregon, the easier it is, versus the middle of Texas."

But the AZA has thus far called only for voluntary sustainability efforts, so progress "all depends on the personality of the person running the institution and his or her point of view," Farinato says. On the whole, serious environmentalism is "more an exception than the norm with zoos around the country, but the AZA tends to make it look like all zoos that are accredited are behaving like this," he says.

Getting Down to Business

How do you go about making a zoo greener? Not all that differently   15
than you would any other business or institution, according to Barbara Batshalom, executive director of the Green Roundtable, a sustainable-development advocacy group and Boston affiliate of the U.S. Green Building Council. The process is familiar: conserve energy, use renewable and clean power, decrease water consumption, reuse gray water, reduce and recycle solid waste, cut the use of harmful chemicals, buy sustainably produced materials and food, use mass transit, practice less destructive landscaping, and educate your employees and the general public about sustainability issues.

Of course, some considerations are zoo-specific. "If a critter needs some sort of animal enrichment item, you can think about using objects that might otherwise get thrown out," says Chin of WCS. Curators at the Brookfield Zoo in Illinois used recycled tires to give the floor in their swamp exhibit a springy, bog-like feel, and they use hydropower to generate the surf crashing through the zoo's coastal ecosystem display, according to Bill Torsberg, the zoo's resource conservation coordinator.

Zoos have "a special advantage in that they're a campus situation. They're controlling a lot of worlds," Batshalom says. "In some cases their procurement standards are higher than at schools. You can use arsenic-treated wood at schools, but not at zoos."

There's mounting interest in holding zoos accountable for their environmental practices. In addition to her work at the Bronx Zoo, Sheppard chairs the AZA's green practices scientific advisory group, which was formed last year [2002]. The group acts as a sustainability clearinghouse and is pushing for more emphasis on environmentalism in the accreditation process. (Zoo accreditation is reviewed every five years.) Over the last several years, accreditation reviewers have begun quizzing institutions on their environmental policies and programs, Sheppard says, though ecological issues are not yet make-or-break accreditation factors.

On many fronts, WCS is setting a high bar. Last spring, the WCS-managed New York Aquarium installed a 200-kilowatt hydrogen fuel cell to supply up to one-fifth of its daily electricity requirement, and, as a byproduct, heat water for some of its buildings and tanks. Even here, there is room for improvement, as the fuel cell is currently powered by natural gas. WCS is looking to add more fuel cells, and to use geothermal, wind, and solar energy where possible. The society has also committed to the expense and headache of continuing its recycling programs despite the withdrawal and phased-in return of New York City's program, and it's heading up efforts to restore the Bronx River watershed from Westchester County into the city.

In addition, WCS is in the midst of some showcase green building 20 projects. As the Bronx Zoo adapts its older buildings to current needs, it is doing so with an eye toward sustainability. For the past couple of decades, the 1903 Lion House, with a Beaux Arts exterior controlled by the city landmarks commission, sat unused; now it's being renovated and is slated to reopen in 2006. The project architects, the appropriately named Fox & Fowle, designed the high-profile 4 Times Square Condé Nast building, among other green structures. The newly redone Lion House will qualify for the U.S. Green Building Council's Leadership in Energy and Environmental Design certification.

Although its plans are ambitious in scope — especially given that they're being hatched in the midst of a recession — WCS isn't just pouring money into expensive statements of institutional concern for the biosphere. Many of the measures have both ecological and economic paybacks and are considered worthwhile investments, according to WCS officials.

It's All Happening at the Zoo

In addition to improving its environmental infrastructure, WCS is calling attention to the ecological impact of human activities — especially local activities. "We can convince people that they need to help us in central Africa because gorillas are at risk, because we have the gorilla standing there and looking at you. That's kind of an easy sell," says Chin. "But how do we have people make that connection that actions here have an impact on the environment and on the world? People think about conservation as being a thing that needs to be done in other places. How do we connect them to here?"

Sheppard echoes this sentiment, saying that visitors "don't always understand that there are a lot of problems here. We educate them about rainforests, exotic pet collecting, hunting in South America, but [habitat] fragmentation is a problem here. One of our [current] exhibits has a wooden sign that says 'For Sale: Adirondack Lots.'"

With this sharper focus on environmentalism at home, WCS and the Bronx Zoo have, in a sense, come full circle. At the turn of the last century, the zoo was among the most progressive in the nation, boasting naturalistic enclosures, the first full-time vet and first animal hospital at a U.S. zoo, and pioneering work in captive breeding. Later, the zoo began emphasizing international conservation and raising awareness of global issues. Now, they're stressing their place in the local ecology.

Other zoos, including those in San Francisco, Seattle, and Syracuse, 25 incorporate environmental awareness to some degree, but usually on a project-by-project basis. By choosing a different strategy — that is, by integrating green priorities into its master plan — WCS is likely to set the standard for zoos and similar institutions across the country and around the globe. Sheppard says WCS's public embrace of sustainability, however imperfect, can invite serious change. She likens it to the species conservation movement in the 1970s: "I was part of the generation that started looking at conservation, even though zoos hadn't really yet. There's been a transformation in the last 25 years. Zoos [initially] thought it was a great idea for PR [but] it attracted people like me, and we . . . drove the whole organization in that direction."

Now that zoos are moving toward sustainability as well as conservation, they can help move society at large in the same direction. "Zoos are in a position to teach their visitors what they want to teach them," says the Humane Society's Farinato.

Understanding the Text

1. Why do zoos generate mixed reactions among environmentalists? What are the environmental benefits and detriments of zoos?

2. How do many zoos define animal welfare? Does the definition need to be expanded? How would you expand the definition?

3. How can zoos become more sustainable? How is this similar to or different from other businesses?

Reflection and Response

4. Why do you think zoos are important to our society and to animals? Alternatively, in what ways do they damage or pose a threat to society and to animals?

5. What role does education play in a zoo? Should this education focus on sustainability? How is this tied to species extinction and other environmental threats?

Making Connections

6. Describe a personal experience you had at a zoo. Was it positive or negative? Did this make you consider animals or the environment in a different way? Do you think this was the zoo's goal?

7. Research a zoo or an aquarium. What is being done to encourage sustainability? Is the zoo or aquarium enacting sustainable practices themselves? Give the zoo or aquarium a grade, and explain why it earned that grade.

Why I Hunt

Rick Bass

Rick Bass was born in Fort Worth, Texas, and studied petroleum geology at Utah State University. He is an environmental activist and award-winning author of dozens of books about natural places. Bass lives in the remote Yaak Valley in Montana, which is featured prominently in his writing.

In this article, Bass uses his own life experiences to explain why and how the environment should be protected. He describes how typical Americans don't need to "hunt and gather" their own food anymore, resorting instead to shopping in supermarkets. He then explains why, in the light of this cultural shift, he still enjoys hunting.

As you read, think about Bass's argument that environmentalists should join forces with hunting and fishing groups. He believes that this would protect the wilderness in which people hunt. Do you agree with him?

I was a hunter before I came far up into northwest Montana, but not to the degree I am now. It astounds me sometimes to step back, particularly at the end of autumn, the end of the hunting season, and take both mental and physical inventory of all that was hunted and all that was gathered from this life in the mountains. The woodshed groaning tight, full of firewood. The fruits and herbs and vegetables from the garden, canned or dried or frozen; the wild mushrooms, huckleberries, thimbleberries, and strawberries. And most precious of all, the flesh of the wild things that share with us these mountains and the plains to the east — the elk, the whitetail and mule deer; the ducks and geese, grouse and pheasant and Hungarian partridge and dove and chukar and wild turkey; the trout and whitefish. Each year the cumulative bounty seems unbelievable. What heaven is this into which we've fallen?

How my wife and I got to this valley — the Yaak — 15 years ago is a mystery, a move that I've only recently come to accept as having been inevitable. We got in the truck one day feeling strangely restless in Mississippi, and we drove. What did I know? Only that I missed the West's terrain of space. Young and healthy, and not coincidentally new-in-love, we hit that huge and rugged landscape in full stride. We drove north until we ran out of country — until the road ended, and we reached Canada's thick blue woods — and then we turned west and traveled until we ran almost out of mountains: the backside of the Rockies, to the wet, west-slope rainforest.

We came over a little mountain pass — it was August and winter was already fast approaching — and looked down on the soft hills, the dense purples of the spruce and fir forests, the ivory crests of the ice-capped peaks, and the slender ribbons of gray thread rising from the chimneys of the few cabins nudged close to the winding river below, and we fell in love with the Yaak Valley and the hard-logged Kootenai National Forest — the way people in movies fall with each other, star and starlet, as if a trap door has been pulled out from beneath them: tumbling through the air, arms windmilling furiously, and suddenly no other world but each other, no other world but this one, and eyes for no one, or no place, else.

Right from the beginning, I could see that there was extraordinary bounty in this low-elevation forest, resting as it does in a magical seam between the Pacific Northwest° and the northern Rockies. Some landscapes these days have been reduced to nothing but dandelions and fire ants, knapweed and thistle, where the only remaining wildlife are sparrows, squirrels, and starlings. In the blessed Yaak, however, not a single mammal has gone extinct since the end of the Ice Age. This forest sustains more types of hunters — carnivores — than any valley in North America. It is a predator's showcase, home not just to wolves and grizzlies, but wolverines, lynx, bobcat, marten, fisher, black bear, mountain lion, golden eagle, bald eagle, coyote, fox, weasel. In the Yaak, everything is in motion, either seeking its quarry, or seeking to avoid becoming quarry.

The people who have chosen to live in this remote valley — few   5 phones, very little electricity, and long, dark winters — possess a hardness and a dreaminess both. They — we — can live a life of deprivation, and yet are willing to enter the comfort of daydreams and imagination. There is something mysterious happening here between the landscape and the people, a thing that stimulates our imagination, and causes many of us to set off deep into the woods in search of the unknown, and sustenance — not just metaphorical or spiritual sustenance, but the real thing.

Only about 5 percent of the nation and 15 to 20 percent of Montanans are hunters. But in this one valley, almost everyone is a hunter. It is not the peer pressure of the local culture that recruits us into hunting, nor even necessarily the economic boon of a few hundred pounds of meat in a cash-poor society. Rather, it is the terrain itself, and one's gradual integration into it, that summons the hunter. Nearly everyone who has lived here for any length of time has ended

Pacific Northwest: a region in western North America bounded by the Pacific Ocean to the west and by the Rocky Mountains to the east.

up — sometimes almost against one's conscious wishes — becoming a hunter. This wild and powerful landscape sculpts us like clay. I don't find such sculpting an affront to the human spirit, but instead, wonderful testimony to our pliability, our ability to adapt to a place.

I myself love to hunt the deer, the elk, and the grouse — to follow them into the mouth of the forest, to disappear in their pursuit — to get lost following their snowy tracks up one mountain and down the next. One sets out after one's quarry with senses fully engaged, wildly alert: entranced, nearly hypnotized. The tiniest of factors can possess the largest significance — the crack of a twig, the shift of a breeze, a single stray hair caught on a piece of bark, a fresh-bent blade of grass.

Each year during such pursuits, I am struck more and more by the conceit that people in a hunter-gatherer culture might have richer imaginations than those who dwell more fully in an agricultural or even post-agricultural environment. What else is the hunt but a stirring of the imagination, with the quarry, or goal, or treasure lying just around the corner or over the next rise? A hunter's imagination has no choice but to become deeply engaged, for it is never the hunter who is in control, but always the hunted, in that the prey directs the predator's movements.

> "All I know is that hunting — beyond being a thing I like to do — helps keep my imagination vital."

The hunted shapes the hunter; the pursuit and evasion of predator and prey are but shadows of the same desire. The thrush wants to remain a thrush. The goshawk wants to consume the thrush and in doing so, partly become the thrush — to take its flesh into its flesh. They weave through the tangled branches of the forest, zigging and zagging, the goshawk right on the thrush's tail, like a shadow. Or perhaps it is the thrush that is the shadow thrown by the light of the goshawk's fiery desire.

Either way, the escape maneuvers of the thrush help carve and shape and direct the muscles of the goshawk. Even when you are walking through the woods seeing nothing but trees, you can feel the unseen passage of pursuits that might have occurred earlier that morning, precisely where you are standing — pursuits that will doubtless, after you are gone, sweep right back across that same spot again and again.

As does the goshawk, so too do human hunters imagine where their prey might be, or where it might go. They follow tracks hinting at not only distance and direction traveled, but also pace and gait and the general state of mind of the animal that is evading them. They plead to the mountain to deliver to them a deer, an elk. They imagine and hope that they are moving toward their goal of obtaining game.

When you plant a row of corn, there is not so much unknown. You can be fairly sure that, if the rains come, the corn is going to sprout. The corn is not seeking to elude you. But when you step into the woods, looking for a deer — well, there's nothing in your mind, or in your blood, or in the world, but imagination.

Most Americans neither hunt nor gather nor even grow their own food, nor make, with their own hands, any of their other necessities. In this post-agricultural society, too often we confuse anticipation with imagination. When we wander down the aisle of the supermarket searching for a chunk of frozen chicken, or cruise into Dillard's department store looking for a sweater, we can be fairly confident that grayish wad of chicken or that sweater is going to be there, thanks to the vigor and efficiency of a supply-and-demand marketplace. The imagination never quite hits second gear. Does the imagination atrophy, from such chronic inactivity? I suspect that it does.

All I know is that hunting — beyond being a thing I like to do — helps keep my imagination vital. I would hope never to be so blind as to offer it as prescription; I offer it only as testimony to my love of the landscape where I live — a place that is still, against all odds, its own place, quite unlike any other. I don't think I would be able to sustain myself as a dreamer in this strange landscape if I did not take off three months each year to wander the mountains in search of game; to hunt, stretching and exercising not just my imagination, but my spirit. And to wander the mountains, too, in all the other seasons. And to be nourished by the river of spirit that flows, shifting and winding, between me and the land.

Understanding the Text

1. How does Bass explain and define hunting? Do you agree or disagree with his perspective?
2. What are the similarities and differences between hunting and gathering, as Bass describes them in this essay?
3. Why do so many people in Yaak Valley become hunters? How does the landscape influence them?

Reflection and Response

4. Do you agree with Bass that hunting can strengthen your imagination? Why or why not?

5. In what ways does hunting seem like a sustainable or an unsustainable practice?

Making Connections

6. Would you enjoy a lifestyle like the one Bass describes in this article? Why or why not?

7. Talk to someone you know who hunts or fishes. What are that person's beliefs and perspectives on conservation, environmentalism, and sustainability? Do those beliefs seem appropriate and in line with their practices?

Let My People Go Surfing

Yvon Chouinard

Yvon Chouinard, born in 1938 in Lewiston, Maine, is considered by *Fortune* to be the most successful outdoor industry businessman in history. Growing up in Maine and Southern California, Chouinard became an avid rock climber, surfer, environmentalist, and businessman. He is the founder and owner of Patagonia, an international clothing and outdoor gear company.

This article begins with personal anecdotes from Chouinard as he explains the purpose of his company, Patagonia. He describes his transition from outdoor athlete to businessman. He then explains how Patagonia worked to become a more sustainable company. As you read, think about the things Patagonia did to become more sustainable, including recycling and reducing pollution.

I had always avoided thinking of myself as a businessman. I was a climber, a surfer, a kayaker, a skier and a blacksmith. We simply enjoyed making good tools and functional clothes that we, and our friends, wanted. My wife, Malinda, and I owned only a beat-up Ford van and a heavily mortgaged, soon-to-be-condemned cabin on the beach. And now, in 1975, we had a heavily leveraged company with employees with families of their own, all depending on us.

After pondering our responsibilities and financial liabilities, it dawned on me one day that I was a businessman, and would probably continue to be one for a long time. It was clear that in order to survive at this game we had to get serious. But I also knew that I would never be happy playing by the normal rules of business. If I had to be a businessman, I was going to do it on my terms.

Work had to be enjoyable on a daily basis. We all had to come to work on the balls of our feet, going up the stairs two steps at a time. We needed to be surrounded by friends who could dress whatever way they wanted, even barefoot. We needed to have flex time to surf the waves when they were good, or ski the powder after a big snowstorm, or stay home and take care of a sick child. We needed to blur that distinction between work and play and family.

From the mid-1980s to 1990, sales at Patagonia° grew from $20 million to $100 million. Malinda and I were not personally any wealth-

---

Patagonia: a Ventura, California–based clothing company, focusing mainly on high-end outdoor clothing. The company, founded by Yvon Chouinard in 1972, is a member of several environmental movements.

Yvon Chouinard (seated), Patagonia's founder, at his home in Ventura, California. The company's flex-time policy allows for surfing when the waves are good.

Copyright Tierney Gearon

ier, as we kept the profits in the company. In many ways the growth was exciting. We were never bored. New employees, including those in the lowest-paid positions in retail stores or the warehouse, could rise rapidly to better-paying jobs. For a few positions we conducted searches — and we could claim our pick of the litter within both the apparel and outdoor industries. But most of the new employees we hired came through a well-rooted and fast-growing grapevine.

Despite our own growth at Patagonia, we were able, in many ways, to keep alive our cultural values. We still came to work on the balls of our feet. People ran or surfed at lunch, or played volleyball in the sandpit at the back of the building.

In growing the business, however, we had nearly outgrown our natural niche, the specialty outdoor market. By the late 1980s the company was expanding at a rate that, if sustained, would have made us a billion-dollar company in a decade.

Can you have it all? The question haunted me as Patagonia evolved. Another problem would come to haunt me more — the deterioration of the natural world. I saw that deterioration first with my own eyes, when I returned to climb or surf or fish in places I knew, like Nepal, Africa or Polynesia, and saw what had happened in the few years since I'd last been there.

In Africa, forests and grassland were disappearing as the population grew. Global warming was melting glaciers that had been part of the continent's climbing history. The emergence of AIDS and Ebola coincided with the clear-cutting of forests and the wholesale pursuit of bush meat, such as infected chimpanzees.

On a kayaking trip to the Russian Far East, before the collapse of the old Soviet Union, I found that the Russians had destroyed much of their country trying to keep up with the U.S. in their arms race.

Closer to home, I saw the relentless paving over of Southern California's remaining coastline and hillsides. In Wyoming, where I spent summers for 30 years, I saw fewer wild animals each year, caught smaller fish, and suffered through weeks of debilitating, record-setting 90-degree heat. But most environmental devastation the eye doesn't see. I learned more by reading about the rapid loss of topsoil and groundwater, about the clear-cutting of tropical forests and the growing list of endangered plant and animal and bird species, and of people in the once pristine Arctic who are now being warned not to eat the local mammals and fish because of toxins from industrial nations.

At the same time, at Patagonia, we slowly became aware that up-hill battles fought by small, dedicated groups of people to save patches of habitat could yield significant results. We began to make regular donations to smaller groups working to save or restore habitat, rather than giving the money to large NGOs° with big staffs, overheads and corporate connections. In 1986, we committed to donate 10 percent of profits each year to these groups. We later upped the ante to 1 percent of sales, or 10 percent of pre-tax profits, whichever was greater. We have kept to that commitment every year, boom or bust.

We also realized that in addition to addressing these external crises, we had to look within the company and reduce our own role as a corporate polluter. We began recycling paper waste in 1984 and conducted an intensive search for a source of paper with a higher percentage of recycled content for our catalog. In 1990, we were the first catalog in the U.S. to use recycled paper. In that first year, switching to recycled paper saved 3,500,000 kilowatt hours of electricity, 6,000,000 gallons of water, kept 52,000 pounds of pollutants out of the air and 1,560 cubic yards of solid waste out of landfills, and it pre-

NGOs: nongovernmental organizations.

vented 14,500 trees from being felled. We also researched and pioneered the use of recycled, reused and less toxic materials in our construction and remodeling projects. We worked with Wellman and Malden Mills to develop recycled polyester for use in our PCP® Synchilla fleece.

All the while we continued to grow. We experienced so much success on so many fronts during the late 1980s that we began to believe the expansion would never end. And we planned to just keep going.

Then, in 1991, after all those years of 30 percent to 50 percent compound annual growth and trying to have it all, Patagonia hit the wall. The United States had entered a recession, and the growth we had always planned on, and bought inventory for, stopped.

The crisis soon deepened. Our primary lender was itself in financial trouble, and it sharply reduced our credit line. To bring our borrowing within the new limits we had to drastically reduce spending. 15

Our own company had exceeded its resources and limitations; we had become dependent, like the world economy, on growth we could not sustain. But as a small company, we couldn't ignore the problem and wish it away. We were forced to rethink our priorities and institute new practices. We had to start breaking the rules.

> "You have to know your strengths and limitations and live within your means. The same is true for a business."

I took a dozen of our top managers to Argentina, to the windswept mountains of the real Patagonia, for a walkabout. In the course of roaming around those wild lands, we asked ourselves why we were in business and what kind of business we wanted Patagonia to be. A billion-dollar company? Okay, but not if it meant we had to make products we couldn't be proud of. And we discussed what we could do to help stem the environmental harm we caused as a company. We talked about the values we had in common, and the shared culture that had brought everyone to Patagonia, Inc., and not another company.

We knew that uncontrolled growth put at risk the values that had made the company succeed so far. Those values couldn't be expressed in a how-to operations manual offering pat answers. We needed philosophical and inspirational guides to make sure we always asked the right questions and found the right answers.

While our managers debated what steps to take to address the sales and cash-flow crisis, I began to lead week-long employee seminars in what we called Philosophies. We'd take a busload at a time to places like Yosemite or the Marin Headlands above San Francisco, camp out, and gather under the trees to talk. The goal was to teach every employee in the company our business and environmental ethics and values.

I realize now that what I was trying to do was to instill in my com- 20 pany, at a critical time, lessons that I had already learned as an indi- vidual — and as a climber, surfer, kayaker and fly fisherman. I had always tried to live my life fairly simply and by 1991, knowing what I knew about the state of the environment, I had begun to eat lower on the food chain and reduce my consumption of material goods. Doing risk sports had taught me another important lesson: never exceed your limits. You push the envelope and you live for those moments when you're right on the edge, but you don't go over. You have to be true to yourself; you have to know your strengths and limitations and live within your means. The same is true for a business. The sooner a company tries to be what it is not, the sooner it tries to "have it all," the sooner it will die.

Understanding the Text

1. Who is Chouinard and how did he develop his business?
2. What did Patagonia do to help the environment?
3. What happened to the company when the country went into recession?

Reflection and Response

4. What are some ways Patagonia could continue to keep its business sustainable?
5. What are some things Chouinard learned from his life experiences? How did his experiences as an outdoorsman and athlete inform his business philosophy?
6. Why would it be financially savvy for an outdoor clothing and equipment company (such as Patagonia) to devote so much attention to sustainability? Is the company's philosophy good business, good ethics, or both?

Making Connections

7. Spend some time browsing Patagonia's Web site, particularly those sections addressing the company's sustainability and environmental impact. What current efforts toward sustainability are they undertaking?
8. Research another company that makes outdoor clothing or equipment. What could that company learn about sustainability from Patagonia? Conversely, what could Patagonia learn from that company?

Climate Revelations

Auden Schendler

Auden Schendler is vice president of sustainability at Aspen Skiing Company. He worked previously in corporate sustainability at Rocky Mountain Institute. His writing has been published in *Harvard Business Review*, the *Los Angeles Times*, *Slate*, *Scientific American*, Atlantic.com, *Huffington Post*, and other sources, and he is the author of the book *Getting Green Done: Hard Truths from the Front Lines of the Sustainability Revolution*. In 2006, Schendler was named a global-warming innovator by *Time* magazine.

In this narrative, Schendler describes his meeting with Walter Bennett, a man who wanted to convince his company to care more about climate change. Schendler explains how their meeting made the author, an atheist, consider the relationship between climate change and religion.

As you read, think about the issues Schendler raises in this narrative. Consider his argument about a relationship between climate change and religion.

One day, a man named Walter Bennett walked into my Aspen, Colorado, office holding a laptop. He was in his mid-to-late fifties, with a graying crew cut, wearing khakis and a button-up shirt. He looked like, and described himself as, a west-Texas redneck. His younger (second) wife accompanied him, saying little. As we chatted, Walter mentioned that his daughter had just given birth to a baby boy — a grandson. Walter reminded me of the aging, Cheney-esque° board members I'd been hoping would die off so we could actually start doing something on climate change. But that was exactly what he wanted to talk about. He set down his laptop and hooked it up to a projector.

"Do you mind if I show you this presentation I've prepared for my senior management?"

"No problem," I said, thinking, *Get me out of here. This is going to hurt.*

I'm a climate guy. I work for a ski resort, Aspen Skiing Company, where my title is "sustainability director." In theory, I work to address all aspects of the resort's environmental impact, from weed control to cage-free eggs, from taking calls about new technologies to handling attacks about what a bunch of hypocrites we are. It's fun. I enjoy it. But, to be brutally honest, I don't care that much about those

---

Cheney-esque: refers to Dick Cheney, 46th U.S. Vice President (2001–2009), who was known for politically conservative views on environmental issues.

subjects. Twenty years ago, I took my first course in climate science. The news I read today is essentially the same. And I believe two things: First, to quote ABC newsman Bill Blakemore, "Climate isn't the story of our time; it's the only story." Second, it seems obvious that a ski resort should both care deeply about climate change and also be in the vanguard of solving it.

Because my job is high profile, people often ask to meet with me   5 about climate, sustainable business, and the environment. That's what Walter Bennett was doing. Walter works for Stihl (pronounced "steel"), the German chainsaw manufacturer. We have a partnership with them. They support free-skiing competitions, and we use Stihl saws on our mountains to cut trails. I didn't expect much from the meeting. After all, we're talking about a chainsaw manufacturer here. But after Walter got his projector set up, he clicked a button and proceeded to blow my mind.

> "Climate change offers us . . . the opportunity to participate in a movement that can fulfill the universal human need for a sense of meaning in our lives."

He had prepared an hour-long multimedia event on climate change, complete with country music overlays, video clips, and charts and graphs, that rivaled any presentation I'd seen from experts in the field, nonprofit heads, and climate PhDs. It got the science exactly right, the challenges, and some of the solutions. Walter's goal was to convince Stihl that it should begin to take action on climate change, in concert with its efforts to develop cleaner burning chainsaws and other power tools.

When Walter was done, I sat in silence. Finally, I asked, "Walter, if you don't mind my asking . . . what was it that moved a self-professed west-Texas redneck to care about climate change at all, let alone try to change an entire corporation's perspective on the issue? You don't really fit the mold of someone who would do this."

Walter said: "Holding my grandchild — holding that little baby in my hands . . ." His voice trailed off. I thought he was going to cry.

• • •

Walter's experience, I believe, is being lived throughout the country, throughout the world, because climate change is a threat the likes of which our society has never seen. Unlike some earlier predictions of doom from environmentalists (the population bomb, for example), this one has uniform scientific agreement. Climate change is happening, and it will get worse. The best science — represented by Rajendra Pachauri of the Intergovernmental Panel on Climate Change and James Hansen at NASA — tells us we have to act in the next few years to cut carbon dioxide emissions 80 percent by midcentury, or the planet will be unrecognizable by end of century.

And yet, somehow, we don't seem to be able to engage this mon- 10 ster adequately. While Aspen Skiing Company has developed a worldwide reputation as a green company, our energy use keeps increasing, despite herculean efforts to reduce it. Not only are other businesses struggling in the same way, but also most of the nations that signed the Kyoto Treaty° are missing their targets. Why? Because our society is entirely based on cheap energy. We can't just retool it overnight. Solving climate change is going to be a bitch.

Given the extreme challenges we face in implementing solutions — whether trying to make mass transit work, fixing the problem of existing buildings, building enough renewable energy to power our operations, or driving federal action on climate policy — it's worth asking the question: what will motivate us to actually pull this off? How will we become, and then remain, inspired for the long slog ahead? Because this battle will take not just political will and corporate action; it will require unyielding commitment and dedication on the part of humanity. *We need to literally remake society.*

We can intellectualize the need for action all we want, but in my experience, in the end our motivation usually comes down to a cliché: our kids and, for want of a better word, our dignity. The journalist Bill Moyers has said, "What we need to match the science of human health is what the ancient Israelites called 'hocma'— the science of the heart . . . the capacity to see . . . to feel . . . and then to act . . . as if the future depended on you. Believe me, it does."

Moyers, who is an ordained Baptist minister, taps into something positively religious about the possibilities in a grand movement to protect the Earth. Climate change offers us something immensely valuable and difficult to find in the modern world: the opportunity to participate in a movement that, in its vastness of scope, can fulfill the universal human need for a sense of meaning in our lives. A climate solution — a world running efficiently on abundant clean energy — by necessity goes a long way toward solving many, if not most, other problems too: poverty, hunger, disease, food and water supply, equity, solid waste, and on and on.

Kyoto Treaty: an international treaty that sets binding obligations on industrialized countries to reduce emissions of greenhouse gases.

Climate change doesn't have to scare us. It can inspire us; it is a singular opportunity to remake society in the image of our greatest dreams.

• • •

What are those dreams? The concept of an ideal society has been a core element in human thought for all of recorded history. In 1516, Thomas More° wrote about a kingdom called Utopia off the coast of the recently discovered Americas; in doing so, he brought the concept of an ideal society out of the realm of religious faith and the afterlife and into the world of the living. For centuries, that utopian ideal had been called by different names but had always existed in some other world: the Garden of Eden, Paradise, the Land of Cockaigne. More's idea that such a place might exist here on Earth was radical, but it came from the same yearning for meaning and betterment that has always driven human beings to new heights. One of the great and hopeful concepts of human history, it carried itself into the present: from the settling and then founding of America and all its promise; to the vision behind Kennedy's City on a Hill and Johnson's Great Society; to Martin Luther King, who said that he might not get there with us, but he had seen the Promised Land.

The absence of that vision is despair.

Barry Lopez° has written, "One of the oldest dreams of mankind is to find a dignity that might include all living things. And one of the greatest of human longings must be to bring such dignity to one's own dreams, for each to find his or her own life exemplary in some way." This longing is a fundamental aspect of human experience. In my work, I see it on a daily basis, in people like Walter Bennett, in the hundreds of college graduates looking for work in the field of sustainability, in people all over the world.

Recently, I received the following e-mail from Bob Janes, an Alaskan tour guide I had met in 2007:

Greetings from Juneau, Auden,

. . . My interests are being drawn more and more towards the global warming issue (whose aren't?). I am able to involve myself both personally and in a business capacity now and into the future, but am definitely in the dark on a specific course . . .

Thomas More: (1478–1535), an English lawyer, social philosopher, and author.
Barry Lopez: (b. 1945), an American writer and environmentalist best known for his book *Of Wolves and Men*.

Do you believe one can actually find a way to earn a bit of a living in this emerging (crisis?), and at the same time go home at night and let the kids know that something good is being accomplished? My business sense tells me there are many grand opportunities, but the field seems to be a tempting invitation to intrusive species and interests. What is reality? What will stand the test of time?

When you get a chance, Auden, could you drop me a line with some thoughts and possible information links . . .

Bob

In a note dashed off after work or between tours in the mayhem of a busy day, Bob was asking some of the most basic, consistent, and profound questions humanity has struggled with. And when I tried to pinpoint exactly what Bob was talking about, I ended up with words that didn't square with the biology background I have, or the empirical perspective the field of sustainability and climate has historically followed. The words I found to describe Bob's goals came from the religious community — words like grace, dignity, redemption, and compassion. And it occurred to me that the environmental, political, and business worlds, in their discussion of climate change and its solutions, have been missing something fundamental.

There have been scores of books published on climate change and sustainable business over the last two decades. Most come from the secular academic or left-leaning environmental community, or they come from the free market–crazed economists at right-wing think tanks. It's either pure science or pure economics. Few of these books address the broader, seemingly glaring point that no such holistically encompassing opportunity as climate change, nothing with so great a promise to achieve universal human goals on so large a scale, has been offered up since the establishment of large, organized religions between two and four thousand years ago. The vision of a sustainable society, with its implications for equity, social justice, happiness, meaning, tolerance, and hope, embodies the aspirations of most religious traditions: a way of living at peace with each other, the world, and our consciences; a graceful existence; a framework for a noble life. Most religions originally evolved to meet a basic human need for community, understanding, and mission. Religion, in its original intent, and the sustainability movement seem to be sourced from the same ancient human wellspring.

Is it any wonder, then, that so many have come at sustainability, 20 and in particular the climate struggle, with an almost religious fervor?

And that many prominent leaders of this movement — leaders like Al Gore, Sally Bingham, Bill Moyers, and Richard Cizek — are either ordained or educated in theology? Indeed, many critics of environmentalism and the current climate "crusade" point out the avid, zealous enthusiasm behind the movement, as if to say, "What a bunch of wackos."

But religion has been one of the most important forces shaping society throughout history. If there are some very clear parallels between the goals of most religious traditions and the goals of a sustainable society, how is it possible to talk about huge philosophical issues that cut to the core of human desire — like climate change, which threatens the very nature and existence of life on Earth — without talking about . . . God?

• • •

My inquiry into religion and climate change began through conversations with my friend Mark Thomas, who was at the time studying for a degree in theology at Berkeley. Mark once said, "To think God is some old guy sitting in a chair, you'd have to be insane." As a member of no religious practice and a lifelong atheist who always felt religion was absurd, the idea was liberating to me. I was guilty of viewing religion in the most simplistic terms.

When I talk about religion, I'm talking about its core founding principles, not what seems to be the bulk of popular modern religious practice in the United States. As Bill McKibben° has pointed out, in America, the evangelical agenda prominent in politics — with its unwavering focus on gay clergy, same-sex union, and abortion — has very little to do with the original teachings of any religious faith, let alone Christianity, despite the fact that roughly 85 percent of U.S. citizens call themselves Christian. He notes that three-quarters of Americans think the line "God helps those who help themselves" comes from the Bible. But Ben Franklin said it, and the notion actually runs counter to the founding ideas of most religions, which focus explicitly on tolerance and helping the poor.

At the same time, the American religious community — even the most unmoored element — is on board with climate action. Leaders typically cite a biblical mandate regarding stewardship, describe Earth as "God's creation," and note Jesus's commandment to "love

---

Bill McKibben: (b. 1960), an American journalist and professor who has written extensively on the impact of climate change.

thy neighbor as thyself." I believe this represents the beginnings of a seismic shift back toward core principles in religion, not contemporary distractions — a shift toward the original, more humble aspects of the Judeo-Christian tradition, and away from making tax cuts permanent. In a way, this makes sense. As we move out of an unprecedented age of abundance and back into a world of scarcity, we are going to need these ideas of tolerance and human dignity that help people work together and coexist peacefully. We are going to need these ideas to solve climate change.

The sustainability movement, too, is arguably seeing a shift to- 25 ward "core principles" in the sense that we're less focused on the microscale and the individual (recycling, paper or plastic, self-righteous SUV-hating) and more focused on the collective (solving climate change as a social, economic, spiritual, and environmental effort).

To get a sense of what might be happening on the leading edge of religion — and how this evolution might relate to the climate struggle — I contacted two young progressive religious thinkers: my friend Mark Thomas, now Director of Mission Integration and Spiritual Care at Providence Hood River Hospital, and Rabbi David Ingber from New York's Kehilat Romemu congregation. I asked them about Lopez's "dignity that includes all living things." In the process of listening to their responses, it became clear to me that Thomas and Ingber had a particular definition of "God" that informed their whole worldview. Further, it had nothing to do with my simplistic understanding of the idea of God. Let me explain.

Two distinct concepts of God have existed in parallel since the origin of religion. Theologian Marcus Borg explains them: Supernatural theism, he says, imagines God as a personlike being. Panentheism, however, "imagines God and the God-world relationship differently. . . . Rather than imagining God as a personlike being 'out there,' this concept imagines God as the encompassing Spirit in whom everything that is, is."

Both Thomas and Ingber used this latter definition, what Father Thomas Keating, a leading thinker on the subject of contemplative prayer, calls the "isness" of the world, or "isness without boundaries." In fact, after conversations with Buddhist leaders, Keating came to a description of God they could all agree on: "ultimate reality." In this context you could also define God as what Lao Tzu called the Tao, or, simply, "the sacred." Similarly, the Talmud says of God, "He is the place of the world; the world is not His place."

When you talk about God as ultimate reality or the sacred, and if you see religion as a way of relating to the world in a dignified way — a broker for grace — then the religion discussion becomes much less charged. Nobody's trying to get you to believe something ridiculous. Instead, we're simply talking about a philosophy of living.

In response to my question about Barry Lopez's "dignity," Ingber and Thomas both described a faith that has the goal of bringing the natural world into harmony with people, bringing the divine to everyday experience. As Ingber writes, "Religion seeks (at its best) to illuminate our eyes, that is to actualize our capacity to realize, apprehend, see (with the eye of Spirit) that there is nothing but G-d, everywhere, now and always."

The idea of the divinization of the world — of our lives — is a powerful and unifying concept tying together religion and the climate challenge. It means that it doesn't matter what direction we come from; most people, religious or secular or something in between, can agree on common goals. An atheist might be envisioning an ideal society running on renewable energy, and others might have the same vision but see that as the true meaning of "God's will be done" on Earth. Heaven must look like a sustainable society.

And yet, for someone like me, the question is, how do you talk about religious ideas, or use words like "grace" and "redemption" and "compassion" in a business context, which is all about return on investment (ROI), net operating income (NOI), cash flow, and year-on-year growth?

Aspen Skiing Company is a good case study. In 1994, our mission, though unstated, was to make money by selling lift tickets. That's not very inspiring. Our incoming CEO at the time, Pat O'Donnell, tapping into the idea that people's lives are, ultimately, a search for meaning, suggested that people won't happily come to work each day to make money for the bossman. Instead, we needed a set of guiding principles that would be based in values, not profits, though business success could certainly become one of those values. What resulted was a core mission for the company that sounds radical to the point of froofiness: "We provide opportunity for the renewal of the human spirit." Come to work to do that, and suddenly things change. Your mission as a company begins to evolve. We're more successful than ever, but that's in part because we've begun to see ourselves, and our mission, differently. Perhaps our role, in part, is providing safe, gratifying work to members of the community, creating fulfilling jobs about which people can be proud. Perhaps business can be *graceful*. If that transition is happening in one corporation, it can happen in others.

And the business community is indeed slowly moving in this direction. It started, in part, with books like Paul Hawken's *The Ecology of Commerce* and his and Amory and Hunter Lovins's *Natural Capitalism*. Their argument was that capitalism is wonderful, but it has never been practiced. We've always discounted the value of the natural (and human) world and the costs of our impacts on it. Making the costs of air pollution, climate change, and fisheries destruction part of the business equation — and recognizing the true value of the natural resources we use as feedstocks — would in fact be a divine act: it would mean the business community finally seeing not just the bottom line but the *entire world* as sacred. It would mean seeing the dignity of the world, the harm in damaging it, and the *vision* of a sustainable future.

It is there. It has always been there. Can we see it? 35

Understanding the Text

1. Who is Walter Bennett? What is his job?
2. What is Aspen Skiing Company's "mission"? How has that mission changed over time?
3. How did Schendler become interested in the relationship between religion and climate change?
4. What is Panentheism? How does it address the intersections of religion and sustainability?

Reflection and Response

5. Do you think there is a correlation between climate change and religion? Explain.
6. What is the great opportunity that climate change offers us as a civilization and as a species?
7. In what ways is sustainability about a particular belief system? Do you think that sustainability is a type of "religion"? Is this a good or a bad thing?

Making Connections

8. Schendler writes that climate change can be a "singular opportunity to remake society in the image of our greatest dreams" (par. 14). Do you agree with this statement? Why or why not?
9. Watch a video interview or lecture about sustainability by some notable figure — such as Al Gore, David Suzuki, Auden Schendler, or another figure who appears in this book. How does the speaker draw on religion in his or her discussions of environmentalism and sustainability? Does this have an impact on you and on other audience members? Do you think the sustainability movement should be grounded in religion, be based entirely on science, or draw on both?

Acknowledgments *(continued from page iv)*

Zorach, Alex. "Sustainability: Building a Consensus between Liberals and Conservatives" from www.cazort.net, June 25, 2010. Copyright © 2010 by Alexander C. Zorach. Reprinted with permission of the author. All rights reserved.

Art Credits

Page 52: Drawing by Lois and Louis Darling, from *Silent Spring* by Rachel Carson. Copyright © 1962 by Rachel L. Carson, renewed 1990 by Roger Christie. Reprinted by permission of Houghton Mifflin Harcourt Publishing Company. All rights reserved.

Page 127: From Dena M. Gromet, Howard Kunreuthera, and Richard P. Larrick, "Political ideology affects energy-efficiency attitudes and choices," PNAS, vol. 110, no. 23, 9314–9319. Reprinted by permission.

Page 128: From Dena M. Gromet, Howard Kunreuthera, and Richard P. Larrick, "Political ideology affects energy-efficiency attitudes and choices," PNAS, vol. 110, no. 23, 9314–9319. Reprinted by permission.

Index of Authors and Titles